PROPHECY
FULFILLED

Jesus Is The Messiah

By

David G. Brown

i

Also by David G. Brown

Miracle, Sign, Symbols and Judgment
Gods Plan for the End Times

It Is All About You
From Eden to Eternity God Never Forgot His Creation

Coming Soon
Still Called:
Serving Faithfully When You Are Not Chosen

PROPHECY FULFILLED

Jesus Is The Messiah

By

David G. Brown

NIV Scripture taken from the Holy Bible, New International Version®, NIV®, Copyright © 1973, 1978, 1984, 2011 by Biblica, Inc.™. Used under the minimum requirement by

Zondervan of 500 verses or less, All right reserved worldwide. www.zondervan.com

The "NIV" and "New International Version" are trademarks registered in the United States Patient and Trade Offices by Biblica, Inc.™

All other quotes are used through the Fair Use Doctrine.

ISBN 979-8-9995981-3-4 (Paperback)

Printed in the United States of America

Acknowledgement

"This work is dedicated to God the Father, who planned redemption; to Jesus Christ, who fulfilled it; and to the Holy Spirit, who empowers His people. May this book bring encouragement to the church and glory to His name until Christ returns. May these lessons inspire hearts to love His Word, proclaim His gospel, and walk in the light of His kingdom."

Preface

As one who loves the Bible and believes that God's Word carries profound meaning—not only in the fulfillment of prophecy but also in guiding our lives day by day—I have long felt the burden to teach others to hear what God is saying to us through His Word. As a teacher of Scripture, it is deeply important to me that each person find his or her own path to understanding what God is revealing.

Sadly, we live in a society that often believes we chart our own direction, independent of God. Against this backdrop, I have felt an urgency to share what Scripture declares about the Messiah and how Jesus fulfills these prophecies—not just one or two, but all of them. It is not merely a handful of verses that point to Him, but hundreds.

J. Barton Payne, in *The Encyclopedia of Biblical Prophecy*, identifies 574 verses in the Old Testament that reference the Messiah or His times. Many scholars agree that Jesus fulfilled around 300–350 distinct prophecies. Some detailed lists, including types, patterns, and indirect foreshadowing, count more than 400 references in all.

One might assume that with such overwhelming evidence, most Christians would be deeply familiar with these prophecies. Yet in my years of ministry, I have observed that biblical illiteracy is greater now than at any time I can remember.

It is for this reason that I undertook the writing of these lessons. While I was tempted to cover every Messianic prophecy, I chose instead to create a year-long study of fifty-two lessons that highlight some of the most important and well-known passages. My hope is that this collection will provide a solid foundation for understanding Jesus as the promised Messiah.

Although the lessons are arranged with the Christian calendar in mind—Advent lessons near Christmas and prophecies of suffering and death near Easter—there is no requirement to follow that order. These prophecies remain relevant throughout the year. If you feel compelled to begin in the middle, that is perfectly fine as well!

I pray that *Prophecies Fulfilled* blesses you as profoundly as it has blessed me while preparing these lessons. May the Lord strengthen you abundantly as you explore His Word, and may you joyfully share your discoveries with those around you. Be bold in your witness, confident in His promises, and rest assured in His care until the day Jesus returns.

God bless each of you. Stay grounded in His Word and courageous in His mission, for He will judge the world, and all who call upon His name will be saved.

52-Week Prophecy Study Plan

Series 1 – Birth & Lineage Prophecies

viii

Lesson:

1. **Sept 7** – Genesis 3:15 – The promise of the seed of the woman ... 1
2. **Sept 14** – Genesis 12:1–3 – Blessing through Abraham's seed ... 6
3. **Sept 21** – Genesis 49:8–12 – The scepter from Judah ... 12
4. **Sept 28** – 2 Samuel 7:12–16 – David's eternal throne ... 19
5. **Oct 5** – Isaiah 11:1–10 – The Branch from Jesse ... 25
6. **Oct 12** – Jeremiah 23:5–6 – The Righteous Branch, King who brings salvation ... 31
7. **Oct 19** – Hosea 11:1 – Out of Egypt I called my son ... 37
8. **Oct 26** – Malachi 3:1 – The messenger prepares the way ... 42
9. **Nov 2** – Psalm 2:6–12 – God's Son enthroned as King ... 48
10. **Nov 9** – Isaiah 42:1–7 – The Servant who brings justice ... 54
11. **Nov 16** – Isaiah 61:1–2 – The Spirit of the Lord upon Me ... 61
12. **Nov 23** – Zechariah 9:9 – The King comes on a donkey ... 67

Series 2 - Advent Season (Christmas Prophecies)

73

13. **Nov 30 (Advent I)** – Isaiah 7:14 – Virgin shall conceive – Immanuel ... 74
14. **Dec 7 (Advent II)** – Micah 5:2 – Ruler from Bethlehem ... 79
15. **Dec 14 (Advent III)** – Isaiah 9:6–7 – A child is born, Prince of Peace ... 84
16. **Dec 21 (Advent IV / Christmas Sunday)** – Matthew 1:18–25 – Immanuel Fulfilled ... 90
17. **Dec 28 – Numbers 24:17 -** A Star and a Scepter: The Rise of the Messiah ... 96

Series 3 – Life & Ministry Prophecies

102

18. **Jan 4** – Psalm 69:9 – Zeal for God's house consumes Him ... 103
19. **Jan 11** – Isaiah 35:5–6 – Healing of the blind and lame ... 109
20. **Jan 18** – Psalm 118:22–26 – The stone the builders rejected ... 114
21. **Jan 25** – Isaiah 8:14 – A stone of stumbling ... 120
22. **Feb 1** – Isaiah 53:3 – Despised and rejected by men ... 126
23. **Feb 8** – Malachi 4:2 – The Sun of Righteousness will rise ... 132
24. **Feb 15** – Psalm 41:9 – Betrayed by a close friend ... 138
25. **Feb 22** – Zechariah 11:12–13 – Thirty pieces of silver ... 144

Series 4 – Suffering & Death Prophecies

150

26. **Mar 1 (Lent I)** – Zechariah 13:7 – Strike the shepherd, sheep scattered ... 151
27. **Mar 8 (Lent II)** – Isaiah 50:6 – Suffering servant beaten and mocked ... 157
28. **Mar 15 (Lent III)** – Psalm 22:1–21 – Forsaken and pierced ... 163
29. **Mar 22 (Lent IV)** – Isaiah 53:4–6 – Wounded for our transgressions ... 170
30. **Mar 29 (Lent V / Passion Sunday)** – Isaiah 53:7–9 – Silent before ... 176

accusers, buried with the rich

31. **Apr 5 (Palm Sunday)** – Zechariah 12:10 – They will look on the one they pierced 182

32. **Apr 12 (Easter Sunday)** – Isaiah 53:10–12 – The Lord's will prospers through suffering & resurrection 188

Series 5 – Resurrection & Exaltation Prophecies

194

33. **Apr 19** – Psalm 34:20 – None of His bones broken 195
34. **Apr 26** – Psalm 16:10 – You will not let your Holy One see decay 200
35. **May 3** – Hosea 6:2 – On the third day He will raise us up 205
36. **May 10** – Isaiah 25:7–9 – He will swallow up death forever 210
37. **May 17** – Psalm 110:1 – Sit at my right hand 217
38. **May 24 (Pentecost)** – Joel 2:28–32 – I will pour out my Spirit on all people 221
39. **May 31 (Trinity Sunday)** – Daniel 7:13–14 – The Son of Man given authority 227

Series 6 – Messianic Kingdom Prophecies

232

40. **Jun 7** – Jeremiah 31:31–34 – The new covenant written on hearts 233
41. **Jun 14** – Ezekiel 36:25–28 – A new heart and a new spirit 239
42. **Jun 21** – Isaiah 2:1–5 – Nations streaming to the Lord's mountain 245
43. **Jun 28** – Isaiah 49:6 – A light to the nations 251
44. **Jul 5** – Ezekiel 37:24–28 – David my servant will be king 256
45. **Jul 12** – Zechariah 14:8–9 – The Lord will be King over all the earth 263
46. **Jul 19** – Habakkuk 2:14 – The earth filled with the knowledge of the Lord 269
47. **Jul 26** – Malachi 4:5–6 – Elijah before the day of the Lord 274
48. **Aug 2** – Psalm 118:17–23 – I will not die but live 279
49. **Aug 16** – Exodus 12:1–30 – The Passover lamb fulfilled in Christ 285
50. **Aug 23** – Numbers 21:4–9 – The bronze serpent lifted up 292
51. **Aug 30** – Daniel 9:24–26 – The Anointed One cut off 298
52. **Sept 6** – Isaiah 65:17–25 – New heavens and a new earth 304

About the Author 310

Introduction

The Importance of Prophecy in the Christian Faith

For a long time, I have desired to emphasize the importance of prophecy in strengthening our faith as we await the return of our Lord and Savior, Jesus Christ. Throughout Scripture, prophecy emerges as one of God's most powerful means of revealing His character, His purposes, and His plan of redemption. Far from being a collection of vague predictions or mystical sayings, biblical prophecy is the living Word of God, delivered through His chosen messengers to lead His people toward faith, obedience, and hope. For Christians, prophecy is central to understanding the Bible and deepening our relationship with Christ, affirming that the God we worship is sovereign over history, faithful to His promises, and committed to accomplishing salvation through His Son.

Prophecy as Revelation of God's Nature

Prophecy is significant because it reveals the nature of God. The God of Israel differentiated Himself from false gods not only through His mighty deeds but also by His ability to declare the end from the beginning. Through Isaiah, He declared: "I am God, and there is no other; I am God, and there is none like me. I make known the end from the beginning, from ancient times, what is still to come" (Isaiah 46:9–10). Prophecy underscores that history is not random but guided by His hand.

For Christians, studying prophecy is not merely about exploring future predictions; it is about deepening our understanding of God Himself. Prophecy is rooted in His covenant faithfulness.

Prophecy and the Fulfillment in Christ

The New Testament affirms the fulfillment of Old Testament prophecy in the life, death, and resurrection of Jesus Christ. Matthew's Gospel, in particular, repeatedly emphasizes how events in Jesus' life occurred "that it might be fulfilled what was spoken by the prophet." Jesus Himself affirmed the reliability of prophecy when He declared, "Do not think that I have come to abolish the Law or the Prophets; I have not come to abolish them but to fulfill them" (Matthew 5:17).

Jesus emphasized this connection. On the road to Emmaus, He explained to His disciples "what was said in all the Scriptures concerning himself" (Luke 24:27). For the apostles, prophecy was foundational to their message. At Pentecost, Peter quoted Joel 2 to explain the coming of the Spirit and Psalm 16 to proclaim the resurrection. In his letters, Paul repeatedly demonstrated how Christ fulfilled God's promises to Israel.

Prophecy and the Future Hope

Finally, prophecy keeps our eyes fixed on the future. The prophets foretold not only Christ's first coming but also His second. They spoke of a day when the knowledge of the Lord would fill the earth as the waters cover the sea (Habakkuk 2:14), when swords would be turned into plowshares (Isaiah 2:4), and when God would create new heavens and a new earth (Isaiah 65:17). Revelation expands on this vision, revealing its fulfillment in Christ's return.

For Christians, this future hope is essential, not optional. Paul refers to it as "the blessed hope—the appearing of the glory of our great God and Savior, Jesus Christ" (Titus 2:13). Prophecy reassures us that history is moving toward God's appointed goal: the reign of Christ and the restoration of all things.

Preparing for the Journey

This study of 52 key prophecies will guide us through the grand narrative of God's plan. We will start in Genesis, where the promise of a Savior first appears, and trace the unfolding promises through the Law, the Prophets, and the Psalms. We will observe how each prophecy finds fulfillment in Christ and how each one strengthens our faith in God's promises.

Our journey will take us from the first gospel in the garden to the promise of new creation in Revelation. Along the way, we will witness God's faithfulness, Christ's central role, and the Spirit's work in bringing God's Word to life. Our goal is not merely to understand prophecy but to be transformed by it—to grow in faith, hope, and love as we behold the God who speaks and fulfills His Word.

As we reflect on the role of prophecy in our faith journey, one truth becomes evident: it is woven into the very fabric of God's redemptive story. Prophecy is not an optional aspect of the Christian faith; it lies at its very heart. It reveals God's character, points us to Christ, assures us of the truth of Scripture, shapes our present lives, and anchors our hope for the future. To study prophecy is to see the unity of God's plan from Genesis to Revelation and to be reminded that our God is faithful, our Savior reigns, and our future is secure.

As we embark on this study, let us approach it with open hearts and eager minds, ready to see how every promise, every prophecy, and every word of God finds its fulfillment in Jesus Christ. For He is the Alpha and the Omega, the beginning and the end—and every prophecy points to Him.

Series 1 – Birth & Lineage Prophecies

PROPHECY FULFILLED - STUDY LESSON - 1

LESSON SCRIPTURE: **GENESIS 3:15**

PROPHECY TITLE

The First Gospel: God's Promise of Victory Over Evil

Introduction

Genesis 3:15, often called the Protoevangelium (PROH-toh-ee-van-JEE-lee-um), is the first announcement of the gospel. Spoken by God in the midst of judgment after the fall, it introduces hope where despair seemed final. God declares enmity between the serpent and the woman, pointing beyond human hostility toward snakes to a deeper, cosmic conflict between evil and humanity, especially those who belong to God.

The promise is remarkable because it speaks of the "seed of the woman," an unusual phrase that anticipates something unique. Christians have long recognized this as a foreshadowing of the virgin birth, where the Messiah would come not by human initiative but by divine power. The prophecy also sets forth the outcome of this conflict: the serpent will strike the offspring's heel—a real but temporary wound— while the offspring will crush the serpent's head, signifying decisive and eternal victory.

This verse becomes the foundation of the redemptive story that runs throughout Scripture. From Abraham's offspring to David's line to the prophecies of Isaiah, every step points back to this promise. Fulfilled in Jesus Christ through His death and resurrection, Genesis 3:15 reminds us that even in judgment God declared hope, and that evil would never have the final word.

Scripture Reference

Genesis 3:15 (NIV)

"And I will put enmity between you and the woman, and between your offspring and hers; he will crush your head, and you will strike his heel."

Big Picture Insights

- Protoevangelium (PROH-toh-ee-van-JEE-lee-um)– first proclamation of the gospel.
- Introduces the cosmic conflict between Satan and humanity.
- Seed of the woman hints at virgin birth.
- Promises ultimate defeat of Satan through Christ.
- Contrasts temporary suffering with final victory.
- Foreshadows covenant promises given to Abraham and David.
- Seen as foundational to messianic expectation.
- Provides hope amid judgment in Eden.
- Echoes in Israel's history (e.g., David and Goliath).
- Reaches final fulfillment in Revelation.

Verse-by-Verse Commentary

Genesis 3:15a — "And I will put enmity between you and the woman…"

- **God's initiative in enmity:** God Himself creates a lasting hostility between the serpent and the woman, asserting sovereign intervention after the fall. This is grace in action: He interrupts sinful alliance and inaugurates a redemptive conflict He intends to win.
- **Beginning of spiritual warfare:** This verse unveils a cosmic struggle that runs through Scripture. The serpent's deception sparks an enduring conflict between evil and the people of God, anticipating Christ's decisive victory and the church's persevering witness in a hostile world.
- **Assurance of a redemptive line:** By instituting enmity, God preserves a faithful lineage. The promised conflict safeguards a seed through whom blessing and deliverance will come, protecting the messianic line from extinction despite human failure and demonic opposition.

Genesis 3:15b — "…and between your offspring and hers…"

-
  Meaning of "offspring/seed": "Offspring" can be collective (God's people across generations) and ultimately singular (the Messiah). Scripture progressively narrows this promise—from Eve to Abraham to David—until it culminates in Christ, the true Seed who embodies Israel's calling.
- **Jewish and Christian readings:** Early Jewish interpretation often emphasized an ongoing struggle between Israel and evil. Christian interpretation affirms that the conflict climaxes in Jesus, whose life, death, and resurrection deliver a decisive blow, while the church continues His triumphal witness.
- **The serpent's "seed":** The serpent's seed represents personal and systemic evil in rebellion against God—spiritual powers and human participants aligned with darkness. This line stands opposed to God's people, yet cannot overturn His purpose or derail the promised redemption.

Genesis 3:15c — "…he will crush your head, and you will strike his heel."

-
  The wounded heel: The serpent's strike prefigures real suffering—Christ's passion and death. The wound is grievous yet not final; God turns apparent defeat into victory through resurrection, exposing evil's fury as ultimately powerless before His saving plan.
-
  The crushed head: Head-crushing signals total, fatal defeat. Christ's cross and empty tomb break the serpent's dominion, disarming principalities and powers. Evil remains active yet mortally wounded, destined for final judgment when Christ consummates His kingdom.
-
  Fulfillment and consummation: Fulfilled at the cross and resurrection, this promise continues to unfold as the church resists evil in the Spirit's power. Its consummation awaits Christ's return, when Satan is cast down forever and creation is restored in righteousness.

Discussion Questions

1. Why does God give hope in the midst of judgment?

2. What significance lies in the phrase "seed of the woman"?

3. 3. How does this verse shape our understanding of redemptive history?

4. What do the serpent's "head" and "heel" imagery teach us?

5. How is this verse echoed in other parts of Scripture?

6. How should this prophecy impact how the church views suffering?

7. What does Genesis 3:15 teach us about God's character?

Narrative Reflection

Genesis 3:15 is often called the first gospel, or the Protoevangelium (PROH-toh-ee-van-JEE-lee-um), because it introduces the promise of redemption at the moment of humanity's fall. In the garden, Adam and Eve confronted guilt, shame, and the curse of sin. Yet, in that dark hour, God spoke words of judgment to the serpent and words of hope for humanity. The promise of enmity between the serpent and the woman was no coincidence; it was a sovereign act of grace, ensuring that evil would never fully dominate humanity. This divine intervention maintained a line of hope that would endure through generations. Even as Adam and Eve were expelled from Eden, they left with the assurance that evil would not have the final say. The verse illustrates a cosmic conflict. The serpent's offspring symbolize the forces of evil and rebellion against God, while the woman's seed ultimately points to a singular figure who will secure ultimate victory. The phrase "seed of the woman" was particularly striking in a patriarchal society that traced lineage through men. Early Jewish interpreters often viewed this as the ongoing struggle between Israel and the forces of idolatry and evil. However, Christians discerned a hint of something extraordinary: a birth that would occur through divine means. This language has long been associated with the virgin birth of Christ, conceived not by human will but by divine initiative. The seed of the woman was not just any descendant but one uniquely chosen to defeat the serpent.

The imagery of the serpent striking the heel and the seed crushing the serpent's head conveys both suffering and victory. A heel wound can be painful and disabling, but it is not fatal. In contrast, a crushed head signifies death and final defeat. This duality encapsulates the essence of the cross and resurrection. At Calvary, Satan struck Christ's heel through suffering, humiliation, and death. Yet, the resurrection three days later revealed that the serpent's apparent victory was merely a temporary setback. The crushing of the serpent's head foreshadows the ultimate triumph when Christ will completely eradicate the powers of sin and death. The New Testament consistently echoes this imagery: Paul reminds the Romans that "the God of peace will soon crush Satan under your feet" (Romans 16:20), and John's Revelation depicts the dragon—the ancient serpent—cast into the lake of fire (Revelation 20:10). The promise first whispered in Eden resonates throughout the entire canon of Scripture.

Throughout history, theologians have returned to this verse as the foundation of redemption. Church fathers like Irenaeus contrasted Eve and Mary, noting that through Eve's disobedience came sin and death, while through Mary's obedience came life and salvation in Christ. The fall and the promise are thus set in parallel: what was broken through disobedience would be restored through faithfulness. Medieval interpreters often linked the bruised heel with the suffering of martyrs and the ongoing struggle between the church and evil. Reformation thinkers emphasized God's sovereign grace in initiating this promise before Adam and Eve repented, underscoring that salvation is rooted in divine action, not human effort.

Theologically, Genesis 3:15 establishes the trajectory of salvation history. It assures believers that hope predates despair and that grace was present even in Eden. It frames human history as a story of conflict—not merely between nations or individuals, but between the kingdom of God and the forces of darkness. This conflict is not evenly matched; the promise clearly states that while the serpent may inflict wounds, the ultimate outcome belongs to God. For Christians today, this shapes our understanding of suffering. Pain and opposition are real, but they are not the end. The bruised heel serves as a reminder that the path of Christ includes suffering, yet the crushed head assures us of certain victory.

Historically, the verse's placement within the creation narrative is significant. Ancient Near Eastern cultures often explained evil through myths of warring gods or cosmic accidents. In contrast, the Bible grounds evil in the rebellion of creatures within God's good creation while asserting that evil is bounded and doomed. This worldview provided Israel with a framework to understand their struggles with idolatrous nations and their hope in God's covenant promises. The genealogies and covenant promises that follow in Genesis can be viewed as manifestations of the "seed" theme, ultimately leading to the Messiah. The story of Israel becomes a narrative of the preservation of the seed until the coming of Christ.

For the modern church, Genesis 3:15 transcends ancient history. It reminds believers that redemption was never an afterthought or a mere fix for a flawed plan. From the beginning, God's design included victory over evil through Christ. It calls the church to live as a people who know that victory has already been secured, even as the conflict continues. It invites believers to view their sufferings not as meaningless wounds but as temporary pains within the larger story of triumph. Just as Christ's heel was struck, so the church experiences opposition; yet just as Christ crushed the serpent, the church shares in His victory.

Genesis 3:15 serves as a testament to God's unwavering faithfulness. He did not abandon humanity at its lowest moment but instead offered the first promise of redemption. This verse is the seedbed of hope, nourished by the prophets, cultivated through the covenants, flourishing in the life, death, and resurrection of Jesus, and awaiting its full fruition in the final victory described in Revelation. For believers today, it is both a call to perseverance and a source of unshakeable hope. Evil is real, but its defeat is certain. The serpent may strike, but its head is already crushed. And from Eden to eternity, the promise endures: God's love and plan for redemption are stronger than humanity's failures and Satan's schemes.

Layers of Understanding

Historical Context

Spoken in Eden immediately after humanity's fall, this verse brings hope into the midst of judgment. While curses are pronounced on the serpent, the woman, and the man, God simultaneously introduces His redemptive plan, ensuring sin would not have the final word.

Jewish Understanding

Early Jewish interpretation viewed this promise corporately, seeing the offspring of the woman as Israel itself. The verse was understood as describing Israel's ongoing struggle with hostile nations, evil powers, and the persistent lure of idolatry opposing God's covenant people.

New Testament Fulfillment

The New Testament repeatedly identifies Christ as the promised seed who defeats Satan. Galatians 4:4 affirms His coming, Romans 16:20 and Hebrews 2:14 highlight victory, while 1 John 3:8 and Revelation 12:9; 20:10 reveal Satan's final judgment and destruction.

Theological Significance Today

For believers, this verse teaches that present suffering and spiritual conflict are real but temporary. Christ's victory at the cross assures us that evil's power is limited, and His eternal triumph guarantees ultimate hope, restoration, and lasting security.

Cross-Reference Connections

- **Romans 16:20** – God will soon crush Satan under your feet.
- **Galatians 4:4** – Fulfillment in Christ, born of a woman.
- **Hebrews 2:14** – Christ breaks the power of the devil through death.
- **1 John 3:8** – The Son of God came to destroy the devil's work.
- **Revelation 12:9** – The serpent identified as Satan in ongoing conflict.
- **Revelation 20:10** – Final defeat of Satan in the lake of fire.

PROPHECY FULFILLED - STUDY LESSON - 2

LESSON SCRIPTURE: GENESIS 12:1-3

PROPHECY TITLE

The Abrahamic Covenant: God's Promise of Blessing to the Nations

Introduction

Genesis 12:1–3 marks a pivotal turning point in Scripture. After humanity's repeated failures in Genesis 1–11—from Adam's sin to the flood, to Babel's arrogance—God begins His redemptive plan anew by calling one man: Abram. Unlike Babel, where people sought to "make a name" for themselves, here God promises to make Abram's name great. These verses are the foundation of the Abrahamic Covenant, one of the most significant covenants in the Bible, shaping the identity of Israel and ultimately the mission of the church.

In this covenant, God calls Abram to leave his country, people, and family, promising him land, descendants, blessing, and protection. More importantly, God declares that through Abram "all peoples on earth will be blessed." This is not only the story of one man's journey of faith but the inauguration of God's plan to bring salvation to the entire world through the Messiah, Jesus Christ.

Christians see Genesis 12:1–3 as a prophecy pointing to the gospel. Abram's offspring ultimately finds its fulfillment in Christ, as Paul explains in Galatians 3:8, 16: "Scripture foresaw that God would justify the Gentiles by faith, and announced the gospel in advance to Abraham: 'All nations will be blessed through you.' … The promises were spoken to Abraham and to his seed. Scripture does not say 'and to seeds,' meaning many people, but 'and to your seed,' meaning one person, who is Christ."

Thus, Genesis 12:1–3 serves as a bridge: it connects God's promises of hope in Eden (Genesis 3:15) to His covenant with Israel and ultimately to the universal blessing accomplished through Jesus Christ.

Scripture Reference

Genesis 12:1-3 (NIV)

"The LORD had said to Abram, "Go from your country, your people and your father's household to the land I will show you. ² I will make you into a great nation, and I will bless you; I will make your name great, and you will be a blessing. ³ I will bless those who bless you, and whoever curses you I will curse; and all peoples on earth will be blessed through you."

Big Picture Insights

- Marks the beginning of the Abrahamic Covenant.
- God calls Abram to leave security and trust in His promises.
- Promise includes land, nationhood, and blessing.

- God Himself guarantees Abram's greatness and protection.
- Blessing extends beyond Israel to "all peoples on earth."
- Foreshadows Christ as the promised "seed" of Abraham.
- Establishes the covenantal theme running through Scripture.
- Contrasts Babel's self-made name with God's gift of a great name.
- Sets Abraham as the model of faith in Hebrews 11.
- Forms the foundation for Israel's identity and the church's mission.

Verse-by-Verse Commentary

Genesis 12:1 — "The LORD had said to Abram, "Go from your country, your people and your father's household to the land I will show you."

- **Divine initiative, human trust:** God's call uproots Abram from security without revealing the destination. Faith is obedience in motion—trusting God's promise more than familiar landscapes, risking loss to gain participation in God's unfolding redemptive plan.

- **Separation for mission:** The command separates Abram from competing loyalties (land, kin, father's house). God forms a new people by calling one man to radical allegiance, modeling how covenant identity precedes geography and reshapes every other attachment.

Genesis 12:2 — "I will make you into a great nation, and I will bless you; I will make your name great, and you will be a blessing. "

- **Grace precedes greatness:** God—not Abram—makes the nation and the name. Promise rebukes Babel's self-exaltation and replaces self-made towers with God-given legacy. Greatness becomes gift, not grasping, secured by covenant rather than human achievement.

- **Blessed to become blessing:** Blessing is not a cul-de-sac but a channel. God enlarges Abram's life so others flourish. True prosperity in Scripture always bends outward, redirecting honor, resources, and influence toward God's purpose for the world.

Genesis 12:3 — "I will bless those who bless you, and whoever curses you I will curse; and all peoples on earth will be blessed through you."

- **Protective solidarity:** God binds Himself to Abram's allies and stands against his adversaries. The promise creates a moral map: how nations treat Abram's line intersects with their experience of God's favor or frustration in history.

- **Global horizon in seed-form:** The universal promise anticipates Christ, Abram's true Seed, through whom the blessing reaches Jew and Gentile. The missionary trajectory of Scripture begins here, culminating in the gospel's worldwide embrace.

Discussion Questions

1. Why does God ask Abram to leave everything familiar before giving the promise?

2. How does Abram's call contrast with the pride of Babel in Genesis 11?

3. In what ways does God's promise to Abraham point forward to Christ?

4. What does it mean to be "blessed to be a blessing" in our lives today?

5. How does this covenant reveal God's heart for the nations?

6. Why is faith essential in responding to God's call, as seen in Abram's obedience?

7. What role does God's protection play in sustaining His promises?

Narrative Reflection

Genesis 12:1–3 is a pivotal passage in Scripture, marking the start of God's covenant plan for redeeming the world. Prior to this, the narrative in Genesis highlights repeated human failures—Adam and Eve in Eden, Cain's murder of Abel, the wickedness of Noah's generation, and the pride at Babel. Each story emphasizes humanity's inability to secure blessing or uphold righteousness independently. Yet, God does not abandon His creation. Instead, He initiates a new phase of His redemptive plan, unfolding not through human ambition but through divine calling and covenant promise. The focus shifts from the broad story of humanity to one man—Abram—through whom God will bless the entire world.

The narrative begins with a startling command: "Go from your country, your people, and your father's household to the land I will show you." In the ancient world, leaving one's homeland, extended family, and household involved more than just relocation; it meant severing ties with sources of identity, protection, and livelihood. Land signified survival, family represented security, and household conferred honor. God calls Abram to relinquish all these, stepping into the unknown with only His word to guide him. This moment underscores a truth that resonates throughout Scripture: faith requires trust in God beyond visible circumstances. Abram's obedience foreshadows the discipleship that Jesus later described when He said, "Whoever wants to be my disciple must deny themselves and take up their cross and follow me" (Mark 8:34). Abram exemplifies radical trust, leaving behind the visible to embrace the promised.

God's call is not merely a demand; it comes with extraordinary promises. God declares, "I will make you into a great nation, and I will bless you; I will make your name great, and you will be a blessing." The reversal of Babel is evident here. In Genesis 11, the people sought to "make a name for ourselves" through prideful ambition, only to be scattered and confounded. In contrast, God promises to make Abram's name great, showing that true greatness is not achieved through self-exaltation but bestowed through divine grace. Abram's greatness will not come from monuments of stone but from a covenantal relationship with the living God.

Central to these promises is the concept of blessing. The word "bless" appears five times in verses 2–3, emphasizing its significance. God promises not only to bless Abram personally but also to make him a conduit of blessing to others. Abram is chosen not for privilege alone, but for purpose: to be the channel through which God's redemptive grace flows to the nations. The covenant looks outward, envisioning a global impact. The culmination comes in verse 3: "All peoples on earth will be blessed through you." This sweeping declaration extends beyond Israel's national identity to a universal mission, ultimately fulfilled in Jesus Christ. As Paul explains in Galatians 3:8, Scripture announced the gospel in advance through Abraham, pointing to Christ as the seed through whom all nations receive blessing.

The promise of blessing and curse also reflects God's sovereign oversight of history: "I will bless those who bless you, and whoever curses you I will curse." This protective assurance means Abram's mission cannot be thwarted by human opposition. Nations and rulers may rise and fall, but God will safeguard His covenant purposes. Throughout Israel's history, this truth played out repeatedly—from Pharaoh's resistance in Egypt to the hostile nations surrounding the land of promise. Ultimately, this protective blessing reaches its climax in Christ, who triumphed over sin and death despite the curse of the cross.

The significance of Genesis 12:1–3 extends far beyond Abram's personal journey. It lays the foundation for Israel's unfolding story, as his descendants become the chosen people through whom God's covenantal purposes are revealed. The promises of land, nationhood, and blessing shape Israel's history: the exodus from Egypt, the conquest of Canaan, the establishment of the Davidic dynasty, and the prophetic vision of a Messiah. Yet Israel's role was never meant to be self-contained. The covenant's universal scope—"all peoples on earth"—anticipates a Messiah who would transcend national boundaries. This universal blessing is realized in Jesus Christ, the ultimate offspring of Abraham, who, through His death and resurrection, brings salvation to both Jew and Gentile.

In the New Testament, the apostles consistently interpret Genesis 12:1–3 in light of Christ. Peter, in Acts 3:25–26, tells his Jewish audience that they are heirs of the covenant God made with Abraham, adding that God has fulfilled this promise by raising Jesus to bless them by turning each of them from their wicked ways. Paul, in Romans 4, presents Abraham as the father not only of Israel but of all who believe, whether Jew or Gentile. Abraham becomes the model of faith for the church, demonstrating that righteousness is credited not by works but by trust in God's promises. Hebrews 11 reinforces this picture, celebrating Abraham as one who went out "not knowing where he was going," trusting in a city with foundations whose architect and builder is God.

For modern believers, Genesis 12:1–3 holds profound theological and practical significance. It teaches that faith often involves costly obedience—leaving behind the familiar to follow God into the unknown. It reminds us that God's blessings are meant to be shared, not hoarded. To be blessed is to be commissioned, entrusted with the mission of extending God's grace to others. The Abrahamic covenant serves as a paradigm for Christian mission: just as Abram was blessed to be a blessing to the nations, so the church is called to bear witness to Christ "to the ends of the earth" (Acts 1:8).

The narrative also challenges the church to embrace God's global vision. In a world fractured by nationalism, division, and prejudice, Genesis 12:3 reminds us that God's redemptive plan encompasses all peoples. The blessing of Abraham is not confined to one ethnicity or culture but extends universally. The church, as the spiritual offspring of Abraham, must embody this expansive vision, breaking down barriers and proclaiming Christ's blessing to every tribe, language, people, and nation.

At a deeper theological level, Genesis 12:1–3 reveals the character of God. Unlike the distant deities of the ancient Near East, the God of Scripture is deeply personal, initiating covenants with humanity, binding Himself to promises, and working through history to accomplish redemption. His call to Abram demonstrates both His sovereignty and His grace—sovereignty in choosing and directing Abram's destiny, and grace because Abram did nothing to earn this call. In this way, the covenant anticipates the gospel itself, where salvation is not achieved by human effort but received as a divine promise.

Finally, Genesis 12:1–3 reassures believers of the reliability of God's word. The promises given to Abram seemed impossible at the time: a barren couple would produce a nation, a wandering nomad would receive land, and one man's descendants would bless the world. Yet every promise was fulfilled in God's timing. This reminds us that God's faithfulness transcends our limitations. His promises may not align with our immediate circumstances, but His word never fails. Just as Abram trusted God's call into the unknown, we too are invited to trust the God who calls us forward into His promises.

Genesis 12:1–3 serves as a cornerstone of biblical theology. It bridges the primeval history of Genesis 1–11 with the covenantal story of Israel and ultimately with the universal gospel of Christ. It reveals a God who calls, a God who blesses, and a God who sends His people into the world to extend His blessing to all nations. For Abram, the journey began with a call to leave and a promise to trust. For the church, the journey continues in Christ, as we live out the covenant's fulfillment by proclaiming His blessing to the ends of the earth. From Abram's tent to the cross of Christ, and from the empty tomb to the church's global mission, the promise rings true: "All peoples on earth will be blessed through you."

Layers of Understanding

Historical Context

In the ancient Near East, land, family, and name were the foundations of security and honor. God's call to Abram upended these categories, demanding trust in His unseen promises. This covenant became Israel's charter of identity, shaping their national destiny and hope.

Jewish Understanding

Early Jewish interpretation emphasized Abram as the father of Israel and the covenantal source of God's blessing to His people. The promise of blessing and protection was seen as God's enduring faithfulness to the patriarchs and their descendants.

New Testament Fulfillment

The New Testament consistently identifies Jesus as the ultimate seed of Abraham. Galatians 3:8, 16 highlights that the blessing of all nations finds its fulfillment in Christ. Romans 4 portrays Abraham as the father of faith for both Jews and Gentiles, while Hebrews 11 presents him as the model of trust in God's promises.

Theological Significance Today

For Christians, Genesis 12:1–3 underscores that salvation is rooted in God's covenantal promises, fulfilled in Christ. It challenges the church to embrace its role as a global community of blessing, extending God's grace to all peoples. It reminds believers that faith often requires costly obedience but leads to eternal reward.

Cross-Reference Connections

- **Galatians 3:8, 16** – Christ as the seed of Abraham bringing blessing to nations.
- **Romans 4:16–17** – Abraham as father of all who believe.
- **Hebrews 11:8–10** – Abraham's faith in God's promises despite uncertainty.
- **Acts 3:25–26** – Fulfillment of the Abrahamic covenant in Christ's resurrection.
- **Genesis 15:5–6** – Abram's faith credited as righteousness.
- **Psalm 67:1–2** – Israel blessed so that God's ways are known on earth.

LESSON SCRIPTURE: **GENESIS 49:8-12**

PROPHECY TITLE

The Scepter of Judah: Promise of the Coming King

Introduction

Genesis 49 records Jacob's final words to his twelve sons, blessings that also serve as prophecies concerning the future of Israel's tribes. Among these blessings, the oracle to Judah (vv. 8–12) stands out as the most significant. While the other sons are described in terms of their character or future fortunes, Judah is uniquely singled out as the one destined for leadership, kingship, and ultimately, messianic fulfillment.

Jacob declares that Judah's brothers will praise him, his enemies will be subdued, and his descendants will hold the scepter — the symbol of royal authority. The prophecy climaxes with the declaration that "the scepter will not depart from Judah, nor the ruler's staff from between his feet, until he to whom it belongs shall come, and the obedience of the nations shall be his" (v. 10). This points beyond Judah's immediate descendants, such as David and Solomon, toward the promised Messiah who would establish an everlasting kingdom.

Christians throughout history have recognized this prophecy as fulfilled in Jesus Christ, the Lion of the tribe of Judah (Revelation 5:5), whose reign extends not only over Israel but over all nations. Genesis 49:8–12 therefore links God's promises from Abraham to David and ultimately to Christ, the eternal King.

Scripture Reference

Genesis 49:8–12 (NIV)

"Judah, your brothers will praise you; your hand will be on the neck of your enemies; your father's sons will bow down to you. [9] You are a lion's cub, Judah; you return from the prey, my son. Like a lion he crouches and lies down, like a lioness—who dares to rouse him? [10] The scepter will not depart from Judah, nor the ruler's staff from between his feet, until he to whom it belongs shall come and the obedience of the nations shall be his. [11] He will tether his donkey to a vine, his colt to the choicest branch; he will wash his garments in wine, his robes in the blood of grapes. [12] His eyes will be darker than wine, his teeth whiter than milk."

Big Picture Insights

- Judah is promised leadership and royal authority among the tribes.
- His line becomes the source of kingship in Israel, fulfilled in David.
- The "scepter" prophecy points to an enduring dynasty.
- Messianic expectation: "he to whom it belongs" is Christ.
- Revelation 5:5 identifies Jesus as the Lion of Judah.
- The imagery of lion conveys strength, majesty, and victory.
- Nations will one day submit to this ruler's authority.
- Abundance and prosperity are pictured in the vine and wine.
- The blessing carries both immediate (Davidic kings) and ultimate (Christ) fulfillment.
- Establishes the link between God's covenant with Abraham, Judah, and David.

Verse-by-Verse Commentary

Genesis 49:8 — "Judah, your brothers will praise you; your hand will be on the neck of your enemies; your father's sons will bow down to you."

- **Preeminence within the family:** Judah receives leadership among the tribes. Praise and homage signal God's choice, anticipating royal authority in Judah's line. This blessing sets the stage for David's throne and, ultimately, the Messiah's greater kingship.

- **Victory with responsibility:** "Hand on the neck of enemies" portrays decisive triumph, yet framed by family language. Dominion is given to serve covenant purposes—protecting, guiding, and uniting God's people under righteous leadership, not self-exalting power.

Genesis 49:9 — "You are a lion's cub, Judah; you return from the prey, my son. Like a lion he crouches and lies down, like a lioness—who dares to rouse him?"

- **Lion imagery of strength and maturity:** Judah grows from cub to commanding lion. Poised rest after victory suggests secure, uncontested rule. The picture communicates courage, wisdom, and stability rather than reckless aggression.

- **Lion of Judah trajectory:** Later Scripture names the Messiah "the Lion of the tribe of Judah" (Rev 5:5). The image links Judah's tribal destiny to Christ's royal authority, where fearless power serves redemptive peace.

Genesis 49:10 — "The scepter will not depart from Judah, nor the ruler's staff from between his feet, until he to whom it belongs shall come and the obedience of the nations shall be his."

- **Enduring royal line:** The scepter and ruler's staff promise continuous governance in Judah. The blessing anticipates the Davidic covenant and looks beyond it to a definitive heir whose right to rule is God-given and permanent.

- **Universal allegiance:** "Obedience of the nations" stretches the vision globally. The coming ruler's authority gathers Gentiles into joyful submission. In the Messiah, Israel's hope expands to the world, fulfilling the mission embedded in Abraham's promise.

Genesis 49:11 — "He will tether his donkey to a vine, his colt to the choicest branch; he will wash his garments in wine, his robes in the blood of grapes."

- **Abundant prosperity:** Vines so plentiful that tying a donkey to them risks no loss; wine flows like water. The Messiah's reign ushers in superabundance—fertility, peace, and security—signs of God's restorative blessing upon creation.

- **Victory and judgment hues:** Garments "washed in wine/blood of grapes" mix abundance with sober imagery of judgment. The conquering king establishes peace through righteousness, where justice purges evil and plenty adorns the land he restores.

Genesis 49:12 — "His eyes will be darker than wine, his teeth whiter than milk."

- **Vitality and beauty:** The language paints vigor, health, and compelling presence. The king's life-giving strength reflects the flourishing he brings—moral clarity, generous provision, and wholesome joy that nourishes his people.

- **A face of blessing:** The imagery hints at the shepherd-king whose countenance reassures and renews. Under his gaze, communities thrive; under his word, God's people taste the goodness of a kingdom marked by truth, abundance, and grace.

Discussion Questions

1. Why is Judah chosen over his older brothers to receive the promise of kingship?

2. How does the imagery of a lion help us understand Christ's role as King?

3. What does the prophecy of the scepter teach about God's covenant faithfulness?

4. In what ways does David's kingship anticipate the greater reign of Christ?

5. How does the obedience of the nations point to the gospel's global mission?

6. What spiritual meaning can be drawn from the imagery of vines, wine, and abundance?

7. How does this prophecy deepen our understanding of Jesus as the Messiah?

Narrative Reflection

Genesis 49:8–12 is one of the most remarkable prophetic blessings in Scripture. Spoken by Jacob in his final hours, these words reach beyond the immediate circumstances of his family, pointing to the future of Israel and, ultimately, the coming of the Messiah. While each of Jacob's twelve sons received blessings reflecting their character or future roles, Judah's blessing is unique in its depth, scope, and significance. It serves as a prophecy of kingship, culminating in the eternal reign of Jesus Christ, the Lion of the tribe of Judah.

The blessing begins with exaltation: "Judah, your brothers will praise you." Jacob's wordplay is intentional—Judah's name means "praise." This moment elevates Judah to a position of honor, not because he is the firstborn (Reuben) or the most beloved (Joseph), but because of God's sovereign choice for leadership. Judah's earlier life was marked by both failure and redemption—he suggested selling Joseph but later offered himself as a substitute for Benjamin (Genesis 44:33). His transformation from self-serving to self-sacrificing made him a worthy ancestor of kings. This theme reflects a pattern throughout Scripture: God chooses unlikely vessels, shaping them by grace for His purposes.

Verse 8 also promises Judah victory over his enemies and the submission of his brothers: "your hand will be on the neck of your enemies; your father's sons will bow down to you." This anticipates the unification of Israel under Judah's leadership. Historically, this was fulfilled when David, a descendant of Judah, was anointed king, and all the tribes pledged allegiance to him (2 Samuel 5:1–3). Beyond David, this prophecy foreshadows the Messiah, before whom every knee shall bow (Philippians 2:10).

The imagery deepens in verse 9: "You are a lion's cub, Judah… like a lion he crouches and lies down, like a lioness—who dares to rouse him?" In the ancient Near East, the lion symbolized strength, courage, and kingship. To call Judah a lion signifies that his tribe will embody royal authority and unchallengeable might. A resting lion represents secure power: it has conquered, fears no rival, and cannot be disturbed. This imagery reverberates throughout Scripture, culminating in Revelation 5:5, where Christ is revealed as the Lion of the tribe of Judah, worthy to open the scroll of God's purposes. The lion imagery reassures believers that Christ's kingship is not fragile or temporary, but unshakable and eternal.

Verse 10 delivers the heart of the prophecy: "The scepter will not depart from Judah, nor the ruler's staff from between his feet, until he to whom it belongs shall come and the obedience of the nations shall be his." The scepter and staff symbolize royal authority, indicating that kingship will permanently be associated with Judah's line. This was first fulfilled in David, to whom God promised an eternal dynasty (2 Samuel 7:12–16). However, David's throne points beyond itself. The phrase "he to whom it belongs" (sometimes translated "Shiloh") is widely understood as a messianic reference, describing the coming one who will hold rightful, everlasting authority, extending beyond Israel to embrace the nations. This verse became foundational for Jewish messianic expectation and for Christian belief that Jesus Christ is the promised king whose reign demands universal obedience.

The prophecy then shifts to imagery of abundance and prosperity in verses 11–12: "He will tether his donkey to a vine, his colt to the choicest branch; he will wash his garments in wine, his robes in the blood of grapes." The picture is almost extravagant: vines so plentiful that one could tie a donkey to them, wine so abundant it could be used like water. This symbolizes overflowing blessing and provision in the kingdom of the promised ruler. Many interpreters also find symbolic meaning here; the imagery of garments washed in wine connects to Christ, whose robes are described as dipped in blood in Revelation 19:13. Wine becomes a symbol, not merely of prosperity, but of redemption, pointing to the blood of Christ poured out for the salvation of the world. Thus, the abundance portrayed is both material and spiritual, fulfilled in the joy and life that flow from Christ's kingdom.

The final verse, "His eyes will be darker than wine, his teeth whiter than milk," depicts vitality, strength, and perfection. It completes the vision of Judah's descendant as the ideal ruler—full of life, vigor, and beauty. In contrast to human kings, who often succumb to weakness and corruption, the Messiah embodies everlasting strength and purity.

This prophecy unfolded in layers across Israel's history. Judah emerged as the leading tribe during the wilderness wanderings. Later, the monarchy was established in David, solidifying Judah's role as the royal line. Even after the Babylonian exile, when kingship seemed lost, prophets like Isaiah and Jeremiah preserved the promise of a future king from David's line who would reign forever (Isaiah 9:6–7; Jeremiah 23:5–6). For centuries, faithful Jews held onto the hope of this ruler. In the fullness of time, that hope was realized in Jesus Christ, born of the tribe of Judah (Matthew 1:2–3), proclaimed King of kings, and now exalted as Lord of all.

For Christians today, Genesis 49:8–12 is not merely an ancient blessing; it is a living testimony to God's covenant faithfulness. It reminds us that God's promises never fail, even when their fulfillment seems delayed. The scepter that passed from David to Solomon and eventually seemed lost in exile was never truly gone; it awaited the coming of Christ, who reigns not only over Israel but over all creation. His kingship calls believers to obedience, not out of fear, but out of joyful allegiance to the Lion of Judah who has conquered sin and death.

The imagery of abundance speaks to believers today. In Christ's kingdom, there is not scarcity but fullness. He provides joy greater than wine and nourishment better than milk. His blood, shed on the cross, becomes the true wine that cleanses and redeems. The extravagant imagery of vines and wine foreshadows the banquet of the Lamb, where His people will rejoice in His presence forever.

Finally, this prophecy challenges the church to live under the authority of Christ's scepter. The obedience of the nations is not merely a distant eschatological hope but a present mission. As the gospel spreads, people from every tribe and tongue are brought into joyful submission to the Lion of Judah. The church participates in this prophecy by proclaiming the good news of Christ's reign and embodying His justice, mercy, and abundance in a world that still longs for true kingship.

This passage is a sweeping vision of hope. It elevates Judah above his brothers, anticipates Israel's monarchy, and points beyond to the Messiah whose reign will never end. Its images of lions, scepters, vines, and wine converge in Jesus Christ, the Lion of Judah, the eternal King. For believers, this passage calls us to praise, trust, and live as citizens of His kingdom. From Jacob's deathbed to Christ's throne, the promise stands: the scepter belongs to Him, and the obedience of the nations shall be His.

Layers of Understanding

Historical Context

Spoken in Jacob's final blessing over his sons, this prophecy outlines Judah's rise to prominence among the tribes. Historically, the monarchy of Israel was established through David, a descendant of Judah, fulfilling the promise of the scepter.

Jewish Understanding

Jewish tradition interprets this passage as pointing to the Davidic dynasty and the expectation of a future Messiah from Judah's line. The "Shiloh" or "he to whom it belongs" was often understood as the anointed one who would bring peace.

New Testament Fulfillment

The New Testament identifies Jesus as the fulfillment of this prophecy. He is the Lion of Judah (Revelation 5:5), the descendant of David (Luke 1:32–33), and the eternal King whose reign draws the nations into obedience (Philippians 2:9–11).

Theological Significance Today

For believers, Genesis 49:8–12 affirms Christ's kingship and eternal reign. It calls the church to live under His authority, proclaim His lordship to the nations, and anticipate the day when His reign is consummated in justice, abundance, and peace.

Cross-Reference Connections

- **2 Samuel 7:12–16** – God's covenant with David, promising an eternal throne.
- **Psalm 72** – Messianic vision of a king who rules in righteousness.
- **Isaiah 9:6–7** – Prophecy of a child born to rule with justice forever.
- **Revelation 5:5** – Jesus as the Lion of the tribe of Judah.
- **Philippians 2:9–11** – Every knee bowing to Christ, Lord of all.
- **Luke 1:32–33** – Jesus as heir to David's throne, reigning forever.

PROPHECY FULFILLED - STUDY LESSON - 4

LESSON SCRIPTURE: **2 SAMUEL 7:12-16**

PROPHECY TITLE

The Eternal Throne: God's Covenant with David

Introduction

Few passages in Scripture carry the weight and scope of 2 Samuel 7:12–16. Here, God speaks to King David through the prophet Nathan, establishing a covenant that reaches far beyond David's lifetime. Though David desired to build a house (temple) for the Lord, God reverses the expectation and promises instead to build a "house" for David—a royal dynasty that will endure forever.

This promise, known as the Davidic Covenant, anchors much of Israel's hope in the Old Testament and forms the backbone of messianic expectation. Though partially fulfilled in David's son Solomon, whose reign included the construction of the temple, the covenant pointed to a far greater son—Jesus Christ—whose kingdom would never end. The covenant links the promises given to Abraham and Judah with the New Testament proclamation that Christ is the Son of David, the eternal King.

Christians see in this passage the clearest Old Testament prophecy of Christ's everlasting reign. The angel Gabriel confirmed this connection when he announced to Mary: "The Lord God will give him the throne of his father David, and he will reign over Jacob's descendants forever; his kingdom will never end" (Luke 1:32–33). The Davidic Covenant is therefore central to understanding the continuity of God's redemptive plan.

Scripture Reference

2 Samuel 7:12–16 (NIV)

"When your days are over and you rest with your ancestors, I will raise up your offspring to succeed you, your own flesh and blood, and I will establish his kingdom. [13] He is the one who will build a house for my Name, and I will establish the throne of his kingdom forever. [14] I will be his father, and he will be my son. When he does wrong, I will punish him with a rod wielded by men, with floggings inflicted by human hands. [15] But my love will never be taken away from him, as I took it away from Saul, whom I removed from before you. [16] Your house and your kingdom will endure forever before me; your throne will be established forever.'"

Big Picture Insights

- Known as the Davidic Covenant, central to biblical theology.
- God promises to build a dynasty ("house") for David.
- Immediate fulfillment through Solomon (temple, kingdom).
- Ultimate fulfillment through Christ, the Son of David.
- Establishes the hope of an eternal throne.

- God's steadfast love contrasts with Saul's rejected kingship.
- Links back to Judah's scepter prophecy (Genesis 49:10).
- Connects forward to New Testament (Luke 1:32–33; Acts 2:30–36).
- Reveals God's initiative: David would not build for God, but God would build for David.
- Grounds the messianic hope in history and covenant faithfulness.

Verse-by-Verse Commentary

2 Samuel 7:12 — **"When your days are over and you rest with your ancestors, I will raise up your offspring to succeed you, your own flesh and blood, and I will establish his kingdom."**

- **Dynasty by promise, not politics:** God sovereignly sustains David's line. The kingdom's security rests on divine covenant, not human maneuvering. Even after David, God Himself will raise up the heir to carry forward His redemptive rule.
- **Seed with a future:** "Offspring" looks to Solomon immediately and to a greater Son ultimately. The promise outlives David, anchoring hope beyond one reign, building expectation for a messianic king who fulfills every covenant word.

2 Samuel 7:13 — **"He is the one who will build a house for my Name, and I will establish the throne of his kingdom forever."**

- **House for God, throne for David:** Solomon builds the temple, yet the "forever" language stretches beyond him. God binds His presence (house) and royal rule (throne) together, hinting that the greater Son will unite worship and kingship perfectly.
- **Forever horizon:** Human kings fail; empires fall. But this oath reaches beyond historical collapse to an everlasting reign, preparing the way for Christ whose resurrection enthronement secures an unending kingdom.

2 Samuel 7:14 — **"I will be his father, and he will be my son. When he does wrong, I will punish him with a rod wielded by men, with floggings inflicted by human hands."**

- **Covenant intimacy with discipline:** God's fatherly bond isn't indulgence. He disciplines errant sons (like Solomon and successors) to preserve the line. Divine correction guards covenant purposes, keeping the royal house from final ruin.
- **Typology fulfilled without flaw:** Later kings falter; the greater Son does not. Jesus embodies perfect sonship, bearing judgment not for His sin but ours, transforming royal discipline into redemptive substitution.

2 Samuel 7:15 — **"But my love will never be taken away from him, as I took it away from Saul, whom I removed from before you."**

- **Steadfast love secures the line:** Unlike Saul's rejected dynasty, David's house is held by covenant loyalty (hesed). God's unwavering commitment, not regal performance, maintains the promise through history's upheavals.
- **Grace stronger than failure:** Even royal sin cannot dissolve divine fidelity. God's covenant love outlasts human weakness, ensuring hope remains for a faithful King who will never forfeit the promise.

2 Samuel 7:16 — "Your house and your kingdom will endure forever before me; your throne will be established forever."

- **Everlasting throne promised:** The triple "forever" nails the certainty. Before God's face, the Davidic line remains. The New Testament identifies Jesus as this eternal King, enthroned by resurrection and reigning until all enemies are subdued.
- **Worshipful assurance:** Israel's hope—and the church's—rests here: an unshakable throne, a righteous King, a future guaranteed by God's oath. History bends toward the Son of David who rules in justice and peace.

Discussion Questions

1. Why did God reverse David's plan to build Him a house, and what does this reveal about divine initiative?

2. How does the Davidic Covenant build on the promises given to Abraham and Judah?

3. What are the differences between Solomon's fulfillment of this prophecy and Christ's?

4. How does the promise of "forever" change our understanding of God's covenant faithfulness?

5. In what ways does Jesus, the Son of David, build a greater "house" than the temple?

6. Why is the contrast with Saul significant in understanding God's promise to David?

7. How should the reality of Christ's eternal throne shape the church's mission today?

Narrative Reflection

The Davidic Covenant, found in 2 Samuel 7:12–16, marks a pivotal moment in the unfolding narrative of redemption. Central to this covenant is a significant reversal. At the peak of his success, David aspired to build a house for the Lord. He had united the tribes, conquered Jerusalem, and brought the ark into the city. His reign symbolized stability, and his wish to honor God with a permanent temple seemed both noble and appropriate. However, God, through the prophet Nathan, rejected David's plan. Instead, God reversed the promise: it would not be David who built a house for God, but God who would build a house for David.

This reversal underscores a profound truth: human intentions, no matter how well-meaning, always take a backseat to God's sovereign purposes. While David sought to do something for God, God aimed to do something through David. The essence of this covenant centers not on human initiative but on divine promise. God Himself commits to establishing David's lineage, ensuring that his throne would endure forever.

The covenant unfolds in layers. Its immediate fulfillment is seen in Solomon, David's son, who succeeded him as king and built the temple in Jerusalem. Verse 13 specifically mentions the construction of a house for God's name, which Solomon completed in grandeur. Yet, the language of an eternal throne extends beyond Solomon, whose reign, though splendid, was temporary and tainted by sin. Following Solomon, the Davidic line experienced division, decline, and ultimately exile. From a human standpoint, the promise seemed broken. Yet God's word remains unfailing. Even during exile, prophets like Isaiah, Jeremiah, and Ezekiel recalled the Davidic covenant, proclaiming that God would raise up a righteous Branch from David's lineage to reign forever in justice and peace (Isaiah 9:6–7; Jeremiah 23:5–6).

The New Testament affirms that Jesus Christ is the ultimate fulfillment of this covenant. The genealogies in Matthew and Luke trace His lineage back to David, confirming Him as the promised heir. When the angel Gabriel announced His birth to Mary, he proclaimed that the Lord God would give Him the throne of His father David and that His kingdom would never end (Luke 1:32–33). On Pentecost, Peter declared that God had raised Jesus to sit on David's throne (Acts 2:30–36). The eternal kingdom promised to David is realized in Christ, who reigns now at the right hand of God.

Verse 14 introduces the father-son relationship: "I will be his father, and he will be my son." While this applied to Solomon in a limited sense, its fullest expression is found in Christ, who is uniquely the Son of God. This covenantal sonship foreshadows the incarnation, where the eternal Son takes on flesh to reign as the perfect King. The clause regarding discipline pertains to Solomon and his descendants, but in Christ, who committed no sin, the punishment clause is transformed—He endured discipline not for His own wrongdoing but for ours (Isaiah 53:5).

The covenant also contrasts David's lineage with Saul's. God affirms that His love will never be removed from David's house, unlike Saul, whose kingdom was taken away. This contrast emphasizes God's steadfast love (*hesed*), His unwavering covenant loyalty. In Christ, this covenant reaches its climax: God's love, exemplified at the cross, secures an unshakeable kingdom that can never be taken from us.

Theologically, the Davidic Covenant is crucial because it unites the promises of the Abrahamic and Mosaic covenants into a royal, messianic hope. From Abraham came the promise of blessing to the nations (Genesis 12:3). From Judah came the promise of the scepter (Genesis 49:10). Now, through David, the promise focuses on an eternal king. This covenant sets the course for the prophets, the psalms, and the messianic hope that permeates the Old Testament.

For the church today, this passage represents more than history; it speaks to our identity. Believers acknowledge Jesus as not only Savior but also as Lord, the eternal Son of David. His throne is established, and His kingdom advances as the gospel spreads among the nations. We navigate the tension of the "already" and the "not yet." Christ reigns now, yet we await the fullness of His kingdom when He returns to judge and renew all things. The promise of 2 Samuel 7 assures us that history is purposeful, directed by God's covenant faithfulness.

This covenant also calls believers to trust in God's promises, even when circumstances seem bleak. When Judah went into exile and the Davidic throne was vacant, it may have appeared that God's word had failed. Yet centuries later, Christ arrived as the fulfillment, demonstrating that no circumstance can nullify God's covenant. For us, in times of waiting, suffering, or uncertainty, the Davidic Covenant reassures us that God's promises in Christ are secure.

Also, the Davidic Covenant teaches us about grace. David aimed to build for God; instead, God chose to build for David. Similarly, salvation is not about what we achieve for God but about what God has accomplished for us in Christ. The eternal throne is not the result of human effort but the gift of divine grace.

2 Samuel 7:12–16 stands as a monumental prophecy in Scripture. It affirms God's sovereignty, His covenant love, and His faithfulness to His promises. It directs our attention from David and Solomon to Christ, the Son of David, the eternal King. For believers, it serves as both reassurance and commission: reassurance that Christ's kingdom is unshakeable and a commission to live as His loyal subjects, proclaiming His reign until He returns. From David's throne in Jerusalem to Christ's throne in heaven, the promise persists: "Your house and your kingdom will endure forever; your throne will be established forever."

Layers of Understanding

Historical Context

Given in the height of David's reign, this covenant established Israel's monarchy as divinely chosen. Though Solomon fulfilled part of it, the ultimate meaning transcends Israel's political history.

Jewish Understanding

For Israel, the Davidic covenant was the cornerstone of messianic expectation. After the exile, prophets drew hope from God's promise that a king would come from David's line. Though Israel's expectations were often misplaced, the covenant found its true fulfillment in God's sovereign purpose through Christ.

New Testament Fulfillment

Jesus Christ is the ultimate Son of David. Luke 1:32–33, Acts 2:30–36, and Revelation 22:16 all affirm His kingship. His resurrection is the guarantee of the eternal throne.

Theological Significance Today

The Davidic Covenant anchors the church's confession of Christ as Lord. It calls believers to trust God's faithfulness, live under Christ's kingship, and proclaim His eternal reign to the nations.

Cross-Reference Connections

- **Psalm 89:3–4, 28–29** – God's covenant faithfulness to David.
- **Isaiah 9:6–7** – The promise of an everlasting kingdom.
- **Jeremiah 23:5–6** – A righteous Branch from David's line.
- **Luke 1:32–33** – Gabriel's announcement of Christ's eternal throne.
- **Acts 2:30–36** – Peter proclaims Jesus seated on David's throne.
- **Revelation 22:16** – Jesus as the Root and Offspring of David.

PROPHECY FULFILLED - STUDY LESSON –5

LESSON SCRIPTURE: **ISAIAH 11:1-10**

PROPHECY TITLE

The Branch from Jesse: The Spirit-Anointed King of Peace

Introduction

Isaiah 11:1–10 is one of the clearest and most beautiful messianic prophecies in the Old Testament. Written during a time of national turmoil and impending judgment, Isaiah paints a picture of hope that goes beyond political deliverance. Though David's dynasty (the "tree of Jesse") seemed destined for destruction, Isaiah promises that from the stump of this seemingly dead tree would come a new shoot—a king unlike any other, Spirit-filled and perfectly righteous.

This prophecy not only affirms the continuity of God's covenant promises to David (2 Samuel 7:12–16) but also expands them. The coming king will not merely rule Israel; He will bring justice for the poor, righteousness for the nations, and a kingdom marked by peace so radical that even nature itself will be transformed.

Christians recognize this passage as pointing directly to Jesus Christ, the descendant of David who came in the power of the Spirit, embodied righteousness, and brought reconciliation between God and humanity. The vision culminates in verse 10: the Root of Jesse will stand as a banner for the peoples, and the nations will rally to Him.

Scripture Reference

Isaiah 11:1–10 (NIV)

"A shoot will come up from the stump of Jesse; from his roots a Branch will bear fruit. ² The Spirit of the LORD will rest on him— the Spirit of wisdom and of understanding, the Spirit of counsel and of might, the Spirit of the knowledge and fear of the LORD— ³ and he will delight in the fear of the LORD. He will not judge by what he sees with his eyes, or decide by what he hears with his ears; ⁴ but with righteousness he will judge the needy, with justice he will give decisions for the poor of the earth. He will strike the earth with the rod of his mouth; with the breath of his lips he will slay the wicked. ⁵ Righteousness will be his belt and faithfulness the sash around his waist. ⁶ The wolf will live with the lamb, the leopard will lie down with the goat, the calf and the lion and the yearling together; and a little child will lead them. ⁷ The cow will feed with the bear, their young will lie down together, and the lion will eat straw like the ox. ⁸ The infant will play near the cobra's den, the young child will put its hand into the viper's nest. ⁹ They will neither harm nor destroy on all my holy mountain, for the earth will be filled with the knowledge of the LORD as the waters cover the sea. ¹⁰ In that day the Root of Jesse will stand as a banner for the peoples; the nations will rally to him, and his resting place will be glorious."

Big Picture Insights

- **The Branch from Jesse** – Messiah arises from David's line, despite apparent ruin.
- **Spirit-filled ruler** – sevenfold Spirit (wisdom, understanding, counsel, might, knowledge, fear, delight).
- **Justice for the poor** – unlike earthly kings, Messiah defends the marginalized.
- **Victory over wickedness** – His word brings judgment.
- **Perfect righteousness** – His reign is marked by faithfulness.
- **Peaceful kingdom** – imagery of wolf, lamb, lion, and child in harmony.
- **Cosmic transformation** – creation itself restored under His rule.
- **Universal mission** – nations rally to the Root of Jesse.
- **Messianic fulfillment** – realized in Christ's first coming, consummated at His return.
- **Hope amid despair** – God's promises remain, even from a "stump."

Verse-by-Verse Commentary

Isaiah 11:1 — "A shoot will come up from the stump of Jesse; from his roots a Branch will bear fruit."

- **Life from apparent death:** David's line looks felled like a stump, yet God brings fresh growth. Renewal is God's specialty—He resurrects hope where monarchy seems finished, preparing a humble, holy King.
- **Back to Jesse, not just David:** By naming Jesse, Isaiah directs attention to the family's roots. The coming King isn't a mere repeat of David but a purer, Spirit-filled fulfillment of the royal ideal.

Isaiah 11:2 — "The Spirit of the LORD will rest on him— the Spirit of wisdom and of understanding, the Spirit of counsel and of might, the Spirit of the knowledge and fear of the LORD—"

- **Sevenfold fullness:** Wisdom, understanding, counsel, might, knowledge, fear of the Lord—complete equipment for perfect rule. The Messiah's authority flows from the Spirit's abiding presence, not from military might or political craft.
- **Delight in holy reverence:** His leadership is anchored in the fear of the Lord—ethical clarity, humble dependence, and joyful obedience, producing justice that reflects God's character.

Isaiah 11:3–5 — "and he will delight in the fear of the LORD. He will not judge by what he sees with his eyes, or decide by what he hears with his ears; ⁴ but with righteousness he will judge the needy, with justice he will give decisions for the poor of the earth. He will strike the earth with the rod of his mouth; with the breath of his lips he will slay the wicked. ⁵ Righteousness will be his belt and faithfulness the sash around his waist."

- **Justice beyond appearances:** He penetrates spin, status, and surface. The poor receive equity; the wicked face truth. Word and breath accomplish judgments that reshape society with integrity and compassion.

- **Righteousness as clothing:** Girded with righteousness and faithfulness, He embodies covenant virtues. His rule protects the vulnerable, restrains oppression, and establishes a moral order aligned with God's heart.

Isaiah 11:6–9 — "The wolf will live with the lamb, the leopard will lie down with the goat, the calf and the lion and the yearling together; and a little child will lead them. [7] The cow will feed with the bear, their young will lie down together, and the lion will eat straw like the ox. [8] The infant will play near the cobra's den, the young child will put its hand into the viper's nest. [9] They will neither harm nor destroy on all my holy mountain, for the earth will be filled with the knowledge of the LORD as the waters cover the sea."

- **Creation reconciled:** Predators and prey dwell peaceably. The curse's hostilities unwind under the Messiah's reign, signaling comprehensive shalom: safety, harmony, and flourishing for all creation.
- **Knowledge of the Lord filling the earth:** Not merely information, but intimate, transforming awareness saturates the world. Violence withers where God is truly known; holiness becomes habitat.

Isaiah 11:10 — "In that day the Root of Jesse will stand as a banner for the peoples; the nations will rally to him, and his resting place will be glorious."

- **Root and rallying point:** He is both source and shoot—origin and heir. Nations turn to His banner, fulfilling the global horizon of the promises to Abraham and David.
- **Resting place glorious:** His presence becomes sanctuary for weary peoples. Mission flows from monarchy; the King draws the world into God's rest.

Discussion Questions

1. Why does Isaiah describe David's line as a "stump," and what hope does this imagery convey?

2. How does the description of the Spirit on the Messiah point us to Christ's ministry?

3. What does it mean that Christ judges with righteousness rather than appearances?

4. How should the vision of a peaceable kingdom shape our understanding of Christ's reign?

5. In what sense has this prophecy already been fulfilled, and in what sense is it still future?

6. Why is it significant that the Root of Jesse is also a banner for the nations?

7. How does this prophecy challenge us to live as people of the kingdom today?

Narrative Reflection

The image of a tender shoot emerging from a cut-down stump offers one of Scripture's most powerful portraits of renewal. In this prophecy, Isaiah reveals the Messiah whose Spirit-filled reign transforms the world with righteousness and peace. At the time Isaiah delivered these words, Judah faced significant threats. The once-mighty Davidic dynasty appeared on the brink of collapse due to invading forces. Isaiah had already warned of impending judgment, predicting that what was once a flourishing tree of David's lineage would be reduced to a mere stump. Yet from that seemingly lifeless stump, God promised new growth.

This new growth signifies not merely a revival of an old monarchy, but the emergence of something far greater: a shoot from Jesse, a Branch that will bear fruit. The imagery is compelling. While cut-down trees seem dead, new shoots often arise from their roots. Similarly, God would bring life from what appeared lifeless. This imagery reflects Christ's humble beginnings. Born not in the palace of Jerusalem but in a manger in Bethlehem, Jesus emerged from obscurity. Though the world did not recognize Him as royalty, He embodied the full weight of God's promises as the heir of David's line.

Verses 2–3 shift the focus to the Messiah's character and empowerment. Unlike human kings, whose authority relies on military strength or political alliances, this king is distinguished by the Spirit of the Lord. The sevenfold description—wisdom, understanding, counsel, might, knowledge, fear of the Lord, and delight in the fear of the Lord—highlights the fullness and perfection of His Spirit-led reign. The Gospels vividly illustrate this: Jesus' ministry begins with the Spirit descending upon Him at His baptism (Matthew 3:16). His teachings demonstrate wisdom beyond human understanding, His miracles reveal divine power, and His obedience reflects perfect reverence for the Lord. Isaiah reminds us that this king rules not through worldly strength but through Spirit-filled faithfulness.

In verses 4–5, the Messiah's reign is characterized by justice and righteousness. He defends the needy, speaks truth, and judges impartially. This stands in stark contrast to many kings of Israel and Judah, who often exploited the poor or relied on appearances. Jesus exemplified this perfectly: He showed compassion to the marginalized, healed the sick, and welcomed those whom society rejected. His authority stemmed not from wealth or status but from righteousness. His words held power, reaching deep into the heart, and His faithfulness became the foundation of His rule.

The most renowned section, verses 6–9, presents a vision of a peaceable kingdom. The wolf and the lamb, the leopard and the goat, the lion and the calf—all coexist harmoniously under the leadership of a child. This imagery is striking, as it defies natural instincts; predators and prey do not typically live side by side. Yet, in the Messiah's kingdom, harmony is restored. This vision signifies not only political peace but also cosmic transformation. Paul echoes this in Romans 8, describing creation itself groaning and waiting for redemption. Under Christ's reign, creation will no longer be marked by hostility but by shalom—comprehensive peace.

The culmination occurs in verse 9: "The earth will be filled with the knowledge of the Lord as the waters cover the sea." This vision extends beyond Israel. The Messiah's reign is not tribal, national, or regional; it is universal. Just as the waters thoroughly cover the sea, so will God's knowledge and glory permeate the entire earth. This sharply contrasts with Isaiah's time when nations worshiped idols, and power seemed to belong to empires like Assyria. Isaiah declares that the true King will one day be recognized by all nations.

Verse 10 ties everything together: "The Root of Jesse will stand as a banner for the peoples; the nations will rally to him." Remarkably, the Messiah is both the shoot from Jesse (a descendant) and the root of Jesse (the source). This paradox points to Christ's divine nature. As a man, He is a descendant of David's line; as God, He is David's Lord (cf. Matthew 22:45; Revelation 22:16). He becomes the rallying point for all nations. In Christ, Gentiles are grafted into the promises once given to Israel, fulfilling God's plan for all nations to be blessed through Abraham.

For Christians today, this prophecy provides both comfort and challenge. It reassures us that God brings life from stumps. When situations seem hopeless—whether in our personal lives, our communities, or the world—God can generate new growth. The Messiah arose from a stump, and He continues to bring resurrection where all seems lost.

It also challenges us because it describes a kingdom defined by righteousness, justice, and peace. As followers of Christ, we are called to embody these values now. We exist in the "already but not yet" of the kingdom—Christ has come, but His reign is not yet fully realized. We are to pursue justice, extend compassion to the poor, seek reconciliation, and live in hope of the day when peace will cover the earth.

This vision also fuels our mission. Isaiah does not conclude with Israel alone; he proclaims that the nations will rally to the Root of Jesse. The gospel is global in scope, and as the church, we are called to proclaim the banner of Christ to all peoples. His resting place is glorious, and all who believe are invited into that glory.

This prophecy is renowned for its sweep from despair to hope, from judgment to restoration, from a lifeless stump to a flourishing branch. It portrays the Messiah not only as Israel's Spirit-filled ruler but also as the King of the nations, the restorer of creation, and the bringer of everlasting peace. For Isaiah's audience, it was the assurance that God had not abandoned His covenant. For us, it is the reminder that

Christ has come, Christ reigns, and Christ will come again to make all things new. The Root and Shoot of Jesse is our King, our Banner, and our Peace.

Layers of Understanding

Historical Context

Isaiah prophesied during a time of Assyrian threat and decline of the Davidic monarchy. The promise of a new Branch from Jesse was a lifeline of hope for a people facing judgment.

Jewish Understanding

Many Jewish interpreters regarded this passage as a messianic prophecy, anticipating a future king from David's line who would rule with wisdom, righteousness, and justice. This expectation was not merely political but also spiritual, envisioning peace, restoration, and harmony throughout Israel and ultimately extending to the nations.

New Testament Fulfillment

Christ fulfills this prophecy as the Spirit-anointed Son of David (Luke 3:23–38; Matthew 3:16). Revelation 5:5 and 22:16 explicitly call Him the Root of David.

Theological Significance Today

For Christians, Isaiah 11 reveals Christ as both the hope of Israel and the Savior of the nations. His kingdom is marked by justice, peace, and renewal—realities we anticipate and live out in part until He comes again.

Cross-Reference Connections

- **Matthew 3:16** – Spirit descends on Jesus at baptism.
- **Romans 15:12** – Paul cites Isaiah 11:10, applying it to Christ's mission to the Gentiles.
- **Revelation 5:5** – Jesus, the Lion of Judah, the Root of David.
- **Revelation 22:16** – Jesus as the Root and Offspring of David.
- **Romans 8:19–21** – Creation waits for renewal.

PROPHECY FULFILLED - STUDY LESSON – 6

LESSON SCRIPTURE: **JEREMIAH 23:5-6**

PROPHECY TITLE

The Righteous Branch: The King Who Brings Salvation

Introduction

Jeremiah ministered during one of the darkest periods in Judah's history. Corrupt kings, faithless prophets, and a disobedient people had pushed the nation to the brink of destruction. In Jeremiah 23, God condemns the failed shepherds of His people—leaders who scattered the flock instead of protecting it. Yet amidst this despair, God offers a promise: He will raise up a righteous king from David's lineage.

This king is known as the "Righteous Branch." Unlike Judah's failed rulers, He will govern with wisdom, justice, and righteousness. His reign will bring safety and salvation, and His name will be *"The Lord Our Righteous Savior."*

For Christians, this prophecy is fulfilled in Jesus Christ. He is the long-awaited Son of David who not only rules in righteousness but also grants righteousness to His people through His death and resurrection. Where earthly kings failed, Christ succeeded; where Judah's leaders brought ruin, Christ brings salvation and restoration.

Scripture Reference

Jeremiah 23:5–6 (NIV) **⁵ "The days are coming," declares the LORD, "when I will raise up for David a righteous Branch, a King who will reign wisely and do what is just and right in the land. ⁶ In his days Judah will be saved and Israel will live in safety. This is the name by which he will be called: The LORD Our Righteous Savior.**

Big Picture Insights

- **God's promise of a Righteous Branch** – a Messianic king from David's line.
- **Contrast to corrupt kings** – unlike Judah's failed rulers, this king rules justly.
- **Wisdom and righteousness** – His reign embodies God's character.
- **Salvation and safety** – His people experience deliverance and peace.
- **Messianic name** – "The Lord Our Righteous Savior" points to Christ's saving work.
- **Fulfilled in Christ** – He is the Son of David and our righteousness (1 Cor. 1:30).
- **Gospel foundation** – Christ not only rules in righteousness but imputes it to His people.
- **Hope amid judgment** – God's covenant with David still stands, even in exile.
- **Future vision** – ultimate safety and peace realized fully in Christ's return.

Verse-by-Verse Commentary

Jeremiah 23:5a — "The days are coming," declares the LORD, "I will raise up for David a righteous Branch …"

- **Branch from the stump:** Isaiah 11:1's "shoot from the stump of Jesse" echoes here. Out of apparent dynastic death, God brings living growth. Exile cannot cancel covenant; divine promise germinates precisely where human prospects wither.
- **Covenant endurance under judgment:** The monarchy's failure invited discipline, but not abandonment. "Branch" signals renewal from God's side—He preserves David's line and moves history toward restoration, proving that judgment serves mercy's larger purpose.
- **Righteousness at the core:** Unlike corrupt kings, this heir embodies God's justice. His character is the antidote to failed shepherds (23:1–2). Integrity is not cosmetic; it defines his person and the order he establishes for God's people.

Jeremiah 23:5b — "…a King who will reign wisely and do what is just and right in the land."

- **Wisdom as divine gift:** The king's discernment recalls Solomon's prayer (1 Kings 3:9), yet surpasses it. Wisdom here is Spirit-shaped governance—decisions aligned with God's will, producing equity rather than expedience.
- **Covenant faithfulness in power:** Past rulers chased self-preservation; this king practices covenant loyalty. "Just and right" describes more than policies—it names a moral atmosphere where truth protects the weak and restrains oppression.
- **Shalom through justice:** His wise rule restores communal well-being. Security, flourishing, and moral clarity spread because authority is exercised as stewardship under God, not as self-advancement over people.

Jeremiah 23:6a — "In his days Judah will be saved and Israel will live in safety."

- **Salvation with substance:** Rescue is spiritual and social—right standing with God and tangible security in the land. His reign integrates forgiveness, order, and peace, healing fractures between God and His people.
- **Beyond temporary reprieves:** Historical returns from exile prefigure, but do not exhaust, the promise. The messianic king secures enduring deliverance that outlasts regimes and circumstances, anchoring hope in God's irrevocable commitment.
- **A shepherded people:** Safety arises where righteous rule prevails. Under his care, scattered sheep are gathered, fears quieted, and communities rebuilt around holiness, truth, and mercy.

Jeremiah 23:6b — "This is the name by which he will be called: 'The LORD Our Righteous Savior.'"

- **YHWH Tsidkenu—righteousness supplied:** The name announces that righteousness is given, not achieved. God Himself becomes our righteousness, covering our lack and establishing a covenant status no human merit can secure.
- **Christ our righteousness:** The title anticipates the New Testament witness—"Christ Jesus…our righteousness" (1 Cor 1:30). He justifies the ungodly, embodying and imparting the right standing His people could never produce.

- **Personal and corporate grace:** The king's name blesses individuals and reconstitutes a holy people. As He shares His righteousness, identity and destiny are reshaped—a community lives safely because it lives under grace.

Discussion Questions

1. Why is the imagery of the "Branch" such a powerful symbol of hope?

2. How does this prophecy contrast with the corrupt kings of Jeremiah's time?

3. What does it mean that the Messiah is called "The Lord Our Righteous Savior"?

4. How does Christ provide righteousness for His people?

5. In what ways has this prophecy been fulfilled already, and how is it still future?

6. How should the promise of a righteous King shape the church's mission today?

7. What encouragement does this prophecy offer believers living in uncertain times?

Narrative Reflection

Jeremiah 23:5–6 presents one of the most striking messianic prophecies in the Old Testament, emerging from a deeply troubling context. Jeremiah, often referred to as "the weeping prophet," ministered during the final years of Judah before its destruction by Babylon. The nation suffered under corrupt leaders who were meant to guide God's people but instead scattered them. Kings like Jehoiakim and Zedekiah epitomized this failure, marked by oppression, injustice, and disobedience to God's covenant. The temple was defiled, the poor were exploited, and idolatry flourished. Amidst this moral and spiritual decay, God spoke through Jeremiah to announce judgment on the false shepherds while promising a coming Shepherd-King who would embody true righteousness.

The prophecy begins with the familiar phrase: "The days are coming." In Jeremiah, this signals a future hope that transcends present despair. God asserts that His covenant promises remain intact, even when Judah's monarchy appears destroyed. The image of the "righteous Branch" builds on earlier prophetic imagery, especially from Isaiah 11:1. Just as Isaiah described a shoot emerging from the stump of Jesse, Jeremiah envisions new life springing from the Davidic line, which seemed like a felled tree. Although Babylon's axe would soon cut down the kingdom, God's purposes would not be thwarted. From apparent death, God would bring new life in the form of a new king.

This Branch is not merely another king in David's lineage but a radically different one. Jeremiah emphasizes that He will "reign wisely and do what is just and right in the land," deliberately contrasting Judah's failed rulers. Kings like Jehoiakim enriched themselves at the expense of their people (Jeremiah 22:13–17), while Zedekiah was weak and indecisive, swayed by fear rather than trust in God. These leaders neglected the poor, oppressed the vulnerable, and led the nation into idolatry. In contrast, the coming King would embody wisdom and justice, His reign reflecting the very character of God—righteousness, equity, compassion, and truth.

Verse 6 expands the promise: "In his days Judah will be saved and Israel will live in safety." This assurance points beyond mere temporary political rescue. Judah's return from exile after seventy years under Babylon was only a shadow of this promise. The ultimate fulfillment would come in Christ, whose salvation transcends national boundaries and political contexts. He saves not only from earthly enemies but also from sin, death, and Satan. In Christ, the people of God—Jew and Gentile alike—find true safety, with the security of eternal life under His lordship.

The most remarkable aspect of this prophecy is the name given to the Messiah: *The LORD Our Righteous Savior* (YHWH Tsidkenu). This name is extraordinary because it directly associates the promised King with the divine name of Yahweh. This is not just a godly man but God Himself come to bring salvation. In Christ, we see this fulfilled: Jesus is both fully man, descended from David, and fully God, the Lord of righteousness.

This name also highlights the heart of the gospel: God's people need righteousness, and He provides it in His Messiah. On our own, we fall short of God's standard. Israel's history repeatedly demonstrated this—law, kingship, and the temple could not produce lasting righteousness. But in Christ, righteousness is not merely demanded; it is given. Paul echoes this in 1 Corinthians 1:30: "It is because of him that you are in Christ Jesus, who has become for us wisdom from God—that is, our righteousness, holiness, and redemption." Through His obedient life, sacrificial death, and victorious resurrection, Christ becomes our righteousness, justifying us by grace through faith and clothing us in His perfect record.

This prophecy thus bridges Israel's history of failed kings and the New Testament gospel of grace. Where David's descendants faltered, Christ succeeded. Where kings oppressed, Christ served. Where rulers led into idolatry, Christ revealed the Father. And where judgment fell, Christ bore it on behalf of His people.

Theologically, Jeremiah 23:5–6 also addresses the already-and-not-yet nature of the kingdom. In Christ's first coming, the Righteous Branch appeared and inaugurated His reign through His death and resurrection. By faith, we receive His righteousness and are transferred into His kingdom. Yet the fullness of Judah's safety and Israel's peace awaits His second coming, when He will establish perfect justice and peace on earth. The imagery of the wolf and lamb from Isaiah 11 finds its consummation here as Christ's reign extends over all creation.

For believers today, this passage offers profound encouragement. It reminds us that God is faithful to His promises, even when circumstances seem hopeless. When the tree appears cut down to a stump, God can bring forth new life. It reassures us that our salvation does not depend on human leaders, governments, or institutions but on Christ, the Lord our Righteousness. In a world plagued by corruption, injustice, and insecurity, we have a King who reigns with wisdom and truth. His reign provides safety, not necessarily by removing trials, but by securing eternal life and hope that cannot be shaken.

This prophecy also challenges us to live as people of righteousness. If Christ is our righteousness, we are called to reflect His character in our lives. We cannot claim Him as our King while embracing the injustice, self-interest, or idolatry that characterized Judah's failed leaders. Instead, we are to live out His righteousness by caring for the poor, defending the vulnerable, and walking humbly with our God.

Jeremiah 23:5–6 stands as a beacon of hope in a time of despair. It promises a King unlike any other—a Branch from David's line who would reign with righteousness, bring salvation, and be called "The Lord Our Righteous Savior." For Jeremiah's audience, it pointed forward to a day of restoration beyond exile. For us, it points to Christ, who has come to secure our righteousness and will come again to establish His reign in fullness. From the ashes of failed kingship, God raised up the true King—Jesus Christ, our righteousness and our salvation.

Layers of Understanding

Historical Context

Jeremiah ministered during one of the darkest times in Judah's history, as the nation faced corruption, idolatry, and impending exile. The failures of kings and prophets left the people hopeless. This prophecy promised that God would not abandon His covenant, but would raise up a faithful Davidic ruler who would shepherd His people rightly.

Jewish Understanding

For Jewish readers, this prophecy was a powerful messianic hope. It envisioned a future king from David's line who would establish justice, righteousness, and peace. In contrast to Judah's failed leaders, this figure would embody God's covenant faithfulness, restoring Israel to blessing and security, and vindicating the promises made to their ancestors.

New Testament Fulfillment

The New Testament identifies Jesus Christ as the fulfillment of Jeremiah's prophecy. He is the "Righteous Branch" from David's line, establishing God's kingdom not by military might but by righteousness and grace. In Him we receive righteousness (1 Cor. 1:30), and through His sacrifice we are made right with God (2 Cor. 5:21).

Theological Significance Today

For believers, this prophecy underscores that salvation and righteousness cannot be earned by works but are gifts received through Christ. It also challenges the church to embody His justice and mercy in a fractured world, living as a witness to God's faithfulness and pointing others to the true King, Jesus Christ.

Cross-Reference Connections

- **Isaiah 11:1** – The shoot from the stump of Jesse.
- **Ezekiel 34:23–24** – God promises to raise up one shepherd, David.
- **Jeremiah 33:15–16** – Parallel prophecy of the Righteous Branch.
- **1 Corinthians 1:30** – Christ our righteousness.
- **2 Corinthians 5:21** – We become the righteousness of God in Him.
- **Revelation 22:16** – Jesus, the Root and Offspring of David.

LESSON SCRIPTURE: HOSEA 11:1

PROPHECY TITLE

Out of Egypt: God's Son Called to Fulfill Redemption

Introduction

Hosea, often referred to as the prophet of steadfast love, wrote during the 8th century B.C., a period marked by idolatry and decline in Israel. His book weaves together messages of judgment and vivid images of God's covenant love for His people. In Hosea 11, God reflects on His relationship with Israel, portraying Himself as a loving father who called His son out of Egypt during the Exodus.

On one level, this verse alludes to Israel's deliverance from slavery under Pharaoh. God chose Israel as His son (Exodus 4:22–23) and redeemed them from bondage, establishing them as His covenant people. However, the Gospel of Matthew applies Hosea 11:1 to Jesus: "And so was fulfilled what the Lord had said through the prophet: 'Out of Egypt I called my son'" (Matthew 2:15). Matthew interprets Jesus' early life—His flight to Egypt and subsequent return—as a recapitulation of Israel's story. Where Israel failed in the wilderness, Jesus succeeded, embodying the true Israel and fulfilling God's purposes perfectly.

Thus, Hosea 11:1 serves both historical and prophetic roles. It reveals God's love for His son Israel, His power to redeem, and ultimately, His plan to bring forth His true Son, the Messiah, out of Egypt to save His people from their sins.

Scripture Reference

Hosea 11:1 (NIV)   "When Israel was a child, I loved him, and out of Egypt I called my son.

Big Picture Insights

- **Historical reference** – recalls the Exodus, God delivering Israel from Egypt.
- **Father–son imagery** – God as a loving father, Israel as His son (Exodus 4:22).
- **Covenant love** – rooted in God's affection, not Israel's merit.
- **Messianic fulfillment** – Matthew 2:15 applies this verse to Christ's return from Egypt.
- **Jesus as true Israel** – embodies Israel's calling, succeeds where Israel failed.
- **Redemptive pattern** – Exodus → Exile → Christ → Salvation.
- **God's faithfulness** – even when His people fail, His love endures.
- **Typology** – Israel's history foreshadows the Messiah's life.
- **Christ's mission** – He retraces Israel's steps to redeem His people.
- **Hope for the church** – God's redeeming love still calls His children out of bondage.

Verse-by-Verse Commentary

Hosea 11:1a — "When Israel was a child, I loved him…"

- **Covenant affection before performance:** God's parental language signals love that precedes merit. From Israel's earliest days, He chose and cherished them. This origin story grounds identity and summons trust, even amid failure, judgment, and exile.
- **Echoes Exodus 4:22 ("firstborn son"):** Hosea recalls Israel's corporate sonship and vocation. As God's "firstborn," Israel was to reflect the Father's character among the nations—carrying both privilege and responsibility within the wider arc of redemptive purpose.
- **Grace initiates, not obedience:** Divine love comes first; obedience follows. Hosea's indictments are framed by steadfast affection. God's calls to return spring from covenant love that disciplines to restore, refusing to relinquish the people He claimed.

Hosea 11:1b — "…and out of Egypt I called my son."

- **Historical Exodus in view:** God's effectual summons brings Israel out of bondage under Moses. The verb "called" stresses divine initiative—freedom as God's act—forming a people for worship, covenant, and mission under His saving lordship.
- **Typology fulfilled in Christ (Matt. 2:15):** Matthew reads this line through Jesus' return from Egypt. Not mere prediction mechanics, but recapitulation—Christ retraces Israel's story so God's faithfulness culminates in the true Son.
- **Jesus embodies Israel's vocation:** Out of Egypt, through waters, into wilderness testing—yet faithful where Israel failed. As representative head, He honors the Father perfectly, becoming the obedient Son whose faithfulness secures our redemption.

Discussion Questions

1. How does Hosea 11:1 reveal God's relationship with Israel as a father to a son?

2. Why is the Exodus central to Israel's identity and to God's covenant promises?

3. How does Matthew 2:15 show Jesus as the fulfillment of Israel's story?

4. In what ways did Jesus succeed where Israel failed?

5. What does this prophecy teach us about God's enduring love despite human unfaithfulness?

6. How does the pattern of Exodus → Christ → Church encourage believers today?

7. How are we, as God's people, still being "called out of Egypt"?

Narrative Reflection

Hosea 11:1 is a brief verse with profound significance. At first glance, it seems like a straightforward historical statement: God loved Israel and delivered them from Egypt. However, when we explore Scripture more deeply, we uncover layers of meaning—historical, theological, and messianic. This verse illustrates God's covenant love, defines Israel's identity as His son, and ultimately points to Christ as the true Son who fulfills God's plan.

The verse opens with, "When Israel was a child, I loved him." This language presents God not as a distant ruler but as a caring father. Right from the beginning of Israel's story, God's relationship with His people is rooted in love. In Exodus 4:22, God instructs Moses to tell Pharaoh, "This is what the Lord says: Israel is my firstborn son." This statement elevates Israel from the status of slaves in Egypt to that of God's cherished child. Their identity is not based on merit or achievement but on God's gracious choice. His love came before their obedience, and His covenant faithfulness persisted despite their unfaithfulness.

The latter part of the verse recalls Israel's pivotal moment: "Out of Egypt I called my son." The Exodus was not merely a political liberation; it was a theological event. God redeemed His son from slavery, led them through the sea, and established them as His covenant people at Sinai. Israel's story of salvation began with God's call out of Egypt. The Passover, the Red Sea crossing, and the wilderness journey became central symbols of God's saving power. Each generation of Israel looked back to the Exodus as the foundation of their identity and faith.

Yet Hosea's prophecy extends beyond history. The Gospel of Matthew, inspired by the Spirit, applies this verse to Jesus: "So was fulfilled what the Lord had said through the prophet: 'Out of Egypt I called my son'" (Matthew 2:15). At first, this may seem surprising—Hosea was referring to Israel, not predicting an event in Jesus' life. However, Matthew perceives a deeper meaning. Jesus, the Son of God, recapitulates

Israel's story. Just as Israel was called out of Egypt, so was Jesus. Just as Israel passed through the Red Sea, Jesus passed through the waters of baptism. Just as Israel was tested in the wilderness for forty years, Jesus faced temptation in the wilderness for forty days. Where Israel grumbled, doubted, and disobeyed, Jesus remained faithful. He is the true Israel, the obedient Son who fulfills the Father's will.

This prefigurative fulfillment reveals that Israel's history was always pointing to Christ. God's son, Israel, foreshadowed God's Son, Jesus. The Exodus signifies a greater deliverance, not from Pharaoh but from sin and death. Thus, Hosea 11:1 becomes a prophecy of Christ's mission: the beloved Son, called out of Egypt, who embodies Israel's calling and brings salvation to the world.

This verse underscores the unbreakable nature of God's love. Despite Israel's repeated turning away, God's love remained steadfast. Hosea 11 continues with God lamenting Israel's unfaithfulness—how they turned to idols and neglected His care. Yet God assures that His compassion will not fail. This covenant love finds its ultimate expression in Christ. God so loved the world that He gave His one and only Son (John 3:16). Just as He called Israel out of Egypt, He calls us out of sin's bondage through Christ.

For the church today, Hosea 11:1 serves as both reassurance and challenge. It reassures us that God's love is not contingent on our faithfulness but on His. He is a Father who calls us His children, even when we falter. It challenges us to recognize ourselves as part of this ongoing story of redemption. Just as God called Israel out of Egypt and Jesus out of Egypt, He calls us out of our own "Egypts"—places of bondage, idolatry, and sin—into the freedom of His kingdom.

This verse also enhances our understanding of Jesus' identity. He is not only the Son of David, the Messiah from Judah's line; He is the true Israel, the Son called out of Egypt. He succeeds where Israel failed, perfectly fulfilling the law, overcoming temptation, and offering salvation. His obedience secures our redemption and restores our relationship with the Father.

Hosea 11:1 is a verse where history, prophecy, and gospel converge. It recalls God's love for His son Israel in the Exodus, anticipates Christ as the true Son called out of Egypt, who embodies and fulfills Israel's mission, and speaks to us today, reminding us of God's steadfast love and His power to call us out of bondage into freedom. From Egypt to the cross, from exile to resurrection, God's love is the thread that binds the story together. Out of Egypt He called His Son, and through His Son, He calls us—into salvation, sonship, and His everlasting kingdom.

Layers of Understanding

Historical Context

This prophecy recalls the Exodus, the defining moment when God delivered Israel from slavery in Egypt and claimed them as His son (Exodus 4:22–23). It reflects both liberation and covenant identity, showing Israel's unique relationship with God as His chosen people, redeemed to serve and worship Him in freedom and faithfulness.

Jewish Understanding

In Jewish tradition, this verse was remembered primarily as a historical reference, celebrating God's covenant love expressed through the Exodus. It reminded Israel of their deliverance, shaping their identity as God's redeemed people. The Exodus became the foundation of hope that God would continue to rescue and preserve His people.

New Testament Fulfillment

Matthew 2:15 applies this verse to Jesus, portraying Him as the true Israel. His journey out of Egypt after Herod's persecution fulfills this prophecy, showing that Christ embodies God's purposes perfectly. Unlike Israel's failures, Jesus lives in full obedience, completing the redemptive mission that Israel's history foreshadowed but could not accomplish.

Theological Significance Today

For Christians, this prophecy highlights God's enduring love and His power to deliver. Just as Israel was brought out of bondage, in Christ we are freed from slavery to sin and death. The church continues the Exodus pattern—redeemed by grace, tested in faith, and led by the faithful Son who secures victory.

Cross-Reference Connections

- **Exodus 4:22–23** – Israel called God's firstborn son.
- **Deuteronomy 7:7–8** – God's love is based on His choice, not merit.
- **Matthew 2:13–15** – Jesus called out of Egypt, fulfilling Hosea 11:1.
- **Matthew 4:1–11** – Jesus' wilderness testing parallels Israel's.
- **Romans 6:17–18** – Believers freed from slavery to sin.
- **1 Peter 2:9–10** – The church as God's chosen people.

LESSON SCRIPTURE: **MALACHI 3:1**

PROPHECY TITLE

The Messenger and the Lord's Coming

Introduction

Malachi, the last prophet of the Old Testament, served around the 5th century B.C., following the return from Babylonian exile and the rebuilding of the temple. During this time, however, the people had become complacent in their worship and unfaithful to their covenant with God. The priests were corrupt, offerings were flawed, and justice was ignored. In this context, Malachi delivers a sobering yet hopeful message: God Himself is coming to His temple, but first, a messenger will prepare the way.

This prophecy addresses both the immediate issues of Malachi's time and the future coming of the Messiah. The "messenger" is later identified as John the Baptist (cf. Matthew 11:10; Mark 1:2; Luke 7:27), who paved the way for Christ's ministry. The "Lord" who comes to His temple is realized in Jesus, who entered the temple in Jerusalem, purified it, and ultimately offered Himself as the final sacrifice.

In this way, Malachi 3:1 serves as a bridge between the Old and New Testaments. It anticipates the day when God would arrive to restore order. The messenger would prepare hearts, and the arrival of the Lord would bring both judgment and salvation.

Scripture Reference

Malachi 3:1 (NIV)
"I will send my messenger, who will prepare the way before me. Then suddenly the Lord you are seeking will come to his temple; the messenger of the covenant, whom you desire, will come," says the LORD Almighty.

Big Picture Insights

- **The last Old Testament prophecy** before 400 years of silence.
- **The messenger** prepares the way → John the Baptist.
- **The Lord Himself** comes to His temple → Jesus Christ.
- **Messenger of the covenant** → Christ as fulfillment of God's promises.
- **Preparation and expectation** → hearts must be ready for His arrival.
- **Judgment and salvation** → His coming purifies, tests, and redeems.
- **Temple focus** → fulfilled in Jesus, the true temple and final sacrifice.
- **Echoes Isaiah 40:3** → voice crying, "Prepare the way of the Lord."
- **Transition prophecy** → closes the Old Testament, opens to the New.
- **Messianic hope** → the long-awaited Lord is coming.

Verse-by-Verse Commentary

Malachi 3:1a - "I will send my messenger, who will prepare the way before me."

- **Points to John the Baptist**, the forerunner who levels paths by preaching repentance (Matt 3:1–3; Isa 40:3). Like royal envoys clearing roads, he prepares hearts and communities for God's approach through confession, renewal, and readiness.
- **Preparation is spiritual**—crooked lives straightened, rough places smoothed. Repentance is not mere sentiment; it is a reordering of loyalties so the Lord's arrival meets uncluttered allegiance, receptive faith, and fruits worthy of repentance.
- **The initiative is God's**: He sends the messenger before coming Himself. The forerunner's ministry signals imminence—mercy offered before judgment—inviting Israel to welcome the Lord with humility rather than be startled unprepared.

Malachi 3:1b - "Then suddenly the Lord you are seeking will come to his temple…"

- **The Lord Himself comes**, not merely a human delegate. Israel's longings converge in a divine visitation. Jesus' temple actions (John 2:13–22) prefigure cleansing, renewal, and the re-centering of worship around the One in whom God dwells bodily.
- **"Suddenly" underscores surprising timing**—long-expected yet arresting in arrival. God's approach exposes pretenses, overturns distortions, and restores true worship, reminding us that divine nearness comforts the humble and unsettles the complacent.
- **The temple is His**—ownership implies authority to purify and to redefine access. In Christ, the locus of God's presence shifts from building to Person; He becomes the true temple where God meets His people in grace and truth.

Malachi 3:1c - "The messenger of the covenant, whom you desire, will come," says the LORD Almighty.

- **Christ is the mediator of the New Covenant** (Heb 8:6)—the One who brings, embodies, and secures covenant blessings. What Israel desired—restoration and faithfulness—arrives personally in Him, not as mere program or reform.
- **His coming brings purification and refining**. Desire for God's nearness entails transformation; the Lord removes dross so covenant life can flourish. The promised presence is inseparable from holiness that heals and reorders the community.
- **Covenant fulfillment is relational**. The people longed for God to act; God answers by coming in the Son. In Him, promises mature from shadow to substance—mercy, justice, and steadfast love gathered into one faithful King.

Discussion Questions

1. Why is it significant that the Old Testament ends with this prophecy of a coming messenger and the Lord?

2. How does John the Baptist fulfill the role of preparing the way?

3. What does it mean that the Lord Himself would come to His temple?

4. How does Christ as the "messenger of the covenant" fulfill God's promises?

5. Why does God call for preparation before His coming?

6. How does this prophecy challenge believers to examine their worship today?

7. What does Malachi 3:1 teach us about God's faithfulness to His covenant people?

Narrative Reflection

Malachi 3:1 is a crucial verse that serves as a bridge between the Old and New Testaments. It represents the final prophetic word before four centuries of silence, setting the stage for the Messiah's arrival. This verse intertwines themes of anticipation, preparation, judgment, and salvation, all centered on the promise that God Himself will come to His temple.

The prophecy begins with God saying, "I will send my messenger, who will prepare the way before me." This imagery reflects ancient practices where kings sent heralds to prepare the roads, announce their arrival, and ensure people were ready. Spiritually, this messenger's role is to call God's people to repentance, clearing away the obstacles of sin and apathy so they can receive the coming King. The New Testament clearly identifies this messenger as John the Baptist. Jesus affirmed in Matthew 11:10, quoting Malachi 3:1, that John fulfilled this prophecy.

John's ministry exemplified this role. He appeared in the wilderness, dressed in camel's hair and eating locusts and wild honey, proclaiming, "Repent, for the kingdom of heaven has come near" (Matthew 3:2). His baptism symbolized repentance, preparing the people to receive Christ. Like a royal herald, John pointed away from himself and toward the One who was to come: "After me comes one more powerful than I" (Mark 1:7). His message was urgent and necessary; without repentance, the people would not be ready for the Lord's arrival.

The second part of the prophecy states, "Then suddenly the Lord you are seeking will come to his temple." This declaration is staggering. God Himself is coming—not just another prophet or king, but the Lord of the covenant. For centuries, Israel had yearned for God to return in glory to His temple. After the exile, the rebuilt temple lacked the visible presence of God's glory that had filled Solomon's temple, leading many to wonder if God had abandoned them. Malachi reassures that the Lord is indeed coming, and He will arrive suddenly, decisively, and unmistakably.

This prophecy was fulfilled in Jesus Christ. He entered the temple, drove out the money changers, and declared it to be His Father's house (Matthew 21:12–13). More profoundly, He Himself was the true temple. In John 2:19–21, Jesus stated, "Destroy this temple, and I will raise it again in three days," referring to His body. The Lord came to His temple not just by entering a building but by becoming the very dwelling place of God among humanity (John 1:14).

The verse concludes with, "The messenger of the covenant, whom you desire, will come." This indicates Christ as the mediator of the New Covenant. Israel longed for restoration and deliverance, desiring the fulfillment of God's promises, even if they did not fully understand how. In Christ, God completed the covenant. Through His blood, He established the New Covenant, fulfilling Jeremiah 31:31–34 and offering forgiveness of sins, new hearts, and the Spirit's indwelling. The covenant mediator had arrived, not only to proclaim God's promises but to secure them.

However, Malachi's prophecy also conveys a tone of warning. The Lord's coming is sudden and purifying. The following verses (Malachi 3:2–3) describe Him as a refiner's fire and launderer's soap. His arrival is confrontational, purging sin and hypocrisy. This was evident in Christ's ministry as He exposed religious corruption, called sinners to repentance, and laid down His life to atone for sin. His coming divides humanity—between those who receive Him in faith and those who reject Him in rebellion.

For believers today, this prophecy offers several lessons. First, it reminds us that God keeps His promises. Centuries elapsed between Malachi's prophecy and John the Baptist's ministry, yet the promise was fulfilled exactly as God declared. His faithfulness is unshakable, and His timing is perfect.

Second, it emphasizes the necessity of preparation. Just as Israel needed John's message of repentance to prepare for Christ's arrival, we too must continually prepare our hearts. Advent particularly reflects this theme of preparation. We prepare not only to celebrate Christ's first coming but to anticipate His second coming, when He will return suddenly and gloriously.

45

Third, this prophecy calls us to recognize Jesus as both the Lord of the temple and the mediator of the covenant. He is God in the flesh, dwelling among us, and He secures for us a new covenant relationship with God. Our salvation relies not on our efforts but on His completed work.

Finally, Malachi 3:1 challenges the church to embody the role of preparation in today's world. Just as John pointed people to Christ, we are called to proclaim the gospel and prepare others for the Lord's return. Our message remains the same: repent and believe the good news, for the King is coming.

Malachi 3:1 serves as a bridge between the testaments. It closes the Old Testament with a promise and opens the New Testament with its fulfillment. It directs our attention to the messenger, John the Baptist, who prepared the way, and to the Lord Himself, Jesus Christ, who came to His temple as the mediator of the covenant. It reminds us of God's faithfulness, the certainty of His word, and the necessity of our readiness for His coming—whether in the first century or at the end of the age. The Lord you are seeking has come, and He will come again.

Layers of Understanding

Historical Context

Malachi's prophecy came after the Babylonian exile, during a period when the temple had been rebuilt but spiritual decline and apathy marked Israel's life. Priests were corrupt, worship was shallow, and the people doubted God's justice. Into this context, God promised His coming to the temple, preceded by a divinely sent messenger.

Jewish Understanding

Jewish interpreters understood this prophecy as a promise of God's decisive intervention in history. Many expected Elijah, or one like him (cf. Malachi 4:5), to prepare the way. Others anticipated a prophetic figure who would announce the Messiah, cleanse the temple, and restore Israel's faithfulness before the Lord's final appearing.

New Testament Fulfillment

The New Testament identifies John the Baptist as the promised messenger (Matthew 11:10; Mark 1:2; Luke 7:27). He prepared the way by calling people to repentance. Jesus Christ is the Lord who comes to His temple, inaugurating the New Covenant (Hebrews 8:6) and fulfilling God's promise of presence and redemption.

Theological Significance Today

This prophecy challenges believers to prepare their hearts continually for Christ's reign, living in readiness and repentance. It also reminds the church of its mission to proclaim His coming with urgency. Above all, it points us to God's unchanging faithfulness—He fulfills His promises perfectly in Jesus Christ, our Lord and Savior.

Cross-Reference Connections

- **Isaiah 40:3** – "A voice of one calling… prepare the way of the Lord."
- **Matthew 11:10** – Jesus identifies John as the messenger.
- **Mark 1:2–3** – Gospel opens with Malachi 3:1 and Isaiah 40:3 fulfilled in John.
- **Luke 7:27** – Jesus applies this prophecy to John the Baptist.
- **John 2:19–21** – Jesus Himself is the true temple.
- **Hebrews 8:6** – Jesus, mediator of the New Covenant.

LESSON SCRIPTURE: PSALM 2: 6-12

PROPHECY TITLE

The Son Enthroned: God's King over All Nations

Introduction

Psalm 2 is one of the most explicitly messianic psalms in Scripture. It details the rebellion of nations against God and His Anointed, outlines the Lord's declaration of His chosen King, and serves as a warning to rulers who oppose Him. In verses 6–12, the psalm shifts to God's decree: He has installed His King on Zion, His holy hill. This King is referred to as God's Son, who will rule the nations with authority and bring blessings to those who seek refuge in Him.

Although Psalm 2 initially connects to Israel's monarchy, its language transcends any earthly king. The promise that nations will be given as an inheritance and the ends of the earth as possession is too vast for David or his descendants alone. The New Testament affirms that Psalm 2 finds its fulfillment in Jesus Christ. At His baptism and transfiguration, the Father declared Jesus as His beloved Son (Matthew 3:17; 17:5). The apostles applied Psalm 2 to Christ's resurrection, exaltation, and authority over all nations (Acts 13:33; Hebrews 1:5).

For the church, Psalm 2 serves as a reminder that Christ is the true King, enthroned by God, and that all people must respond to Him. It offers both a warning and hope: those who resist His reign will face judgment, while those who embrace Him will find refuge and blessing.

Scripture Reference

Psalm 2:6–12 (NIV) "I have installed my king on Zion, my holy mountain." [7] I will proclaim the LORD's decree: He said to me, "You are my son; today I have become your father. [8] Ask me, and I will make the nations your inheritance, the ends of the earth your possession. [9] You will break them with a rod of iron; you will dash them to pieces like pottery." [10] Therefore, you kings, be wise; be warned, you rulers of the earth. [11] Serve the LORD with fear and celebrate his rule with trembling. [12] Kiss his son, or he will be angry and your way will lead to your destruction, for his wrath can flare up in a moment. Blessed are all who take refuge in him.

Big Picture Insights

- **Coronation psalm** – originally read at enthronement of Israel's kings.
- **Messianic fulfillment** – transcends earthly kings; fulfilled in Christ.
- **Sonship** – God declares Messiah as His Son (cf. Matthew 3:17).
- **Universal rule** – nations and earth as inheritance.
- **Authority and judgment** – Messiah rules with rod of iron (Rev. 19:15).

- **Warning to rulers** – submit or face judgment.
- **Invitation to refuge** – blessing for all who trust in Him.
- **Already/Not yet** – Christ reigns now, full consummation at His return.
- **Tension** – warning of wrath, promise of blessing.
- **The gospel in a psalm** – repent and take refuge in the Son.

Verse-by-Verse Commentary

Psalm 2:6 - "I have installed my king on Zion, my holy mountain."

- God declares His sovereign choice of the true King, emphasizing His authority above human rulers. Zion symbolizes God's dwelling and covenant promises, anchoring His kingdom in holiness rather than earthly power.
- This points to the Davidic covenant (2 Samuel 7:12–16) but finds ultimate fulfillment in Christ, the Messiah who reigns not from political conquest but through God's eternal plan of redemption.
- God's decision silences opposition; human rebellion cannot undo His enthronement of the chosen King. Zion becomes the spiritual center of God's reign, drawing nations to His authority in the end times.

Psalm 2:7 - "I will proclaim the LORD's decree: He said to me, 'You are my son; today I have become your father.'"

- This decree affirms the intimate father-son relationship between God and His chosen king. Historically tied to Israel's kings, it is fully realized in Jesus, the eternal Son of God (Hebrews 1:5).
- "Today" signifies the moment of royal installation, ultimately fulfilled at Christ's resurrection and exaltation, when He was declared with power to be God's Son (Romans 1:4).
- The title "Son" goes beyond adoption—it conveys divine identity, authority, and mission, marking Jesus as both King and Savior.

Psalm 2:8 - "Ask me, and I will make the nations your inheritance, the ends of the earth your possession."

- God promises universal dominion to His Son, extending far beyond Israel's borders. The Messiah's reign is global in scope, encompassing every tribe and tongue.
- Jesus fulfills this through His Great Commission (Matthew 28:18–20), receiving authority over heaven and earth and sending disciples to proclaim His kingship worldwide.
- The inheritance is not merely land but the redemption of peoples, bringing the nations into God's family through Christ's rule of grace and truth.

Psalm 2:9 - "You will break them with a rod of iron; you will dash them to pieces like pottery."

- The imagery reveals the severity of Christ's authority. Rebellion against Him will not stand; His rule brings both salvation and judgment.
- The rod of iron conveys unbreakable strength and absolute sovereignty, unlike fragile earthly powers. Nations that oppose God's King face inevitable collapse.
- Revelation 19:15 echoes this verse, portraying Christ as the warrior-king who executes final judgment, crushing evil and establishing His eternal reign.

Psalm 2:10–11 - "Therefore, you kings, be wise; be warned, you rulers of the earth. Serve the LORD with fear and celebrate his rule with trembling."

- Earthly leaders are exhorted to humility and obedience, recognizing God's greater authority. Wisdom means surrender, not resistance, to His appointed King.
- The paradox of fear and joy reflects reverent worship—celebrating God's reign while trembling at His holiness. True service requires both devotion and awe.
- These verses remind us that no position exempts one from accountability. Kings and rulers must bow before Christ, just as ordinary people must.

Psalm 2:12 - "Kiss his son, or he will be angry and your way will lead to your destruction, for his wrath can flare up in a moment. Blessed are all who take refuge in him."

- "Kiss" symbolizes submission, loyalty, and covenant faithfulness. To refuse the Son is to invite judgment, but to embrace Him is to find mercy and life.
- The suddenness of wrath highlights the urgency of repentance. God's patience is real, but His justice cannot be indefinitely delayed.
- The psalm closes with hope: those who take refuge in the Son experience blessing, security, and eternal joy under His reign.

Discussion Questions

1. What does it mean that God has "installed" His King on Zion?

2. How do the New Testament writers apply Psalm 2 to Jesus?

3. Why is the declaration of sonship central to this prophecy?

4. What does Messiah's inheritance of the nations teach us about God's plan?

5. How do verses 10–12 serve as both a warning and an invitation?

6. What does it mean today to "take refuge" in Christ as King?

7. How does this psalm challenge modern nations and rulers?

Narrative Reflection

Psalm 2:6–12 presents a powerful affirmation of God's sovereign authority and His selection of the Messiah as the true King. At its heart, the psalm declares that God has already acted: "I have installed my king on Zion, my holy mountain." In response to the rebellion of nations and rulers, God proclaims His decree, reminding the world that His purposes cannot be thwarted.

The proclamation begins with the enthronement of the King in verse 6. For Israel, this likely referred to the coronation of David or his descendants. However, even at this level, it points beyond human kingship to divine appointment. The king of Israel was not self-made but chosen by God, serving as His representative on earth. The New Testament expands this understanding, identifying the true King not as David or Solomon, but as Jesus Christ, who is seated at the right hand of God. His enthronement resulted not from political power but from His resurrection and exaltation (Acts 2:32–36).

Verse 7 introduces the theme of sonship: "You are my son; today I have become your father." In Israel's monarchy, kings were recognized as "sons" of God at their coronation, symbolizing their covenant relationship and divine authority. However, the ultimate Son is Christ, the eternal Son by nature. The New Testament applies this verse to significant moments in His life. At His baptism and transfiguration, the Father's voice from heaven affirmed His identity as the beloved Son. After the resurrection, Paul declared that Christ was publicly vindicated as the Son of God in power, referencing Psalm 2:7 (Acts 13:33). This sonship is not merely ceremonial but essential—Jesus is the eternal Son, the second person of the Trinity, now revealed as the enthroned Messiah.

Verses 8–9 broaden the scope of His reign: "Ask me, and I will make the nations your inheritance, the ends of the earth your possession." This promise extends far beyond the limited geographic reign of Israel's kings. The Messiah's authority encompasses all nations, stretching to the ends of the earth. His dominion is illustrated with striking imagery: "You will break them with a rod of iron; you will dash them to pieces like pottery." Rebellion against the King is ultimately futile; human power is fragile, much like clay vessels shattered by iron. This imagery reappears in Revelation 2:27 and 19:15, where Christ is described as ruling the nations with a rod of iron. His kingdom is not partial or temporary but universal and eternal.

Verses 10–11 shift from proclamation to exhortation: "Therefore, you kings, be wise; be warned, you rulers of the earth." The psalm challenges the arrogance of human power, urging rulers to humble themselves before the true King. Wisdom is found not in self-reliance but in submission to God's authority. The call is to "serve the Lord with fear and celebrate his rule with trembling." This blend of reverence and joy captures the essence of worship—acknowledging God's majesty while rejoicing in His reign.

The psalm culminates in verse 12 with both warning and promise: "Kiss his son, or he will be angry and your way will lead to your destruction, for his wrath can flare up in a moment. Blessed are all who take refuge in him." To "kiss" the Son signifies homage, a gesture of allegiance and submission. The choice is clear: resist Him and face judgment, or embrace Him and find refuge. The final message is one of blessing: those who take refuge in the Son are safe, secure, and blessed.

For Christians, this psalm conveys profound truths about Christ's reign. First, it reminds us that God has already installed His King. The resurrection and ascension of Jesus signify His enthronement. He reigns now, even amidst worldly resistance. This truth anchors the church's hope; regardless of the chaos among nations, Christ is on the throne.

Second, it emphasizes Christ's universal authority. The nations belong to Him, not to human powers. Our mission as the church stems from this reality: we proclaim Christ as King to all peoples, affirming that He is Lord of all. Evangelism is not about persuading people to accept a possibility but about announcing a fact: Christ reigns.

Third, it challenges today's rulers and nations. Political powers continue to resist God's authority, pursuing their own agendas. Psalm 2 confronts them with the reminder that their power is temporary and fragile. True wisdom lies in bowing before Christ. This applies not only to governments but also to individuals. Each person must respond to the Son—rejecting Him leads to judgment, while trusting Him offers refuge.

Finally, the psalm reassures believers with the promise of blessing. To take refuge in Christ is to find unshakeable security. His wrath is real, but so is His mercy. Those who trust in Him experience the blessings of forgiveness, reconciliation, and eternal life.

Psalm 2:6–12 serves as a royal decree that resonates through history. It proclaims the enthronement of God's Son, warns rulers to submit, and invites all to find refuge in Him. While it was partly understood in the context of Israel's kings, it is fully realized in Jesus Christ. Today, it calls us to worship, obedience, and mission. The King is installed on Zion. He is the Son of God, the ruler of the nations, and the refuge of His people. Blessed indeed are all who take refuge in Him.

Layers of Understanding

Historical Context

Psalm 2 is a royal psalm, probably used during coronations of Davidic kings. It declared God's covenant faithfulness to David's line, affirming that Israel's king ruled under divine authority. In a world of hostile nations, the psalm reminded God's people that their security rested in His chosen ruler, not human power.

Jewish Understanding

For Jewish readers, Psalm 2 celebrated God's appointment of Israel's king as His anointed one. While it reflected immediate political realities, it also carried messianic overtones, anticipating a greater future ruler. The expectation grew that God's ultimate Messiah would overthrow opposition, establish justice, and bring peace to Israel and the nations.

New Testament Fulfillment

The New Testament applies Psalm 2 directly to Jesus. At His baptism and transfiguration, the Father's voice confirmed Him as the beloved Son. Apostolic preaching linked it to His resurrection and exaltation (Acts 13:33; Hebrews 1:5). Revelation portrays its final fulfillment when Christ reigns universally as King over all nations and peoples.

Theological Significance Today

For Christians, Psalm 2 affirms Christ's present reign at God's right hand and warns against resisting His authority. It assures believers that God's plan cannot fail despite earthly opposition. The psalm also promises blessing and refuge for those who submit to Christ, calling the church to live in faith, hope, and obedience.

Cross-Reference Connections

- **2 Samuel 7:12–16** – Davidic covenant promise.
- **Matthew 3:17; 17:5** – Father declares Jesus His Son.
- **Acts 13:33** – Psalm 2:7 applied to resurrection.
- **Hebrews 1:5** – Sonship applied to Christ's exaltation.
- **Revelation 2:27; 19:15** – Christ rules with rod of iron.

PROPHECY FULFILLED - STUDY LESSON - 10

LESSON SCRIPTURE: **ISAIAH 42: 1-7**

PROPHECY TITLE

The Servant of the Lord: Light to the Nations

Introduction

Isaiah 42:1–7 introduces the first of the "Servant Songs" in Isaiah, with additional references in chapters 49, 50, and 52–53. These passages depict the enigmatic Servant of the Lord, chosen by God, empowered by the Spirit, and tasked with bringing justice and salvation. In contrast to earthly rulers who depend on power and force, this Servant achieves His mission through gentleness, humility, and compassion.

The New Testament explicitly connects this Servant to Jesus Christ. Matthew 12:18–21 cites Isaiah 42:1–4, applying it to Jesus' ministry of healing and quiet authority. Jesus fulfilled this prophecy by embodying Spirit-filled service, demonstrating compassion for the weak, and proclaiming justice not only to Israel but to all nations.

Isaiah 42 portrays a Servant who restores sight, liberates captives, and establishes a covenant with His people. It foreshadows the mission of Christ, who came not to oppress the broken but to redeem them, shining as the light of the world.

Scripture Reference

Isaiah 42:1–7 (NIV) **"Here is my servant, whom I uphold, my chosen one in whom I delight; I will put my Spirit on him, and he will bring justice to the nations. ² He will not shout or cry out, or raise his voice in the streets. ³ A bruised reed he will not break, and a smoldering wick he will not snuff out. In faithfulness he will bring forth justice; ⁴ he will not falter or be discouraged till he establishes justice on earth. In his teaching the islands will put their hope." ⁵ This is what God the LORD says— the Creator of the heavens, who stretches them out, who spreads out the earth with all that springs from it, who gives breath to its people, and life to those who walk on it: ⁶ "I, the LORD, have called you in righteousness; I will take hold of your hand. I will keep you and will make you to be a covenant for the people and a light for the Gentiles, ⁷ to open eyes that are blind, to free captives from prison and to release from the dungeon those who sit in darkness.**

Big Picture Insights

- **God's Servant introduced** – chosen, upheld, delighted in by God.
- **Spirit-empowered mission** – fulfills the promise of Isaiah 11:2.
- **Gentle and compassionate** – does not break the bruised reed.
- **Justice to the nations** – mission extends beyond Israel.

- **Faithful perseverance** – He will not falter until justice is established.
- **Covenant for the people** – Messiah embodies the new covenant.
- **Light to the Gentiles** – salvation for all nations, not Israel alone.
- **Healing and deliverance** – sight for the blind, freedom for captives.
- **Fulfilled in Christ** – quoted in Matthew 12, embodied in His ministry.
- **Theological cornerstone** – Christ's kingdom is marked by both compassion and justice.

Verse-by-Verse Commentary

Isaiah 42:1 - "Here is my servant, whom I uphold, my chosen one in whom I delight; I will put my Spirit on him, and he will bring justice to the nations."

- God introduces His Servant with words of delight and affirmation, revealing divine favor. Unlike human leaders chosen for strength or status, this Servant is upheld by God Himself, empowered uniquely by the Spirit to accomplish His redemptive mission.
- The Servant's calling is global in scope, extending far beyond Israel. His reign establishes justice throughout the nations, bringing hope where oppression, corruption, and human failure have reigned. His Spirit-filled authority ensures lasting righteousness rooted in God's eternal will.
- At Jesus' baptism, the Spirit descended upon Him and the Father declared, "This is my beloved Son" (Matthew 3:16–17). These words confirm that Christ fulfills this prophecy, inaugurating His Spirit-filled ministry as God's chosen Servant for the nations.

Isaiah 42:2 - "He will not shout or cry out, or raise his voice in the streets."

- The Servant's mission is marked by humility and quiet strength rather than noisy proclamation or political display. His authority does not depend on public spectacle or human approval but flows from God's Spirit resting upon Him.
- Unlike earthly rulers who dominate through power, intimidation, or loud self-promotion, the Servant embodies gentleness. His ministry reaches the broken and humble, showing God's kingdom advances not by force but through compassion, healing, and self-sacrificial love.
- Jesus fulfilled this verse through His earthly ministry, drawing people not with worldly clamor but with words of truth and acts of mercy. His gentle authority revealed divine power clothed in humility and grace.

Isaiah 42:3 - "A bruised reed he will not break, and a smoldering wick he will not snuff out. In faithfulness he will bring forth justice."

- The Servant does not crush the weak or discard those society deems worthless. Instead, He restores, strengthens, and lifts up the brokenhearted, demonstrating justice that is merciful and faithful rather than harsh and destructive.
- The reed and wick imagery highlight fragility. A bruised reed easily snaps and a dim flame quickly dies, yet the Servant protects both. He values human weakness and redeems it rather than allowing it to be extinguished.
- Jesus embodied this compassion by healing the sick, forgiving sinners, and embracing the marginalized. His faithful justice restores rather than destroys, proving God's kingdom seeks to redeem broken lives rather than discard them as useless.

Isaiah 42:4 - "He will not falter or be discouraged till he establishes justice on earth. In his teaching the islands will put their hope."

- Despite opposition, suffering, and apparent setbacks, the Servant remains steadfast in His mission. His perseverance ensures that God's justice will not fail but will ultimately be established across the entire earth.
- The reference to "islands" symbolizes distant nations, pointing to the Gentiles who would find hope in His teaching. The Servant's influence is not limited to Israel but expands worldwide, revealing God's universal plan of salvation.
- Jesus fulfilled this by sending His disciples to the nations (Matthew 28:18–20). His unwavering determination ensures the spread of His teaching, inspiring hope even in the most distant places and forgotten corners of the world.

Isaiah 42:5 - "This is what God the LORD says—the Creator of the heavens, who stretches them out, who spreads out the earth with all that springs from it, who gives breath to its people, and life to those who walk on it:"

- God grounds the Servant's mission in His identity as Creator and sustainer of all life. The One who made heaven and earth affirms and guarantees the success of the Servant's divine calling.
- The reminder of God's creative power ensures confidence. The Servant is not sent by a weak deity but by the Maker of the universe, who provides breath, life, and purpose to all creation.
- This verse assures that the Servant's mission is unstoppable. As God gives life to all, so He empowers His Servant to bring spiritual renewal and redemption that cannot be thwarted by human rebellion.

Isaiah 42:6 - "I, the LORD, have called you in righteousness; I will take hold of your hand. I will keep you and will make you to be a covenant for the people and a light for the Gentiles."

- God personally calls, upholds, and sustains the Servant, promising divine support through every step of His mission. The Servant is chosen in righteousness, reflecting God's holiness and fulfilling His perfect plan.
- Unlike earlier covenants delivered through human mediators, the Servant Himself becomes the covenant. He embodies God's promises, ensuring redemption and relationship with His people through His very life, death, and resurrection.
- The Servant's light extends to the Gentiles, showing God's covenant love is not confined to Israel. Jesus fulfills this as the light of the world (John 8:12), drawing all nations to God's salvation.

Isaiah 42:7 - "To open eyes that are blind, to free captives from prison and to release from the dungeon those who sit in darkness."

- The Servant's mission is liberation, both physical and spiritual. He heals blindness, delivers captives, and brings light to those imprisoned in darkness. His work restores freedom, dignity, and vision to those in bondage.
- This prophecy points to Jesus' miracles of healing, opening blind eyes, and setting free those oppressed by sin and demonic powers. His ministry demonstrated the reality of God's kingdom breaking into the world.

- Ultimately, Christ fulfills this in salvation, freeing humanity from spiritual blindness and captivity to sin. His resurrection guarantees lasting freedom for those who trust Him, delivering them from darkness into light.

Discussion Questions

1. How does Isaiah 42 describe the character of the Messiah's mission?

2. What does it mean that God delights in His Servant?

3. How do verses 2–3 contrast Christ's ministry with worldly rulers?

4. Why is it significant that the Servant is a "light for the Gentiles"?

5. In what ways did Jesus fulfill this prophecy in His ministry?

6. How does this passage encourage those who feel weak or broken?

7. How should the church reflect the Servant's mission today?

Narrative Reflection

Isaiah 42:1–7 beautifully describes the Messiah's mission, presenting Him as the Servant of the Lord who arrives not with forceful power but with Spirit-filled gentleness and compassion. At a time when nations relied on military strength and rulers showcased power through conquest, Isaiah offers a radically different perspective on leadership. The Servant is chosen and upheld by God, delights the Father's heart, and fulfills His mission with humility, perseverance, and a global vision.

The prophecy opens with God's declaration: "Here is my servant, whom I uphold, my chosen one in whom I delight; I will put my Spirit on him." This echoes Jesus' baptism in the Jordan River, where the Spirit descended like a dove and the Father's voice proclaimed, "This is my Son, whom I love; with him I am well pleased" (Matthew 3:17). Isaiah emphasizes that the Servant's authority derives not from human power but from divine selection and Spirit empowerment. His mission is universal—He will bring justice to all nations, not just Israel.

The following verses highlight His gentleness: "He will not shout or cry out, or raise his voice in the streets. A bruised reed he will not break, and a smoldering wick he will not snuff out." This imagery illustrates the tenderness of Christ's ministry. The bruised reed portrays those fragile and near collapse, while the smoldering wick depicts believers whose faith is weak and barely burning. Rather than crush or extinguish them, Christ restores and strengthens them. The Gospels depict Him embodying this compassion: He welcomed children, touched lepers, restored outcasts, and forgave sinners. Unlike rulers who gain power by oppressing the weak, Jesus elevates them.

However, His gentleness is not weakness. Verse 4 states, "He will not falter or be discouraged till he establishes justice on earth. In his teaching the islands will put their hope." Despite facing opposition, misunderstanding, and rejection, the Servant perseveres, ensuring that His mission will succeed. The mention of "the islands" signifies the farthest reaches of the earth, indicating that His message of hope will resonate globally—a promise fulfilled as the gospel spread from Jerusalem to Judea, Samaria, and beyond (Acts 1:8).

Verses 5–7 anchor the Servant's mission in the authority of the Creator. God, who made heaven and earth and gives breath to all people, commissions His Servant to bring life and redemption. This connection is profound: the Creator who gave life in the beginning now brings new life through His Servant. The Servant is called "in righteousness," upheld by God, and appointed to be "a covenant for the people and a light for the Gentiles." This indicates that the Servant is not merely a messenger of the covenant but its embodiment. In Christ, God's promises are fulfilled; He is the mediator of the new covenant (Hebrews 8:6).

The Servant's mission encompasses opening blind eyes, freeing captives, and releasing those who sit in darkness. Jesus fulfilled these words both literally and spiritually. He healed the blind, as seen in John 9, where He gave sight to a man born blind, demonstrating that He is the light of the world. He proclaimed freedom for the oppressed during His inaugural sermon in Nazareth (Luke 4:18–19, quoting Isaiah 61). Ultimately, He liberated people from the captivity of sin and the power of death through His cross and resurrection.

For the New Testament writers, Isaiah 42 was a pivotal prophecy about Jesus. Matthew 12:18–21 directly quotes the first four verses, applying them to Christ's healing ministry and His refusal to quarrel or raise

His voice in public. The Servant's quiet authority, compassion for the weak, and global mission were all realized in Jesus.

For Christians today, Isaiah 42 offers profound encouragement. It reassures us that Christ's mission is gentle and compassionate. Many of us may feel like bruised reeds or smoldering wicks—weak, weary, and struggling. Yet Christ does not cast us aside; He heals, restores, and strengthens us. His compassion invites us to bring our brokenness to Him, knowing He will not break us further but renew us.

This passage also challenges us to reflect His mission as the church. If Christ embodies justice with compassion, then His followers are called to do the same. We must advance the gospel not through force or coercion but with humility, mercy, and perseverance. We are to be a light to the nations, directing people to the Christ who delivers from darkness.

Isaiah 42 underscores the global scope of the gospel. The Servant was sent not only for Israel but as a light to the Gentiles. This has always been God's plan: to bless all nations through Abraham's seed (Genesis 12:3), fulfilled in Christ. Today, the church continues that mission, proclaiming the gospel to all peoples, confident that in His teaching, the nations will find hope.

A final look at Isaiah 42:1–7 portrays the Messiah as the Spirit-filled Servant who brings justice with compassion, embodies God's covenant, and shines as a light to the nations. It reveals a Savior who restores the weak, perseveres in His mission, and brings deliverance to those in darkness. For Isaiah's audience, it was a promise of hope amidst uncertainty. For us, it illustrates Christ's ministry and calls us to reflect His character. The Servant has come, the light has dawned, and the mission continues through His people until He establishes justice on the earth.

Layers of Understanding

Historical Context

Isaiah's prophecy was given during the looming threat of Assyria, when Israel sought political and military deliverance. Instead of promising a warrior or conqueror, God revealed a Servant who would bring justice in an unexpected way—through humility, gentleness, and divine empowerment. This vision contrasted with Israel's longing for immediate national rescue.

Jewish Understanding

Jewish interpretation often wrestled with the Servant's identity. Some saw the Servant as Israel itself, called to embody God's justice and light before the nations. Others understood it as a messianic figure, uniquely chosen to restore righteousness. Over time, this expectation deepened into hope for a coming deliverer who would embody God's covenant promises.

New Testament Fulfillment

The New Testament explicitly connects Jesus with this Servant prophecy. Matthew 12:18–21 quotes Isaiah 42:1–4, presenting Christ as the one who fulfills the mission of bringing justice and hope to the nations. Through His compassion, healings, and sacrificial death, Jesus embodies the Servant's role as healer of the broken and light to all peoples.

Theological Significance Today

For believers today, Isaiah's Servant points to Christ's compassion and restorative mission. His example calls the church to live with humility and reflect His justice in the world. This passage reassures us that Christ restores the weak and faltering, and challenges us to carry His light into places of darkness and despair.

Cross-Reference Connections

- **Isaiah 11:2** – The Spirit of the Lord rests on the Messiah.
- **Matthew 3:16–17** – Jesus' baptism fulfills Spirit-anointing and divine delight.
- **Matthew 12:18–21** – Direct citation of Isaiah 42 in reference to Jesus.
- **Luke 4:18–19** – Jesus proclaims freedom for the oppressed.
- **John 8:12** – "I am the light of the world."
- **Hebrews 8:6** – Christ as mediator of the new covenant

PROPHECY FULFILLED - STUDY LESSON 11

LESSON SCRIPTURE: ISAIAH 61: 1-2

PROPHECY TITLE

The Spirit of the Lord: Good News to the Poor

Introduction

Isaiah 61:1–2 stands out as one of the most powerful messianic prophecies in the Old Testament, outlining the mission of the Servant of the Lord. This mission includes bringing good news to the poor, healing the brokenhearted, proclaiming freedom for the captives, and announcing the year of the Lord's favor.

Centuries later, Jesus entered the synagogue in His hometown of Nazareth, opened the scroll of Isaiah, and read this very passage (Luke 4:16–21). He then declared, *"Today this Scripture is fulfilled in your hearing,"* identifying Himself as the Spirit-anointed Servant who brings salvation, freedom, and hope.

This prophecy highlights the compassionate heart of the Messiah's mission. In contrast to worldly rulers who seek wealth and power, the Spirit-filled Christ offers restoration to the poor, oppressed, and broken. His mission began with His first coming and will reach its fulfillment when He returns to bring final judgment and complete restoration.

Scripture Reference

Isaiah 61:1–2 (NIV)   "'The Spirit of the Sovereign LORD is on me, because the LORD has anointed me to proclaim good news to the poor. He has sent me to bind up the brokenhearted, to proclaim freedom for the captives and release from darkness for the prisoners," [2] to proclaim the year of the LORD's favor and the day of vengeance of our God, to comfort all who mourn,

Big Picture Insights

- **Spirit-anointed mission** – Messiah empowered by the Spirit (fulfilled at Jesus' baptism).
- **Good news to the poor** – salvation reaches the humble, needy, and broken.
- **Healing the brokenhearted** – Christ's ministry restores hope and wholeness.
- **Freedom for captives** – liberation from sin, death, and spiritual bondage.
- **Year of the Lord's favor** – echoes Jubilee (Leviticus 25), symbolizing release and renewal.
- **Day of vengeance** – future judgment upon sin and evil.
- **Partial fulfillment now, complete later** – Jesus stopped mid-verse in Luke 4, highlighting the "already/not yet" of prophecy.
- **Compassionate Messiah** – focuses on healing and restoration rather than conquest.
- **Kingdom ethic** – the church continues Christ's mission of good news.
- **Hope for all generations** – promise of freedom and comfort for those in Christ.

Verse-by-Verse Commentary

Isaiah 61:1a – "The Spirit of the Sovereign Lord is on me"

- This phrase establishes divine authority. The Servant is not self-appointed but Spirit-anointed, empowered to accomplish God's mission. His strength does not come from human wisdom or earthly power but directly from the Spirit resting upon Him.
- At Jesus' baptism the Spirit descended visibly, confirming His identity as the anointed Servant (Luke 3:22). His ministry from the beginning was Spirit-driven, a model of dependence on God's empowering presence for accomplishing redemption.

Isaiah 61:1b – "because the Lord has anointed me to proclaim good news to the poor."

- The anointing is purposeful, tied to proclamation of the gospel. The poor here include both economically disadvantaged and spiritually needy, those most aware of dependence on God's mercy.
- Jesus fulfilled this in Luke 4:18–21 when He declared this prophecy completed in Himself. The gospel is good news because it brings hope, forgiveness, and restoration where despair and oppression once reigned.

Isaiah 61:1c – "He has sent me to bind up the brokenhearted"

- The Servant's mission is healing, not only of physical wounds but of spiritual and emotional fractures. God's redemption mends lives shattered by sin, grief, and injustice, bringing restoration to the whole person.
- Jesus demonstrated this in His compassionate ministry—welcoming outcasts, forgiving sinners, and comforting mourners. His words and works reveal the Father's heart for restoration, binding up hearts that otherwise remain crushed and hopeless.

Isaiah 61:1d – "to proclaim freedom for the captives and release from darkness for the prisoners"

- Captivity includes both literal bondage, such as Israel's exile, and spiritual enslavement under sin and death. The Servant's mission is release, shining light into darkness and granting true freedom.
- Jesus fulfilled this by liberating those oppressed by sin, demons, and fear. His death and resurrection broke the power of bondage forever, offering lasting freedom: "So if the Son sets you free, you will be free indeed" (John 8:36).

Isaiah 61:2 – "to proclaim the year of the Lord's favor and the day of vengeance of our God, to comfort all who mourn."

- The "year of the Lord's favor" points to Jubilee imagery—an age of release, restoration, and grace. It is fulfilled in Christ's first coming, where He inaugurated the kingdom of God through salvation.
- The "day of vengeance" refers to God's justice, a reminder that grace and judgment belong together. Jesus paused before this line in Luke 4, showing His first mission was favor, with final judgment reserved for His second coming.
- Comfort flows from both favor and justice. The Servant brings hope to mourners, assuring them that God's redemption will ultimately reverse grief, restore joy, and wipe away every tear.

Discussion Questions

1. Why is it significant that Jesus read this prophecy at the start of His ministry?

2. How does the Spirit's anointing define the Messiah's mission?

3. What does "good news to the poor" mean for the church today?

4. How do we see Christ binding up the brokenhearted in His ministry?

5. Why did Jesus stop reading before "the day of vengeance of our God" in Luke 4?

6. How does this passage reveal the "already/not yet" nature of God's kingdom?

7. How are believers called to continue Christ's mission of freedom and healing?

Narrative Reflection

For one of the clearest depictions of the Messiah's mission in the Old Testament, one need only look to Isaiah 61:1–2. Addressed to a weary people longing for restoration after exile, this prophecy promises not merely political renewal but deep spiritual healing and lasting freedom. Its message echoes throughout history and finds its ultimate fulfillment in the ministry of Jesus Christ. The prophecy opens with the statement, "The Spirit of the Sovereign Lord is on me, because the Lord has anointed me." This identifies the Servant as someone chosen and empowered by God for a divine purpose. The Hebrew term for "anointed" is *mashiach*, the root of our word "Messiah." Anointing was reserved for kings, priests, and prophets, marking them for God's purposes. In this context, it signifies that the Messiah is divinely appointed, filled with the Spirit, and uniquely empowered to bring about salvation. The connection to Jesus is clear; at His baptism, the Holy Spirit descended upon Him like a dove, and the Father proclaimed Him as His beloved Son (Luke 3:21–22). Isaiah's words anticipate this commissioning moment.

The mission is characterized by proclamation and healing. The Messiah is sent "to proclaim good news to the poor." In Isaiah's context, "the poor" included not only those facing material deprivation but also those marginalized and oppressed, who humbly seek God. Jesus embodied this mission by offering hope to those society overlooked—lifting up the lowly, including the poor, women, children, lepers, tax collectors, and sinners. The Beatitudes reflect this theme: "Blessed are the poor in spirit, for theirs is the kingdom of heaven" (Matthew 5:3). The good news is that God's kingdom is given to the humble and broken, not the proud and powerful.

The prophecy continues: "He has sent me to bind up the brokenhearted." This imagery evokes a healer tending to wounds. Jesus exemplified this throughout His ministry—comforting the grieving, restoring dignity to the outcast, and offering forgiveness to the burdened. The brokenhearted among Isaiah's audience would have been those suffering from exile and disobedience. In Christ, we see this mission fulfilled in a profound way: He heals the deepest wounds of the human soul.

The next phrase, "to proclaim freedom for the captives and release from darkness for the prisoners," echoes the Jubilee year in Israel's law, when debts were forgiven and slaves were freed (Leviticus 25). For the exiles, it meant liberation from Babylonian bondage. For humanity, it foreshadows the greater deliverance Christ brings from sin, Satan, and death. Jesus stated, "If the Son sets you free, you will be free indeed" (John 8:36). His liberation is not merely political but spiritual and eternal.

Verse 2 shifts focus: "to proclaim the year of the Lord's favor and the day of vengeance of our God." The contrast between favor and vengeance is striking. The "year of the Lord's favor" recalls Jubilee, a time of renewal and release, symbolizing God's grace entering history. In Luke 4:16–21, Jesus read from Isaiah 61 in the synagogue but stopped short before mentioning "the day of vengeance." This was intentional. In His first coming, Christ initiated an era of grace and good news. The day of vengeance, representing final judgment, is reserved for His second coming. This illustrates the prophetic pattern of "already/not yet," indicating that while the prophecy speaks of one mission, it encompasses two horizons: Christ's first advent of grace and His second advent of judgment.

The dual nature of the prophecy holds significant theological implications. It reminds us that God's salvation and judgment are intertwined. The same Messiah who offers freedom and healing also enacts justice and judgment against sin. Yet, in His mercy, God has postponed judgment to extend grace. We currently live in the "year of the Lord's favor," a time when the gospel is proclaimed and salvation is offered to all who believe.

For the church today, Isaiah 61:1–2 defines both identity and mission. Just as Christ was Spirit-anointed, so too are His followers. The Spirit that rested on Him was poured out on the church at Pentecost (Acts 2). Our calling is to continue His mission: proclaim good news, bind up the brokenhearted, set captives free, and declare the Lord's favor. This entails preaching the gospel, caring for the poor, comforting the hurting, and advocating for justice. We are called to embody Christ's compassion in tangible ways.

Isaiah's prophecy also brings hope to individuals. Many of us experience brokenness, feeling captive to sin or fear, or trapped in darkness. This passage reassures us that Christ came for us. He does not overlook the poor, the weak, or the hurting. He actively seeks them out, bringing freedom, healing, and light. His mission is not abstract but deeply personal.

Finally, Isaiah 61:1–2 leads us toward the ultimate fulfillment of Christ's mission. The year of favor has begun, but the day of vengeance is coming. This is both sobering and hopeful. Sobering, as it reminds us that sin will be judged; hopeful, as it assures us that evil will not prevail forever. Christ will return to complete the work He began, bringing justice and restoration to the world.

Isaiah 61:1–2 is a prophetic declaration of the Messiah's mission, fulfilled in Christ's first coming and awaiting completion at His return. It proclaims good news to the poor, healing to the brokenhearted, freedom to captives, and God's favor to the world. Jesus embraced this prophecy as His mission statement, and the church is called to live it out until His return. The Spirit of the Lord rests upon Him, and through Him, upon us. The good news continues to be proclaimed, the broken are still being healed, and the captives are still being set free.

Layers of Understanding

Historical Context

Isaiah 61:1–2 was spoken to a people returning from Babylonian exile, weary from loss and hardship. While they longed for national and political restoration, the prophecy pointed beyond these immediate hopes. It envisioned a deeper renewal—healing of broken hearts, release for captives, and lasting freedom found only in God's Spirit-anointed work.

Jewish Understanding

Within Jewish tradition, this prophecy was read as a vision of messianic restoration. It portrayed God's favor poured out on His people through the coming of the Messiah. Israel anticipated one who would proclaim liberty, bring justice, and establish peace, signaling not just survival after exile but true spiritual renewal and hope.

New Testament Fulfillment

Jesus explicitly connected Himself to this passage when He read it in the synagogue at Nazareth (Luke 4:16–21). Declaring, "Today this Scripture is fulfilled in your hearing," He identified His mission with the Spirit-anointed servant. His ministry of healing, teaching, and deliverance embodied the prophetic vision and brought God's promises into reality.

Theological Significance Today

For believers today, this prophecy affirms Christ's compassion for the poor, oppressed, and brokenhearted. It calls the church to continue His Spirit-filled mission of proclaiming good news and practicing justice. It also assures us of God's favor in the present while reminding us that final judgment and full restoration are yet to come.

Cross-Reference Connections

- **Leviticus 25:10** – Year of Jubilee, liberty proclaimed throughout the land.
- **Isaiah 11:2** – The Spirit of the Lord rests upon the Messiah.
- **Luke 4:16–21** – Jesus reads Isaiah 61 in the synagogue.
- **Matthew 5:3–4** – Blessing for the poor and those who mourn.
- **John 8:36** – The Son sets captives free.
- **Acts 2:17–18** – Spirit poured out at Pentecost, empowering the church.
- **Revelation 19:11–16** – The day of vengeance at Christ's return.

PROPHECY FULFILLED - STUDY LESSON - 12

LESSON SCRIPTURE: ZECHARIAH 9: 9

PROPHECY TITLE

The Humble King: Salvation on a Donkey

Introduction

Zechariah prophesied in the late 6th century B.C., following the return from Babylonian exile and during the temple's reconstruction. His messages blended encouragement for the present with visions of God's future kingdom. In Zechariah 9:9, the prophet vividly describes the coming King, who enters Jerusalem not on a warhorse, but on a donkey—righteous and victorious, yet humble.

This prophecy was fulfilled during Jesus' triumphal entry into Jerusalem (Matthew 21:4–5; John 12:14–15). Riding a donkey symbolizes peace, humility, and service. Unlike conquering kings who arrive with power and military force, Jesus came to offer salvation through sacrifice.

Zechariah 9:9 highlights the paradox of the Messiah's kingship: He is the righteous, victorious King who brings salvation, yet His victory is characterized by humility rather than domination. The cross and resurrection illustrate that His kingdom is not of this world but is founded on love and self-giving.

Scripture Reference

Zechariah 9:9 (NIV) "Rejoice greatly, Daughter Zion! Shout, Daughter Jerusalem! See, your king comes to you, righteous and victorious, lowly and riding on a donkey, on a colt, the foal of a donkey. "

Big Picture Insights

- **Messianic promise** – the King comes to Jerusalem.
- **Call to rejoice** – joy marks His arrival.
- **Righteous and victorious** – true justice and salvation belong to Him.
- **Lowly and humble** – not a conquering warrior but a gentle King.
- **Donkey symbol** – peace, service, humility (contrast with warhorse).
- **Palm Sunday fulfillment** – Jesus' entry into Jerusalem (Matthew 21:4–5).
- **Paradox of kingship** – power through humility, victory through suffering.
- **Foreshadows cross** – salvation comes not by conquest but by sacrifice.
- **Invitation to worship** – rejoice in the King who brings peace.
- **Advent connection** – points toward the coming of Christ as the humble King.

Verse-by-Verse Commentary

Zechariah 9:9a – "Rejoice greatly, Daughter Zion! Shout, Daughter Jerusalem!"

- The prophecy begins with a call to rejoice. Zion and Jerusalem represent God's people, invited to celebrate the arrival of their King. Joy replaces despair, marking the coming of salvation as both corporate and deeply personal.
- This joyful summons is not grounded in temporary victories but in God's promise of a righteous ruler. The language anticipates a Messianic fulfillment where celebration is not optional—it is the appropriate response to divine intervention.

Zechariah 9:9b – "See, your king comes to you, righteous and victorious"

- The king's coming is personal—"to you." Unlike distant monarchs, this ruler arrives for His people's sake. His righteousness and victory demonstrate moral integrity, divine favor, and deliverance beyond political power.
- The prophecy anticipates Christ's triumph, not through conquest but through obedience to the Father. His victory is over sin and death, not merely over earthly enemies, fulfilling the deeper needs of humanity.

Zechariah 9:9c – "lowly and riding on a donkey"

- Unlike kings who rode warhorses, this ruler enters humbly, rejecting displays of earthly dominance. His donkey signifies peace, humility, and accessibility, contrasting worldly expectations of power and grandeur.
- Jesus fulfilled this directly at His triumphal entry (Matthew 21:4–5). Crowds welcomed Him with palm branches, yet His humble mount revealed a kingdom of peace rather than military conquest.

Zechariah 9:9d – "on a colt, the foal of a donkey."

- The repetition underscores humility, stressing the king's peaceful intent. A young donkey, unused for war, highlights innocence and purity, reinforcing the prophetic picture of meekness clothed with authority.
- Jesus' fulfillment of this detail shows God's sovereignty in every aspect. Nothing is accidental— the Messiah's entry on a colt confirms His identity and mission, signaling that God's plan unfolds with precision.

Discussion Questions

1. Why does Zechariah call God's people to rejoice at the King's coming?

2. How do righteousness and humility define Christ's kingship?

3. What is the significance of the donkey in this prophecy?

4. How does Jesus' triumphal entry fulfill this prophecy?

5. What does this prophecy teach us about God's kingdom compared to earthly kingdoms?

6. How does Christ's humility challenge our ideas of power and success?

7. What does it mean to welcome Jesus as King in our lives today?

Narrative Reflection

Zechariah 9:9 is a vivid and significant messianic prophecy that captures both the joy of the King's arrival and the paradox of His humility. This prophecy emerged at a time when God's people were fragile, having recently returned from exile and struggling to rebuild their city, temple, and identity. Into this weariness, Zechariah proclaimed hope: their King would come, bringing righteousness, salvation, and peace.

The verse opens with a call to joy: "Rejoice greatly, Daughter Zion! Shout, Daughter Jerusalem!" The coming of the King is a cause for celebration, not fear. Unlike oppressive rulers or foreign conquerors, this King comes for the good of His people. The imperative to rejoice reflects the gospel itself—good news that demands a response of worship and gladness. Centuries later, Palm Sunday embodied this call as crowds shouted "Hosanna!" and waved palm branches to welcome Jesus into Jerusalem (John 12:13).

At the heart of the prophecy is the King's arrival: "See, your king comes to you." This is remarkable because it emphasizes God's initiative; the people are not told to seek their King, but He comes to them.

This reflects God's grace throughout Scripture—He comes to Adam and Eve in the garden, to Abraham with promises, to Israel in Egypt, and ultimately to humanity in Christ. Salvation is always initiated by God.

The King is described as "righteous and victorious," and these qualities are inseparable. His righteousness signifies His covenant faithfulness, justice, and holiness. Unlike human rulers who often pursue self-interest, this King's reign will reflect God's character. His victory is achieved not through military conquest but through salvation. The Hebrew word for "victorious" can also mean "saved" or "vindicated." This King embodies victory by delivering His people rather than destroying enemies in the conventional sense.

The most surprising description follows: "lowly and riding on a donkey, on a colt, the foal of a donkey." This would have defied expectations. Kings in the ancient world typically entered cities on horses or chariots, symbols of military strength. A donkey, in contrast, symbolizes humility, service, and peace. In Israel's history, donkeys were used for peaceful royal occasions, as when Solomon rode David's mule at his coronation (1 Kings 1:33). By choosing this imagery, Zechariah portrays a King whose authority is rooted not in domination but in humility.

Jesus fulfilled this prophecy in striking detail. On Palm Sunday, He instructed His disciples to bring Him a colt, the foal of a donkey, and rode it into Jerusalem (Matthew 21:1–7). The Gospel writers explicitly cite Zechariah 9:9 to show that Jesus was fulfilling the prophecy. The crowds recognized its significance, crying out "Hosanna to the Son of David!" (Matthew 21:9). However, their expectations were mixed; many hoped for a political deliverer who would overthrow Rome. But Jesus came not to conquer with the sword but to establish a kingdom of peace through His death and resurrection.

The humility of this prophecy highlights the paradox of the gospel. The King is righteous and victorious, yet His victory is marked by lowliness. He brings salvation not through force but through sacrifice. His triumph comes not from wielding power but from laying down His life. The donkey ride into Jerusalem foreshadowed the cross, where the humble King would achieve ultimate victory over sin and death.

Theologically, Zechariah 9:9 captures the tension between the "already" and "not yet" of Christ's kingdom. In His first coming, He arrived humbly, bringing salvation and peace. In His second coming, He will return in glory, riding not a donkey but a white horse (Revelation 19:11), symbolizing judgment and final victory. Together, these images reveal the fullness of His kingship—humble Savior and reigning Lord.

For the church today, this prophecy offers several key lessons. First, it calls us to rejoice. Worship and joy are the proper responses to the King who comes. Christianity is not primarily about duty or fear but about joy rooted in the good news of Christ's reign.

Second, it challenges our notions of power and success. The King who saves does not come with pomp or military might but with humility and service. This upends worldly values. As Paul writes in Philippians 2:6–8, Christ "made himself nothing, taking the very nature of a servant… he humbled himself by becoming obedient to death—even death on a cross." If our King reigns through humility, His followers must embody the same.

Third, it invites us to welcome Christ personally. The crowds on Palm Sunday welcomed Jesus with shouts but later turned against Him. We are called not only to celebrate His arrival but to submit to His reign. Welcoming the King means acknowledging His authority in every aspect of life, finding salvation in His sacrifice, and living as citizens of His kingdom.

Finally, it points us forward with hope. The King has come, humble and righteous, bringing salvation. He will come again, victorious in glory, bringing final justice and peace. In the meantime, we live between Palm Sunday and Revelation, rejoicing in the already and longing for the not yet.

Zechariah 9:9 is a prophecy that truly captures the heart of the gospel. The King comes not in might but in meekness, not to conquer nations by war but to conquer sin by sacrifice. His humility is His glory, His lowliness is His strength, and His cross is His victory. Rejoice, Daughter Zion! Your King has come, and He will come again.

Layers of Understanding

Historical Context

This prophecy was spoken after the exile to bring encouragement to a disheartened people with the promise of a coming King. Unlike earthly rulers who secured power through violence and force, this King would bring salvation through humility and peace, offering hope of true renewal under God's sovereign hand.

Jewish Understanding

For Jewish readers, this verse was understood as a messianic promise pointing to a future deliverer. Many expected a political leader who would overthrow foreign oppressors and restore Israel's independence. The prophecy stirred nationalistic hopes, yet it also hinted at a deeper kind of redemption rooted in God's covenant faithfulness.

New Testament Fulfillment

The New Testament explicitly connects this prophecy to Jesus' triumphal entry into Jerusalem, recorded in Matthew 21:4–5 and John 12:14–15. Riding humbly on a donkey, Jesus revealed Himself as the promised King. Yet His kingdom would not be established through military conquest, but through sacrifice, obedience, and the cross.

Theological Significance Today

This prophecy reminds believers that Christ's kingdom is marked by humility and peace, not worldly power. It calls us to rejoice in His reign, to welcome Him as King in our hearts, and to imitate His humility in how we live, serve, and bear witness to the gospel.

Cross-Reference Connections

- **1 Kings 1:33** – Solomon's peaceful coronation on a mule.
- **Philippians 2:6–8** – Christ's humility and self-emptying.
- **Matthew 21:1–9** – Jesus rides into Jerusalem on a donkey.
- **John 12:13–15** – Palm Sunday crowds fulfill Zechariah 9:9.
- **Revelation 19:11** – Christ returns on a white horse for judgment.

Series 2 - Advent Season (Christmas Prophecies)

PROPHECY FULFILLED - STUDY LESSON - 13

LESSON SCRIPTURE: **ISAIAH 7: 14**

PROPHECY TITLE

The Virgin Shall Conceive: God with Us

Introduction

Isaiah 7:14 is one of the most recognized messianic prophecies in the Old Testament. Delivered during King Ahaz's reign, Judah was in a state of deep political crisis, facing threats of invasion from neighboring nations. In his fear and unbelief, Ahaz sought human alliances instead of trusting in God's promise. In this moment of doubt, Isaiah proclaimed that the Lord Himself would provide a sign. This assurance was intended not only to calm Ahaz but also to remind God's people that their hope must rest in His faithfulness rather than in human schemes.

However, the prophecy's significance extends beyond its immediate context. Isaiah foretold a miraculous birth: a virgin conceiving and bearing a son named *Immanuel*, which means "God with us." While the sign had near-term implications for Judah, the language points to something far greater than any child born in Isaiah's time. The promise encompasses God's plan for ultimate deliverance and restoration.

Matthew's Gospel makes this connection explicit by applying Isaiah 7:14 to the birth of Jesus Christ (Matthew 1:22–23). In Jesus, the prophecy finds its ultimate fulfillment, for He is Immanuel in the fullest sense—God made flesh, dwelling among His people. More than just a temporary sign for a fearful king, this verse becomes a timeless declaration of God's presence with humanity through His Son. It assures believers that God's faithfulness is not confined to history but continues through Christ, who came once in humility and will come again in glory.

Scripture Reference

Isaiah 7:14 (NIV) **"Therefore the Lord himself will give you a sign: The virgin [h] will conceive and give birth to a son, and will call him Immanuel."**

Big Picture Insights

- **Immediate context** – reassurance to King Ahaz during political crisis.
- **The sign** – a miraculous birth that signals God's intervention.
- **Virgin birth** – fulfilled in Mary, mother of Jesus (Matthew 1:23; Luke 1:26–35).
- **Immanuel** – "God with us," the heart of the Incarnation.
- **Dual fulfillment** – near-term sign for Ahaz, ultimate fulfillment in Christ.

- **Messianic identity** – Jesus is both son of David and Son of God.
- **God's presence** – not just deliverance from enemies, but God dwelling with His people.
- **Theological cornerstone** – affirms Christ's divinity and humanity.
- **Christmas prophecy** – central to Advent and the Nativity story.
- **Hope for believers** – God has not abandoned us; He is with us.

Verse-by-Verse Commentary

Isaiah 7:14a – "Therefore the Lord himself will give you a sign:…"

- God declares that He, not human effort, will provide the sign. This emphasizes His sovereignty in salvation, removing human boasting. A divine sign assures Judah—and ultimately all humanity—that deliverance comes by God's initiative.
- In context, King Ahaz faced political fear and doubted God's promises. Yet God promised a miraculous sign beyond the crisis of the day, pointing to His faithfulness to accomplish redemption despite human unbelief.

Isaiah 7:14b – "…The virgin will conceive and give birth to a son…"

- This prophecy's striking nature lies in its impossibility. A virgin conceiving defies natural explanation, proving that God alone can bring about this promised deliverance. It foreshadows Christ's miraculous birth through Mary by the Holy Spirit.
- The son promised is no ordinary child but the Messiah. Matthew 1:22–23 explicitly connects this verse to Jesus' birth, showing the fulfillment of Isaiah's prophecy in the incarnation of the Son of God.

Isaiah 7:14c – "…and will call him Immanuel."

- The name "Immanuel" means "God with us," revealing the mystery of incarnation. God does not remain distant but enters human history, dwelling among His people in the form of His Son.
- In Christ, God is present not only to comfort but to save. His presence signifies covenant faithfulness and enduring companionship, assuring believers that God is both near and actively involved in their redemption.

Discussion Questions

1. How does understanding the original context of Ahaz help us appreciate the prophecy's significance?

2. Why is the virgin birth essential to Christian faith?

3. What does the name "Immanuel" reveal about God's character and purposes?

4. How does Matthew's use of Isaiah 7:14 deepen our understanding of Jesus' identity?

5. How does this prophecy encourage us in times of fear and uncertainty?

6. What does it mean for the church today to live as the people of "God with us"?

7. How does this prophecy shape the way we celebrate Christmas?

Narrative Reflection

Isaiah 7:14 is one of the most cherished and significant prophecies in Scripture. It connects Israel's ancient struggles to the gospel narrative of Christ's birth, providing hope both in its immediate context and in its ultimate fulfillment.

This prophecy was first delivered to King Ahaz during a time of great fear, as the kings of Aram (Syria) and Israel (Ephraim) had formed an alliance and threatened to invade Judah. Ahaz, fearful and lacking faith, considered seeking help from Assyria instead of trusting God. Isaiah confronted him, urging him to remain steadfast in faith and offering him a sign from the Lord. When Ahaz hypocritically refused, God declared that He would provide a sign: "The virgin will conceive and give birth to a son, and will call him Immanuel."

For Ahaz, the sign was meant to reassure him that Judah would not be destroyed by its enemies. Within a short time—before the child would be old enough to discern right from wrong—the threat from Aram and Ephraim would diminish. Historically, this proved true as Assyria conquered both nations. However, the sign carried greater significance than Ahaz realized. While it addressed his immediate situation, it also pointed to a future fulfillment that only God could accomplish.

The phrase "the virgin will conceive" is pivotal. In Hebrew, the term *almah* (pronounce like ahl-MAH refers to a young woman of marriageable age, which could imply virginity but does not necessitate it. However, the Septuagint (the Greek translation of the Old Testament) used the word *Parthenos* (pronounced as PAR-theh-nos), which explicitly means "virgin." Matthew, inspired by the Holy Spirit, utilized this Greek term to demonstrate that the ultimate fulfillment of Isaiah 7:14 is found in the miraculous conception of Jesus by the Virgin Mary. This was no ordinary birth; it was the Incarnation— the eternal Son of God taking on human flesh.

Mary's response to the angel Gabriel in Luke 1 underscores the miracle: "How will this be," she asked, "since I am a virgin?" (Luke 1:34). Gabriel explained that the Holy Spirit would come upon her, and the power of the Most High would overshadow her, so the child would be called the Son of God. This captures the essence of Isaiah's prophecy: God intervening to bring salvation in a way only He could. The virgin birth highlights that salvation is not a result of human effort but of divine action. Christ was not born of human will but of God's sovereign grace.

The name Immanuel is equally significant. In Ahaz's time, it symbolized God's presence with His people amid threats from enemies. In its ultimate fulfillment, it reveals the mystery of the Incarnation: Jesus is God with us. John captures this in his Gospel: "The Word became flesh and made his dwelling among us" (John 1:14). In Christ, God is not distant but present; He is not abstract but personal, not aloof but near. He entered our world, shared in our humanity, and experienced our sufferings.

The significance of "God with us" cannot be overstated. In Christ, God fully identifies with His people. He does not save from a distance but engages deeply in human existence. He knows hunger, weariness, rejection, and grief. Yet He also brings healing, forgiveness, and eternal life. Immanuel is not merely a title; it is a transformative reality. In Christ, God is present in our joys and sorrows, struggles and victories, births and deaths.

Isaiah 7:14 also carries eschatological hope. The birth of Immanuel marked the beginning of God's kingdom breaking into the world, but the fullness of "God with us" awaits Christ's return. Revelation 21:3 proclaims, "Now the dwelling of God is with men, and he will live with them. They will be his people, and God himself will be with them and be their God." What began in the manger will culminate in the new heavens and new earth, when God's presence fills all creation.

For the church today, this prophecy offers both comfort and challenge. It comforts us by reminding us that God has not abandoned us. Regardless of our fears, the promise of Immanuel assures us of His presence. Just as God was with Judah in its crisis and with Mary in her calling, He is with us in every circumstance. His presence is our peace.

It also challenges us to live as people who embody Immanuel. If God is with us, our lives should reflect His presence. We are called to be a people of hope, joy, and holiness, demonstrating to the world that God dwells with His people. Advent and Christmas are not merely traditional seasons but opportunities to proclaim that God has come in Christ and will come again in glory.

Theologically, Isaiah 7:14 emphasizes two essential truths: the full humanity and full divinity of Christ. As the virgin-born Son, He shares in our humanity. As Immanuel, He is fully divine. This union represents the mystery of the Incarnation, the foundation of our salvation. Only one who is both God and man could reconcile God and humanity. As Paul writes in Colossians 2:9, "In Christ all the fullness of the Deity lives in bodily form."

As we conclude this lesson on Isaiah 7:14 it represents more than a Christmas verse; it is the heart of the gospel. It intertwines history and prophecy, fear and hope, judgment and salvation. It reminds us that God is faithful to His promises, that His ways surpass human understanding, and that His love is so great that He came to dwell among us. From Ahaz's trembling court to Mary's humble home, from the manger in Bethlehem to the cross at Calvary, the promise of Immanuel resounds: God is with us.

Layers of Understanding

Historical Context

This prophecy was given to King Ahaz during the Syro-Ephraimite crisis (735–732 B.C.), when Judah faced military threats from neighboring kingdoms. In his fear, Ahaz looked to foreign alliances rather than trusting God. Through Isaiah, the Lord reassured Judah that He was present, sovereign, and in control of their destiny.

Jewish Understanding

For Jewish readers, Isaiah 7:14 was viewed as a sign of God's immediate intervention during Ahaz's crisis. It testified that God had not abandoned His covenant people and that His promises would endure. Over time, the verse also came to embody Israel's broader hope for God's faithfulness and ultimate deliverance.

New Testament Fulfillment

Matthew 1:22–23 explicitly cites Isaiah 7:14 as fulfilled in the virgin birth of Jesus Christ, identifying Him as Immanuel—"God with us." Luke 1:26–35 records Gabriel's announcement to Mary, affirming that her child would be conceived by the Holy Spirit, making this prophecy central to the New Testament narrative.

Theological Significance Today

This verse affirms the mystery of the Incarnation: Jesus Christ is fully God and fully man, dwelling among His people. It reassures believers of God's continual presence through Christ and the Spirit. It also challenges the church to live faithfully as those who belong to Immanuel, bearing witness in a broken world.

Cross-Reference Connections

- **Exodus 4:22–23** – Israel as God's son, foreshadowing Christ as true Son.
- **Isaiah 9:6–7** – Prophecy of the child who is Mighty God, Prince of Peace.
- **Matthew 1:22–23** – Direct citation of Isaiah 7:14 fulfilled in Jesus' birth.
- **Luke 1:26–35** – Virgin conception announced by Gabriel.
- **John 1:14** – The Word became flesh and dwelt among us.
- **Revelation 21:3** – Final fulfillment of Immanuel in the new creation.

LESSON SCRIPTURE: **MICAH 5: 2**

PROPHECY TITLE

The Ruler from Bethlehem: Eternal King from Humble Beginnings

Introduction

Micah prophesied in the 8th century B.C. during the reigns of Jotham, Ahaz, and Hezekiah in Judah. His ministry coincided with that of Isaiah and addressed issues such as corruption in Jerusalem, idolatry, and injustice among God's people. Amid warnings of impending judgment, Micah also conveyed a message of hope for restoration.

Micah 5:2 stands out as one of the most explicit messianic prophecies in Scripture. It predicts that the Messiah, the future ruler of Israel, would be born in Bethlehem, a small and seemingly insignificant town. The phrase "origins are from of old, from ancient times" not only highlights His Davidic lineage but also points to His eternal nature.

The New Testament clearly applies this prophecy to Jesus. When the Magi visited Herod, inquiring about the birthplace of the Christ, the religious leaders cited Micah 5:2 (Matthew 2:5–6). This connection directly links the identity of the Messiah with His birthplace, showcasing God's sovereignty in choosing humble Bethlehem to bring forth the King of kings and emphasizing that He often works through the unexpected to fulfill His promises.

Scripture Reference

Micah 5:2 (NIV)   "But you, Bethlehem Ephrathah, though you are small among the clans of Judah, out of you will come for me one who will be ruler over Israel, whose origins are from of old, from ancient times."

Big Picture Insights

- **Bethlehem identified** – specific prophecy of Messiah's birthplace.
- **Small town, great ruler** – God uses the humble and unexpected.
- **Davidic connection** – Bethlehem was the city of David (1 Sam. 16:1).
- **Divine ruler** – "origins from of old" hint at Messiah's eternal nature.
- **God's sovereignty** – place, time, and lineage chosen by Him.
- **Fulfilled in Jesus** – born in Bethlehem (Luke 2:4–7).
- **Recognized by Magi** – Matthew 2:5–6 cites this prophecy directly.

- **Hope in exile** – assurance that God's plan for David's line endures.
- **Theological depth** – Christ is both child of Bethlehem and eternal Lord.
- **Advent theme** – God comes humbly yet reigns eternally.

Verse-by-Verse Commentary

Micah 5:2a – "But you, Bethlehem Ephrathah, though you are small among the clans of Judah,…"

- Bethlehem, an insignificant village, is chosen for greatness. Its smallness highlights God's pattern of using what the world overlooks to accomplish His purposes. David's birthplace becomes the cradle of the promised Messiah.
- The contrast between insignificance and destiny underscores divine sovereignty. God chooses the lowly to shame the proud, ensuring that His plan unfolds according to grace, not human merit or status.

Micah 5:2b – "…out of you will come for me one who will be ruler over Israel,…"

- The prophecy points to a divinely appointed ruler. Unlike kings who seek self-interest, this one comes "for me," fulfilling God's will rather than personal ambition. His authority is God-centered, not man-centered.
- This anticipates Christ as the true Shepherd-King, who rules not by force but by sacrificial love. His mission was always to glorify the Father, bringing salvation and righteousness to His people.

Micah 5:2c – "…whose origins are from of old, from ancient times."

- The ruler's origins stretch beyond history, pointing to eternity. This reveals the Messiah's preexistence, distinguishing Him from all other human leaders. His coming is not new invention but eternal plan.
- John 1:1 affirms this truth: "In the beginning was the Word, and the Word was with God, and the Word was God." Christ is both eternal and incarnate, fulfilling Micah's prophecy perfectly.

Discussion Questions

1. Why is it significant that God chose Bethlehem, a small town, as the Messiah's birthplace?

2. How does this prophecy connect the Messiah to David?

3. What does it mean that the ruler's "origins are from of old, from ancient times"?

4. How do Matthew 2:5–6 and Luke 2 confirm the fulfillment of this prophecy?

5. What does this passage teach us about God's sovereignty in salvation history?

6. How does Micah 5:2 encourage us when we feel small or insignificant?

7. How does this prophecy shape our celebration of Advent and Christmas?

Narrative Reflection

Micah 5:2 stands out for its precision, hope, and theological depth. In a time when Judah faced threats from Assyria and experienced spiritual decline, Micah delivered both warnings of judgment and promises of restoration. Among these promises is the prophecy that the Messiah, the ruler of Israel, would arise from Bethlehem.

At first glance, Bethlehem might seem an unlikely choice. As a small village, it appeared insignificant compared to Jerusalem, the political and religious center of Judah. Yet, God often works through the humble and unexpected. Bethlehem holds historical significance as the birthplace of David, Israel's greatest king. By choosing Bethlehem, God reaffirmed His covenant with David, promising that a ruler from his line would reign forever (2 Samuel 7:16). The Messiah would not emerge from a powerful capital but from a humble town, highlighting that God's ways differ from our own.

The prophecy states, "Out of you will come for me one who will be ruler over Israel." The phrase "for me" is essential. The Messiah is not merely a political leader but God's chosen ruler, appointed for His divine purposes. Unlike Judah's corrupt kings, this ruler will embody God's will and establish His reign.

In the New Testament, Jesus fulfills this prophecy perfectly. He is not self-appointed; rather, He is sent by the Father. His kingship is rooted not in earthly power but in divine mission.

Perhaps the most profound line in the prophecy is, "whose origins are from of old, from ancient times." This suggests the Messiah's connection to the ancient promises given to David and Abraham. However, it also implies something deeper—the eternal nature of the coming ruler. The Hebrew text can be interpreted as referencing eternity past. In Christ, this is fulfilled: "In the beginning was the Word, and the Word was with God, and the Word was God" (John 1:1). The child born in Bethlehem is no ordinary ruler but the eternal Son of God, entering history to redeem His people.

The New Testament confirms the fulfillment of Micah 5:2 with striking clarity. In Matthew 2, when the Magi came seeking the one born King of the Jews, Herod consulted the chief priests and teachers of the law, who immediately referenced Micah 5:2, stating that the Messiah would be born in Bethlehem. Luke's Gospel recounts how Joseph and Mary traveled to Bethlehem due to Caesar's census, where Jesus was born (Luke 2:4–7). Every detail aligns with God's sovereign plan, demonstrating His orchestration of history to fulfill His word.

This prophecy reveals much about God's character. Firstly, it highlights His faithfulness. Despite Israel's unfaithfulness, God remained committed to His promises. The line of David appeared broken, but God had not forgotten. In Bethlehem, the city of David, He raised up the true King.

Secondly, it illustrates God's sovereignty. He determined the place, time, and lineage of the Messiah's birth. Even Caesar's decree, intended for taxation, served God's purpose in bringing Mary and Joseph to Bethlehem. Nothing can thwart God's plans.

Thirdly, it reflects God's humility. The eternal ruler entered the world not in splendor but in simplicity. He was born not in a palace but in a manger, not in Jerusalem but in Bethlehem. This pattern of choosing the lowly to achieve great things is consistent throughout Scripture—Abraham, a nomad; David, a shepherd; Mary, a young woman from Nazareth. As Paul later wrote, "God chose the foolish things of the world to shame the wise" (1 Corinthians 1:27).

For believers today, Micah 5:2 offers profound encouragement. Many of us may feel small or insignificant, much like Bethlehem. Yet, God delights in using the humble for His glory. Just as Bethlehem was chosen to bring forth the Messiah, God works through our lives, no matter how modest, to accomplish His purposes.

The prophecy also deepens our worship of Christ. He is not only the child of Bethlehem but the eternal King. His birth in a small village highlights His humility, while His eternal origins affirm His divinity. Together, these truths remind us that the Incarnation represents the mystery of God made flesh—fully human, fully divine.

During Advent and Christmas, Micah 5:2 invites us to marvel at God's faithfulness and humility. The child born in Bethlehem is the fulfillment of ancient promises, the eternal ruler, and the Savior of the world. His coming reassures us that God keeps His word, works through the unexpected, and brings salvation at the perfect time.

Much more than a geographical detail Micah 5:2 is about Christ's birthplace. It serves as a window into God's character and plan. It reveals His faithfulness to David, His sovereignty over history, His preference for the humble, and His ultimate purpose of sending His eternal Son into the world. Bethlehem, though small, became the center of the universe's story because there the eternal Word became flesh. Out of Bethlehem came the ruler who now reigns forever—the King of kings and Lord of lords.

Layers of Understanding

Historical Context

This prophecy was spoken during the time of Judah's decline under the looming shadow of Assyrian power. In the midst of fear and instability, Isaiah pointed to Bethlehem, the city of David, as the birthplace of a future ruler. This promise offered hope that God's covenant with David would endure.

Jewish Understanding

For the Jewish people, Micah 5:2 was interpreted as a messianic prophecy rooted in Bethlehem, David's hometown. It affirmed God's covenant promises, assuring them that a deliverer would arise from humble beginnings. This expectation grew into a central part of Israel's messianic hope for restoration, justice, and God's kingdom reign.

New Testament Fulfillment

The Gospel writers directly connect Micah 5:2 to the birth of Jesus. Matthew 2:5–6 cites it in response to Herod's inquiry, affirming Bethlehem as the Messiah's birthplace. Luke 2 records Joseph and Mary's journey to Bethlehem, fulfilling prophecy through divine providence, confirming Jesus as the promised Davidic ruler and Savior.

Theological Significance Today

Micah 5:2 reminds believers of God's faithfulness, sovereignty, and humility in accomplishing His purposes. The Messiah came not from a seat of worldly power but from an ordinary town. This encourages the church to trust that God works through the small and overlooked to accomplish extraordinary things for His glory and kingdom.

Cross-Reference Connections

- **1 Samuel 16:1** – David anointed in Bethlehem.
- **2 Samuel 7:16** – David's throne established forever.
- **Matthew 2:5–6** – Micah 5:2 quoted regarding Christ's birth.
- **Luke 2:4–7** – Jesus born in Bethlehem because of the census.
- **John 7:42** – The people recognized Messiah must come from Bethlehem.
- **John 1:1–14** – The eternal Word became flesh.

PROPHECY FULFILLED – STUDY LESSON 15

LESSON SCRIPTURE: **ISAIAH 9: 6-7**

PROPHECY TITLE

The Child Who Is King: Wonderful Counselor, Mighty God, Prince of Peace

Introduction

Isaiah prophesied during a dark period in Judah's history, marked by the looming threat of Assyria and failed leadership, casting a shadow over the land. Yet, in this darkness, God delivered a message of radiant hope: a child would be born, endowed with divine authority and destined to bring everlasting peace.

Isaiah 9:6–7 stands out as one of the clearest messianic prophecies in the Old Testament. It foretells a child whose titles reveal His divine essence: *Wonderful Counselor, Mighty God, Everlasting Father, Prince of Peace.* His reign will be established on David's throne, extending beyond time and human limitations.

The New Testament identifies Jesus Christ as the fulfillment of this prophecy. His birth in Bethlehem marked the arrival of the promised child; His ministry demonstrated divine wisdom and power; His death and resurrection secured lasting peace; and His eventual return will establish His reign in its fullness. During Advent, this passage reminds us that the baby in the manger is also the eternal King who brings light into the world's darkness.

Scripture Reference

Isaiah 9:6–7 (NIV)   For to us a child is born, to us a son is given, and the government will be on his shoulders. And he will be called Wonderful Counselor, Mighty God, Everlasting Father, Prince of Peace. [7] Of the greatness of his government and peace there will be no end. He will reign on David's throne and over his kingdom, establishing and upholding it with justice and righteousness from that time on and forever. The zeal of the LORD Almighty will accomplish this.

Big Picture Insights

- **Darkness to light** – prophecy of hope in Judah's darkest hour.
- **Child is born** – fully human; son is given – divine gift.
- **Government on His shoulders** – authority and rule belong to Him.
- **Four titles** – each reveals His divine nature and kingly role.
- **Davidic covenant** – reign rooted in God's promise to David (2 Sam. 7).
- **Eternal reign** – unlike human kingdoms, His has no end.
- **Justice and righteousness** – core values of His kingdom.

- **Zeal of the Lord** – God Himself ensures fulfillment.
- **Already/Not yet** – fulfilled in Christ's first coming, completed at His return.
- **Advent focus** – hope, peace, and joy embodied in Christ.

Verse-by-Verse Commentary

Isaiah 9:6a – "For to us a child is born, to us a son is given,…"

- The prophecy emphasizes both humanity and divinity. The child is born, marking His human nature, while the Son is given, signifying divine origin. God's gift of His Son fulfills the promise of redemption.
- This verse stresses personal possession: "to us." Salvation is not abstract but given directly to God's people. The Messiah's coming is God's gracious intervention on behalf of a world in desperate need of hope.

Isaiah 9:6b – "…and the government will be on his shoulders…"

- The imagery of government on His shoulders reflects authority, responsibility, and kingship. Unlike corrupt rulers, this King carries His people with justice, wisdom, and compassion, establishing God's perfect order.
- Jesus' authority extends beyond earthly realms, encompassing heaven and earth (Matthew 28:18). His shoulders bear the weight of God's kingdom, ensuring eternal peace and righteousness for all who submit to His reign.

Isaiah 9:6c – "…And he will be called Wonderful Counselor, Mighty God, Everlasting Father, Prince of Peace."

- These titles describe His character and mission. As Wonderful Counselor, He brings divine wisdom; as Mighty God, He embodies deity; as Everlasting Father, He shows covenant care; as Prince of Peace, He reconciles humanity with God.
- The fourfold name anticipates Christ's multifaceted role as Savior and King. His reign offers guidance, strength, security, and peace, surpassing anything offered by human rulers or philosophies.

Isaiah 9:7a – "Of the greatness of his government and peace there will be no end…"

- The Messiah's kingdom is eternal, unlike earthly kingdoms that rise and fall. His peace is not temporary but everlasting, rooted in God's unchanging nature and eternal covenant promises.
- Jesus fulfills this promise through His resurrection and reign at God's right hand. His kingdom expands through the gospel and will culminate in eternal peace at His second coming.

Isaiah 9:7b – "…He will reign on David's throne and over his kingdom, establishing and upholding it with justice and righteousness from that time on and forever…"

- The prophecy ties the Messiah to David's line, fulfilling God's covenant (2 Samuel 7:12–16). His reign is marked by justice and righteousness, correcting the failures of previous kings.
- Christ is the true heir to David's throne, ruling not merely over Israel but over all creation. His reign is eternal, characterized by perfect justice, holiness, and covenant faithfulness.

Isaiah 9:7c – "…The zeal of the LORD Almighty will accomplish this."

- The prophecy closes with assurance. God's zeal—His passionate commitment—guarantees fulfillment. Human failure cannot undo His plan; His kingdom is secured by divine determination.
- The incarnation, life, death, and resurrection of Christ prove that God's zeal brings promises to completion. The future hope of His eternal reign is certain, anchored in God's unfailing

Discussion Questions

1. How does this prophecy bring hope to people in darkness?

2. What is the significance of the child's humanity and divinity?

3. Which of the four titles (Wonderful Counselor, Mighty God, Everlasting Father, Prince of Peace) speaks most to you, and why?

4. How is Jesus' government different from earthly governments?

5. In what ways has Christ already fulfilled this prophecy?

6. How will this prophecy be completed at His second coming?

7. What does it mean that the zeal of the Lord will accomplish this?

Narrative Reflection

There are many rich messianic passages in Scripture, but few rival Isaiah 9:6–7. Frequently read during Christmas services and immortalized in music such as Handel's *Messiah*, its power lies in both poetic beauty and prophetic depth. Spoken in a time of deep despair, it points forward to Christ, the eternal King, whose reign brings lasting hope, peace, and justice.

The context of Isaiah 9 is one of darkness. The people of Judah were fearful of Assyria, and their leaders were corrupt. Earlier in Isaiah, gloom is depicted as covering the land, with people walking in darkness. However, Isaiah announces that a great light will shine, taking the form of a child. This reveals the mystery of God's plan: His response to the world's darkness is not another military leader, but a humble child.

The opening phrase captures the dual nature of the Messiah: "For to us a child is born, to us a son is given." The child's birth emphasizes His full humanity—He enters the world as we do. Yet He is also "given," a divine gift. The Son is not created but given by the Father, underscoring His divinity and eternal pre-existence. Jesus Christ embodies both truths: fully man, born of Mary; fully God, given from eternity.

The prophecy continues: "The government will be on his shoulders." Ancient rulers bore the weight of government, symbolized by a key placed on the shoulder (Isaiah 22:22). In Christ, this signifies that the entire kingdom of God rests on Him. Unlike human leaders who may falter under responsibility, He bears it perfectly. His government brings a peace and justice that no earthly ruler can achieve.

Isaiah then lists four titles, each revealing an aspect of the Messiah's identity. Wonderful Counselor reflects divine wisdom; Jesus is the one in whom all treasures of wisdom and knowledge are hidden (Colossians 2:3). His counsel surpasses human understanding. Mighty God unmistakably affirms His deity. This child is no ordinary ruler but God Himself incarnate, possessing the power to save. Everlasting Father signifies His eternal care and provision. While distinct from God the Father in Trinitarian theology, this title highlights Christ's fatherly role as protector and sustainer of His people. Prince of Peace (Hebrew *shalom*) denotes wholeness, harmony, and reconciliation. Jesus fulfills this through His death on the cross, reconciling us to God and offering true peace.

Verse 7 expands the promise: "Of the greatness of his government and peace there will be no end." Unlike human kingdoms that rise and fall, Christ's reign is eternal. This was echoed in Gabriel's words to Mary: "He will reign over Jacob's descendants forever; his kingdom will never end" (Luke 1:33). His throne is established on David's line, fulfilling the covenant God made with David (2 Samuel 7:16), yet His reign surpasses David's, extending over all creation.

The defining characteristics of His kingdom are justice and righteousness. While human governments often fail in these areas, Christ's reign will be marked by fairness, truth, and holiness. His justice is restorative and redemptive, free from corruption or self-serving motives. His righteousness ensures that His kingdom will embody integrity and purity.

The passage concludes with assurance: "The zeal of the Lord Almighty will accomplish this." This is significant. The fulfillment of this prophecy does not rely on human strength or effort but on God's passionate determination. His zeal guarantees the arrival of the Messiah and the establishment of His kingdom.

In the New Testament, we see this prophecy fulfilled in Christ. His birth in Bethlehem brought the promised child into the world. His ministry revealed divine wisdom and power as He healed the sick, taught with authority, and forgave sins. His death and resurrection secured peace with God. His ascension and reign at the right hand of the Father affirm His ongoing kingship, and His return will bring the fullness of justice and righteousness to earth.

For Christians today, Isaiah 9:6–7 offers both comfort and challenge. It comforts us by reminding us that Christ reigns even now. In a world filled with darkness, injustice, and turmoil, we have hope because the Prince of Peace is on the throne. His government brings order, purpose, and peace.

It challenges us to live as citizens of His kingdom. If His reign is characterized by justice and righteousness, then His people must reflect those values in their lives. The church is called to embody His peace, extend His justice, and proclaim His wisdom.

During Advent and Christmas, this prophecy reminds us that the baby in the manger is not merely a symbol of innocence but the eternal King. The titles given to Him—Wonderful Counselor, Mighty God, Everlasting Father, Prince of Peace—are not poetic exaggerations but profound truths about His identity. He is the divine King who reigns forever.

Isaiah 9:6–7 is a prophecy that shines as brightly today as it did in Isaiah's time. It proclaims that in the midst of darkness, God has given us a child who is also the eternal Son—a King whose reign is just, righteous, and everlasting. His kingdom brings peace, His wisdom directs us, His power saves us, and His zeal guarantees the fulfillment of God's promises. This is the hope of Advent: the King has come, the King reigns, and the King will come again to gather His people as recipients of the eternal reward prepared for all who call upon His name.

Layers of Understanding

Historical Context

Isaiah 9:1–7 was spoken during the dark days of Assyrian oppression, when fear and despair overshadowed God's people. Into this context of political turmoil and spiritual decline, Isaiah proclaimed a message of hope. He promised that God would send a ruler who would bring light, peace, and lasting deliverance.

Jewish Understanding

For Jewish audiences, this prophecy was understood as a messianic promise of a coming ruler from David's line. He would reign with justice and righteousness, establishing peace for Israel. Many saw it as a pledge that God's covenant faithfulness remained unbroken, even when their circumstances seemed marked by weakness and defeat.

New Testament Fulfillment

The New Testament applies Isaiah 9 directly to Jesus Christ. Luke 2:11 declares His birth as the arrival of the promised Savior, while Matthew 4:15–16 describes His ministry as light dawning in Galilee. The titles—Wonderful Counselor, Mighty God, Everlasting Father, Prince of Peace—are fulfilled in His life, death, resurrection, and reign.

Theological Significance Today

For the church, this prophecy assures us of Christ's present reign and future hope. Believers are called to live according to His kingdom values of peace, justice, and righteousness. It also points us forward to His return, when He will establish God's rule fully and bring everlasting peace to creation.

Cross-Reference Connections

- **2 Samuel 7:16** – God's covenant with David, throne established forever.
- **Luke 1:32–33** – Gabriel's promise to Mary: eternal reign of David's heir.
- **Matthew 4:15–16** – Light dawns in Galilee, quoting Isaiah 9.
- **Colossians 2:3** – Christ holds all wisdom and knowledge.
- **Philippians 4:7** – Peace of God surpasses understanding.
- **Revelation 11:15** – "The kingdom of the world has become the kingdom of our Lord."

PROPHECY FULFILLED - STUDY LESSON 16

LESSON SCRIPTURE: MATTHEW 18: 18-25

PROPHECY TITLE

Immanuel Fulfilled: God With Us

Introduction

Matthew 1:18–25 narrates the birth of Jesus from Joseph's perspective, emphasizing the fulfillment of prophecy and God's intervention in history. While Luke highlights Mary's experience, Matthew centers on Joseph, who faces a dilemma upon discovering Mary's pregnancy. In a dream, an angel reveals that the conception is by the Holy Spirit and instructs Joseph to marry Mary and name the child Jesus, for He will save His people from their sins.

Matthew explicitly links this miraculous birth to Isaiah 7:14: *"The virgin will conceive and give birth to a son, and they will call him Immanuel" (which means 'God with us').* In Christ, the ancient prophecy reaches its ultimate fulfillment.

This passage teaches that Jesus is both Savior ("He will save His people from their sins") and Immanuel ("God with us"). It underscores the supernatural nature of His birth, the fulfillment of God's promises, and the profound truth that God has entered human history to dwell among His people.

Scripture Reference

Matthew 1:18–25 (NIV)

"This is how the birth of Jesus the Messiah came about: His mother Mary was pledged to be married to Joseph, but before they came together, she was found to be pregnant through the Holy Spirit. [19] Because Joseph her husband was faithful to the law, and yet did not want to expose her to public disgrace, he had in mind to divorce her quietly. [20] But after he had considered this, an angel of the Lord appeared to him in a dream and said, "Joseph son of David, do not be afraid to take Mary home as your wife, because what is conceived in her is from the Holy Spirit. [21] She will give birth to a son, and you are to give him the name Jesus, [t] because he will save his people from their sins." [22] All this took place to fulfill what the Lord had said through the prophet: [23] "The virgin will conceive and give birth to a son, and they will call him Immanuel" [w] (which means "God with us"). [24] When Joseph woke up, he did what the angel of the Lord had commanded him and took Mary home as his wife. [25] But he did not consummate their marriage until she gave birth to a son. And he gave him the name Jesus."

Big Picture Insights

- **Virgin birth** – miraculous conception by the Holy Spirit.
- **Joseph's righteousness** – faithful to the law, yet merciful toward Mary.

- **Angel's assurance** – divine explanation of the miracle.
- **Name "Jesus"** – means "The Lord saves"; mission to save from sin.
- **Fulfillment of Isaiah 7:14** – prophecy of Immanuel realized.
- **Dual identity** – Jesus as Savior and God-with-us.
- **Davidic connection** – Joseph, "son of David," links Jesus to David's line.
- **Faithful obedience** – Joseph obeys despite social and personal cost.
- **Divine initiative** – salvation begins with God's action, not human effort.
- **Advent climax** – Christmas is the arrival of God Himself into the world.

Verse-by-Verse Commentary

Matthew 1:18–19 – "This is how the birth of Jesus the Messiah came about: His mother Mary was pledged to be married to Joseph, but before they came together, she was found to be pregnant through the Holy Spirit. Because Joseph her husband was faithful to the law, and yet did not want to expose her to public disgrace, he had in mind to divorce her quietly."

- Matthew sets the stage with a surprising, even scandalous situation—Mary, pledged to Joseph, is pregnant before marriage. The divine origin is revealed: her pregnancy is by the Holy Spirit, confirming Jesus' identity as God's Son.
- Joseph is portrayed as both righteous and compassionate. He seeks to uphold the law yet avoid shaming Mary. His dilemma reflects the tension between legal obligation and merciful love, qualities God Himself perfectly embodies.
- Joseph's quiet plan shows integrity under trial. Though confused, his actions reveal a heart inclined toward mercy, preparing him to play a crucial role in God's redemptive plan.

Matthew 1:20–21 – "But after he had considered this, an angel of the Lord appeared to him in a dream and said, 'Joseph son of David, do not be afraid to take Mary home as your wife, because what is conceived in her is from the Holy Spirit. She will give birth to a son, and you are to give him the name Jesus, because he will save his people from their sins.'"

- Divine reassurance comes through the angel's message. Joseph is called "son of David," reminding him of his role in the Messianic line. The angel affirms Mary's purity and the divine nature of the child.
- The angel gives the child's name: Jesus (Yeshua, "the Lord saves"). The name captures His mission—not political liberation, but salvation from sin. This sets the foundation for His redemptive work.
- Joseph is commanded to take Mary as his wife and name the child. By doing so, he legally adopts Jesus, anchoring Him in David's lineage, fulfilling prophecy, and participating in God's eternal plan.

Matthew 1:22–23 – "All this took place to fulfill what the Lord had said through the prophet: 'The virgin will conceive and give birth to a son, and they will call him Immanuel' (which means 'God with us')."

- Matthew ties the miraculous conception directly to Isaiah 7:14. This is not a new story but the fulfillment of an ancient prophecy, proving God's promises never fail.
- The virgin birth signals God's supernatural intervention. The Messiah's arrival is not by human will but by divine action, confirming His identity as both fully human and fully divine.

- The name Immanuel declares God's presence among His people. Through Jesus, God is no longer distant but has entered human experience to redeem, restore, and dwell with His creation.

Matthew 1:24–25 – "When Joseph woke up, he did what the angel of the Lord had commanded him and took Mary home as his wife. But he did not consummate their marriage until she gave birth to a son. And he gave him the name Jesus."

- Joseph responds in obedience. Though initially hesitant, he accepts God's command fully, taking Mary as his wife and naming the child Jesus. His obedience demonstrates trust in God's word despite cultural risk.
- The restraint shown until after Jesus' birth underscores the miraculous nature of the virgin conception. Joseph's faithful compliance validates both prophecy and divine plan.
- By naming Jesus, Joseph affirms Him legally as his son, securing His Davidic lineage and demonstrating the human partnership God uses to fulfill divine promises.

Discussion Questions

1. What does Joseph's response to Mary's pregnancy reveal about his character?

2. Why is the virgin birth central to Christian faith?

3. What does the name "Jesus" reveal about His mission?

4. How does Matthew show the fulfillment of Isaiah 7:14?

5. Why is it significant that Jesus is both Savior and Immanuel?

6. How does Joseph's obedience encourage us to trust God in difficult situations?

7. What does it mean for us today that God is truly "with us"?

Narrative Reflection

Matthew 1:18–25 connects the promises of the Old Testament with their fulfillment in the New Testament. This passage narrates the story of Jesus' birth from Joseph's perspective, in contrast to Luke's account from Mary's viewpoint. It emphasizes themes of obedience, faith, and God's faithfulness.

The narrative begins with a dilemma: Mary, betrothed to Joseph, is found to be pregnant "through the Holy Spirit." To Joseph, this appears scandalous, as betrothal in Jewish culture is legally binding, and unfaithfulness could lead to severe repercussions. Although Joseph is described as "faithful to the law," he chooses not to expose Mary to public disgrace. His intention to divorce her quietly reflects both his integrity and compassion.

In Joseph's distress, God intervenes. An angel visits him in a dream, addressing him as "son of David." This title is significant, linking Joseph—and thus Jesus—to David's royal lineage. The angel reveals that the child conceived in Mary is from the Holy Spirit, highlighting Jesus' divine origin. He is not merely the child of human parents but the Son of God, conceived by God's Spirit.

The angel also articulates the child's purpose: "You are to give him the name Jesus, because he will save his people from their sins." The name Jesus (*Yeshua*) (pronounced Ye-shua) means "The Lord saves." From the outset, His mission is clarified—not political liberation from Rome but spiritual salvation from sin. The angel reshapes messianic expectations, identifying sin as the true enemy rather than foreign oppressors.

Matthew pauses to connect these events to prophecy: "All this took place to fulfill what the Lord had said through the prophet: 'The virgin will conceive and give birth to a son, and they will call him Immanuel'" (Isaiah 7:14). In Jesus' birth, the ancient promise of Immanuel is fulfilled. He is not only the Savior but also "God with us." The Incarnation is central to this passage: God enters human history, taking on flesh to dwell among His people.

Joseph's response exemplifies faithful obedience. He accepts Mary as his wife despite societal stigma and names the child Jesus, legally adopting Him into David's lineage. Through his obedience, Joseph plays a crucial role in God's plan, mirroring Abraham's faith in difficult circumstances.

This passage carries profound theological significance. It affirms the virgin birth, a cornerstone of Christian doctrine, and underscores that salvation originates from God. Humanity cannot produce the

Savior on its own; only divine intervention can bring forth salvation. Jesus' birth, wholly the work of God's Spirit, illustrates that salvation is by grace.

The passage also emphasizes Jesus' dual identity as Savior and Immanuel. As Savior, He delivers us from sin, addressing our deepest needs. As Immanuel, He embodies God's presence among His people, demonstrating that God is not distant but intimately involved in our lives. These identities are inseparable; He can save because He is God with us.

For Advent, this passage holds special significance. It reminds us that Christmas is about God's decisive action in history, not merely sentiment or tradition. The child born in Bethlehem fulfills ancient prophecy, serves as the Savior from sin, and represents the God who dwells among His people. His coming calls for a response—like Joseph, we are invited to trust and obey, even at a cost.

For the church today, Matthew 1:18–25 is both comforting and challenging. It reassures us that God is with us; no matter our struggles, we are not alone. The Incarnation means that God understands our condition—He has shared our humanity and experienced our suffering. It also challenges us to live faithfully, like Joseph, especially when obedience demands sacrifice.

Ultimately, this passage directs us to the gospel. The virgin-born Son is both fully God and fully man, uniquely suited to bridge the gap between God and humanity. His mission is salvation from sin, and His presence reassures us of God's love. At Christmas, we celebrate not only His birth but also the fulfillment of God's promises, the arrival of the Savior, and the reality of Immanuel: God with us.

Layers of Understanding

Historical Context

Joseph and Mary's betrothal occurred in a Jewish culture where honor, purity, and obedience to the law were highly valued. A miraculous virgin birth was unprecedented and shocking, yet God's plan broke through human expectations. This event revealed that salvation would come not by human initiative but by divine intervention.

Jewish Understanding

Isaiah 7:14 was long regarded as a sign of God's covenant faithfulness and presence with His people. In its original setting, it reassured Judah of divine help. By the time of Matthew, this prophecy was understood messianically, and he declares its ultimate fulfillment in Christ's birth as Immanuel, "God with us."

New Testament Fulfillment

Matthew 1:22–23 explicitly identifies Jesus' birth as the fulfillment of Isaiah's prophecy. Conceived by the Holy Spirit and born of the virgin Mary, Jesus is revealed as both Savior and Immanuel. The Gospel writers present this miraculous event as central to God's redemptive plan, highlighting Christ's unique divine and human nature.

Theological Significance Today

This prophecy affirms the Incarnation, the virgin birth, and Christ's mission to save humanity. It reminds believers that God is not distant but present with us in every circumstance. Jesus, our Immanuel, embodies God's love and presence, calling us to live faithfully with confidence in His promises and saving power.

Cross-Reference Connections

- **Isaiah 7:14** – Virgin birth prophecy fulfilled.
- **Luke 1:26–38** – Annunciation to Mary by Gabriel.
- **Luke 2:11** – Savior born, Christ the Lord.
- **John 1:14** – The Word became flesh and dwelt among us.
- **Philippians 2:6–8** – Christ humbled Himself to become man.
- **Hebrews 2:14–15** – Jesus shared in our humanity to defeat death.

PROPHECY FULFILLED - STUDY LESSON - 17

LESSON SCRIPTURE: **NUMBERS 24: 17**

PROPHECY TITLE

A Star and a Scepter: The Rise of the Messiah

Introduction

Numbers 24:17 is one of the most striking messianic prophecies in the Pentateuch, the first five books of the Bible, delivered by an unexpected source: the pagan prophet Balaam. Hired by Balak, the king of Moab, to curse Israel, Balaam found his intentions overruled by God, who compelled him to speak blessings instead. What was meant for harm transformed into a proclamation of hope, highlighting God's sovereignty and faithfulness.

The imagery in this prophecy is particularly remarkable. Balaam speaks of a star rising from Jacob and a scepter emerging from Israel. Both symbols carry royal and messianic significance: the star represents light, guidance, and glory, while the scepter denotes authority and kingship. Together, they foreshadow a ruler unlike any before, one who would conquer God's enemies and establish enduring dominion.

For Israel, these words foretold future victories under leaders like David, who subdued Moab. However, the prophecy's profound meaning extends far beyond the historical monarchy of Israel. It ultimately points to Christ, the true star and eternal king, whose reign offers salvation to the nations and judgment upon sin. In this lesson, we will explore how Numbers 24:17 connects the story of Israel to the person and work of Jesus, and how its message of hope resonates with us today as we anticipate the full coming of His kingdom.

Scripture Reference

Numbers 24:17 (NIV)

"I see him, but not now; I behold him, but not near. A star will come out of Jacob; a scepter will rise out of Israel. He will crush the foreheads of Moab, the skulls of all the people of Sheth."

Big Picture Insights

- **Divine instrument** – God uses even Balaam, an unwilling prophet, to declare His sovereign purposes.
- **Star imagery** – Symbolizes divine light, hope, and the dawning of God's promised deliverer.
- **Scepter authority** – Points to the rise of a king, fulfilled in David and ultimately in Christ.
- **Covenant faithfulness** – God's promises to Israel include triumph and blessing, not just survival.
- **Immediate and ultimate** – The prophecy has near fulfillment in Israel's history and greater fulfillment in the Messiah.

- **Light of the world** – The star imagery anticipates Christ as the guiding light breaking into darkness.
- **Judging ruler** – The scepter reflects not only rule but judgment over Israel's enemies.
- **Scriptural unity** – This prophecy connects to Bethlehem's star and Christ's eternal kingship.
- **Hope and power** – Christ embodies both saving hope for His people and power against His foes.
- **Kingdom confidence** – Believers today can live with assurance in Christ's coming reign.

Verse-by-Verse Commentary

Numbers 24:17a – "I see him, but not now; I behold him, but not near…"

- Balaam speaks prophetically of a distant figure, not immediate in his day but certain in God's timing. This vision stretches beyond Israel's present history to the coming Messiah.
- The "not now…not near" emphasizes prophetic distance. God reveals a future hope beyond current struggles, teaching Israel to trust His long-range purposes. Fulfillment rests in Christ, whose coming was prepared across centuries.

Numbers 24:17b – "…A star will come out of Jacob;…"

- The "star" symbolizes guidance, glory, and divine kingship. In ancient culture, stars were signs of destiny. This prophecy connects to Christ as the true guiding light for the nations.
- The Magi's star (Matthew 2:1–2) directly recalls this prophecy. The star above Bethlehem announced the Messiah's birth, confirming Jesus as the long-awaited King from Jacob's line.

Numbers 24:17c – "…a scepter will rise out of Israel…"

- The scepter symbolizes rule, authority, and kingship. This prophecy anticipates a powerful ruler who arises from Israel to govern with divine authority, greater than all earthly kings.
- Ultimately fulfilled in Christ, the true King of Israel, whose reign is righteous, eternal, and unshakable. Revelation 19:15 portrays Him ruling the nations with a rod of iron.

Numbers 24:17d – "…He will crush the foreheads of Moab, the skulls of all the people of Sheth."

- The prophecy shifts to judgment. The coming King defeats Israel's enemies, symbolized by Moab and Sheth, representing resistance to God's kingdom.
- Christ fulfills this in a greater way—not merely military conquest but final victory over sin, Satan, and all spiritual powers opposed to God. His reign brings justice and peace through triumph.

Discussion Questions

1. Why do you think God chose to reveal such a clear messianic prophecy through Balaam, a reluctant and compromised prophet? What does this show about God's sovereignty?
2. How does the imagery of a star and a scepter deepen your understanding of Christ's role as both light of the world and eternal King?

3. In what ways does Balaam's prophecy point first to David and ultimately to Christ? How does this dual fulfillment strengthen the case for messianic prophecy?

4. The prophecy says, "not now… not near." How does this tension between delay and certainty encourage believers as we wait for Christ's return?

5. How does the connection between Numbers 24:17 and the magi's following of the star in Matthew 2 strengthen your faith in Scripture's unity?

6. What comfort can we take today from the promise that Christ's scepter will crush all opposition, including sin and death?

7. How should this prophecy influence the way the church proclaims Christ today—as both Savior and King whose rule demands our obedience?

Narrative Reflection

Numbers 24:17 contains one of the most striking and far-reaching prophecies in the Old Testament. Spoken by Balaam, a prophet of ambiguous allegiance who was hired to curse Israel but instead compelled by God to bless them, this verse looks well beyond Balaam's own time. It envisions a future ruler, symbolized by a star and a scepter, who will rise from Israel to exercise dominion and bring judgment upon Israel's enemies. The imagery is rich, the scope cosmic, and the fulfillment is unmistakably linked to the Messiah, Jesus Christ.

The story of Balaam is unique. Summoned by Balak, the king of Moab, to curse Israel as they camped on the plains of Moab, Balaam is restrained by God. Instead of uttering curses, he is compelled to pronounce blessings. By the time we reach his fourth and final oracle in Numbers 24, Balaam speaks not only of Israel's immediate future but also of a distant horizon. His words transcend the moment, becoming some of the earliest and most direct messianic prophecies in the Torah.

The prophecy begins with an acknowledgment of temporal distance: "I see him, but not now; I behold him, but not near." Balaam realizes that the figure he envisions is not an immediate king of Israel but a future one. This sets the stage for a prophecy with dual horizons: it has a near-term fulfillment in Israel's history and a long-term fulfillment in the coming of Christ. This dual perspective is common in prophecy. Like mountain peaks viewed from afar, events that are centuries apart can appear side by side. Balaam sees a coming ruler, and although Israel would soon have kings like David and Solomon, the ultimate horizon is the Messiah Himself.

The central imagery is powerful: "A star will come out of Jacob; a scepter will rise out of Israel." In the ancient world, stars often symbolized rulers or deities. In biblical thought, the star signifies a radiant figure who will guide, conquer, and rule. It is not merely a celestial object but a metaphor for a person of extraordinary significance. The scepter represents kingship, authority, and dominion. Together, these images describe a future king who will rise from Israel with divine authority and everlasting rule.

In Israel's immediate history, this prophecy pointed to David's victories. David defeated Moab and subdued surrounding nations, fulfilling the aspect of crushing the heads of enemies. However, the imagery of the star and scepter extends beyond David to a greater king. This prophecy is echoed later in Jacob's blessing to Judah (Genesis 49:10), which foretells that the scepter will not depart from Judah until the one to whom it belongs comes. Both passages converge on the Messiah, who alone fulfills them perfectly.

The mention of the star has long intrigued interpreters. Early Jewish tradition sometimes connected this prophecy to a coming deliverer. The Dead Sea Scrolls and writings from Qumran refer to a "Star of Jacob" in their messianic expectations. Later, during the failed revolt of Simon bar Kokhba in the second century A.D., his name—meaning "son of the star"— was deliberately linked to this prophecy. However, the revolt ended in tragedy, demonstrating that only Christ is the true fulfillment.

The New Testament connection becomes clear in Matthew's Gospel. The magi, guided by a star, come seeking the newborn king of the Jews (Matthew 2:2). While the star they saw may not have been a direct fulfillment of Balaam's prophecy, the parallel is striking. The Messiah, described as a star rising from Jacob, was literally announced by a star in the heavens. The imagery of heavenly light leading Gentiles to the King of Israel directly ties to the universal scope of Christ's mission. Revelation 22:16 makes this identification explicit: Jesus declares, "I am the Root and the Offspring of David, and the bright Morning Star."

The prophecy also foretells judgment: "He will crush the foreheads of Moab, the skulls of all the people of Sheth." This language recalls Genesis 3:15, our very first lesson in this series, the promise that the seed of the woman would crush the serpent's head. The crushing of foreheads signifies the total defeat of the enemy. David subdued Moab, but the ultimate crushing of enemies belongs to Christ. His victory is not merely over earthly foes but over sin, death, and Satan himself. What David accomplished in part, Jesus fulfills in whole.

Theologically, this prophecy reveals the sovereignty of God. Balaam, a man hired to curse Israel, becomes the mouthpiece of blessing and messianic promise. God demonstrates His power to turn curses into blessings and His ability to overrule human intentions for His redemptive plan. If God can use Balaam to declare Christ, He can use any circumstance to fulfill His purposes.

For believers today, Numbers 24:17 offers assurance and hope. It reminds us that God's plan of salvation has been unfolding from the very beginning. Centuries before Christ, God declared that a star and scepter would rise out of Jacob. In Jesus, that star has risen; in Him, the scepter has appeared. His kingdom has come, and although we await its full consummation, we live in the light of its present reality.

This prophecy also challenges us to respond rightly to the Messiah. The star shining from Jacob calls us to follow His light, as the magi did, leaving behind our own kingdoms to worship Him. The scepter rising from Israel demands our submission. Christ is not only Savior but King, and His rule extends over every part of our lives.

Finally, Numbers 24:17 teaches us to see prophecy as both promise and fulfillment. In its original context, it assured Israel of victory and a future king. In its ultimate sense, it points us to Jesus, the bright Morning Star, whose light scatters darkness, whose reign brings justice and peace, and whose victory ensures the crushing of every enemy.

Though Balaam spoke these words under compulsion, God's Spirit ensured they pointed to Christ. This verse, nestled within the unusual story of a reluctant prophet, shines with messianic hope. A star has risen, a scepter has come, and His name is Jesus. For those who believe, the prophecy is not distant but present, fulfilled in Christ who reigns today.

Layers of Understanding

Historical Context

Numbers 24 records Balaam's fourth oracle, spoken over Israel while they camped near Moab. Though hired to curse them, he was compelled by God's Spirit to bless. This final prophecy points beyond Davidic victories to a messianic king who would arise from Jacob.

Jewish Understanding

Jewish interpreters saw in this passage both immediate fulfillment in David's conquests and future messianic expectation. The Dead Sea Scrolls and later writings applied the "Star of Jacob" to the Messiah. Some falsely applied it to leaders like Simon bar Kokhba, but Christians see its true fulfillment in Jesus.

New Testament Fulfillment

Matthew 2 shows Gentile magi guided by a star to the Messiah, recalling Balaam's vision. John 19 and Revelation 22 identify Christ as the true ruler and "bright Morning Star." His scepter of authority fulfills both this prophecy and Genesis 49:10.

Theological Significance Today

Numbers 24:17 assures us of God's sovereign plan and its fulfillment in Christ. It calls us to trust His promises, follow His light, and submit to His reign. It assures us that the enemies of God will ultimately be crushed under Christ's victorious scepter.

Cross-Reference Connections

- **Genesis 49:10** –Scepter not departing from Judah connects directly with Balaam's vision.
- **2 Samuel 7:12–16** – God's covenant with David about an eternal throne.
- **Psalm 2:6–9** – The Messiah's authority echoes the imagery of the ruling scepter.
- **Isaiah 9:6–7** – The child born expands on Balaam's vision of a coming king.
- **Matthew 2:1–2** – The Magi saw His star, tying directly to this prophecy.
- **Luke 1:32–33** – Gabriel's announcement that Jesus will reign forever on David's throne.
- **Revelation 22:16** – Jesus identifies Himself as "the bright Morning Star,".

Series 3 - Life & Ministry Prophecies

PROPHECY FULFILLED - STUDY LESSON - 18

LESSON SCRIPTURE: **PSALM 69: 9**

PROPHECY TITLE

Zeal for God's House Consumes Him

Introduction

Psalm 69 is a lament attributed to David, in which the psalmist expresses his anguish under persecution, isolation, and suffering for God's sake. Verse 9 stands out: "For zeal for your house consumes me, and the insults of those who insult you fall on me."

The New Testament directly connects this verse to Christ. When Jesus cleansed the temple by driving out the money changers, John 2:17 notes that the disciples recalled Psalm 69:9: "Zeal for your house will consume me." Later, Paul references the latter part of the verse in Romans 15:3 to illustrate Christ's willingness to endure reproach for God's glory.

This prophecy reveals that Jesus not only faced opposition for God's sake but also exemplified perfect devotion to God's dwelling. His zeal was characterized not by reckless passion but by a holy determination to purify worship and honor His Father. The insults aimed at God were ultimately directed at Him, culminating at the cross.

Scripture Reference

Psalm 69:9 (NIV)   "for zeal for your house consumes me, and the insults of those who insult you fall on me."

Big Picture Insights

- **Psalm of lament** – David suffers for his devotion to God.
- **Zeal for God's house** – deep passion for God's presence and worship.
- **Applied to Christ** – disciples recall this verse after temple cleansing (John 2:17).
- **Christ's mission** – bearing reproach and opposition for God's glory (Romans 15:3).
- **House of God** – ultimately fulfilled in Christ Himself and His church (John 2:19–21).
- **Foreshadows cross** – insults directed at God fell fully on Christ.
- **Messianic pattern** – David's suffering anticipates Christ's greater suffering.
- **Passion with purpose** – zeal rightly directed toward holiness, not self.
- **Identity of the church** – as God's temple, we are to embody His holiness.
- **Practical challenge** – what consumes our zeal: self, or God's glory?

Verse-by-Verse Commentary

Psalm 69:9a – "For zeal for your house consumes me,…"

- The psalmist expresses deep devotion to God's dwelling, willing to endure personal cost for God's honor. This intensity foreshadows the Messiah's passion for true worship and the purity of God's temple.
- Jesus fulfilled this at the cleansing of the temple (John 2:15–17). His zeal for His Father's house drove Him to oppose corruption, showing His commitment to holiness and God's glory.
- Ultimately, His zeal consumed Him at the cross, where He bore reproach to restore humanity to God's presence. His suffering becomes the cost of restoring God's true dwelling with His people.

Psalm 69:9b – "…and the insults of those who insult you fall on me."

- The psalmist identifies with God so fully that attacks aimed at the Lord are felt personally. Suffering is not for wrongdoing but for standing faithfully with God's purposes.
- Paul applies this verse to Christ in Romans 15:3, showing that Jesus bore reproach on behalf of God, enduring scorn intended for the Father by absorbing humanity's hostility on Himself.
- In Christ, this prophecy reaches its fulfillment. The insults directed at God's holiness were carried by the Son, who endured rejection and shame to secure redemption for all who trust Him.

Discussion Questions

1. What does it mean to be consumed with zeal for God's house?

2. How did Jesus embody this verse during His ministry?

3. Why do insults against God "fall on" His faithful servants?

4. How does this verse connect David's experience with Christ's greater mission?

5. What does this teach us about bearing reproach for Christ today?

6. In what ways is the church called to reflect zeal for God's holiness?

7. What consumes your zeal—worldly pursuits or devotion to God?

Narrative Reflection

Notable for its raw honesty and its anticipation of Christ's sufferings and mission, Psalm 69 is one of the most remarkable psalms in the Old Testament. Attributed to David, this psalm of lament expresses his deep anguish under persecution, isolation, and rejection. It articulates the pain of one who suffers not for wrongdoing but for faithfulness to God. Among its many verses, Psalm 69:9 stands out as a prophetic insight into the Messiah's devotion and the reproach He would endure: "For zeal for your house consumes me, and the insults of those who insult you fall on me."

The first half of the verse highlights the intensity of David's passion for God's house. In his time, this likely referred to the tabernacle—the tent where God's presence was manifested among His people and where sacrifices were offered. Later generations would associate this with the temple, the permanent dwelling of God's glory in Jerusalem. To love God's house was to love God Himself, as the sanctuary represented His covenant presence and holy rule in Israel. David's zeal for God's dwelling consumed him; his desire for God's honor profoundly shaped his life. However, this same devotion made him a target. His passion for holiness and worship drew the scorn of those indifferent to God. In David's experience, zeal came at a cost.

Yet David's lament transcends his personal struggles. In God's providence, his words became prophetic, pointing to the ultimate Son of David, the Messiah, whose devotion to God's house would be perfect and complete. When Jesus entered the temple in Jerusalem and found it corrupted by money changers and merchants, He acted decisively. John records that He made a whip, drove them out, and commanded, "Stop turning my Father's house into a market!" (John 2:16). In that moment, the disciples recalled Psalm 69:9: "Zeal for your house will consume me." They realized that Jesus' actions were not merely those of a reformer outraged by corruption; they were the actions of the Servant-King whose consuming passion was for His Father's glory and the purity of His worship. Christ's zeal was not reckless or uncontrolled anger but a holy determination to honor God's dwelling.

The second half of Psalm 69:9 carries equally profound significance: "And the insults of those who insult you fall on me." Here, David conveys the reality that devotion to God often brings reproach. When God is mocked, His servants feel the sting. David internalized the insults directed at God as if they were aimed at him personally. However, the verse finds its fullest meaning in Christ. Paul quotes it in Romans 15:3 to illustrate Jesus' humility: "For even Christ did not please himself but, as it is written: 'The insults of those who insult you have fallen on me.'" Jesus bore not only the opposition of sinners but also the shame and hostility directed at His Father. The insults hurled at God fell squarely upon the Son, culminating at the cross, where Christ absorbed the full weight of humanity's sin and rebellion.

Thus, this verse offers a glimpse into the heart of the Messiah. His passion for God's glory consumed Him, and His willingness to bear reproach defined His mission. He endured shame, scorn, and hostility not because He failed but precisely because He was faithful. His life exemplified complete devotion to God's purposes, even to the point of death.

For believers today, Psalm 69:9 carries profound theological and practical implications. First, it teaches us that zeal for God's house is costly. Living with passion for God's holiness and worship invites opposition from a world that rejects Him. David experienced it, Christ embodied it, and the church must expect it. Faithfulness often leads to reproach. Yet that reproach is not meaningless—it unites us with Christ, who bore insults for His Father's glory.

Second, this verse reshapes our understanding of "God's house." In David's time, it was the tabernacle. In Christ's time, it was the temple in Jerusalem. However, Jesus transformed this understanding when He declared, "Destroy this temple, and I will raise it again in three days" (John 2:19). He was referring to His body, the true dwelling place of God. Through His resurrection, Christ became the cornerstone of a new spiritual temple. The apostles teach that the church, as Christ's body, is now God's house. Believers are described as "living stones" being built into a spiritual temple (1 Peter 2:5). Zeal for God's house today translates to zeal for the holiness, unity, and mission of the church. It compels us to uphold the purity of worship, pursue holiness, and bear witness to the world as God's dwelling place on earth.

Third, Psalm 69:9 points us to Christ's role as the suffering servant whose devotion consumed Him and whose reproach brought salvation. His passion for God's house was inseparable from His passion for God's people. He cleansed the temple because He desired pure worship. He bore insults because He willingly took upon Himself the sin of the world. He was consumed not only by zeal for His Father's glory but also by love for the people He came to redeem. His zeal carried Him all the way to the cross, where the insults of sinners became the suffering of the Savior.

For the Advent and Christmas seasons, this verse beautifully connects to the broader story of Christ's coming. The child born in Bethlehem grew up to be the Messiah whose zeal consumed Him. His incarnation marked the beginning of a life characterized by holy passion and costly obedience. From the manger to the temple to the cross, His mission was to glorify God and redeem His people. Psalm 69:9 reminds us that His zeal was not a fleeting emotion but a consuming fire that defined His life and death.

Practically, this verse challenges us to reflect on our own zeal. What consumes us? Many people are driven by ambition, wealth, or comfort. Others are passionate about causes that may be good but not ultimate. For Christians, the call is clear: our zeal must be for God's glory, His worship, and His mission. Like David, we may face reproach. Like Christ, we may bear insults for His name. But such zeal is not wasted—it is participation in the mission of the Messiah.

Finally, Psalm 69:9 offers encouragement. It assures us that when we face reproach for our devotion to God, we are not alone. Christ has gone before us. The insults that fall on us have already fallen on Him, and He has borne them to the cross. Our faithfulness, even in suffering, glorifies God and unites us with Christ's mission.

Thus, Psalm 69:9 bridges David's lament with Christ's fulfillment. It portrays a Savior whose zeal for God's house consumed Him and who bore the insults of sinners for the glory of His Father. It calls the church to share in that zeal, embrace reproach for Christ's sake, and live as God's house in the world. It assures us that God's promises are certain: the zeal of the Lord Almighty will accomplish His purposes, and His glory will fill His house forever.

Layers of Understanding

Historical Context

Psalm 69 reflects David's deep devotion to God, a devotion that brought him scorn and suffering from those who rejected God's ways. His personal lament over unjust reproach becomes prophetic, foreshadowing the Messiah's even greater zeal for God's house and the rejection, insults, and opposition He would ultimately endure.

Jewish Understanding

Jewish readers often understood Psalm 69 primarily as the psalmist's personal cry of lament, expressing the pain of a righteous sufferer. At the same time, it also came to be viewed as a picture of the faithful servant of God, one who bore insults and rejection because of unwavering devotion.

New Testament Fulfillment

The New Testament explicitly applies Psalm 69:9 to Jesus. John 2:17 identifies His zeal in cleansing the temple as a direct fulfillment of the verse. Romans 15:3 highlights Christ's willingness to bear reproach for God's sake. Together, they show the psalm's prophetic fulfillment in His life, ministry, and sacrificial mission.

Theological Significance Today

Psalm 69:9 challenges believers to share Christ's zeal for God's glory, even when it brings reproach. As God's living temple, the church is called to pursue holiness, purity in worship, and bold witness. Enduring opposition for Christ's name unites us with Him and demonstrates the reality of God's presence in the world.

Cross-Reference Connections

- **John 2:17** – Disciples recall Psalm 69:9 at the temple cleansing.
- **Romans 15:3** – Christ bore insults directed against God.
- **John 2:19–21** – Jesus as the true temple.
- **1 Peter 2:5** – Believers as living stones in God's spiritual house.
- **Hebrews 13:13** – Call to bear the reproach of Christ.

PROPHECY FULFILLED - STUDY LESSON - 19

LESSON SCRIPTURE: ISAIAH 35: 5-6

PROPHECY TITLE

The Messiah Heals: Eyes Open, Lame Walk, Tongues Sing

Introduction

Isaiah 35 presents a vision of restoration, illustrating how God transforms deserts into flourishing lands and sorrow into joy. Central to this renewal are verses 5–6: "Then will the eyes of the blind be opened and the ears of the deaf unstopped. Then will the lame leap like a deer, and the mute tongue shout for joy."

This prophecy promises both physical healing and spiritual renewal, anticipating a time when suffering will be reversed and wholeness restored. The New Testament explicitly connects this prophecy to Jesus' ministry. When John the Baptist inquired if Jesus was the Messiah, Jesus responded by highlighting these very signs: "The blind receive sight, the lame walk, those who have leprosy are cleansed, the deaf hear, the dead are raised, and the good news is proclaimed to the poor" (Matthew 11:5).

For Christians, Isaiah 35:5–6 underscores Jesus as the One who brings God's kingdom through His words and actions. His miracles are not merely acts of compassion; they are signs of His messianic identity, foreshadowing the complete restoration that will occur at His return.

Scripture Reference

Isaiah 35:5–6 (NIV) **"Then will the eyes of the blind be opened and the ears of the deaf unstopped.**
⁶ Then will the lame leap like a deer, and the mute tongue shout for joy. Water will gush forth in the wilderness and streams in the desert. "

Big Picture Insights

- **Kingdom renewal** – suffering reversed, creation restored.
- **Physical healings** – blind, deaf, lame, mute transformed.
- **Spiritual dimension** – blindness and deafness symbolize spiritual dullness.
- **Messianic signs** – fulfilled in Jesus' ministry (Matthew 11:5).
- **Kingdom inaugurated** – miracles foreshadow final restoration.
- **Isaiah's hope** – God intervenes to save and renew.
- **Jesus' identity** – miracles confirm Him as Messiah.
- **Foreshadows resurrection** – life bursting forth like streams in desert.
- **Already/not yet** – partial now in Christ, complete at His return.
- **Mission of the church** – proclaim kingdom in word and deed.

Verse-by-Verse Commentary

Isaiah 35:5 – "Then will the eyes of the blind be opened and the ears of the deaf unstopped."

- The prophecy describes God's restorative power breaking into a broken world. Physical healing symbolizes the reversal of sin's effects and the renewal of creation through the coming of the Messiah.
- Jesus literally fulfilled this verse by healing blind men (Mark 8:22–25; John 9:6–7) and opening deaf ears (Mark 7:32–35). His miracles revealed that the Messianic age had dawned with His ministry.
- Beyond physical sight and hearing, Christ restores spiritual perception. Through Him, the blind see God's truth and the deaf hear His Word, showing salvation as both physical renewal and inner transformation.

Isaiah 35:6 – "Then will the lame leap like a deer, and the mute tongue shout for joy. Water will gush forth in the wilderness and streams in the desert."

- The lame leaping and mute shouting reflect complete healing, turning weakness into joy. These images portray the fullness of God's kingdom, where broken bodies and broken spirits are restored in abundance.
- Jesus fulfilled this in healing paralytics (Mark 2:11–12; John 5:8–9) and giving speech to the mute (Matthew 9:32–33). These acts confirmed Him as Messiah and revealed God's compassionate heart for the suffering.
- The imagery of waters in the wilderness points to new creation and the Spirit's outpouring. In Christ, barren places are renewed, and those once hopeless find life, joy, and abundance in Him.

Discussion Questions

1. How do Isaiah's images of healing reflect God's kingdom?

2. Why does Jesus point to these signs when asked if He is the Messiah?

3. What do physical healings teach us about spiritual renewal?

4. How do Jesus' miracles connect to His identity as Savior?

5. What does it mean to live in the "already/not yet" of this prophecy?

6. How should the church embody kingdom restoration today?

7. Where do you long to see God's streams flow into your deserts?

Narrative Reflection

Isaiah 35:5–6 vividly depicts God's kingdom entering a world filled with suffering and brokenness. In these verses, the prophet envisions the blind receiving sight, the deaf hearing, the lame leaping, and the mute singing—a complete transformation where human weakness and sorrow turn into strength and joy.

For Isaiah's original audience, this prophecy offered hope amid despair. Israel faced powerful enemies and the judgment of exile. Yet Isaiah 35 presents a vision of ultimate restoration: deserts blooming, sorrow replaced by joy, and bodies healed from afflictions. God Himself would intervene to bring salvation and renewal.

The New Testament reveals that this promise was fulfilled in the ministry of Jesus Christ. When John the Baptist, imprisoned and doubting, sent messengers to ask Jesus, "Are you the one who is to come?" Jesus responded by pointing to the signs of Isaiah 35: "The blind receive sight, the lame walk, the lepers are cleansed, the deaf hear, the dead are raised, and the good news is proclaimed to the poor" (Matthew 11:5). Jesus' miracles were not mere acts of kindness; they were deliberate signs that He was the promised Messiah.

Consider the healings recorded in the Gospels. In John 9, Jesus opened the eyes of a blind man, symbolizing both physical and spiritual sight. He healed a deaf and mute man in Mark 7, restoring his hearing and speech. In Mark 2, He made a paralyzed man walk, forgiving his sins and demonstrating His authority. Each miracle echoes Isaiah 35, illustrating God's kingdom breaking into the world through the Messiah.

These healings also carry deep spiritual significance. Blindness and deafness in Scripture often represent spiritual dullness. Jesus not only healed physical ailments but also opened spiritual eyes to perceive God's truth and ears to hear His word. Lameness and muteness symbolize humanity's inability to walk in righteousness or praise God. In Christ, these conditions are reversed—He empowers His followers to walk in His ways and proclaim His praise.

The imagery of water in the desert enhances this theme of renewal. Isaiah 35:6 states, "Water will gush forth in the wilderness and streams in the desert." In a barren land, water signifies life. Spiritually, this foreshadows the living water Jesus offers in John 7:37–39—the Holy Spirit, who brings life and refreshment to weary souls. Just as streams transform deserts into gardens, the Spirit transforms barren hearts into fruitful lives.

Theologically, Isaiah 35:5–6 reveals the nature of God's kingdom: a kingdom of restoration, wholeness, and joy. Jesus inaugurated this kingdom during His first coming, demonstrating its reality through miracles. Yet its fullness is still to come. We live in the "already/not yet." Already, Christ heals, restores, and renews; not yet, the world continues to groan, awaiting final redemption (Romans 8:22–23). When Christ returns, the blind will see, the lame will leap, and the mute will sing forever in the new creation.

For the church today, this passage offers both comfort and a calling. It reassures us that God is in the business of restoration. Whatever deserts we encounter—illness, sorrow, spiritual dryness—Christ brings streams of living water. His miracles remind us that brokenness is not the final word.

It also urges us to participate in His mission. As His body, the church is called to reflect His kingdom through acts of compassion, healing, and proclamation. We are not miracle workers in ourselves, but we point others to the One who heals. By caring for the poor, comforting the broken, and sharing the gospel, we embody the reality of Isaiah 35 in the present.

Isaiah 35:5–6 is thus both a prophecy and a promise. It foretells the fulfillment of prophecy in Jesus' earthly ministry, confirming Him as the Messiah. It also represents a promise awaiting full realization when Christ returns to make all things new. In the meantime, we live with hope, experiencing the streams of living water while longing for the day when deserts will fully bloom.

The prophecy of Isaiah 35:5–6 identifies the Messiah as the one who alone heals and restores. His miracles signify the kingdom, and His Spirit becomes the living water, and His return will bring final fulfillment. For now, we rejoice in the glimpses of renewal we witness and hold fast to the hope of complete restoration to come.

Layers of Understanding

Historical Context

Isaiah 35:5–6 was spoken to Israel during a period of judgment and looming exile. The nation faced despair and devastation, yet the prophet's words looked beyond present suffering. He promised a future of renewal, where God Himself would bring healing, joy, and restoration to His broken people and their land.

Jewish Understanding

For Jewish readers, this passage was received as a vision of messianic restoration. It described a time when God would act decisively to heal His people, opening blind eyes and unstopping deaf ears. The prophecy also portrayed creation itself being renewed, signaling that divine salvation would extend far beyond Israel's borders.

New Testament Fulfillment

The New Testament identifies Isaiah 35:5–6 as fulfilled in Jesus' ministry. When John the Baptist's disciples questioned His identity, Jesus pointed to His healings as evidence that the kingdom had come (Matthew 11:5). Every miracle—opening blind eyes, making the lame walk—demonstrated that He was the promised Messiah bringing God's salvation.

Theological Significance Today

For Christians today, this prophecy inspires hope that renewal is possible in Christ. It calls the church to embody His ministry of restoration through compassion and service. It assures believers that ultimate healing awaits at His return, when every brokenness will be mended and God's people will rejoice in everlasting joy.

Cross-Reference Connections

- **Isaiah 61:1–2** – Spirit of the Lord brings good news and healing.
- **Matthew 11:5** – Jesus cites Isaiah's signs to affirm His identity.
- **John 9:1–7** – Healing of the man born blind.
- **Mark 7:31–37** – Healing of the deaf and mute man.
- **John 7:37–39** – Jesus offers living water.
- **Revelation 21:4** – Final healing: no more death, mourning, crying, or pain.

LESSON SCRIPTURE: PSALM 118:22-26

PROPHECY TITLE

The Rejected Stone Becomes the Cornerstone

Introduction

Psalm 118 is a psalm of thanksgiving, likely sung during temple worship and festival processions. In verses 22–26, the psalmist emphasizes how God transforms what is rejected into something central: "The stone the builders rejected has become the cornerstone." This imagery of reversal illustrates God's power to turn weakness into strength and humiliation into glory.

The New Testament frequently connects this prophecy to Jesus Christ. Rejected by religious leaders, condemned, and crucified, He became the foundation of God's redemptive plan through His resurrection. The apostles often reference this passage to affirm that salvation is found only in Him (Matthew 21:42; Acts 4:11; 1 Peter 2:7).

Additionally, the psalm anticipates joy and salvation. Verses 24–25 call for rejoicing in the day the Lord has made, while verse 26 foreshadows the triumphal entry: "Blessed is he who comes in the name of the Lord." Together, these verses highlight the paradox of the gospel—rejection leads to exaltation, suffering leads to salvation, and Christ, the cornerstone, secures God's eternal kingdom.

Scripture Reference

Psalm 118:22–26 (NIV)   "The stone the builders rejected has become the cornerstone; 23 the LORD has done this, and it is marvelous in our eyes. 24 The LORD has done it this very day; let us rejoice today and be glad. 25 LORD, save us! LORD, grant us success! 26 Blessed is he who comes in the name of the LORD. From the house of the LORD we bless you."

Big Picture Insights

- **Reversal of rejection** – God makes the rejected stone central.
- **Messianic prophecy** – applied to Christ in multiple New Testament passages.
- **Cornerstone imagery** – foundation and alignment of God's building.
- **Marvelous work of God** – salvation comes by divine initiative.
- **The day of the Lord** – fulfilled in resurrection and new creation.
- **Hosanna cry** – "Lord, save us!" connects to Palm Sunday.
- **Triumphal entry** – crowds quote verse 26 in Matthew 21:9.
- **Christ-centered worship** – joy and thanksgiving in God's salvation.

- **Continuity with temple worship** – now fulfilled in Christ as true temple.
- **Hope for believers** – rejection by the world cannot undo God's purposes.

Verse-by-Verse Commentary

Psalm 118:22 – "The stone the builders rejected has become the cornerstone;"

- The image of the rejected stone symbolizes one dismissed as unworthy but chosen by God for ultimate honor. Human judgment is overturned by divine purpose, showing God's sovereignty in exalting the unexpected.
- Jesus directly fulfills this prophecy (Matthew 21:42; Acts 4:11). Though rejected by religious leaders and crucified, He became the cornerstone of God's redemptive plan, the foundation of salvation for all believers.
- The cornerstone is essential, aligning and supporting the entire structure. Christ unites Jew and Gentile into one spiritual house, anchoring the Church upon Himself as the foundation stone.

Psalm 118:23 – "the LORD has done this, and it is marvelous in our eyes."

- The psalmist acknowledges that this reversal is God's work, not human achievement. What seemed impossible or foolish to human wisdom becomes marvelous when seen as divine intervention.
- The resurrection of Jesus epitomizes this marvel. God raised the rejected One to glory, confirming His identity and establishing salvation. The Church marvels at the wonder of redemption accomplished through the cross.
- This verse invites worship and awe. God's ways overturn human rejection, transforming apparent defeat into eternal victory, stirring gratitude and reverence among His people.

Psalm 118:24 – "The LORD has done it this very day; let us rejoice today and be glad."

- The psalmist calls for joy in response to God's decisive action. Salvation history pivots on God's intervention, making each day of deliverance a cause for rejoicing.
- The resurrection day especially embodies this verse. Believers rejoice because Christ's victory has inaugurated a new creation, turning sorrow into gladness and despair into hope.
- Joy becomes a command as well as a response. God's saving work demands gladness, reminding His people to celebrate His faithfulness continually.

Psalm 118:25 – "LORD, save us! LORD, grant us success!"

- This plea for salvation ("Hosanna") reflects dependence upon God for deliverance and prosperity. It acknowledges human inability and calls upon the Lord as the only true source of blessing.
- During Jesus' triumphal entry, the crowds shouted "Hosanna" (Matthew 21:9), directly echoing this verse. Their cry revealed messianic hope, though their understanding was incomplete.
- In Christ, this prayer is answered fully. He is salvation incarnate, granting success not as worldly conquest but as eternal redemption.

113

Psalm 118:26 – "Blessed is he who comes in the name of the LORD. From the house of the LORD we bless you."

- This verse celebrates the arrival of God's appointed one. To come "in the name of the LORD" signifies divine authority and mission, affirming the legitimacy of the servant sent by God.
- The crowds proclaimed this of Jesus at His triumphal entry, identifying Him as the Messiah. Their blessing acknowledged His role as God's chosen representative, even if they misunderstood His mission.
- This verse also anticipates Christ's return, when all nations will bless the One who comes in God's name, recognizing His reign with joy and worship.

Discussion Questions

1. What does the cornerstone imagery reveal about Christ's role in salvation?

2. Why is it significant that the rejected stone became central?

3. How does this passage reveal God's power to reverse human rejection?

4. In what ways is Psalm 118 fulfilled in Jesus' triumphal entry?

5. What does it mean to rejoice in "the day the Lord has made"?

6. How does the cry "Hosanna" shape our prayers for salvation today?

7. What encouragement does this give when believers face rejection for Christ's sake?

Narrative Reflection

Psalm 118:22–26 is a theologically rich passage, weaving together themes of rejection, divine reversal, salvation, and joy. Originally sung during temple liturgy, it celebrated God's deliverance and the establishment of His people. Ultimately, its fulfillment is found in the Messiah, Jesus Christ, the cornerstone of God's kingdom.

The passage opens with a striking image: "The stone the builders rejected has become the cornerstone." In construction, builders evaluate stones to choose those suitable for the foundation, discarding any deemed unsuitable. Yet, here, the very stone rejected becomes the most crucial one—the cornerstone, which aligns and holds the entire structure together. This reversal emphasizes God's sovereignty: human judgment is overturned by divine choice.

In the New Testament, this verse is consistently applied to Christ. Jesus quotes it in Matthew 21:42 after telling the parable of the tenants, where the builders (the religious leaders) reject the Son but are judged by God. Peter boldly proclaims it in Acts 4:11 before the Sanhedrin, asserting that Jesus—though rejected and crucified—is the cornerstone of salvation. Later, in 1 Peter 2:7, he reminds believers that this stone is precious to those who trust in Him, even as it causes others to stumble.

For the early church, this verse encapsulated the paradox of the gospel: Jesus' rejection and crucifixion were not the end but the very means through which God established salvation. The rejected stone became the foundation of a new spiritual house—the church.

Verse 23 states: "The Lord has done this, and it is marvelous in our eyes." The marvel lies not only in the reversal itself but also in its divine origin. Salvation results from God's action, not human wisdom or effort. The resurrection, in particular, is the marvelous work of God that vindicated Jesus as Messiah and secured salvation. To perceive this through the eyes of faith is to marvel at grace.

Verse 24 continues: "The Lord has done it this very day; let us rejoice today and be glad." For Israel, this referred to a day of deliverance, possibly linked to a military victory or festival celebration. For Christians, it resonates deeply with Easter—the day of Christ's resurrection. The day the Lord has made is the day He raised His Son from the dead, conquering sin and death. Each Sunday worship echoes this joy, celebrating the resurrection.

Verse 25 captures the cry: "Lord, save us! Lord, grant us success!" The Hebrew word "Hosanna" (save us now) became a ritualistic plea in temple worship. At the triumphal entry, the crowds in Jerusalem shouted this very word, waving palm branches as they welcomed Jesus (Matthew 21:9; John 12:13). They recognized in Him the fulfillment of this psalm: the long-awaited King bringing salvation.

Verse 26 adds: "Blessed is he who comes in the name of the Lord." Originally a blessing for pilgrims arriving at the temple, it evolved into a messianic acclamation. When the crowds shouted it on Palm Sunday, they proclaimed Jesus as the one sent by God. In John's Gospel, the Pharisees observed this and

115

despaired, acknowledging the growing recognition of Jesus' authority. Later, Jesus stated that Jerusalem would not see Him again until they uttered these words (Matthew 23:39), connecting this psalm to His ultimate return in glory.

Theologically, this passage highlights God's ability to transform rejection into glory. Jesus, despised and crucified, became the foundation of God's plan of salvation. His resurrection vindicated Him as the cornerstone. For believers, this offers encouragement: rejection by the world does not thwart God's purposes. What is despised by people can be chosen and exalted by God.

It also reminds us that salvation is God's work, not ours. "The Lord has done this, and it is marvelous in our eyes." We marvel not at our achievements but at God's grace. The day of salvation is His doing, and our response should be one of joy and thanksgiving.

Finally, this passage invites us to worship. The cries of "Hosanna" and "Blessed is he who comes" are not just historical echoes but ongoing invitations. We continue to welcome Christ into our lives and communities, declaring Him blessed and rejoicing in His salvation.

Psalm 118:22–26 connects Old Testament worship with New Testament fulfillment. It reveals Christ as the rejected yet exalted cornerstone, the marvel of God's salvation, the source of Easter joy, and the King welcomed with Hosannas. For the church, it serves both as a prophecy fulfilled and a promise still unfolding, as we await the day when the rejected stone returns as the reigning Lord.

Layers of Understanding

Historical Context

Psalm 118:22–26 belongs to the Hallel psalms, sung during temple festivals such as Passover. It celebrated God's deliverance, blessing pilgrims as they approached the sanctuary with prayers for salvation. This psalm carried strong communal significance, reminding Israel of God's covenant faithfulness and His power to vindicate His people against their enemies.

Jewish Understanding

For Jewish worshipers, these verses were a thanksgiving for God's dramatic reversals, whether Israel's vindication over hostile nations or a king's unexpected victory. The rejected stone becoming the cornerstone symbolized God's power to overturn human judgment. The psalm reinforced confidence in God's ability to raise up His chosen servant against opposition.

New Testament Fulfillment

The New Testament repeatedly applies Psalm 118:22–26 to Jesus. Though rejected by Israel's leaders, He is exalted as the cornerstone (Matthew 21:42; Acts 4:11; 1 Peter 2:7). Verses 25–26 echo in the triumphal entry, when crowds shouted "Hosanna!" welcoming Christ as the promised King who brings salvation and establishes God's kingdom.

Theological Significance Today

These verses assure believers that rejection is never the final word. God exalts the despised and vindicates His chosen. Christ, the rejected stone, is now the foundation of salvation and the church's cornerstone. Believers are called to worship Him with joy, celebrating the day of His resurrection as God's glorious victory.

Cross-Reference Connections

- **Isaiah 28:16** – God lays a chosen cornerstone in Zion.
- **Matthew 21:42** – Jesus identifies Himself as the rejected stone.
- **Acts 4:11** – Peter proclaims Christ as cornerstone to the Sanhedrin.
- **1 Peter 2:7** – Believers honor the stone rejected by others.
- **John 12:13** – Palm Sunday crowds cry "Hosanna!" from Psalm 118.
- **Revelation 7:9–10** – Hosanna cry fulfilled in eternal worship.

PROPHECY FULFILLED - STUDY LESSON - 21

LESSON SCRIPTURE: ISAIAH 8:14

PROPHECY TITLE

A Stone of Stumbling and a Rock of Offense

Introduction

Isaiah 8 depicts a time of fear and crisis for Judah as the nation faced threats from foreign powers. God admonished His people to place their trust solely in Him rather than in human alliances. In verse 14, Isaiah presents a vivid image: the Lord will be a sanctuary for some, but a stone of stumbling for others.

The New Testament connects this prophecy to Christ, with both Peter and Paul citing Isaiah 8:14 to illustrate that Jesus is the stone over which many stumble (Romans 9:33; 1 Peter 2:7–8). For believers, He serves as the cornerstone and refuge; for those who reject Him, He becomes an obstacle that leads to their downfall.

This prophecy underscores a crucial truth about the Messiah: His arrival does not bring neutrality. He divides humanity—acting as either Savior and refuge or stumbling block and offense. Faith leads to salvation, while unbelief results in judgment and ruin.

Scripture Reference

Isaiah 8:14 (NIV)   He will be a holy place; for both Israel and Judah he will be a stone that causes people to stumble and a rock that makes them fall. And for the people of Jerusalem he will be a trap and a snare.

Big Picture Insights

- **Dual imagery** – God is both sanctuary and stumbling stone.
- **Crisis of faith** – trust in God brings safety; rejection brings downfall.
- **Messianic fulfillment** – applied to Christ in NT (Romans 9:33; 1 Peter 2:7–8).
- **Cornerstone vs. stumbling stone** – same stone, different response.
- **Division of humanity** – belief or unbelief determines destiny.
- **Sanctuary** – God Himself is the true refuge for His people.
- **Stumbling** – rejection of God's plan leads to judgment.
- **Foreshadows rejection of Christ** – religious leaders stumble over Him.
- **The gospel's offense** – grace confronts human pride and self-righteousness.
- **Theological tension** – Christ comforts and offends at the same time.

Verse-by-Verse Commentary

Isaiah 8:14a – "He will be a holy place;…"

- God is portrayed as a sanctuary, offering protection and security to those who trust Him. This emphasizes His role as refuge for the faithful, a place of safety amid fear, opposition, and judgment.
- The holy place is not merely a temple but God Himself. For those who seek Him in faith, He becomes the ultimate dwelling of peace, sustaining them when worldly structures fail.

Isaiah 8:14b – "…for both Israel and Judah he will be a stone that causes people to stumble and a rock that makes them fall…"

- The same God who is sanctuary becomes a stumbling stone for those who resist Him. Israel and Judah, meant to trust Him, falter because of unbelief and misplaced reliance on human alliances.
- This dual imagery highlights human responsibility. Rejection of God's truth turns a refuge into an obstacle. The difference lies not in God's nature but in people's response to Him.
- The New Testament applies this directly to Christ. Paul notes that Israel stumbled over the "stone" because they pursued righteousness by law instead of faith (Romans 9:32–33).

Isaiah 8:14c – "…And for the people of Jerusalem he will be a trap and a snare."

- The imagery intensifies: not only stumbling but entrapment. For those hardened in unbelief, God becomes the very snare that exposes and judges rebellion. Jerusalem, the holy city, is not exempt.
- Jesus fulfilled this by confronting religious leaders. Their rejection of Him became their downfall, proving that unbelief blinds and ensnares even those closest to God's covenant promises.
- God's holiness is inescapable. Those who resist His truth find themselves caught in judgment, while those who embrace Him find safety in His sanctuary.

Discussion Questions

1. What does it mean for God to be both a sanctuary and a stumbling stone?

2. How is this prophecy fulfilled in Jesus Christ?

3. Why do people stumble over Christ and the gospel?

4. How do faith and unbelief produce such different outcomes from the same "stone"?

5. What does this passage reveal about the offense of grace?

6. In what ways is Jesus a sanctuary for believers today?

7. How can the church embody Christ as sanctuary while acknowledging the offense of the cross?

Narrative Reflection

Isaiah 8:14 presents a striking paradox in prophetic writings: "He will be a holy place; for both Israel and Judah he will be a stone that causes people to stumble and a rock that makes them fall. And for the people of Jerusalem, he will be a trap and a snare." In this single verse, God is depicted as both a sanctuary and a stumbling stone, serving as a refuge for the faithful while becoming a snare for the rebellious. This tension permeates Scripture and finds its fullest expression in Christ, who is both the cornerstone of salvation and the stumbling block of judgment.

To grasp this prophecy, we must place it in its historical context. Isaiah prophesied during the reign of King Ahaz, a time of political upheaval and spiritual decline. Judah was embroiled in the Syro-Ephraimite crisis around 735–732 B.C., when Israel (Ephraim) and Aram (Syria) conspired against Judah. Rather than trusting in God, Ahaz sought security through alliances with foreign powers, particularly Assyria. Isaiah urged him to have faith and fear the Lord instead of earthly rulers, emphasizing that only God could protect Judah. However, Ahaz ignored Isaiah's counsel and relied on human power. In this context, Isaiah proclaimed that God would be both sanctuary and stumbling stone: a holy refuge for those who trusted Him, but a stone of ruin for those who rejected Him, even among His own people.

This imagery would have resonated deeply with Isaiah's audience. Stones held significant symbolism in Israel's religious life. Altars were made of uncut stones, the covenant was inscribed on stone tablets, and the temple's foundation was built on massive stones. To refer to God as a "stone" evoked ideas of strength, permanence, and stability. However, the same stone could also trip, wound, or crush. It served as both a foundation and a stumbling block, offering life or leading to death. The response of those encountering the stone determined its effect.

Jewish tradition sustained this tension. Many interpreted Isaiah 8:14 as a warning: God would be a sanctuary for the faithful remnant, but a source of judgment for the unfaithful majority. Later Jewish writings continued to explore the "stone" imagery, connecting it with verses like Psalm 118:22 ("The stone the builders rejected has become the cornerstone") and Isaiah 28:16 ("See, I lay a stone in Zion, a tested stone, a precious cornerstone"). Together, these verses highlighted a pattern: God's chosen foundation is often rejected, yet it is through this rejection that His purposes advance. This theme of the stone evolved into a messianic expectation: one would come who would serve as both the sure foundation of God's kingdom and a dividing line of judgment.

New Testament writers picked up this prophetic thread and applied it to Jesus. Paul quotes Isaiah 8:14 in Romans 9:33, stating: "See, I lay in Zion a stone that causes people to stumble and a rock that makes them fall, and the one who believes in him will never be put to shame." For Paul, Christ embodies both aspects. To believers, He is the cornerstone of salvation, providing security and honor. However, to those who reject Him, He becomes a stumbling stone that reveals unbelief and leads to judgment.

Peter expands on this theme in 1 Peter 2:7–8. Addressing believers facing persecution, he reassures them that Christ, though despised by men, is chosen and precious to God. By quoting both Isaiah 28:16 and Isaiah 8:14, Peter illustrates that Christ is the cornerstone of God's spiritual house. Those who trust in Him find refuge and life, while those who disobey stumble over Him, fulfilling the prophecy. The same stone produces opposite outcomes based on faith or unbelief.

This imagery also informs Paul's theology in 1 Corinthians 1:23: "We preach Christ crucified: a stumbling block to Jews and foolishness to Gentiles." The cross is offensive because it defies human expectations. Many Jews yearned for a political Messiah to overthrow Rome and restore Israel's independence. Instead, Jesus came in humility, preaching forgiveness, serving the outcast, and enduring the shame of crucifixion. For those equating God's power with earthly triumph, the cross appeared scandalous. Yet, in that apparent weakness lies the wisdom and power of God. What causes others to stumble becomes the foundation of salvation.

Thus, the theological significance of Isaiah 8:14 is that Christ cannot be encountered neutrally. He demands a response—either as sanctuary or stumbling stone, refuge or ruin. The same stone offers stability to one person while bringing destruction to another. The difference lies in faith: to trust in Him is to find life; to reject Him is to stumble into death. This reality stems not from Christ seeking harm, but from His embodiment of God's decisive plan. Rejecting Christ equates to rejecting salvation.

For the church today, this verse holds profound significance. First, it offers comfort: Christ is our sanctuary. In a world filled with fear, uncertainty, and opposition, He is our holy refuge. Just as Isaiah promised that God would be a sanctuary for the faithful remnant, Christ assures His presence and protection for those who trust Him. We are not alone in navigating life's dangers; we are supported by the cornerstone of God's eternal kingdom.

Second, it presents a sobering challenge. The gospel will always be a stumbling block for some. Its message of grace confronts human pride, asserting that salvation is a gift, not earned through heritage, works, or achievement. It dismantles all human boasting and calls for repentance and humility. Many stumble because the gospel disrupts self-sufficiency and challenges worldly wisdom. The church must resist the urge to dilute or remove this offense; to do so is to strip the cross of its power. Our mission is to faithfully proclaim Christ, understanding that some will find refuge while others will stumble.

Third, Isaiah 8:14 highlights our identity as the temple of God. Jesus referred to His body as the true temple (John 2:19–21), and through His death and resurrection, He became the meeting place between God and humanity. Believers, as living stones, are now integrated into a spiritual house (1 Peter 2:5). Zeal for God's house today means commitment to the holiness, unity, and mission of the church. We must reflect Christ's presence as His sanctuary in a hostile world, embodying His purity and compassion.

Finally, this prophecy conveys a message for every generation: Christ is the dividing line of history. Nations rise and fall, ideologies come and go, but the essential question remains: what will we do with the stone God has laid in Zion? Will we stumble in unbelief or find sanctuary in faith? The answer shapes not only our present but also our eternal destiny.

During Advent and Christmas, Isaiah 8:14 resonates even more. The child born in Bethlehem was both sanctuary and stumbling stone. He came as Immanuel—God with us—bringing light to darkness and hope to despair. Yet that same child grew to be despised and rejected, a man of sorrows familiar with suffering. His presence comforted the humble while bringing judgment to the proud. The paradox of His mission is encapsulated in this prophecy: He is both the holy place and the stone of stumbling.

Ultimately, Isaiah 8:14 reminds us that Christ is unavoidable. He will either be our refuge or our ruin. The gospel demands a choice. For those who trust Him, He is life, security, and sanctuary. For those who reject Him, He is the stone that reveals unbelief and leads to judgment. As His followers, we are called to share in His reproach, proclaim His salvation, and live as His holy temple. The stone laid in Zion is both the foundation of our faith and the measure by which every human heart is tested.

Layers of Understanding

Historical Context

Isaiah delivered this prophecy during the Syro-Ephraimite crisis, when Judah faced military threats from neighboring nations and spiritual decline within its borders. The people were tempted to rely on alliances with Assyria rather than trusting in God. Through Isaiah, the Lord declared that He would be a sanctuary for the faithful but a stumbling stone for those who rejected Him.

Jewish Understanding

Jewish interpreters read Isaiah 8:14 as a sober warning. God Himself, the covenant protector, could become the downfall of His people if they placed confidence in human strength, foreign powers, or idols instead of relying on Him. The prophecy reminded Israel that rejecting God's ways inevitably led to judgment and ruin.

New Testament Fulfillment

The apostles apply Isaiah 8:14 directly to Christ. Romans 9:33 and 1 Peter 2:7–8 identify Him as both the cornerstone and stumbling stone. Israel's leaders rejected Him, and His crucifixion displayed that rejection. Yet in resurrection, He was vindicated as the foundation of God's redemptive plan, fulfilling Isaiah's paradoxical prophecy.

Theological Significance Today

Isaiah 8:14 reminds believers that Christ is both sanctuary and offense. He is our holy refuge, offering protection and life to those who trust Him. Yet the gospel inevitably confronts human pride, dividing those who believe from those who stumble. The church must embrace Christ fully while faithfully proclaiming His saving truth.

Cross-Reference Connections

- **Isaiah 28:16** – God lays a chosen cornerstone in Zion.
- **Psalm 118:22** – The rejected stone becomes the cornerstone.
- **Romans 9:32–33** – Israel stumbles over the "stone" of Christ.
- **1 Peter 2:7–8** – Believers honor Him, unbelievers stumble.
- **1 Corinthians 1:23** – Christ crucified: stumbling block and foolishness.
- **John 2:19–21** – Christ as the true temple, sanctuary for His people.

LESSON SCRIPTURE ISAIAH 53:3

PROPHECY TITLE

Despised and Rejected: The Man of Sorrows

Introduction

Isaiah 53 is the clearest Old Testament prophecy of the Messiah's suffering and redemptive death. Verse 3 paints a portrait of the Servant as one despised, rejected, and deeply acquainted with grief: "He was despised and rejected by mankind, a man of suffering, and familiar with pain."

This prophecy points directly to Jesus Christ, who was rejected by His own people, betrayed by His disciples, mocked by leaders, and crucified by Rome. His sorrow was not merely personal but carried the weight of the world's sin. The New Testament repeatedly identifies Isaiah 53 with Jesus' passion (Matthew 8:17; John 12:38; Acts 8:32–35).

For believers, this verse reveals both the depth of Christ's identification with human suffering and the reality of His rejection as the chosen Messiah. He bore our griefs so that we might know His healing.

Scripture Reference

Isaiah 53:3 (NIV)   "He was despised and rejected by mankind, a man of suffering, and familiar with pain. Like one from whom people hide their faces he was despised, and we held him in low esteem.

Big Picture Insights

- **Messianic Servant** – prophecy of Christ's humiliation and rejection.
- **Despised and rejected** – foreshadows rejection by Israel and leaders.
- **Man of sorrows** – acquainted with grief, suffering deeply.
- **Familiar with pain** – Christ's full identification with human suffering.
- **Hiding faces** – imagery of shame and revulsion.
- **Low esteem** – the Messiah judged unworthy by men.
- **New Testament fulfillment** – applied to Christ's rejection, passion, and cross.
- **Reversal** – the despised Servant becomes exalted Lord (Philippians 2:9–11).
- **Pastoral comfort** – Christ understands our pain because He has borne it.
- **Gospel paradox** – salvation comes through rejection and sorrow.

Verse-by-Verse Commentary

Isaiah 53:3a – "He was despised and rejected by mankind,…"

- The Servant experiences rejection by those He came to save. Rather than receiving honor, He is despised, dismissed as insignificant, and pushed aside by human judgment. His humility contrasts with expectations of a conquering king.
- Jesus fulfilled this in His ministry. Religious leaders opposed Him, crowds turned against Him, and even His own disciples abandoned Him. Humanity's rejection revealed its blindness to God's chosen Messiah.

Isaiah 53:3b – "…a man of suffering, and familiar with pain…"

- The Servant is described not by power but by suffering. Pain is not occasional but constant, marking His entire life experience. He identifies fully with human brokenness and frailty.
- In Christ, this was fulfilled through His rejection, betrayal, trials, crucifixion, and death. Yet His suffering was not meaningless—it prepared Him to bear humanity's deepest wounds and sorrows.

Isaiah 53:3c – "…Like one from whom people hide their faces he was despised, and we held him in low esteem."

- The Servant's suffering was so intense that people turned away, unwilling to look upon His pain. He was not only despised but considered unworthy of honor or respect.
- At the cross, many mocked, jeered, or stood at a distance, unwilling to identify with Him. Humanity's low regard revealed sin's depth—yet through this rejection came the world's salvation.

Discussion Questions

1. Why is it important that the Messiah was despised and rejected?

2. How does Jesus' suffering fulfill this verse?

3. What does it mean that Christ is "familiar with pain"?

4. How does this verse comfort us in our own grief?

5. Why did people hide their faces from Him?

6. How does the paradox of rejection leading to salvation shape our faith?

7. How can we identify with Christ in rejection and suffering today?

Narrative Reflection

Isaiah 53:3 vividly depicts the humiliation and rejection of the Servant of the Lord: "He was despised and rejected by mankind, a man of suffering, and familiar with pain. Like one from whom people hide their faces he was despised, and we held him in low esteem." Centuries before Christ's birth, Isaiah presented a vision of the Messiah that defies human expectations. Rather than embodying triumph and honor, this Servant would endure sorrow, rejection, and shame. Yet, through this very rejection, God's plan for redemption was fulfilled.

The prophecy begins: "He was despised and rejected by mankind." From the outset of His ministry, Jesus faced this reality. Although He drew large crowds who were amazed by His teachings and miracles, many soon turned away when His demands became too challenging. John notes that after Jesus referred to Himself as the bread of life, "many of his disciples turned back and no longer followed him" (John 6:66). The religious leaders scorned Him, accusing Him of blasphemy, breaking the Sabbath, and being possessed by a demon. In His hometown of Nazareth, He was rejected when He proclaimed the fulfillment of Isaiah's prophecy; His neighbors drove Him out and even attempted to kill Him (Luke 4:28–29). John encapsulates this tragic irony: "He came to that which was his own, but his own did not receive him" (John 1:11).

This rejection peaked during the passion. One of His closest disciples, Judas, betrayed Him with a kiss. Peter, who had boldly professed his loyalty, denied Him three times out of fear. The other disciples scattered, abandoning Him in His darkest hour. The same crowds that once shouted "Hosanna!" turned against Him, demanding His crucifixion. At His trial, He was mocked, spat upon, scourged, and crowned with thorns. On the cross, He endured not only the physical agony of crucifixion but also the humiliation of public shame, abandonment, and rejection. He bore the scorn of sinners, despised and rejected by those He came to save.

Isaiah continues: "a man of suffering, and familiar with pain." In the language the Hebrew conveys the notion of someone intimately acquainted with grief, living closely with sorrow. Jesus' life was marked by suffering long before the cross. He wept at Lazarus' tomb, even knowing He would raise him, demonstrating His deep empathy with human grief (John 11:35). He lamented over Jerusalem's hardness of heart, longing to gather the people like a hen gathers her chicks, but they refused (Luke 13:34). In Gethsemane, He agonized in prayer, and His sweat fell like drops of blood as He faced the weight of sin and the cup of God's wrath. His compassion for the suffering was not theoretical; it stemmed from His own experience of pain. Ultimately, His greatest suffering occurred at Calvary, where He bore not only physical torment but the spiritual burden of the world's sin, crying out in forsakenness: "My God, my God, why have you forsaken me?" (Matthew 27:46).

The next phrase deepens this portrayal: "like one from whom people hide their faces." This evokes an image of someone viewed as cursed, afflicted, or too repulsive to look at. In the ancient world, visible suffering was often interpreted as evidence of God's judgment. Job's friends assumed his losses resulted from sin; similarly, those who witnessed Jesus beaten and crucified presumed He was under divine curse. Crucifixion was designed to strip victims of dignity, leaving them exposed and mocked. As Isaiah later states in verse 4, people thought He was "stricken by God, smitten by him, and afflicted." At the cross, many turned away, unable to bear the sight of His disfigured form. Paul highlights the scandal in Galatians 3:13: "Christ redeemed us from the curse of the law by becoming a curse for us." The Servant willingly bore the stigma, fully embracing the weight of human shame.

Isaiah concludes: "He was despised, and we held him in low esteem." This verse underscores not only the world's rejection but also humanity's misjudgment. The Servant was seen as insignificant, unworthy, even cursed. His humility and suffering led people to dismiss Him as powerless. Yet, in God's economy, what the world despises, He exalts. Paul reflects on this paradox in Philippians 2:8–9: "He humbled himself by becoming obedient to death—even death on a cross! Therefore God exalted him to the highest place and gave him the name that is above every name." The despised Servant became the exalted Lord.

From a pure theologically point of view, Isaiah 53:3 reveals the mystery of salvation: redemption comes through rejection, humiliation, and sorrow. The Messiah was not embraced as a hero but dismissed as a criminal. Yet through His humiliation, He achieved what no earthly conqueror could—atonement for sin. The Servant's suffering was purposeful; it was God's chosen path for salvation. As Paul writes, the message of the cross is "foolishness to those who are perishing, but to us who are being saved it is the power of God" (1 Corinthians 1:18). This is the marvelous reversal at the heart of the gospel.

For believers, Isaiah 53:3 provides profound comfort. It assures us that Christ understands our sorrows firsthand. He is not a distant God but One who has entered our pain. He knows rejection, loneliness, and grief, for He has endured them Himself. Hebrews 4:15 reminds us that we have a high priest who can sympathize with our weaknesses, having been tested in every way, yet without sin. When we face rejection, we know Christ has gone before us. When we grieve, we know He is acquainted with grief. When we suffer, we know He is with us, having borne greater suffering for our sake.

This verse also challenges us to reassess our values. Humanity despised the Servant because He did not conform to worldly standards of greatness. He was not wealthy, glamorous, or politically powerful. Instead, He was humble, lowly, and suffering. If we follow Him, we should expect the same. Jesus warned His disciples that the world would hate them because it hated Him first (John 15:18). The church must be ready to walk the path of the cross, bearing reproach for Christ's name and seeking God's approval above human esteem.

The New Testament frequently references Isaiah 53:3 to explain Christ's life and mission. Matthew 8:17 cites Isaiah 53 to interpret Jesus' healing ministry: "He took up our infirmities and bore our diseases." John 12:37–38 connects the people's unbelief to Isaiah 53:1–3, illustrating how their rejection of Christ fulfilled prophecy. In Acts 8, the Ethiopian eunuch reads from Isaiah 53, and Philip clarifies that it points to Jesus, leading to the eunuch's conversion. The early church viewed Isaiah 53 not as vague poetry but as a direct prophecy fulfilled in Christ's suffering and rejection.

Ultimately, Isaiah 53:3 directs us to the cross, where Christ bore our griefs and carried our sorrows. He was despised and rejected, seen as cursed and insignificant, yet through His rejection, we are accepted. Through His sorrow, we receive joy. Through His pain, we are healed. The man of sorrows is our Savior, and the one held in low esteem is the cornerstone of our faith.

Isaiah 53:3 invites us to contemplate the paradox of God's plan: salvation through suffering, glory through shame, exaltation through humiliation. For the world, this remains a stumbling block. For believers, it is the deepest source of comfort and hope. The Servant was despised so that we might be accepted. He was rejected so that we might be received. He was acquainted with grief so that our joy might be full.

Layers of Understanding

Historical Context

Isaiah's prophecy was spoken to a people facing exile, despair, and oppression. It introduced a Servant figure who would not conquer with power but instead carry griefs, endure rejection, and suffer on behalf of the people. This vision reframed redemption, showing salvation would come through sorrow rather than triumph.

Jewish Understanding

Within Jewish tradition, Isaiah 53 was often read as a description of Israel itself—the suffering nation bearing the sins of others—or of a faithful remnant enduring affliction. Over time, some interpreters connected it to a coming righteous figure, though Christians uniquely understand the Servant as fulfilled in the Messiah.

New Testament Fulfillment

The New Testament directly applies Isaiah 53:3 and its context to Jesus Christ. Matthew 8:17 explains His healing ministry as fulfillment of bearing infirmities. John 12:38 interprets Israel's unbelief through Isaiah's words. In Acts 8, Philip declares to the Ethiopian eunuch that the Servant's rejection, suffering, and death find their fulfillment in Jesus.

Theological Significance Today

Isaiah 53:3 assures believers that Christ identifies with rejection, grief, and suffering. His humiliation secured salvation, transforming weakness into victory. For the church, it provides comfort that our Savior knows our pain, and confidence that God exalts what the world despises, calling us to embrace the cross-shaped path of discipleship.

Cross-Reference Connections

- **John 1:11** – He came to His own, but His own did not receive Him.
- **Matthew 8:17** – He took up our infirmities and bore our diseases.
- **John 12:38** – Isaiah 53 explains unbelief in Jesus' ministry.
- **Acts 8:32–35** – Philip explains Isaiah 53 as fulfilled in Jesus.
- **Hebrews 4:15** – Christ sympathizes with our weaknesses.
- **Philippians 2:8–9** – Rejected yet exalted by God.
- **Galatians 3:13** – Christ became a curse for us.

PROPHECY FULFILLED - STUDY LESSON - 23

LESSON SCRIPTURE: **MALACHI 4:2**

PROPHECY TITLE

The Rising Sun of Righteousness

Introduction

Malachi, the final prophet of the Old Testament, addresses a time of spiritual decline following the return from exile. The people had grown weary, the priests were corrupt, and hope appeared dim. Nevertheless, Malachi concludes with a vision of God's imminent day. While the arrogant and wicked will face judgment, those who honor God's name will experience healing and joy.

Malachi 4:2 states: "But for you who revere my name, the sun of righteousness will rise with healing in its rays. And you will go out and frolic like well-fed calves." This prophecy heralds the dawn of a new era, fulfilled in the coming of Christ, who brings righteousness, healing, and joy. The imagery of the rising sun evokes messianic hope: Jesus is the light of the world, the morning star, and the one who ushers in eternal day.

For believers, this prophecy reassures us that Christ's coming signifies not only judgment for the wicked but also salvation for the faithful. His righteousness shines upon us, His healing restores us, and His presence fills us with joy.

Malachi 4:2 (NIV) **"But for you who revere my name, the sun of righteousness will rise with healing in its rays. And you will go out and frolic like well-fed calves."**

Big Picture Insights

- **Contrast of destinies** – judgment for the wicked, healing for the faithful.
- **Sun of righteousness** – Christ as the dawning light of salvation.
- **Healing rays** – restoration of body, soul, and creation.
- **Joyful freedom** – image of calves leaping in open pasture.
- **Messianic dawn** – connects to Luke 1:78–79, Jesus as rising sun.
- **Light over darkness** – fulfillment in Christ the Light of the World.
- **Holistic salvation** – righteousness and healing go together.
- **Advent theme** – hope and joy in the coming of Christ.
- **Already/not yet** – fulfilled in Christ's first coming, consummated in His return.
- **Encouragement** – calls us to persevere in reverence until the dawn breaks.

Verse -by-Verse Commentary

Malachi 4:2a – "But for you who revere my name,…"

- The promise is directed to those who honor God with reverence. Unlike the arrogant who face judgment, the faithful receive assurance of blessing. God's covenant faithfulness is tied to those who fear Him in truth.
- Reverence involves more than outward practice; it is heartfelt obedience and awe. This sets apart those who belong to God, ensuring that His coming brings hope rather than terror.

Malachi 4:2b – "…the sun of righteousness will rise with healing in its rays…"

- The imagery of the sun signifies light, life, and renewal. Righteousness shines forth, dispelling darkness and bringing wholeness. Healing suggests restoration of both physical and spiritual brokenness.
- Early Christians saw this fulfilled in Christ, the Light of the World (John 8:12). His resurrection brought dawn after the darkness of the cross, radiating righteousness and healing for all who believe.

Malachi 4:2c – "…And you will go out and frolic like well-fed calves."

- The picture is one of freedom, joy, and vitality. Just as calves leap in open pasture, God's people are released from bondage into abundant life, celebrating His deliverance.
- This exuberant joy reflects salvation's fullness. Christ not only redeems from sin but fills life with new vitality, transforming sorrow into gladness and restoring creation to flourish under God's reign.

Discussion Questions

1. What does the image of the "sun of righteousness" teach us about the Messiah?

2. How is Christ's coming both judgment and salvation in Malachi's prophecy?

3. In what ways did Jesus bring "healing in His rays" during His ministry?

4. How does this prophecy connect to the New Testament (Luke 1:78–79; John 8:12)?

5. What does the joyful image of frolicking calves teach us about life in Christ?

6. How can we live in hope while waiting for the final dawn of His return?

7. Where do you need the healing rays of Christ in your life today?

Narrative Reflection

Malachi 4:2 presents a radiant vision of hope at the conclusion of the Old Testament: "But for you who revere my name, the sun of righteousness will rise with healing in its rays. And you will go out and frolic like well-fed calves." This verse serves as both a promise and a striking contrast. Just one verse earlier, Malachi proclaimed that the day of the Lord would arrive like a furnace, consuming the arrogant and wicked like stubble (Malachi 4:1). The imagery is sobering—fire, destruction, judgment. Yet immediately afterward, the prophet depicts a vastly different scene. For those who fear the Lord, that same day will not bring darkness, but dawn; not destruction, but healing; not terror, but joy.

This dual imagery lies at the heart of biblical prophecy. The day of the Lord divides humanity: it signifies wrath for the rebellious and redemption for the reverent. Thus, Malachi's prophecy concludes the Old Testament canon by extending hope to the faithful remnant who cling to God's name. For them, the promise is not annihilation but renewal; not curse but blessing; not night but sunrise.

The image of the "sun of righteousness" is particularly striking. After centuries of spiritual decline and prophetic silence, Malachi announces that a new dawn is approaching. Just as the sun ends the night, bringing warmth, light, and life to the earth, so the Messiah will rise to deliver righteousness, healing, and joy to God's people. This metaphor would have resonated deeply with Malachi's audience. In the ancient Near Eastern world, the sun was often associated with power, vitality, and divine presence. However, Malachi carefully redirects this symbolism: it is not the sun itself that is worshiped, but the God whose righteousness shines like the sun. This imagery elevates the Lord as the true source of life and light, distinguishing Him from pagan sun deities and foreshadowing the arrival of His anointed one.

In the New Testament, this imagery finds its fulfillment in Jesus Christ. Zechariah, the father of John the Baptist, echoes Malachi's prophecy in his song of praise recorded in Luke 1:78–79: "Because of the tender mercy of our God, by which the rising sun will come to us from heaven to shine on those living in darkness and in the shadow of death, to guide our feet into the path of peace." Here, the rising sun is directly linked to the Messiah, the one who brings divine light into human darkness. Jesus Himself identifies with this imagery when He declares, "I am the light of the world. Whoever follows me will never walk in darkness, but will have the light of life" (John 8:12). The apostle John expands on this theme in his Gospel: "The true light that gives light to everyone was coming into the world" (John 1:9). In Christ, the long night of sin is shattered, and the dawn of salvation begins.

The phrase "healing in its rays" enhances the imagery. As the rising sun emits beams of light, the Messiah's coming radiates restoration. Throughout His earthly ministry, Jesus healed the blind, the lame, the deaf, and the lepers. He cast out demons, comforted the brokenhearted, and raised the dead. Each miracle served not merely as an act of compassion but as a signpost of something greater: the inbreaking of God's kingdom and the ultimate healing of sin. Isaiah had foretold, "By his wounds we are healed" (Isaiah 53:5), and Peter echoes this truth, declaring, "By his wounds you have been healed" (1 Peter 2:24). The healing rays of the sun of righteousness extend beyond physical cures to encompass spiritual renewal—reconciliation with God, forgiveness of sin, and the promise of a restored creation.

This healing is both present and future. Christ's death and resurrection have already secured forgiveness and new life for believers. His Spirit renews hearts, comforts the sorrowful, and binds up wounds. Yet not all is complete; we still inhabit a broken world where disease, grief, and pain persist. The healing rays shine now as a foretaste but will reach their full strength upon Christ's return. On that day, every wound will be healed, every tear wiped away, and creation itself liberated from its bondage to decay (Romans 8:21). Malachi's promise thus transcends time, offering hope not only to his generation but to ours: the dawn has begun, but the full day is still to come.

The second half of the verse shifts the imagery from light to joy: "You will go out and frolic like well-fed calves." To ancient listeners, this would have evoked a vivid and delightful picture. Calves confined during winter were joyfully released into the fields in spring, leaping and bounding with exuberance. This image conveys freedom, abundance, and uncontainable joy. For God's people, the coming of the Messiah signifies liberation from captivity—freedom from sin's bondage, joy in salvation, and new life in God's presence. The image of frolicking calves encapsulates the essence of redeemed humanity—free, joyful, and flourishing under the light of God's righteousness.

This prophecy also highlights the dual nature of Christ's coming. The same dawn that brings joy to the faithful reveals judgment for the wicked. Malachi articulates this tension clearly: the arrogant will be consumed like stubble in fire, while the reverent will be healed and set free. The New Testament echoes this duality. Christ is both cornerstone and stumbling stone (1 Peter 2:6–8). His light exposes darkness, revealing both salvation and sin. His righteousness confronts pride, humbling the exalted while exalting the humble. The same Christ who saves also judges, and the distinction lies in the response: reverence or rebellion.

For believers today, Malachi 4:2 provides profound comfort. It reassures us that Christ is our rising sun, illuminating our darkness. Regardless of the griefs or wounds we endure, His rays bring healing.

133

Whatever despair clouds our path, His dawn promises hope. His resurrection is the first light of the new creation, and His promised return guarantees the full sunrise. We live in the "already but not yet," experiencing the warmth of His rays now while anticipating the day when darkness is banished forever.

At the same time, this verse challenges us. The promise is given specifically to those who "revere my name." Reverence entails more than outward respect; it implies awe, loyalty, and wholehearted devotion. To revere God's name is to live in constant awareness of His holiness, to honor Him in word and deed, and to align our lives with His will. In a culture that frequently trivializes or mocks God, Malachi calls the faithful to stand apart, marked by reverence. The healing dawn is not for the indifferent but for those who treasure His name above all.

This prophecy also informs the church's mission. As recipients of the sun's rays, we are called to reflect His light into the world. Jesus instructed His disciples, "You are the light of the world. A town built on a hill cannot be hidden" (Matthew 5:14). The healing we receive is not solely for ourselves but for the world, as we carry the message of Christ's light into dark places. Just as the sun spreads its beams across the earth, the church is called to radiate Christ's love, truth, and healing into every corner of society.

Malachi 4:2 thus concludes the Old Testament with a promise that points directly to Christ. The sun of righteousness has risen in His incarnation, shone brightly in His ministry, radiated healing through His death and resurrection, and will blaze in fullness at His return. For now, His rays sustain, strengthen and fill us with joy, even as we await the day when dawn breaks fully.

This passage is a prophecy of hope and contrast. For the wicked, the day of the Lord is fire; for the faithful, it is sunrise. For those who revere God's name, the sun of righteousness rises with healing in its rays, bringing freedom and joy like calves leaping from their stalls. In Christ, this promise is fulfilled. He is the light of the world, the healer of the broken, and the source of everlasting joy. His rays continue to shine until the day when darkness is no more and His light fills the new heavens and the new earth.

Layers of Understanding

Historical Context

Malachi prophesied after the exile, around the fifth century B.C., when the temple had been rebuilt but spiritual decline remained widespread. The people wrestled with disillusionment, questioning God's justice and covenant faithfulness. Malachi 4 contrasts the fate of the wicked—burned like stubble—with the hope of the faithful. For those who revered the Lord's name, the promise was sunrise after darkness, healing after affliction, and joy after sorrow. The imagery of the rising sun symbolized God's decisive intervention to bring renewal, assuring the faithful remnant that the day of the Lord would be salvation, not destruction.

Jewish Understanding

Within Jewish tradition, this verse was read as a message of comfort and vindication for the faithful. The "sun of righteousness" was often associated with God's justice, shining brightly to restore what was broken and reward those who feared His name. Some saw it as a metaphor for national renewal and deliverance from foreign oppression. Others connected it to messianic expectation—the hope of a coming figure through whom God's light would shine. In all cases, the imagery emphasized divine intervention, contrasting the fate of the arrogant with the blessings promised to those who lived in reverence and covenant loyalty.

New Testament Fulfillment

The New Testament writers apply Malachi 4:2 directly to the ministry and person of Christ. Zechariah, the father of John the Baptist, echoes its imagery when he proclaims that "the rising sun will come to us from heaven" (Luke 1:78–79). Jesus identifies Himself as "the light of the world" (John 8:12), the one who shines into darkness and guides His people into peace. John 1:9 declares Him the true light for all humanity. The "healing in its rays" is fulfilled in Christ's earthly ministry—His miracles of physical healing, His forgiveness of sins, and His reconciling work on the cross. Through His resurrection, He secures ultimate restoration, and at His return the full sunrise of this prophecy will be complete.

Theological Significance Today

For believers, Malachi 4:2 offers assurance and challenge. It assures us that Christ is our rising sun, shining light into our darkness and bringing healing to our wounds. His rays reach into every corner of life—body, soul, and creation—offering renewal and hope. Yet the promise is given specifically to those who "revere" God's name, calling us to live in awe, obedience, and faithfulness. This verse also shapes the mission of the church: as recipients of the sun's light, we are called to reflect it, becoming witnesses of His healing and joy in a darkened world. Ultimately, Malachi 4:2 points us forward to the new creation, when Christ's light will banish all darkness, and God's people will rejoice with the freedom and exuberance of calves leaping from their stalls.

Cross-Reference Connections

- **Luke 1:78–79** – Zechariah's prophecy of the rising sun.
- **John 1:9** – Christ as the true light coming into the world.
- **John 8:12** – Jesus, the light of the world.
- **Isaiah 53:5** – By His wounds we are healed.
- **1 Peter 2:24** – Christ bore our sins, bringing healing.
- **Revelation 22:5** – No more night; the Lord Himself is the light.

PROPHECY FULFILLED - STUDY LESSON - 24

LESSON SCRIPTURE: PSALM 41:9

PROPHECY TITLE

Betrayed by a Close Friend

Introduction

Psalm 41, attributed to David, weaves together gratitude for God's deliverance and sorrow over betrayal and opposition. Verse 9 emotionally expresses the anguish of being betrayed by a trusted friend: "Even my close friend, someone I trusted, one who shared my bread, has turned against me."

In its original context, David laments the treachery of a close companion, likely Ahithophel (2 Samuel 15–17), who sided with Absalom during the rebellion. The New Testament interprets this verse as prophetic, anticipating Judas Iscariot's betrayal of Jesus. John 13:18 directly quotes Psalm 41:9, and the act of sharing bread during the Last Supper underscores Judas's role as the betrayer.

This prophecy enriches our understanding of Christ's suffering. He faced not only opposition from His enemies but also betrayal from one of His own disciples—someone who walked with Him, shared meals, and earned His trust. This experience of betrayal fulfills Scripture and serves as a poignant reminder that He deeply understands the pain of human treachery.

Scripture Reference

Psalm 41:9 (NIV) "Even my close friend, someone I trusted, one who shared my bread, has turned against me."

Big Picture Insights

- **David's betrayal** – likely Ahithophel, his trusted counselor.
- **Friendship broken** – betrayal by one who shared bread.
- **Messianic fulfillment** – applied directly to Judas in John 13:18.
- **Depth of suffering** – betrayal from within the circle of trust.
- **Shared table** – symbol of intimacy turned into treachery.
- **Christ's foreknowledge** – He knew betrayal was coming, yet submitted.
- **Scripture fulfilled** – betrayal was not accidental but part of God's plan.
- **Parallel to the cross** – betrayal leads directly to Christ's arrest and death.
- **Pastoral comfort** – Jesus knows the sting of betrayal personally.
- **Call to faithfulness** – disciples are warned against treachery and called to loyalty.

Verse-by-Verse Commentary

Psalm 41:9a – "Even my close friend..."

- Betrayal is most painful when it comes from someone within one's inner circle. The psalmist laments that not an enemy, but a close companion, is the one who turned against him.
- This prophecy foreshadows Judas, who walked with Jesus as a disciple. His betrayal stung deeply because it came from someone close, underscoring that Christ suffered treachery not from strangers but from trusted fellowship.

Psalm 41:9b – "...someone I trusted..."

- Trust amplifies the wound of betrayal. The psalmist highlights the intimacy of confidence shared, making the act not only disloyal but deeply violating. Broken trust pierces the heart more than open opposition.
- Judas was entrusted with responsibilities, even the money bag (John 12:6). His betrayal was not casual but a breaking of confidence, showing how greed and sin corrupt even relationships built on trust.

Psalm 41:9c – "...one who shared my bread..."

- To share bread was a sign of fellowship and peace in the ancient world. The betrayal violates hospitality, one of the strongest cultural bonds, deepening the treachery with shocking dishonor.
- Jesus recalled this verse during the Last Supper (John 13:18), identifying Judas as the betrayer. The very act of shared bread became the moment where prophecy and betrayal intersected in fulfillment.

Psalm 41:9d – "...has turned against me."

- The betrayal is not passive but active opposition. A friend becomes an adversary, weaponizing closeness to cause pain. The psalmist's grief points to the ultimate rejection Christ endured from Judas.
- Judas' betrayal culminated in his kiss in Gethsemane (Luke 22:47–48). This act, outwardly affectionate, revealed treachery at its darkest, fulfilling prophecy and setting in motion Christ's path to the cross.

Discussion Questions

1. Why is betrayal by a close friend more painful than by an enemy?

2. How does Psalm 41:9 connect David's experience with Christ's?

3. What does Judas' betrayal reveal about the fulfillment of prophecy?

4. How does Jesus' willingness to be betrayed reveal His submission to God's plan?

5. What comfort does it bring that Jesus understands betrayal?

6. How can believers guard against betraying Christ through disloyalty?

7. What does it mean to remain faithful at Christ's table?

Narrative Reflection

Psalm 41:9 presents one of the most emotional and personal prophecies fulfilled in the passion of Jesus Christ. Unlike verses that address opposition from enemies or persecution by outsiders, this prophecy highlights the betrayal from within—the pain of treachery by a trusted companion. David's lament over betrayal, written centuries before Christ, finds its fullest expression in the Messiah, who was betrayed not by strangers but by one of His own disciples.

In David's life, betrayal came from Ahithophel, his trusted counselor. Scripture describes Ahithophel as a man of exceptional wisdom, whose advice was regarded as if it came directly from God (2 Samuel 16:23). For many years, Ahithophel faithfully advised David, sharing in the intimate circle of the king's leadership. However, when Absalom rebelled against David and sought to seize the throne, Ahithophel defected, siding with the rebellious son against the king he had once served loyally (2 Samuel 15:31).

This betrayal was not merely political; it was deeply personal. David understood the sting of enemy attacks, but being betrayed by a trusted advisor cut even deeper. The pain was exacerbated by the

138

closeness of their relationship: one who had shared counsel, companionship, and loyalty turned against him. The poetic language of Psalm 41:9 captures this anguish with vivid imagery: a close friend who "shared my bread" has "lifted his heel against me." Sharing bread signified loyalty and fellowship, while lifting the heel conveyed hostility and contempt.

David's experience foreshadowed the ultimate betrayal—the betrayal of Christ by Judas Iscariot. Judas was not an outsider but one of the Twelve, chosen by Jesus Himself. He walked with the Lord for three years, witnessed His miracles, heard His teachings, and participated in His ministry. He was entrusted with the responsibility of managing the money bag (John 12:6). Most significantly, he shared meals with Jesus, including the Last Supper.

In this context, Psalm 41:9 finds its prophetic fulfillment. In John 13:18, Jesus quotes this very verse: "But this is to fulfill this passage of Scripture: 'He who shared my bread has turned against me.'" Jesus explicitly identifies Judas' betrayal as the fulfillment of David's lament. The treachery unfolds at the most intimate moment—during the Passover meal, when fellowship and loyalty should have been at their peak.

In the ancient world, sharing bread symbolized peace, trust, and friendship. To break bread with someone was to pledge loyalty and protection. Yet, in this moment of fellowship, Judas revealed his treachery. Jesus dipped the bread and gave it to Judas (John 13:26), a gesture that should have signified intimacy but instead exposed betrayal. What should have been the deepest bond of trust became the deepest wound of treachery.

Theologically, this prophecy highlights the profound depth of Christ's suffering. He was not only rejected by the crowds, opposed by religious leaders, and condemned by political authorities, but also betrayed by a friend. The sting of betrayal amplified the burden of His passion. He endured not only the physical agony of crucifixion but also the emotional anguish of shattered trust.

It is crucial to recognize that Jesus was not taken by surprise. He knew the prophecy, anticipated the betrayal, and willingly submitted to it. His foreknowledge did not diminish the pain but revealed His obedience. Even betrayal was intricately woven into God's redemptive plan. Jesus fully embraced the path of suffering, understanding that betrayal would lead to the cross, and the cross to salvation.

Judas' betrayal raises profound theological questions about the relationship between divine sovereignty and human freedom. Judas acted freely, motivated by greed and hardened by sin. He chose to betray Jesus for thirty pieces of silver (Matthew 26:14–16). Yet, his actions fulfilled what God had foretold. Peter declared in Acts 1:16: "The Scripture had to be fulfilled in which the Holy Spirit spoke long ago through David concerning Judas."

This tension does not excuse Judas' guilt. Jesus Himself stated, "The Son of Man will go just as it is written about him. But woe to that man who betrays the Son of Man! It would be better for him if he had not been born" (Matthew 26:24). Judas bears full responsibility for his choice. Yet, in the mystery of God's sovereignty, even his treachery became an instrument for redemption. God transformed human evil into divine good, intertwining betrayal within the tapestry of salvation.

For believers, this prophecy offers both comfort and caution. It comforts us because Jesus understands the pain of betrayal. Many have experienced the wounds of broken trust—by friends, family, or colleagues. Such betrayal can feel isolating and unbearable. Yet Christ empathizes with this pain because He endured it Himself. He knows what it means to be abandoned and betrayed. In Him, we find not only forgiveness for our sins but also companionship in our suffering. He is the faithful friend who never fails, the one who comprehends betrayal's sting and offers healing grace.

However, this verse also serves as a warning. Betrayal is not solely Judas' sin; it lurks as a potentiality in every heart. While few may betray Christ in such a dramatic manner, disloyalty can manifest in various forms—compromise with the world, denial under pressure, hypocrisy in witness, or apathy in devotion. The church is called to continually examine itself, asking whether we are walking in loyalty or drifting toward betrayal. Paul exhorts believers: "Examine yourselves to see whether you are in the faith; test yourselves" (2 Corinthians 13:5). Psalm 41:9 reminds us of the seriousness of faithfulness and the peril of disloyalty.

At last, Psalm 41:9 points us to the cross. Judas' betrayal initiated the chain of events that led to Jesus' arrest in Gethsemane, His trial before Caiaphas and Pilate, and His crucifixion at Calvary. The close friend who turned against Him became the instrument through which the Lamb of God was handed over. What appeared to be a triumph of treachery was, in fact, the triumph of God's plan.

The betrayal that seemed to seal Christ's fate became the means of fulfilling prophecy. Through Judas' actions, the Scriptures were realized, and redemption unfolded. What humans intended for evil, God intended for good (Genesis 50:20). Through betrayal came crucifixion; through crucifixion came atonement; and through atonement came salvation. The treachery of a friend became the pathway to reconciliation with God.

Psalm 41:9 reveals the depth of betrayal and the greater depth of God's faithfulness. The close friend who turned against Jesus fulfilled the Scripture, but Jesus transformed betrayal into redemption. He was despised, rejected, and betrayed; yet through His suffering, He brought reconciliation.

For us, this prophecy serves as both comfort and challenge. It assures us that Christ understands betrayal and walks with us in our pain. It challenges us to remain faithful, resist disloyalty, and cling to the One who endured betrayal for our sake. Jesus is the faithful friend who never abandons us, even when others fail. The betrayed Savior has become the cornerstone of our salvation, demonstrating that even in the darkest acts of treachery, God's light shines, and His plan prevails

Layers of Understanding

Historical Context

Psalm 41:9 reflects David's deep lament over betrayal during Absalom's rebellion, most likely by Ahithophel, his trusted counselor. Once a close friend who shared meals and counsel, Ahithophel turned against the king, compounding David's grief. This historical moment illustrates the devastating pain of treachery from within the circle of trust.

Jewish Understanding

Jewish readers primarily viewed Psalm 41:9 as David's personal lament, but also within the larger biblical theme of the righteous sufferer. The psalmist's experience of betrayal became representative of how God's servants often suffer unjustly. Such laments pointed beyond individual pain to God's unfolding work of justice and ultimate deliverance.

New Testament Fulfillment

The New Testament applies Psalm 41:9 directly to Jesus. At the Last Supper, He cites the verse to identify Judas' betrayal (John 13:18). Sharing bread, a sign of loyalty and friendship, becomes the very act of treachery. Acts 1:16 further confirms Judas' role as fulfillment of David's prophetic lament.

Theological Significance Today

For believers, this prophecy offers comfort and challenge. It assures us that Christ fully understands the anguish of betrayal. It challenges us to examine our loyalty to Him, resisting compromise or denial. Above all, it reminds us that even acts of treachery cannot thwart God's redemptive purposes, which prevail in Christ.

Cross-Reference Connections

- **2 Samuel 15:31** – Ahithophel's betrayal of David.
- **John 13:18–19** – Jesus quotes Psalm 41:9 concerning Judas.
- **John 13:26–27** – Judas identified at the Last Supper.
- **Matthew 26:14–16** – Judas agrees to betray Jesus for thirty silver coins.
- **Acts 1:16** – Peter affirms that Judas' betrayal fulfilled Scripture.
- **Hebrews 4:15** – Jesus sympathizes with our weaknesses, including betrayal.

LESSON SCRIPTURE: ZECHARIAH 11:12-13
PROPHECY TITLE

Thirty Pieces of Silver: The Price of Betrayal

Introduction

Zechariah 11 is one of the most enigmatic prophecies in the Old Testament. In a symbolic act, the prophet embodies a shepherd who is rejected by his flock. When his service is deemed worthless, he sarcastically asks for his wages, receiving thirty pieces of silver—the price of a slave. God then instructs him to throw the money into the house of the Lord, to the potter.

This peculiar prophetic sign finds a startling fulfillment in Judas Iscariot's betrayal of Jesus. Judas agrees to hand over Jesus for thirty pieces of silver (Matthew 26:15). Later, filled with remorse, he throws the coins into the temple. The chief priests, unwilling to return the blood money to the treasury, use it to purchase the potter's field (Matthew 27:3–10).

This prophecy underscores the worthlessness with which Christ was appraised, the fulfillment of God's sovereign word, and the tragedy of betrayal. What the world deemed cheap, God exalted, for the rejected Shepherd is the true Savior.

Scripture Reference

**Zechariah 11:12–13 (NIV)   "I told them, "If you think it best, give me my pay; but if not, keep it."
So they paid me thirty pieces of silver. [13] And the LORD said to me, "Throw it to the potter"—the
handsome price at which they valued me! So I took the thirty pieces of silver and threw them to the
potter at the house of the LORD."**

Big Picture Insights

- **Rejected shepherd** – Zechariah acts out Israel's rejection of God's shepherd.
- **Thirty silver coins** – price of a slave (Exodus 21:32), symbolizing insult.
- **Prophetic irony** – "handsome price" is bitter sarcasm.
- **Thrown into the temple** – fulfilled when Judas casts the money back.
- **Potter's field** – priests buy a field with the coins, fulfilling prophecy.
- **Christ undervalued** – betrayed for a trivial sum.
- **Human contempt, divine plan** – man devalues the Messiah, God exalts Him.
- **Foreknowledge of God** – prophecy fulfilled centuries later.
- **Tragedy of Judas** – remorse without repentance ends in despair.
- **Comfort for believers** – God's purposes stand even in betrayal.

Verse-by-Verse Commentary

Zechariah 11:12a – "I told them, 'If you think it best, give me my pay; but if not, keep it…'"

- The prophet speaks symbolically for God, addressing Israel's rejection of His care. By asking for "pay," He confronts their attitude toward His shepherding, exposing how little they value His covenant faithfulness and guidance.
- This anticipates Israel's dismissal of Christ. Instead of embracing Him as the Good Shepherd, they measured His worth cheaply, foreshadowing His betrayal for a sum that insulted His true value.

Zechariah 11:12b – "…So they paid me thirty pieces of silver."

- Thirty pieces of silver was the compensation for a slave (Exodus 21:32), underscoring the contempt shown toward God's chosen Shepherd. The Messiah's value, in the eyes of His people, is reduced to the price of servitude.
- This finds fulfillment in Judas, who agreed with the chief priests to betray Jesus for thirty pieces of silver (Matthew 26:14–15). The sum reveals humanity's devaluation of Christ's immeasurable worth.

Zechariah 11:13a – "And the LORD said to me, 'Throw it to the potter'—the handsome price at which they valued me!…"

- The Lord speaks with irony, calling it a "handsome price," highlighting the insult of undervaluing the Shepherd. Throwing it to the potter signifies rejection and contempt, as though the payment were worthless.
- Matthew 27:9–10 records Judas' remorse and the chief priests using the silver to buy the potter's field. This fulfilled the prophecy with precise detail, showing God's sovereignty even in betrayal.

Zechariah 11:13b – "…So I took the thirty pieces of silver and threw them to the potter at the house of the LORD."

- The act of discarding the money at the temple connects rejection of God's Shepherd with the center of worship. The betrayal becomes not just personal but a religious offense against God's covenant.
- Judas threw the silver back into the temple before his death (Matthew 27:5). The priests then used it for the potter's field, fulfilling this prophecy exactly, underscoring both judgment and God's foreordained plan.

Discussion Questions

1. Why do you think Zechariah's symbolic act used thirty pieces of silver?

2. What does this reveal about how humanity valued Christ?

3. How does the New Testament show this prophecy fulfilled in Judas?

4. What lessons can we learn from Judas' remorse and despair?

5. How does God turn an act of contempt into part of His redemptive plan?

6. What does this prophecy teach us about God's sovereignty in salvation history?

7. How should believers respond when the world undervalues Christ?

Narrative Reflection

Zechariah 11:12–13 presents specific messianic prophecies fulfilled during Christ's passion. The imagery is vivid, the symbolism profound, and the fulfillment in Jesus' betrayal is undeniable. In this passage, the prophet enacts a symbolic drama, portraying a shepherd who embodies God's care for His people. However, the flock rejects him, responding to his faithful service with disdain. In a tone bordering on sarcasm, the shepherd asks for his wages: "If you think it best, give me my pay; if not, keep it." Their payment? Thirty pieces of silver—the price of a slave.

The book of Zechariah is rich with visions and symbolic actions, many of which foreshadow the Messiah. In chapter 11, Zechariah takes on the role of a shepherd, symbolizing God's leadership and protection over His people. Instead of receiving gratitude or loyalty, however, the flock turns against him, culminating in their offering of thirty pieces of silver as his wages.

This amount is significant. According to Exodus 21:32, thirty shekels was the compensation for the death of a slave. By paying the shepherd this sum, the people effectively reduce him to the status of a slave—an act of profound insult. The sarcasm is evident in God's response: "Throw it to the potter—the handsome price at which they valued me!" The irony is striking; the Lord of glory is appraised at the lowest value possible. The shepherd's work is scorned, and in that scorn, the people reject God Himself.

Zechariah's action continues as he throws the silver into the house of the Lord, to the potter. While the full significance of this act was unclear at the time, it eerily anticipates the details of Judas' betrayal of Christ.

The New Testament reveals the prophetic depth of Zechariah's actions. Judas Iscariot, one of Jesus' twelve disciples, conspired to betray Him to the chief priests for thirty pieces of silver (Matthew 26:14–16). For the religious leaders, this was a convenient way to dispose of the troublesome Galilean rabbi at a bargain price. For Judas, it was a temptation he could not resist, though it ultimately filled him with regret.

The amount carries prophetic weight. Just as Zechariah's shepherd was valued at the price of a slave, so the Messiah was betrayed for the same contemptible sum. The one who healed the sick, raised the dead, calmed storms, and preached the kingdom of God was sold for the price of a common servant. Humanity placed little worth on the One of infinite value.

The fulfillment becomes even more distressing when considering what followed. Overwhelmed by remorse after witnessing Jesus' condemnation, Judas returned the silver to the priests, confessing, "I have sinned, for I have betrayed innocent blood" (Matthew 27:4). The priests, hardened in their rejection, dismissed him coldly. In despair, Judas threw the coins into the temple and went away to end his life (Matthew 27:5).

The priests, unwilling to return blood money to the treasury, used the coins to purchase a field from a potter. That field became known as the "Field of Blood" (Matthew 27:6–10). Every detail aligns with Zechariah's prophecy: the thirty coins, the throwing of the silver into the house of the Lord, and the involvement of a potter's field. Matthew explicitly cites this, attributing it to Jeremiah as a summary of the prophetic tradition (Matthew 27:9–10), though the wording clearly reflects Zechariah 11.

Theologically, Zechariah 11:12–13 reveals humanity's deep contempt for Christ. The eternal Son of God, the Good Shepherd who came to lay down His life for the sheep, was valued at the price of a slave. This valuation was not merely Judas' estimation or the priests' appraisal—it symbolized the world's rejection of God's Messiah. Yet what humanity despised, God exalted. As Peter boldly declared in Acts 4:11, "The stone you builders rejected, which has become the cornerstone." The insult of thirty pieces of silver sets the stage for the glory of Christ's exaltation.

This prophecy also underscores God's sovereignty over history. Judas acted freely, motivated by greed and later by despair. The priests acted wickedly, driven by hatred of Christ. Yet their actions fulfilled what God had already spoken through Zechariah. Betrayal, contempt, and rejection became the very path by which Christ went to the cross, accomplishing redemption. What seemed like chaos was, in fact, the outworking of God's eternal plan.

At the same time, this prophecy confronts us with the tragedy of Judas' story. His remorse was real, but it did not lead to repentance. He regretted his actions but did not turn to Christ for forgiveness. Instead, he sank into despair and self-destruction. His life serves as a sobering reminder that sorrow without repentance leads to death (2 Corinthians 7:10). Judas stands as a warning against hardening our hearts, undervaluing Christ, and turning away from the grace that alone can heal and restore.

For believers, Zechariah 11:12–13 offers profound comfort alongside its warning. It reminds us that Christ endured rejection, betrayal, and contempt. He understands what it means to be undervalued and despised. Many believers throughout history have experienced devaluation by the world—treated as expendable, scorned for their faith, or regarded as worthless in society. Yet the Lord Himself shared in that experience. He bore the insult of being valued at a slave's price so that we might be valued as children of God.

Moreover, the fulfillment of this prophecy reassures us of God's faithfulness. Every detail unfolded exactly as foretold. The thirty coins, the throwing of the silver into the temple, and the purchase of the potter's field all came to pass. This meticulous fulfillment assures us that God's Word never fails. If He fulfilled this prophecy with such precision, we can trust Him to fulfill all His promises—to be with us, redeem us, raise us, and bring us into His eternal kingdom.

Ultimately, Zechariah 11:12–13 points us to the paradox of redemption through rejection. The Messiah was sold for the price of a slave, despised and devalued, yet through that very betrayal, He accomplished salvation. The contempt of men became the means of God's glory. The price of betrayal became the cost of salvation.

What the world treated as worthless, God made priceless. What was cast aside, God exalted. The rejected Shepherd became the cornerstone of a new covenant. In this way, the prophecy of Zechariah is not just about betrayal—it is about the triumph of God's love over human scorn, the sovereignty of His plan over human rebellion, and the faithfulness of His Son in the face of ultimate rejection.

Layers of Understanding

Historical Context

In Zechariah's prophetic drama, the shepherd represents God's care for His people. Instead of gratitude, the flock rejects him and appraises his service at thirty pieces of silver—the price of a slave in Exodus 21:32. This shocking undervaluation symbolized Israel's contempt for God's leadership and foreshadowed the ultimate rejection of the Messiah.

Jewish Understanding

Jewish interpreters first viewed Zechariah's vision as a symbolic portrayal of Israel's dismissal of God's prophets and shepherds. The insult of thirty silver coins expressed the people's disdain for divine care. Over time, the passage gained messianic significance, understood as anticipating the rejection of God's chosen Shepherd, who would suffer contempt and betrayal.

New Testament Fulfillment

The New Testament records this prophecy fulfilled with remarkable precision. Judas betrayed Jesus for thirty silver coins (Matthew 26:15). Overcome with guilt, he threw the money into the temple, fulfilling Zechariah's imagery. The priests then purchased a potter's field with the coins (Matthew 27:5–10), perfectly echoing the prophet's enacted sign.

Theological Significance Today

This prophecy confronts humanity's undervaluing of Christ, betrayed for the price of a slave. Yet God exalted Him as cornerstone and Lord. It assures us that even betrayal was within God's sovereign plan of redemption. At the same time, it warns that sorrow without repentance, as with Judas, leads to destruction.

Cross-Reference Connections

- **Exodus 21:32** – Price of a slave set at thirty shekels.
- **Matthew 26:14–16** – Judas agrees to betray Jesus for thirty silver coins.
- **Matthew 27:3–10** – Judas throws the money into the temple; priests buy potter's field.
- **Acts 1:18–20** – Judas' death and the field of blood.
- **Zechariah 13:7** – Strike the shepherd, sheep scattered.
- **Acts 4:11** – The rejected stone becomes the cornerstone.

Series 4 – Suffering & Death Prophecies

LESSON SCRIPTURE: ZECHARIAH 13:7

PROPHECY TITLE

Strike the Shepherd, the Sheep Will Scatter

Introduction

Zechariah 13 explores themes of cleansing, renewal, and judgment among God's people. In verse 7, the prophet conveys a divine command: "Awake, sword, against my shepherd, against the man who is close to me!" declares the Lord Almighty. "Strike the shepherd, and the sheep will be scattered, and I will turn my hand against the little ones."

This verse emphasizes both divine initiative and human response. God Himself calls for the sword to strike His Shepherd, referring to the suffering and death of Christ, who is closest to the Father. The immediate result is the scattering of the sheep, which occurs when the disciples flee after Jesus' arrest in Gethsemane (Matthew 26:31; Mark 14:27).

However, within this judgment is a promise of hope. God's hand remains upon the "little ones," His remnant people, as He preserves them through their scattering and refines them through suffering. Thus, the prophecy encompasses both the passion of Christ and the preservation of His church.

Scripture Reference

Zechariah 13:7 (NIV) "Awake, sword, against my shepherd, against the man who is close to me!" declares the LORD Almighty. "Strike the shepherd, and the sheep will be scattered, and I will turn my hand against the little ones.

Big Picture Insights

- **Divine command** – God Himself calls for the striking of the Shepherd.
- **The Shepherd** – messianic figure, close to God, fulfilled in Christ.
- **The sword** – symbol of judgment, suffering, and death.
- **Sheep scattered** – fulfilled in the disciples fleeing after Jesus' arrest.
- **God's sovereignty** – even betrayal and scattering are within His plan.
- **Little ones** – God preserves a remnant despite disruption.
- **Christ's intimacy with the Father** – "the man close to me."
- **Passion prophecy** – Jesus cites this verse before His arrest.
- **Judgment and grace** – both striking and preservation occur together.
- **Comfort** – God's hand remains with His people even in scattering.

Verse-by-Verse Commentary

Zechariah 13:7a – "Awake, sword, against my shepherd, against the man who is close to me!" declares the LORD Almighty..."

- God commands the sword to awaken, signifying judgment falling on His chosen Shepherd. The "man close to me" highlights intimacy with God, pointing to the Messiah's unique relationship as both divine and human.
- Jesus fulfills this as the Good Shepherd (John 10:11). Though innocent, He is struck down by divine will, bearing judgment on behalf of His people, showing God's justice and mercy intertwined.

Zechariah 13:7b – "...Strike the shepherd, and the sheep will be scattered,..."

- The Shepherd's striking leads to dispersion. Israel's leaders rejected Christ, and at His arrest, His disciples fled in fear (Matthew 26:56), fulfilling this prophecy precisely.
- The scattering reveals human weakness, yet it is temporary. Though shaken, the disciples would later be regathered and empowered by the Spirit at Pentecost, continuing the Shepherd's mission.

Zechariah 13:7c – "...and I will turn my hand against the little ones..."

- God's hand of discipline falls on the "little ones," indicating the refining of His people. Trials and persecution test their faith, yet God's purpose is purification, not destruction.
- Early believers endured scattering and suffering, but through it, the church grew strong. God's refining hand ensured their faith became more resilient, preparing them for future witness.

Zechariah 13:7d – "...In the whole land," declares the LORD,"

- The prophecy widens to national scope. The Shepherd's striking impacts not just disciples but the covenant community, revealing the far-reaching consequences of rejecting God's appointed One.
- Ultimately, the verse points forward to both judgment and restoration—Israel's rejection of Christ led to scattering, yet God's plan continues, ensuring that through the Shepherd's sacrifice, salvation extends to all nations.

Discussion Questions

1. Why does God Himself summon the sword against His Shepherd?

2. How does this verse reveal both divine sovereignty and human responsibility?

3. In what ways was Jesus "the man close to God"?

4. Why did the disciples scatter, and what does this teach us about fear and faith?

5. How does God's hand remain with His people even in times of scattering?

6. How does this prophecy deepen our understanding of the cross?

7. What encouragement can we take from knowing God preserves His flock through trial?

Narrative Reflection

Zechariah 13:7 presents a clear messianic prophecy that highlights both the suffering of Christ and the repercussions of His arrest on His followers. The verse's language is striking: God Himself calls for the sword against His Shepherd, the one closest to Him. This moment brings forth both judgment and redemption, scattering and preservation.

The verse begins: "Awake, sword, against my shepherd, against the man who is close to me!" declares the Lord Almighty." Here, the sword symbolizes divine judgment, and notably, God summons it Himself. This underscores that Christ's suffering was not merely a historical accident or a result of human betrayal but an integral part of God's sovereign plan. Jesus' death was foreordained, the Lamb slain from the foundation of the world (Revelation 13:8).

The Shepherd referred to is the Messiah, who is intimately connected to God. This closeness emphasizes Christ's unique relationship with the Father; He is not a distant servant but the beloved Son, eternally one with the Father (John 10:30). Striking the Shepherd allows suffering to fall on the one most precious to God, revealing both the cost of redemption and the depth of divine love: God did not spare His own Son but gave Him up for us all (Romans 8:32).

The next phrase states: "Strike the shepherd, and the sheep will be scattered." Jesus quotes this verse on the night of His arrest, telling His disciples in Matthew 26:31: "This very night you will all fall away on account of me, for it is written: 'I will strike the shepherd, and the sheep of the flock will be scattered.'" Mark 14:50 records its fulfillment: "Then everyone deserted him and fled."

The scattering of the sheep symbolizes the disciples' fear and failure. Despite their pledges of loyalty, they fled when danger arose. Peter, who vowed he would never deny Jesus, denied Him three times. Their scattering highlights human frailty, yet even in this moment, Scripture was fulfilled.

The scattering also illustrates that God's people are never exempt from testing. The disciples' collapse served to strip them of self-confidence and prepare them to become faithful witnesses. Their restoration after the resurrection demonstrates that even failure can play a role in God's redemptive plan, transforming what seemed like shame into the foundation for a Spirit-empowered mission.

The final phrase adds: "and I will turn my hand against the little ones." This indicates that the scattering was not abandonment but a form of refinement. God's hand remains with His people, even in discipline. The early disciples were shaken but not destroyed; they were gathered again after the resurrection, restored by the risen Christ, and empowered by the Spirit at Pentecost. What appeared to be a disaster became the seed of the church's mission.

This image of God's hand "against" the little ones serves as a reminder that discipline does not equate to rejection. Hebrews 12:6 states: "The Lord disciplines the one he loves, and he chastens everyone he accepts as his son." For the disciples, the scattering refined their faith. For the church today, seasons of scattering, persecution, or weakness often serve as God's means of drawing us into deeper dependence on Him.

This verse reveals several profound Theologically truths. First, it emphasizes God's sovereignty over the cross. The Shepherd was struck not outside of God's will but in accordance with it. Jesus willingly laid down His life, fulfilling the Father's plan (Acts 2:23). This assures us that even the darkest events remain under God's control.

Second, it underscores the intimacy between the Father and the Son. The one struck is "close to me," indicating that the cross was not a moment of abandonment but a unified act of the triune God to accomplish salvation. The Father gave, the Son offered, and the Spirit empowered. The cross represents divine harmony rather than conflict.

Third, it teaches us about the frailty of human discipleship. Even those nearest to Jesus fled, reminding us that faithfulness relies not on human strength but on God's grace. This also brings comfort, as those who fled were later restored. Failure does not define us when God's hand remains upon His people.

Finally, it offers hope to believers experiencing scattering today. The church often faces disruption through persecution, division, or fear, yet God's hand stays upon the "little ones." He refines, restores, and regathers His flock. Just as the disciples were reunited after the resurrection, so God continues to preserve His people until the end.

For the persecuted church worldwide, this verse conveys significant meaning. The scattering of God's people is painful but never final. Christ, the struck Shepherd, guarantees that the flock will ultimately be preserved. For local congregations facing decline or conflict, it provides encouragement: God's hand is still at work. The same Shepherd who was struck now reigns as the risen Lord, ensuring that His scattered sheep are always under His care.

In this prophecy there is a reminder that the cross was part of God's plan, that Christ bore the judgment we deserved, and that God's hand sustains us even in weakness. It calls the church to humility, dependence, and hope. We may be scattered but are never abandoned; struck down but never destroyed. The Shepherd who was struck has gathered us into His fold and will preserve His flock until the end of the age.

Layers of Understanding

Historical Context

Zechariah's prophecy draws on shepherd imagery familiar in Israel's history, where kings and leaders were seen as shepherds of God's flock. By declaring that the Shepherd would be struck by God's command, Zechariah portrays both divine judgment on sin and the refining process through which God would preserve a faithful people.

Jewish Understanding

Jewish interpreters often viewed this verse as judgment upon Israel's leaders and people, where the striking of the shepherd resulted in scattering. Yet this scattering was not final; it also implied God's refining work, through which a purified remnant would emerge. The prophecy balanced themes of discipline, hope, and covenant preservation.

New Testament Fulfillment

Jesus explicitly cites this prophecy in Matthew 26:31, applying it to His impending arrest and the disciples' desertion. The scattering fulfilled Zechariah's words as the Shepherd was struck. Christ's passion demonstrates that His suffering was foreseen and purposeful, showing Him as the Good Shepherd who lays down His life for His sheep.

Theological Significance Today

This verse reassures believers that Christ's death was part of God's sovereign plan, not human accident. It humbles us by reminding us of human weakness, even among devoted disciples, while also comforting us with God's preserving hand. Even in seasons of scattering, fear, or failure, the Lord restores, regathers, and strengthens His flock.

Cross-Reference Connections

- **Matthew 26:31** – Jesus quotes Zechariah 13:7 before His arrest.
- **Mark 14:27–50** – Fulfillment in the disciples' flight.
- **John 10:11** – Jesus as the Good Shepherd who lays down His life.
- **Acts 2:23** – Jesus' death according to God's set purpose.
- **Romans 8:32** – God did not spare His own Son.
- **Revelation 13:8** – The Lamb slain from the foundation of the world.

PROPHECY FULFILLED - STUDY LESSON - 27

LESSON SCRIPTURE: ISAIAH 50:6

PROPHECY TITLE

The Servant Who Endures Shame and Suffering

Introduction

Isaiah 50 presents the third of the Servant Songs, highlighting the Lord's Servant's unwavering obedience in the face of rejection and suffering. In verse 6, the Servant vividly describes offering His back to those who beat Him, His cheeks to those who pulled out His beard, and His face to those who mocked and spat on Him.

This passage serves as a clear prophecy of Jesus' passion. The Gospels recount how He was scourged, mocked, spat upon, and struck before His crucifixion (Matthew 26:67; 27:26–30; Mark 14:65; John 19:1–3). The Servant submitted to this humiliation not out of a lack of power to resist, but out of obedience to God's mission.

For Christians, Isaiah 50:6 illustrates the depth of Christ's endurance, the reality of His humiliation, and the obedience that ultimately led Him to the cross. He endured shame and pain so that we might be restored and honored in God's presence.

Scripture Reference

Isaiah 50:6 (NIV)   I offered my back to those who beat me, my cheeks to those who pulled out my beard; I did not hide my face from mocking and spitting.

Big Picture Insights

- **Servant's obedience** – willingly submits to suffering.
- **Physical abuse** – beaten, beard pulled, mocked, spat upon.
- **Fulfilled in Christ** – passion narratives echo these details.
- **Humiliation** – shame was as real as the pain.
- **Willing sacrifice** – not forced, but freely given.
- **Contrast** – the Servant's dignity vs. human cruelty.
- **Messianic identity** – early Christians saw this fulfilled in Jesus.
- **The cross pathway** – suffering precedes vindication.
- **Pastoral comfort** – Christ identifies with those humiliated or shamed.
- **Pattern for disciples** – endurance in suffering for God's sake.

Verse Commentary

Isaiah 50:6a – "I offered my back to those who beat me…"

- The phrase "I offered" highlights the Servant's voluntary submission. He was not overpowered or caught by surprise but willingly gave Himself to suffering, fulfilling God's purpose. This reveals obedience, courage, and determination to accomplish redemption through pain.
- The prophecy finds fulfillment in Jesus' scourging by Roman soldiers before His crucifixion (John 19:1). The lashes tore His flesh, a brutal punishment meant for criminals. Yet Christ bore it willingly, embodying the suffering Servant foretold by Isaiah.
- This submission shows not helplessness but trust in God's plan. By offering His back, Christ exemplified perfect obedience. His silence and endurance teach believers that suffering can serve a redemptive purpose when surrendered to God's will.

Isaiah 50:6b – "…my cheeks to those who pulled out my beard…"

- In the ancient Near East, striking or tearing a beard symbolized deep insult and humiliation. This act degraded a man publicly, attacking his dignity. The Servant endured such dishonor, bearing shame as part of His mission.
- Christ's willingness to suffer this humiliation underscores His identification with human shame. He did not shield Himself but absorbed the indignity, showing that He came not only to bear sin but also to bear reproach on behalf of His people.
- By enduring this insult, Jesus fulfilled the image of the despised Servant. His humiliation reveals the world's rejection of God's chosen One and foreshadows how true obedience often encounters ridicule and dishonor.

Isaiah 50:6c – "…I did not hide my face from mocking and spitting."

- The Gospels confirm this prophecy, recording that Jesus was spit upon, mocked, and struck during His trial (Matthew 26:67; Mark 14:65). These acts conveyed contempt, treating Him as worthless and stripped of honor.
- The Servant does not retaliate or shrink back but faces the humiliation with resolve. This reveals the depth of His commitment to the Father's mission, enduring ridicule without vengeance in order to accomplish salvation for the world.
- Such scenes reveal the costliness of redemption. Christ bore not only physical pain but also emotional and social shame. He became the target of human scorn so that those who trust Him might be freed from everlasting shame.

Discussion Questions

1. Why does the Servant willingly offer Himself to suffering and shame?

2. How do the details of this verse point to Jesus' passion?

3. What is the significance of the phrase "I offered"?

4. How does Christ's endurance of humiliation comfort those who suffer shame today?

5. What does this verse reveal about the obedience of Christ?

6. How does it challenge us to endure trials faithfully?

7. Why is it important that Jesus' suffering was both physical and humiliating?

Narrative Reflection

Isaiah 50:6 presents a striking prophecy of the Messiah's humiliation and suffering, forming part of the third of Isaiah's Servant Songs. These passages detail the mission, obedience, and sacrifice of the Servant of the Lord. In this song, the Servant is depicted not as a helpless victim, but as one who willingly submits to suffering. Each phrase emphasizes His voluntary acceptance; He does not resist, retaliate, or shy away. Instead, He offers His back, cheeks, and face to abuse and shame.

This element of choice is crucial. The Servant does not inadvertently stumble into suffering; instead, He embraces it as integral to His mission of redemption. He remains obedient to the Father's plan, confident that vindication will come from God. This prophetic image is fulfilled in Jesus Christ, who accepted suffering as the pathway to salvation for His people.

The opening phrase highlights this choice: "I offered my back." The Servant is not unexpectedly seized or overpowered; He intentionally submits Himself to be struck. This willingness is most clearly exemplified in Jesus. On the night of His arrest, when Peter drew his sword to defend Him, Jesus instructed him to put it away, reminding him that He could summon over twelve legions of angels. Yet, He chose not to escape but yielded.

This prophecy was realized when Jesus was flogged at Pilate's command. Roman flogging was infamous for its brutality, with whips made of leather straps embedded with bone or metal that could tear through flesh, often leaving victims near death before crucifixion. John's Gospel records this event simply: "Then Pilate took Jesus and had him flogged." Isaiah had foretold this centuries prior. Christ's submission was not an act of weakness but of obedience; He offered His back because He was committed to the Father's redemptive purpose. His pain was real but endured purposefully, to bear the judgment of sin and accomplish salvation.

The prophecy deepens with the phrase: "my cheeks to those who pulled out my beard." In ancient Near Eastern culture, a man's beard symbolized dignity and honor. Striking or pulling it out was not merely a physical assault but a calculated act of public humiliation. Isaiah reveals that the Servant accepted this indignity willingly. Although the Gospels do not specifically mention His beard being pulled, they describe acts of equal significance: striking, mocking, spitting, and slapping. These actions represented not only physical abuse but also a symbolic rejection of His identity and mission.

This detail illustrates that the Servant's suffering extended beyond physical pain to profound humiliation. He endured contempt and insult, experiencing suffering of heart and mind as well as body. Christ, the eternal Son of God, allowed Himself to be treated as worthless, fully entering the human experience of shame and dishonor.

The prophecy concludes with, "I did not hide my face from mocking and spitting." In the ancient world, spitting in someone's face was the ultimate sign of disdain. To be mocked and spat upon was to face public shame. The Gospels vividly record this fulfillment. Matthew recounts soldiers spitting in Jesus' face, striking Him, and mocking Him as a false prophet. Later, Roman soldiers crowned Him with thorns, dressed Him in a scarlet robe, bowed in mock homage, and spat on Him again. Throughout, Jesus did not turn away; He faced humiliation head-on, choosing to endure disgrace rather than shield Himself.

This passage highlights Christ's obedience. His suffering was not due to powerlessness but to perfect submission. Paul echoes this truth in Philippians, stating that Christ humbled Himself by becoming obedient to death, even death on a cross. His willingness to endure shame reflects His total surrender to the Father's will.

Isaiah's prophecy also emphasizes the depth of Christ's identification with humanity. He endured not only physical suffering but also the anguish of disgrace. Many believers throughout history have faced ridicule, mockery, and humiliation for their faith. Isaiah 50:6 reassures us that Christ has gone before us, understanding the sting of insults, the pain of injustice, and the anguish of rejection. The letter to the Hebrews encourages us to fix our eyes on Jesus, who endured the cross, disregarding its shame, and now reigns at God's right hand.

157

The paradox of the cross is evident here: humiliation leads to exaltation, suffering brings salvation, and disgrace transforms into glory. What appeared as defeat in the eyes of the world was, in God's plan, the means of victory. The Servant's humiliation became the pathway to redemption.

For the early church, Isaiah 50:6 confirmed that Jesus' passion fulfilled prophecy. The flogging, mocking, and spitting were not random acts of cruelty but foretold elements woven into God's redemptive plan. Peter reflected on this when he wrote that when insults were hurled at Christ, He did not retaliate; when He suffered, He made no threats, but entrusted Himself to the One who judges justly.

For us today, this passage serves as both comfort and challenge. It comforts us by affirming that Christ identifies with our pain. If you have ever faced mockery, shame, or contempt, you are not alone. Jesus endured the same—and more—to redeem you from everlasting shame. It challenges us as His example compels us to endure. The Servant did not retaliate or hide His face but entrusted Himself to God. Likewise, we are called to bear reproach for His sake, enduring mistreatment without bitterness, trusting that God will vindicate us.

The church today often encounters ridicule or marginalization. Isaiah 50:6 reminds us that this is part of the Servant's journey. Yet, it assures us that humiliation is not the end; vindication and glory await, just as Christ was raised and exalted after His suffering.

For us, this prophecy is more than a historical account; it is a living testimony of God's plan. It reassures us that Christ understands our sorrows, comforts us in our shame, and challenges us to walk in faithful obedience. His humiliation secured our salvation, and His endurance serves as our example.

In Christ, the words of Isaiah 50:6 are not only fulfilled but transformed into a call: to follow the Servant who suffered for us, to endure with the confidence that glory follows shame, life follows death, and vindication follows suffering.

Layers of Understanding

Historical Context

Isaiah's Servant Song highlights the obedience of God's chosen Servant even in the face of suffering, humiliation, and rejection. In contrast to Israel's repeated failures, the Servant remains faithful. This prophecy prepared God's people to expect a deliverer who would accomplish redemption not through power, but through suffering.

Jewish Understanding

Jewish interpreters often understood this Servant Song as describing Israel itself, enduring suffering in exile, or as the righteous sufferer who remains faithful despite persecution. Christians, however, recognize its fullest meaning in the Messiah, whose life and death uniquely embody voluntary obedience, humiliation, and ultimate vindication by God.

New Testament Fulfillment

The Gospels record Jesus being mocked, spat upon, struck, and scourged before His crucifixion (Matthew 26:67; 27:26–30; Mark 14:65; John 19:1–3). These accounts directly fulfill Isaiah's prophecy, showing Christ's willing obedience. His silence and submission reveal that He accepted suffering not as defeat, but as God's ordained path to salvation.

Theological Significance Today

Isaiah 50:6 reveals Christ's willing obedience and His endurance of humiliation for our redemption. He identifies with our pain, proving that He understands the sting of rejection and scorn. Believers are called to endure suffering faithfully, following His example, and to trust that God will vindicate His people in the end.

Cross-Reference Connections

- **Matthew 26:67–68** – Jesus mocked, struck, and spat upon.
- **Matthew 27:26–30** – Jesus scourged, mocked, and crowned with thorns.
- **Mark 14:65** – Guards spit on and beat Him.
- **John 19:1–3** – Roman soldiers flog, mock, and strike Him.
- **Philippians 2:8** – Christ humbled Himself to obedience, even to death.
- **Hebrews 12:2–3** – Jesus endured shame, setting an example for believers.

PROPHECY FULFILLED - STUDY LESSON - 28

LESSON SCRIPTURE: **PSALM 22:1-21**

PROPHECY TITLE

Forsaken and Pierced: The Suffering Messiah

Introduction

Psalm 22 is a psalm of David, yet its language extends beyond his personal experience. It opens with a cry of abandonment and unfolds with vivid descriptions of humiliation, mockery, and physical torment. Phrases such as "They pierce my hands and my feet" *and* "They divide my clothes among them and cast lots for my garment" find direct fulfillment in the crucifixion of Jesus.

Jesus quoted the opening line while on the cross: "My God, my God, why have you forsaken me?" (Matthew 27:46). The Gospels also document the fulfillment of the casting of lots (John 19:24) and the mocking by onlookers (Matthew 27:39–43). Psalm 22 serves as a prophetic lens for viewing the crucifixion, demonstrating that Christ's suffering was foreseen by God and embraced by the Messiah.

For believers, this psalm assures us that the cross was not a random tragedy but part of a divine plan. Christ was forsaken so that we might be accepted; He was pierced so that we might be healed.

Scripture Reference

Psalm 22:1–21 (NIV "My God, my God, why have you forsaken me? Why are you so far from saving me, so far from my cries of anguish? [2] My God, I cry out by day, but you do not answer, by night, but I find no rest. [3] Yet you are enthroned as the Holy One; you are the one Israel praises. [4] In you our ancestors put their trust; they trusted and you delivered them. [5] To you they cried out and were saved; in you they trusted and were not put to shame. [6] But I am a worm and not a man, scorned by everyone, despised by the people. [7] All who see me mock me; they hurl insults, shaking their heads. [8] "He trusts in the LORD," they say, "let the LORD rescue him. Let him deliver him, since he delights in him." [9] Yet you brought me out of the womb; you made me trust in you, even at my mother's breast. [10] From birth I was cast on you; from my mother's womb you have been my God. [11] Do not be far from me, for trouble is near and there is no one to help. [12] Many bulls surround me; strong bulls of Bashan encircle me. [13] Roaring lions that tear their prey open their mouths wide against me. [14] I am poured out like water, and all my bones are out f joint. My heart has turned to wax; it has melted within me. [15] My mouth is dried up like a potsherd, and my tongue sticks to the roof of my mouth; you lay me in the dust of death. [16] Dogs surround me, a pack of villains encircles me; they pierce g my hands and my feet. [17] All my bones are on display; people stare and gloat over me. [18] They divide my clothes among them and cast lots for my garment. [19] But

you, L<small>ORD</small>, do not be far from me. You are my strength; come quickly to help me. ²⁰ Deliver me from the sword, my precious life from the power of the dogs. ²¹ Rescue me from the mouth of the lions; save me from the horns of the wild oxen."

Big Picture Insights

- **Cry of abandonment** – words spoken by Jesus on the cross.
- **Mockery fulfilled** – bystanders jeered at Jesus as He hung on the cross.
- **Pierced hands and feet** – prophecy of crucifixion.
- **Casting lots** – fulfilled in soldiers dividing Jesus' garments.
- **Messianic suffering** – foreshadows the passion in vivid detail.
- **Davidic lament → messianic prophecy** – David's suffering points forward to Christ.
- **Theology of the cross** – Christ bears both physical and spiritual agony.
- **God's plan** – not accident, but fulfillment of Scripture.
- **Pastoral assurance** – Christ knows the depths of human suffering.
- **Hope emerges** – suffering leads to deliverance and future praise (rest of Psalm).

Verse Commentary

Psalm 22:1–2 – "My God, my God, why have you forsaken me? Why are you so far from saving me, so far from my cries of anguish? ² My God, I cry out by day, but you do not answer, by night, but I find no rest."

- David cries out in anguish, expressing abandonment and unanswered prayer. His lament sets the tone of suffering yet maintains faith by addressing God as "my God." Jesus echoes this on the cross, uniting David's experience with His own.
- The sense of forsakenness reflects the depth of human suffering under sin's curse. On the cross, Christ bore this ultimate alienation, entering into humanity's despair so that reconciliation with God could be accomplished through His sacrifice.

Psalm 22:3–5 – "Yet you are enthroned as the Holy One; you are the one Israel praises. ⁴ In you our ancestors put their trust; they trusted and you delivered them. ⁵ To you they cried out and were saved; in you they trusted and were not put to shame."

- Despite feeling forsaken, David recalls God's holiness and His faithfulness to Israel's ancestors. This shift models how lament should turn toward trust, even when circumstances seem hopeless.
- Christ fulfills this by trusting the Father throughout His suffering. Even while experiencing abandonment, He rested on God's character and plan, embodying perfect obedience where humanity so often wavers.

Psalm 22:6–8 – "But I am a worm and not a man, scorned by everyone, despised by the people. ⁷ All who see me mock me; they hurl insults, shaking their heads. ⁸ "He trusts in the L<small>ORD</small>," they say, "let the L<small>ORD</small> rescue him. Let him deliver him, since he delights in him."

- David describes scorn and ridicule, treated as less than human. The imagery of mockery points forward to Christ's trial, where He was ridiculed, beaten, and called false names.

- Verse 8 is quoted directly at the crucifixion: "He trusts in the Lord, let the Lord rescue him." The taunts hurled at Jesus fulfill this prophecy, showing rejection from both leaders and bystanders.

Psalm 22:9–11 – "Yet you brought me out of the womb; you made me trust in you, even at my mother's breast. ¹⁰ From birth I was cast on you; from my mother's womb you have been my God. ¹¹ Do not be far from me, for trouble is near and there is no one to help."

- David appeals to God's lifelong care, remembering His providence from birth. This reflects covenant faithfulness: God has been near from the beginning, so David asks Him not to abandon him now.
- For Christ, this echoes His unique relationship with the Father. From His incarnation, He was set apart for the mission of redemption. Yet on the cross He bore the mystery of separation, fulfilling God's plan for salvation.

Psalm 22:12–15 – "Many bulls surround me; strong bulls of Bashan encircle me. ¹³ Roaring lions that tear their prey open their mouths wide against me. ¹⁴ I am poured out like water, and all my bones are out f joint. My heart has turned to wax; it has melted within me. ¹⁵ My mouth is dried up like a potsherd, and my tongue sticks to the roof of my mouth; you lay me in the dust of death."

- The imagery of strong bulls, lions, and dogs conveys the overwhelming power of enemies. David feels encircled, helpless, and near death. This points to Christ's arrest, trial, and crucifixion, surrounded by hostile forces.
- Verses 14–15 describe physical collapse—poured out like water, bones out of joint, tongue parched. These details foreshadow the physical realities of crucifixion, fulfilled when Jesus thirsted on the cross and His body hung in agony.

Psalm 22:16–18 – "Dogs surround me, a pack of villains encircles me; they pierce ^g my hands and my feet. ¹⁷ All my bones are on display; people stare and gloat over me. ¹⁸ They divide my clothes among them and cast lots for my garment."

- The piercing of hands and feet aligns unmistakably with crucifixion, a method unknown in David's time but fulfilled in Christ's death. This detail shows the prophetic precision of the psalm.
- Verse 18 is fulfilled when soldiers cast lots for Jesus' clothing (Matthew 27:35; John 19:23–24). What seemed like cruelty and chance was in fact foretold by Scripture, demonstrating God's sovereign plan.

Psalm 22:19–21 – "But you, LORD, do not be far from me. You are my strength; come quickly to help me. ²⁰ Deliver me from the sword, my precious life from the power of the dogs. ²¹ Rescue me from the mouth of the lions; save me from the horns of the wild oxen."

- The psalm shifts from lament to urgent prayer for deliverance. David's cry anticipates God's intervention, even when death seems near. This turning point foreshadows resurrection hope.
- For Christ, the petition culminates in His ultimate vindication. Though He was struck down, God answered Him by raising Him from the dead, transforming the cry of anguish into triumph and eternal salvation for all who believe.

Discussion Questions

1. Why is it significant that Jesus quotes Psalm 22:1 from the cross?

2. How do the details of this psalm confirm the crucifixion was foreseen by God?

3. What does it mean that Christ was "forsaken" for our sake?

4. How does this psalm connect David's suffering with Christ's?

5. In what ways does Psalm 22 deepen our understanding of the cross?

6. How can this passage comfort us in times of suffering and abandonment?

7. How does God's faithfulness in fulfilling prophecy strengthen our faith?

Narrative Reflection

Psalm 22 is a prophetic description of the crucifixion found in the Old Testament. Written by David nearly a thousand years before Christ, its imagery aligns closely with the events of Good Friday, leading the early church to recognize it as a direct prophecy of the passion. Rather than being a random lament, this psalm serves as a Spirit-inspired foreshadowing of the Messiah's suffering, humiliation, and ultimate vindication. When read alongside the Gospel accounts, the connections become so precise that it is evident this psalm serves as a window into the cross, long before crucifixion was even practiced.

The psalm begins with one of the most haunting cries in Scripture: "My God, my God, why have you forsaken me?" David's words encapsulate the anguish of feeling abandoned, unheard, and enveloped in despair. Centuries later, Jesus echoed these very words while hanging on the cross (Matthew 27:46). His cry expresses not only the pain of physical suffering but also the profound spiritual weight of sin. By bearing the sins of the world, He experienced the full alienation that sin creates between God and humanity. This does not imply that the Father abandoned the Son in essence—since the Trinity cannot be divided—but rather that Jesus endured the forsakenness of sin's judgment. He entered the depths of human despair so that we might never be forsaken. His cry was not one of unbelief, but of faith expressed in lament, clinging to "my God" even in His darkest hour.

The psalm swiftly transitions from the cry of forsakenness to a remembrance of God's past faithfulness: "In you our ancestors put their trust; they trusted and you delivered them." David reflects on God's faithfulness to His people throughout history, yet he feels as though deliverance is absent in his present plight. Likewise, Jesus recalled God's faithfulness as He bore the weight of suffering. His cry on the cross was set against the backdrop of God's covenant promises. This tension—between despair and trust—lies at the heart of Psalm 22, beautifully encapsulating the mystery of the cross: grief and faith existing together in a single moment.

From verse 6 onward, the psalm vividly depicts humiliation and ridicule: "But I am a worm and not a man, scorned by everyone, despised by the people. All who see me mock me; they hurl insults, shaking their heads." The imagery extends beyond David's own experience to the mockery that Christ faced during His trial and crucifixion. Matthew's Gospel recounts that passersby and religious leaders derided Him, saying, "He saved others, but He can't save Himself!" (Matthew 27:42). Verse 8's taunt—"He trusts in the Lord; let the Lord rescue him"—echoes almost verbatim in their insults, leaving no doubt that the psalm anticipated the events at Calvary. The Servant of the Lord endured not only pain but also the bitter sting of ridicule and rejection.

The psalm then shifts tone: "Yet you brought me out of the womb; you made me trust in you, even at my mother's breast." Here, David recalls God's intimate involvement from birth, affirming divine providence amid despair. For Christ, this reality was paramount. From His incarnation, He was dedicated to the mission of salvation. Even in Gethsemane, as He prayed for the cup to pass, He entrusted Himself entirely to the Father's will. The intimacy between Father and Son is evident—God's hand has been present from the beginning, even as the Son bore the agony of apparent abandonment.

In verses 12–15, the psalm employs imagery of overwhelming danger and physical collapse: "Many bulls surround me; strong bulls of Bashan encircle me. Roaring lions tear their prey, open their mouths wide against me." David feels besieged by enemies, as if devouring beasts are ready to consume him. For Christ, this imagery was fulfilled in the hostile crowds, the mocking soldiers, and the religious leaders conspiring for His death. The intensity of the description continues: "I am poured out like water, and all my bones are out of joint. My heart has turned to wax; it has melted within me." This foreshadows the very physical realities of crucifixion. Hanging by nails caused dislocated joints, dehydration parched His tongue, and the strain of asphyxiation weakened His heart. John records Jesus crying out, "I thirst" (John 19:28), fulfilling the agony described here.

Verse 16 introduces perhaps the most striking detail: "They pierce my hands and my feet." Although crucifixion was unknown in David's time, the Spirit inspired him to describe it with startling clarity. Jesus' hands and feet were nailed to the cross, providing a literal fulfillment of this ancient prophecy. This detail alone confirms the prophetic nature of Psalm 22, and the psalm continues with even more specificity. Verse 18 states, "They divide my clothes among them and cast lots for my garment." The Gospels record this with precision: the soldiers divided Jesus' garments but cast lots for His seamless tunic (John 19:23–24). What seemed like a minor, random act was foretold centuries earlier, demonstrating God's sovereignty over even the smallest details of Christ's passion.

The closing verses of this section (19–21) shift toward prayer: "But you, Lord, do not be far from me. You are my strength; come quickly to help me." Despite being surrounded by enemies, David cries out for God's nearness. This anticipates the resurrection hope embedded within the psalm. For Christ, the Father's answer did not come in deliverance from death but through resurrection after death. "Rescue me from the mouth of the lions" becomes a plea that God answered on Easter morning, vindicating the Suffering Servant and transforming His cry of abandonment into triumph.

Psalm 22:1–21 reveals the full scope of Christ's suffering: the anguish of forsakenness, the humiliation of ridicule, the agony of crucifixion, and the shame of being stripped and despised. Yet, this was not random cruelty; it was the fulfillment of God's redemptive plan. The Servant bore the penalty of sin, willingly submitting to judgment so that sinners might be saved. The psalm demonstrates that the cross was no accident of history but was written into the story of salvation from the beginning.

For believers, this psalm offers both comfort and challenge. It comforts us by reminding us that Christ has entered into our deepest suffering. When we feel abandoned, mocked, or crushed, we know He has walked that path before us. Hebrews 4:15 assures us that we have a high priest who sympathizes with our weaknesses, having endured them Himself. It challenges us to endure reproach and suffering for His sake, trusting that God will vindicate us just as He vindicated His Son.

Although Psalm 22:1–21 focuses on lament, it does not end there. Beginning in verse 22, the tone shifts dramatically to praise, hope, and worldwide proclamation. This mirrors the arc of the gospel itself— despair giving way to triumph, the cross leading to resurrection, death yielding to life. The suffering Servant of verses 1–21 transforms into the risen King of verses 22–31. In Christ, this movement finds its ultimate fulfillment: the one who was forsaken is now enthroned, and those who mocked Him are called to worship.

Thus, Psalm 22 is more than a lament; it is a prophecy of redemption. It reveals a Messiah who was forsaken, mocked, pierced, and stripped, yet steadfast in His obedience. His cry of dereliction anchors His suffering in Scripture, assuring us that all of it was according to God's plan. For us, it is both a sobering reminder of the cost of our redemption and a comforting assurance that Christ has entered into our suffering to bring us salvation. The cross fulfills the lament, and the resurrection fulfills the hope.

Layers of Understanding

Historical Context

David's psalm reflects deep personal anguish in the face of rejection, humiliation, and mortal danger. His cry of forsakenness arises from real suffering yet transcends his own experience. By divine inspiration, his lament foreshadows the Messiah's ultimate suffering, providing a prophetic foundation for understanding Christ's passion and crucifixion.

Jewish Understanding

Traditionally interpreted as the prayer of the righteous sufferer, this psalm gave voice to the faithful who endured persecution and mockery while clinging to God. Over time, its vivid imagery was increasingly associated with messianic expectation, anticipating a figure who would bear suffering on behalf of the people and secure deliverance.

New Testament Fulfillment

The psalm finds direct fulfillment in Jesus' crucifixion: His cry of forsakenness (Matthew 27:46), the mocking of bystanders (Matthew 27:39–43), the piercing of His hands and feet (John 20:25–27), and the soldiers casting lots for His garments (John 19:24). These details confirm God's sovereign orchestration of prophecy and redemption.

Theological Significance Today

Psalm 22:1–21 reveals the depth of Christ's suffering on behalf of sinners, assuring believers that He truly understands our pain. It offers comfort in trials, demonstrating that suffering has meaning within God's plan and always points toward vindication, hope, and ultimate resurrection through Jesus Christ's saving work.

Cross-Reference Connections

- **Matthew 27:46** – Jesus quotes Psalm 22:1 on the cross.
- **Matthew 27:39–43** – Mocking fulfills Psalm 22:7.
- **John 19:23–24** – Casting lots for garments fulfills Psalm 22:18.
- **John 20:25–27** – Pierced hands and feet.
- **Hebrews 4:15** – Christ sympathizes with our weaknesses.
- **Philippians 2:8** – Obedient to death on a cross.

PROPHECY FULFILLED - STUDY LESSON - 29

LESSON SCRIPTURE: **ISAIAH 53:4-6**

PROPHECY TITLE

Wounded for Our Transgressions

Introduction

Isaiah 53 stands out as one of the most profound prophecies regarding the Messiah's suffering and atoning work. Verses 4–6 serve as the focal point of the passage, transitioning from the Servant's rejection to the deeper theological significance of His suffering.

In these verses, Isaiah emphasizes that the Servant's pain is not due to His own actions, but rather ours: "Surely he took up our pain and bore our suffering … he was pierced for our transgressions … the Lord has laid on him the iniquity of us all." This clearly illustrates the concept of substitution—Christ endures our punishment, allowing us to attain peace and healing.

The New Testament frequently references this passage to elucidate the meaning of the cross (Matthew 8:17; 1 Peter 2:24–25). It encapsulates the essence of the gospel: Jesus carried our sin, judgment, and curse, granting us forgiveness and restoration.

Scripture Reference

Isaiah 53:4–6 (NIV) Surely he took up our pain and bore our suffering, yet we considered him punished by God, stricken by him, and afflicted. ⁵ But he was pierced for our transgressions, he was crushed for our iniquities; the punishment that brought us peace was on him, and by his wounds we are healed. ⁶ We all, like sheep, have gone astray, each of us has turned to our own way; and the LORD has laid on him the iniquity of us all.

Big Picture Insights

- **Substitution** – the Servant suffers in our place.
- **Human misunderstanding** – people thought He was punished by God for His own sin.
- **Pierced and crushed** – vivid images fulfilled in Christ's crucifixion.
- **Peace and healing** – benefits of His atoning work.
- **Universal need** – all have gone astray like sheep.
- **Divine initiative** – God lays our sin on Him.
- **Core of the gospel** – penal substitution in prophecy.
- **NT fulfillment** – cited in Matthew 8:17, 1 Peter 2:24–25.
- **Pastoral comfort** – our guilt transferred, our healing secured.
- **Christ-centered focus** – no salvation apart from His atonement.

Verse Commentary

Isaiah 53:4 – "Surely he took up our pain and bore our suffering, yet we considered him punished by God, stricken by him, and afflicted."

- The Servant does not carry His own griefs but enters fully into ours, taking upon Himself the pain, sorrow, and brokenness of humanity so that He might redeem and restore us through His suffering.
- Matthew 8:17 identifies this prophecy with Christ's ministry of healing, showing that His work extended beyond physical miracles to the ultimate bearing of our sin, sickness, and spiritual need on the cross.
- Humanity misjudged Him as one cursed and rejected by God, when in truth He suffered not for His own sins but for ours, willingly accepting affliction to accomplish God's redemptive plan.

Isaiah 53:5 – "But he was pierced for our transgressions, he was crushed for our iniquities; the punishment that brought us peace was on him, and by his wounds we are healed."

- "Pierced" points directly to Christ's crucifixion—His hands and feet nailed, His side pierced with a spear—suffering not randomly but intentionally as a substitution for human sin, bearing the punishment we deserved.
- The word "crushed" emphasizes the severity of sin's burden laid upon Him. The Servant endured not only physical torment but the crushing weight of divine judgment against human rebellion.
- Punishment fell on Him so that peace might be ours. His suffering reconciles us to God, bridging the gap caused by sin and restoring fellowship through His blood.
- His wounds bring both spiritual healing and a foretaste of ultimate wholeness. Though physical healing may not be immediate, His suffering secures forgiveness now and complete restoration in the new creation.

Isaiah 53:6 – "We all, like sheep, have gone astray, each of us has turned to our own way; and the LORD has laid on him the iniquity of us all."

- This verse confesses the universality of sin: all humanity is guilty, wandering from God's path. None are exempt; each has turned aside in rebellion and selfishness.
- The sheep imagery conveys helplessness, vulnerability, and lostness apart from the Shepherd. Humanity cannot save itself but desperately needs God's intervention through His appointed Servant.
- God Himself places our iniquity on the Servant, revealing the doctrine of substitutionary atonement. He bore what we could not, suffering in our place to reconcile us to God.
- The New Testament affirms this fulfillment in Christ. Peter applies it directly in 1 Peter 2:24–25, declaring that Jesus bore our sins on the cross, bringing us back to the Shepherd of our souls.

Discussion Questions

1. How do these verses describe the meaning of Christ's suffering?

2. Why did people misunderstand the Servant's suffering as God's judgment on Him?

3. What does it mean that He was pierced for our transgressions?

4. How do we experience the "peace" and "healing" His suffering secured?

5. What does the imagery of sheep teach us about our need for a Savior?

6. How does this prophecy deepen your understanding of the cross?

7. In what ways does this passage give comfort when we feel guilty or burdened?

Narrative Reflection

Isaiah 53:4–6 lies at the core of the Servant Song, presenting one of the clearest expressions of the gospel in the Old Testament. In these verses, the prophet not only describes the Servant's sufferings but also clarifies their purpose and the people for whom He suffered. His pain was not random, accidental, or merely the outcome of injustice; it was intentional and substitutionary. He bore the weight of human sin and suffering so that His people might be healed, restored, and reconciled to God.

The opening line asserts, "Surely he took up our pain and bore our suffering." The Servant is depicted as taking on the burdens of others rather than carrying His own grief. He willingly shoulders the anguish, sickness, and sin that belong to humanity. This act is not distant or merely symbolic; the Servant fully enters into human brokenness. His suffering is real and shared in solidarity with the people of God.

This prophecy finds partial fulfillment in Jesus' ministry, long before the crucifixion. Matthew 8:16–17 tells us that Jesus healed the sick and cast out demons, fulfilling Isaiah's words: "He took up our infirmities and bore our diseases." Each act of healing and compassion was a sign of His mission to carry humanity's burdens. However, the ultimate fulfillment occurred not in the villages of Galilee but on the hill of Golgotha, where Jesus bore the ultimate burden: the guilt and penalty of sin.

Yet, the world misunderstood this truth. Isaiah notes, "yet we considered him punished by God, stricken by him, and afflicted." To human perception, the Servant's suffering appeared as divine judgment. During the crucifixion, bystanders mocked Jesus, assuming His agony proved He was cursed. Deuteronomy 21:23 states that anyone hung on a tree is under God's curse. The religious leaders and Roman authorities believed His death confirmed His falsehood, but their judgment was tragically flawed. He was not cursed for His own sins but for ours. Paul clarifies this in Galatians 3:13: "Christ redeemed us from the curse of the law by becoming a curse for us." Humanity misinterpreted the cross, yet the truth remains: God's Servant bore judgment on behalf of His people.

Verse 5 transitions from misunderstanding to revelation: "But he was pierced for our transgressions, he was crushed for our iniquities." Here, the substitutionary nature of the Servant's suffering becomes unmistakable. He endured not vague suffering but specific punishment. He was pierced through His hands, feet, and side when nailed to the cross and later pierced by a Roman spear. The term "crushed" conveys the immense weight of guilt and judgment He bore. This suffering was not merely physical but included the crushing burden of divine wrath against sin, with the punishment that rightfully belonged to us transferred to Him.

The outcome of this exchange is described as one of peace and healing: "the punishment that brought us peace was on him, and by his wounds we are healed." The Servant's suffering is not only substitutionary but also transformative. What He endured brought peace with God to those who believe. Paul echoes this in Romans 5:1: "Therefore, since we have been justified through faith, we have peace with God through our Lord Jesus Christ." Believers are no longer alienated, estranged, or under wrath; they are reconciled to their Creator. By His wounds—not in spite of them but through them—we are healed. This healing encompasses not only the physical but also the spiritual and relational; we are restored to life, forgiven, and made whole in God's presence.

Verse 6 broadens the scope of salvation: "We all, like sheep, have gone astray; each of us has turned to our own way." This confession is comprehensive and inclusive. No one is exempt; all humanity shares in the guilt of sin. The sheep metaphor illustrates helplessness and waywardness. Sheep cannot find their way back on their own; they wander until rescued by a shepherd. Humanity is lost, each person following selfish desires and straying from God's path.

However, the verse does not conclude with despair. "And the LORD has laid on him the iniquity of us all." This encapsulates the essence of substitutionary atonement. God Himself places the full weight of sin upon the Servant. The guilt of many rests on the One. Jesus bore what we could not bear and endured what we could not endure. He carried our iniquity to the cross, making atonement once for all. Peter cites this directly in 1 Peter 2:24–25: "He himself bore our sins in his body on the cross... 'For you were like sheep going astray,' but now you have returned to the Shepherd and Overseer of your souls."

These verses are foundational to Christian theology. The doctrine of substitutionary atonement—Christ dying in our place, bearing the penalty of sin—is firmly rooted in Isaiah 53:4–6. The sacrificial system of Israel foreshadowed this truth, where animals bore guilt symbolically in temple rituals. Isaiah points to the true fulfillment in the Messiah, who would bear the sins of the world once for all. The cross was not an accident of history but the culmination of God's eternal plan.

For believers, these verses provide profound assurance. Our sins are real, and our guilt undeniable, but the Servant has borne them. He was pierced for our transgressions and crushed for our iniquities. His punishment has secured our peace, and His wounds have brought our healing. This truth comforts the guilty conscience, assuring us that forgiveness is secure in Christ. It strengthens the weary soul, reminding us that reconciliation with God has been accomplished.

These verses also highlight the paradox of the cross. To human eyes, the crucifixion appeared as a shameful defeat. Yet, in God's eyes, it was the triumph of love. What seemed like weakness was power; what looked like judgment was salvation; what appeared to be the end of hope was the beginning of eternal life. The Servant's humiliation paved the way for exaltation, and His wounds became the source of our healing.

Moreover, Isaiah 53:4–6 calls us to humility. "We all, like sheep, have gone astray." The universality of sin levels all human pride. None can claim righteousness independently. Every person, regardless of status or culture, needs the Shepherd who bore our iniquity. This shared confession invites all to receive His gift. There is no sin too great, no guilt too heavy, that has not been laid on Him.

Finally, these verses encourage us to imitate Christ. His willingness to bear pain for others serves as a model for His followers. While we cannot atone for sin, we are called to carry one another's burdens, enter into suffering with compassion, and live sacrificially in light of His example. The church is shaped by the cross, embodying its paradox of power through weakness and glory through suffering.

This passage serves as a prophetic lens into the cross of Christ. It reveals the Servant bearing pain, carrying guilt, and enduring punishment—not for Himself but for us. His suffering was substitutionary, His wounds redemptive, and His death reconciling. Through Him, we receive peace with God, healing of our souls, and the hope of restoration. This is the gospel foretold in prophecy, the heart of God's eternal plan, and the comfort of every believer.

Layers of Understanding

Historical Context

Isaiah's words were addressed to a people suffering in exile, burdened with the consequences of their rebellion. The Servant Song offered hope not through political deliverance but through a suffering figure who would carry their guilt and bear judgment. His obedience would bring redemption where human efforts had failed.

Jewish Understanding

Many in Jewish tradition interpreted this Servant as Israel itself, suffering unjustly among the nations yet chosen to reveal God's purposes. Others saw the Servant as a righteous remnant. Christians understand the prophecy as messianic, pointing to a single individual whose suffering would accomplish salvation for all.

New Testament Fulfillment

The New Testament applies these verses directly to Jesus Christ. Matthew 8:17 sees His healing ministry as fulfillment. Peter explains that He "bore our sins" on the cross (1 Peter 2:24–25). Paul adds that He became a curse for us (Galatians 3:13). The imagery of piercing and crushing finds literal realization in His crucifixion.

Theological Significance Today

This passage is the heart of the gospel. Christ bore our pain, carried our guilt, and endured punishment on our behalf. His wounds secured our peace and healing. Believers find assurance of forgiveness in His sacrifice and are called to live with humility and trust in the Shepherd who bore our iniquity.

Cross-Reference Connections

- **Matthew 8:17** – Christ bore our infirmities.
- **Romans 5:1** – Peace with God through Christ's sacrifice.
- **Galatians 3:13** – Christ became a curse for us.
- **1 Peter 2:24–25** – He bore our sins; we were straying sheep.
- **John 19:34** – Pierced side fulfills "pierced for our transgressions."
- **2 Corinthians 5:21** – He became sin for us so we might become righteous.

PROPHECY FULFILLED - STUDY LESSON - 30

LESSON SCRIPTURE: ISAIAH 53: 7-9

PROPHECY TITLE

Silent, Condemned, and Buried with the Rich

Introduction

Isaiah 53:7–9 portrays the humility and injustice of the Servant's suffering. He is oppressed and afflicted yet remains silent, like a lamb led to slaughter. He is cut off from the land of the living, dying for the sins of others. Though assigned a grave with the wicked, He is buried in the tomb of a rich man.

The New Testament reveals how these details are fulfilled in Jesus' passion. He remained silent before His accusers (Matthew 26:62–63; 27:12–14) and was unjustly condemned despite having committed no violence or spoken deceitfully. Although crucified between criminals, His body was laid in the tomb of Joseph of Arimathea, a wealthy disciple (Matthew 27:57–60).

These verses underscore both the injustice of Christ's death and the sovereignty of God in fulfilling prophecy. They demonstrate that even in death, the Servant willingly bore our sins and fulfilled God's redemptive plan.

Scripture Reference

Isaiah 53:7–9 (NIV)   He was oppressed and afflicted, yet he did not open his mouth; he was led like a lamb to the slaughter, and as a sheep before its shearers is silent, so he did not open his mouth. [8] By oppression and judgment he was taken away. Yet who of his generation protested? For he was cut off from the land of the living; for the transgression of my people he was punished. [9] He was assigned a grave with the wicked, and with the rich in his death, though he had done no violence, nor was any deceit in his mouth.

Big Picture Insights

- **Silent submission** – Servant does not resist but submits willingly.
- **Lamb imagery** – evokes Passover and sacrificial system.
- **Unjust trial** – oppression and false judgment.
- **Death for others** – punished for the people's transgressions.
- **Burial paradox** – condemned with criminals but buried with the rich.
- **Innocence affirmed** – no violence or deceit in Him.
- **New Testament fulfillment** – Jesus' silence, unjust condemnation, and burial in Joseph's tomb.
- **Redemptive significance** – suffering was voluntary and purposeful.
- **Christ as sacrificial Lamb** – fulfilled in John 1:29; Revelation 5:6.
- **Hope through injustice** – God works salvation through the darkest injustice.

Verse-by-Verse Commentary

Isaiah 53:7 – "He was oppressed and afflicted, yet he did not open his mouth; he was led like a lamb to the slaughter, and as a sheep before its shearers is silent, so he did not open his mouth."

- Jesus' silence before the Sanhedrin and Pilate (Matthew 26:62–63; 27:12–14) fulfills Isaiah's prophecy. Though falsely accused, He offered no defense, entrusting Himself to the Father's plan rather than seeking human vindication.
- His silence reveals submission and willingness, not weakness. Jesus chose the path of suffering deliberately, bearing injustice without retaliation. In His restraint, He demonstrated obedience to God's redemptive will, offering Himself as a willing sacrifice for humanity's sin.
- The imagery of the lamb underscores His role as the ultimate Passover sacrifice. Just as lambs were led silently to slaughter, Christ bore sin without protest, fulfilling John's declaration: "Behold, the Lamb of God, who takes away the sin of the world" (John 1:29).

Isaiah 53:8 – "By oppression and judgment he was taken away. Yet who of his generation protested? For he was cut off from the land of the living; for the transgression of my people he was punished."

- This verse highlights the miscarriage of justice. Jesus endured betrayal, false witnesses, and an unjust trial before religious and Roman authorities. Though innocent, He was condemned, illustrating the oppression that Isaiah foretold centuries earlier.
- "Cut off from the land of the living" points unmistakably to His death. Isaiah saw not only the trial but its outcome: the Servant removed by violent execution, severed from life though guiltless, fulfilling God's redemptive purpose.
- His death was substitutionary: "for the transgression of my people he was punished." Christ did not die for His own crimes but for the sins of humanity, bearing the penalty we deserved and accomplishing atonement through His suffering.

Isaiah 53:9 – "He was assigned a grave with the wicked, and with the rich in his death, though he had done no violence, nor was any deceit in his mouth."

- Executed between two criminals (Luke 23:32–33), Jesus was treated as a common criminal. His association with the wicked fulfilled Isaiah's prophecy, showing that He bore the shame of sinners though Himself without sin.
- Yet His burial defied expectation. Joseph of Arimathea, a wealthy disciple, placed Jesus in his new tomb (Matthew 27:57–60). This fulfilled Isaiah's paradox: condemned as wicked but honored in burial, proving God's hand guided every detail.
- The verse emphasizes His innocence: "no violence was in his mouth." Though accused of blasphemy and rebellion, He committed no sin. His spotless life contrasts with His condemned death, affirming Him as the righteous Servant who bore guilt not His own.

Discussion Questions

1. Why is the Servant's silence before His accusers important?

2. How does the lamb imagery connect to the sacrificial system and Christ's death?

3. What does verse 8 teach us about the injustice of Jesus' trial?

4. Why is it significant that He was "cut off" for the transgressions of others?

5. How does His burial in a rich man's tomb confirm God's sovereignty in prophecy?

6. What does this passage reveal about the innocence of Christ?

7. How does Christ's willing submission challenge our response to suffering?

Narrative Reflection

Isaiah 53:7–9 continues the profound depiction of the Messiah's suffering in the Servant Song, transitioning from His substitutionary wounds to His silent submission and unjust death. These verses deliver a prophetic portrait of Jesus' passion with remarkable clarity, describing not only the physical aspects of His trial and crucifixion but also their theological implications.

The passage begins: "He was oppressed and afflicted, yet he did not open his mouth." Here, silence is not a sign of weakness but an act of willing submission. The Servant does not argue, seek escape, or resist His oppressors; instead, He offers Himself.

This is vividly illustrated in Jesus' trial before the Sanhedrin. As false witnesses brought accusations, the high priest pressed Him for a defense, yet "Jesus remained silent" (Matthew 26:62–63). Before Pilate, when asked to respond to the charges, He gave no reply, astonishing the governor (Matthew 27:12–14). To human eyes, His silence appeared as helplessness, but Scripture reveals it as divine obedience. He was not overpowered; He willingly surrendered.

Isaiah deepens this imagery: "He was led like a lamb to the slaughter, and as a sheep before its shearers is silent, so he did not open his mouth." In Jewish memory, the lamb holds great significance. At Passover, each household sacrificed a lamb, its blood marking their deliverance from judgment (Exodus 12). The Servant is likened to that lamb—submissive, silent, and sacrificial. John the Baptist declared, "Behold, the Lamb of God, who takes away the sin of the world!" (John 1:29). Isaiah foresaw Christ as the ultimate Passover Lamb, with His silence emphasizing His role as the chosen sacrifice.

The Servant's silence also highlights the contrast between human instinct and divine purpose. Human instinct resists humiliation; Jesus embraced it. Human instinct defends innocence; Jesus set His aside. By His silence, He bore our guilt without protest, willingly walking to the cross.

The prophecy continues: "By oppression and judgment he was taken away." The Hebrew suggests a miscarriage of justice, an enforced removal under the pretense of legal process. Jesus was arrested at night, in secrecy, through betrayal. He was dragged before the Sanhedrin, where false witnesses contradicted one another. Jewish law prohibited trials at night and required consistent testimony, yet both were ignored. Later, He was handed to Pilate, condemned not for guilt but due to pressure from the crowd.

Isaiah emphasizes the lack of intervention: "Who of his generation protested?" His followers fled; Peter denied Him; the crowds demanded His crucifixion. Humanly speaking, He stood alone. Yet this isolation fulfilled prophecy. The Servant would be forsaken, left defenseless in the courts of men, to bear judgment in the court of God.

The verse adds: "He was cut off from the land of the living." This phrase signifies a violent death, pointing beyond humiliation to execution. Jesus was not merely shamed or imprisoned; He was killed. The Servant's destiny was death—not for His own crimes but for ours. Isaiah declares, "for the transgression of my people he was punished." This presents the doctrine of substitution with piercing clarity. He bore punishment not His own, suffering in the place of the guilty.

This truth resonates throughout the New Testament. Paul writes in 2 Corinthians 5:21, "God made him who had no sin to be sin for us, so that in him we might become the righteousness of God." Peter echoes, "He himself bore our sins in his body on the cross" (1 Peter 2:24). Isaiah foresaw this substitutionary atonement: the Servant punished so that the people might be forgiven.

The prophecy then presents a paradox: "He was assigned a grave with the wicked, and with the rich in his death." Typically, executed criminals were discarded, their bodies left unburied or thrown into common graves. Jesus, crucified between two criminals (Luke 23:32–33), appeared destined for such dishonor. Yet instead, He was buried in a new tomb owned by Joseph of Arimathea, a wealthy disciple (Matthew 27:57–60). Condemned as a criminal yet honored in burial—this paradox fulfills Isaiah's words with exactness.

Every detail attests to God's sovereignty. Jesus' death was no accident or tragic twist of fate. Even the location of His burial was prophesied. What men intended for shame, God transformed into honor, ensuring His Son was laid to rest with dignity.

Isaiah adds: "though he had done no violence, nor was any deceit in his mouth." This is the testimony of His innocence. Pilate declared, "I find no basis for a charge against him" (John 18:38). The thief on the cross confessed, "This man has done nothing wrong" (Luke 23:41). Jesus was condemned not for guilt but for grace—He bore judgment for others.

These verses highlight the Servant as the sacrificial Lamb. His silence before accusers, His unjust trial, His violent death, and His paradoxical burial all point to His role as the substitute. He took upon Himself what belonged to us—our guilt, our shame, our punishment—so that we might receive what belonged to Him: peace, righteousness, and life.

They also reveal God's sovereignty over suffering. To human eyes, Jesus' arrest and execution appeared chaotic and defeatist. But Isaiah shows that every detail was foreseen and divinely directed. His silence, His condemnation, His grave—all were part of the redemptive script. This assures believers that even the darkest events in life are not beyond God's plan.

For Christians, these verses offer profound comfort. Many understand what it is to suffer injustice, to be silenced, or to bear undeserved shame. Jesus intimately knows this path; He faced false accusations, endured humiliation, and suffered innocently. When we encounter trials, we remember that He has gone before us, and His Spirit sustains us.

At the same time, these verses challenge us. The Servant's silence is not only prophetic but also exemplary. Peter writes, "When they hurled their insults at him, he did not retaliate; when he suffered, he made no threats. Instead, he entrusted himself to him who judges justly" (1 Peter 2:23). We too are called to entrust ourselves to God during times of injustice, reflecting Christ's submission and trust.

Finally, these verses elevate the glory of substitutionary atonement. He was cut off so that we could be grafted in. He was condemned so that we could be justified. He was buried so that we could rise. Isaiah's words are not mere poetry; they are the gospel written in advance.

Isaiah 53:7–9 is a prophetic masterpiece fulfilled in Jesus Christ. The Servant's silence before His accusers, His unjust condemnation, His violent death, and His paradoxical burial reveal the depth of His obedience and the perfection of God's plan. Innocent yet punished, silent yet victorious, condemned yet exalted—He bore our sins in willing submission.

For us, these verses are not only a fulfilled prophecy but also a source of assurance. They remind us that Christ's suffering was for our sake, that His silence was for our defense, that His death was our redemption, and that His burial preceded resurrection. Isaiah's vision culminates here: the Servant suffers not in vain but to accomplish salvation. In His silence, death, and burial, the voice of God's love speaks most powerfully.

Layers of Understanding

Historical Context

Isaiah's Servant Song portrays a figure oppressed yet silent, suffering willingly in obedience to God's will. While originally echoing Israel's own suffering under oppression, Christians understand its fullest meaning in the Messiah, who endured humiliation, injustice, and death with remarkable silence, fulfilling God's redemptive plan through submission.

Jewish Understanding

Traditionally, Jewish interpretation saw the Servant as Israel itself—suffering corporately among the nations—or as a righteous remnant bearing hardship faithfully. Some also viewed the Servant as a prophet-like figure. Christians, however, recognize this prophecy uniquely fulfilled in Jesus' passion, His trial, execution, and burial aligning precisely with Isaiah's words.

New Testament Fulfillment

The New Testament repeatedly identifies Jesus as the Servant of Isaiah 53. He remained silent before His accusers (Matthew 26:62–63; 27:12–14). Executed with criminals (Luke 23:32–33), buried in Joseph of Arimathea's tomb (Matthew 27:57–60), His innocence confirmed by Pilate (John 18:38). Every detail matches Isaiah's prophecy, affirming divine fulfillment.

Theological Significance Today

This passage reveals Christ as the Lamb of God, silent and submissive in suffering for our redemption. It assures us that God is sovereign even in apparent defeat, comforts us when we face injustice, and challenges believers to endure trials with faith, trusting God's ultimate vindication and Christ's example.

Cross-Reference Connections

- **John 1:29** – Behold the Lamb of God.
- **Matthew 26:62–63; 27:12–14** – Jesus silent before accusers.
- **Luke 23:32–33** – Executed between criminals.
- **Matthew 27:57–60** – Buried in Joseph's rich tomb.
- **John 18:38** – Pilate: "I find no basis for a charge against him."
- **1 Peter 2:22–23** – He committed no sin, no deceit in His mouth.

PROPHECY FULFILLED - STUDY LESSON - 31

LESSON SCRIPTURE: ZECHARIAH 12: 10

PROPHECY TITLE

They Will Look on the One They Pierced

Introduction

Zechariah 12 speaks of a future day when God will defend Jerusalem and pour out His Spirit. In verse 10, the prophecy becomes deeply personal: "They will look on me, the one they have pierced, and they will mourn for him as one mourns for an only child."

This prophecy intertwines suffering, piercing, and ultimate repentance. The speaker is God Himself, who refers to being pierced—foretelling the crucifixion of Christ, where the eternal Son was wounded for our sins. The New Testament directly identifies this fulfillment: John 19:37 references this verse after a soldier pierced Jesus' side. Revelation 1:7 also echoes it, linking it to Christ's return, when all will see Him and mourn.

For believers, this prophecy illustrates the paradox of the gospel: the rejected and pierced Messiah becomes the source of salvation. It serves as a reminder that true repentance arises from witnessing Christ's crucifixion—looking upon Him who was pierced evokes both sorrow for sin and hope for redemption.

Scripture Reference

Zechariah 12:10 (NIV)   "And I will pour out on the house of David and the inhabitants of Jerusalem a spirit ᵖ of grace and supplication. They will look on me, the one they have pierced, and they will mourn for him as one mourns for an only child, and grieve bitterly for him as one grieves for a firstborn son."

Big Picture Insights

- **Spirit poured out** – God initiates repentance through His Spirit.
- **The pierced one** – astonishing prophecy of God Himself being pierced.
- **Mourning** – grief as deep as losing an only son.
- **Fulfilled at the cross** – Jesus pierced by nails and spear (John 19:34–37).
- **Future fulfillment** – all nations will see and mourn at His return (Revelation 1:7).
- **Repentance and grace** – sorrow leads to renewal and salvation.
- **Messianic paradox** – humiliation leads to glory.
- **House of David** – emphasizes messianic lineage and covenant.
- **Theological depth** – combines divine suffering, human guilt, and divine grace.
- **Pastoral comfort** – we mourn our sin but rejoice in Christ's pierced love.

Verse-by-Verse Commentary

Zechariah 12:10a "**And I will pour out on the house of David and the inhabitants of Jerusalem a spirit ᵖ of grace and supplication…**"

- Repentance always begins with God's initiative, not human resolve. He pours out His Spirit, opening blind eyes to grace and moving hardened hearts toward prayer, confession, and genuine dependence on Him.
- The Spirit works to soften human resistance, enabling contrite mourning over sin and producing heartfelt supplication. Without God's Spirit, repentance is impossible; with Him, the soul is drawn to plead for mercy and forgiveness.
- This prophecy is fulfilled at Pentecost when the Spirit was poured out (Acts 2), leading thousands to be cut to the heart, grieve their sin, and turn to Christ in repentance and faith.

Zechariah 12:10b "**…They will look on me, the one they have pierced…**"

- The language is astonishing: God Himself speaks in the first person, declaring, "me." This reveals the incarnation, where the eternal God took on flesh and was pierced for the sins of His people.
- Fulfilled in Jesus Christ, God incarnate, who was literally pierced on the cross by nails and spear. In Him, the paradox of divine suffering and human salvation finds its clearest expression.
- John 19:37 cites this prophecy directly after the soldier pierced Jesus' side with a spear, confirming that this Old Testament vision pointed precisely to the crucifixion of the Messiah.

Zechariah 12:10c "**…and they will mourn for him as one mourns for an only child, and grieve bitterly for him as one grieves for a firstborn son.**"

- Zechariah uses the strongest grief imagery known in the ancient world: the loss of an only child, conveying a sorrow so deep it pierces the heart and strips away hope.
- This mourning anticipates Israel's future repentance when they recognize that the Messiah they rejected and pierced was indeed God's chosen Redeemer. Their grief will be national, sincere, and transformative.
- For believers today, this grief mirrors the sorrow of realizing that our sins pierced Christ. Yet such mourning is redemptive, producing repentance, gratitude, and deeper love for the Savior who bore our guilt.

Discussion Questions

1. Why is it significant that God says "they will look on me, the one they have pierced"?

2. How was this prophecy fulfilled at the crucifixion of Jesus?

3. What role does the Spirit play in leading people to repentance?

4. Why is the imagery of mourning for an only child so powerful here?

5. How does looking on the pierced Christ bring both grief and healing?

6. How does Revelation 1:7 connect this prophecy to Christ's return?

7. How should this verse shape our personal repentance and worship?

Narrative Reflection

Zechariah 12:10 is a profound and theologically rich prophecies in the Old Testament, intertwining themes of divine suffering, human guilt, repentance, and salvation within a single verse. It not only anticipates Christ's crucifixion but also highlights the Spirit's role in repentance and the ultimate hope of redemption. This prophecy masterfully connects the incarnation, the cross, and the outpouring of God's Spirit, leaving readers in awe of its depth.

The verse begins with divine initiative: "I will pour out on the house of David and the inhabitants of Jerusalem a spirit of grace and supplication." Repentance does not stem from human will but from God's gracious action. The outpouring of the Spirit enables both the recognition of sin and the turning of the heart toward God.

The "spirit of grace" signifies God's empowering presence that opens blind eyes to His mercy. Repentance is impossible without grace. By nature, humanity resists God, but His Spirit softens hearts, convicts consciences, and awakens faith. The "spirit of supplication" indicates a response of prayer, confession, and seeking mercy. Together, these elements describe God's work in guiding His people to repentance.

This prophecy finds partial fulfillment at Pentecost, when the Spirit was poured out upon the disciples and the crowds who heard Peter's preaching. Cut to the heart, they asked, "Brothers, what shall we do?" (Acts 2:37). The Spirit's convicting power resulted in supplication, repentance, and the establishment of the church. However, Zechariah's vision also looks toward a future day when Israel, as a nation, will receive this spirit and turn to Christ in repentance, as Paul anticipated in Romans 11:26.

At the center of the verse is the staggering statement: "They will look on me, the one they have pierced." This declaration is extraordinary because God Himself is speaking. How can the Almighty, the eternal Lord, be pierced? This paradox points directly to the incarnation, when the Word became flesh and dwelt among us (John 1:14).

Christians recognize this prophecy as one of the clearest anticipations of the crucifixion. In His humanity, Jesus could be pierced; in His divinity, God claims those wounds as His own. John's Gospel recounts that when a Roman soldier thrust his spear into Jesus' side, blood and water flowed out (John 19:34). John adds, "These things happened so that the Scripture would be fulfilled: 'They will look on the one they have pierced'" (John 19:37). Thus, the cross is not only a historical event but also the divine fulfillment of Zechariah's prophecy.

The piercing is not merely an act of violence; it is a revelation of sin. It was not only the Roman soldiers who pierced Him nor merely Judas who betrayed Him or the Sanhedrin who condemned Him. It was humanity as a whole. Our sins pierced Him. Every transgression, selfish act, and rebellion against God found its dreadful expression in those nails and that spear. To look upon the pierced Messiah is to witness not only God's suffering love but also the reality of our own guilt.

The response to the piercing is grief: "They will mourn for him as one mourns for an only child, and grieve bitterly for him as one grieves for a firstborn son." In the ancient world, the death of an only child represented the deepest imaginable sorrow, extinguishing the family's hope and future. This imagery conveys the intensity of the sorrow God's people will feel upon realizing what they have done to their Messiah.

This mourning is both corporate and personal. It anticipates Israel's future repentance, as the nation will recognize that the One they rejected is the Savior sent by God. Simultaneously, it reflects each individual's experience when confronted with the crucified Christ. True repentance is not a casual acknowledgment but a profound grief, a sorrow that pierces the heart. Like Peter, who wept bitterly after denying Jesus (Luke 22:62), the believer sees the cost of sin and mourns.

Yet this mourning is not despair. It is a sorrow that leads to repentance, which in turn leads to life (2 Corinthians 7:10). When the Spirit opens our eyes to see Christ pierced for us, we grieve over our sin, but we also find grace in that very moment. The pierced One is not only the object of grief but also the source of forgiveness.

The New Testament applies Zechariah 12:10 in two directions: the crucifixion and the Second Coming. John applies it directly to the cross in John 19:37, showing that the piercing of Christ's side fulfills the prophecy. Revelation 1:7 expands its scope: "Look, he is coming with the clouds, and every eye will see him, even those who pierced him; and all peoples on earth will mourn because of him."

At Christ's first coming, a small group stood by the cross and literally looked upon Him pierced. At His second coming, every eye will see Him, and all peoples will mourn. Some will mourn in repentance unto salvation; others will mourn in terror unto judgment. But none will remain indifferent.

This verse captures the paradox of the gospel. God declares, "They will look on me, the one they have pierced." The Almighty humbled Himself to be wounded by His own creations. Divine suffering becomes the means of human salvation. The grief of sin opens the gateway to grace.

This prophecy also emphasizes the necessity of the Spirit in repentance. People do not naturally mourn for their sin or recognize their guilt. Only when God pours out His Spirit of grace and supplication do hearts break and turn toward Him. Salvation is thus wholly God's work: the Spirit convicts, the Son is pierced, and the Father forgives.

Eventually, the prophecy highlights the hope of redemption. Israel will one day look upon the pierced Messiah and mourn, leading to national restoration. The church already looks back at the cross with both grief and gratitude, finding in the pierced Christ the source of forgiveness and life. At His return, the whole world will look upon Him, and His wounds will either condemn or comfort, depending on whether one has received His grace.

For Christians today, Zechariah 12:10 is both sobering and comforting. It reminds us that our sins pierced Christ. Every lie, every act of pride, every selfish desire contributed to what nailed Him to the cross. To meditate on His wounds is to grasp the seriousness of sin.

Yet it also brings comfort because those same wounds are the source of our healing. The pierced Christ is not only the object of our grief but also the assurance of our forgiveness. His death secures our life; His wounds bring us peace. Looking upon Him crucified awakens sorrow but also fills us with gratitude and hope.

This verse calls us to proclaim Christ to the world. Just as the Spirit was poured out at Pentecost to lead thousands to repentance, we are called to bear witness to the pierced Messiah today. Our message is simple: look upon Him who was pierced, mourn your sin, and receive His grace.

Zechariah 12:10 is a prophecy fulfilled at the cross, applied by the Spirit, and awaiting consummation at Christ's return. It declares that God Himself would be pierced, that His people would mourn, and that His Spirit would lead them to repentance. For us, it calls us to gaze upon the crucified Christ, to grieve the sins that pierced Him, and to rejoice in His pierced love that brings salvation.

The pierced Messiah stands at the center of history—His wounds testify to humanity's guilt and to God's grace. One day, every eye will see Him, and every heart will reckon with His wounds. For those who trust Him, those wounds will be their eternal joy.

Layers of Understanding

Historical Context

Zechariah prophesied to a weary, post-exilic Judah, where discouragement lingered despite the rebuilding of the temple. His words pointed beyond immediate struggles to God's ultimate plan. Zechariah 12:10 shifts the focus toward a future messianic age, when God Himself would intervene decisively to bring repentance, restoration, and salvation.

Jewish Understanding

In Jewish tradition, this verse was often interpreted as God vindicating His people after suffering under foreign powers. The piercing was seen metaphorically as Israel's pain. Christians, however, understand its fullest meaning in the Messiah—pierced not for His own sins but for ours, bringing redemption through suffering.

New Testament Fulfillment

The Gospel of John explicitly cites this prophecy after Jesus' side was pierced by the soldier's spear (John 19:37). Revelation 1:7 applies it universally to Christ's Second Coming, when all will see Him. At Pentecost (Acts 2), the Spirit of grace was poured out, leading many to repentance.

Theological Significance Today

Zechariah 12:10 reminds believers of the terrible cost of sin and the depth of God's love revealed in the pierced Christ. It calls us to repentance by looking upon the crucified Lord. It also strengthens hope, assuring us that one day every eye will see Him returning in glory.

Cross-Reference Connections

- **John 19:34–37** – Jesus' side pierced, prophecy fulfilled.
- **Revelation 1:7** – Every eye will see Him, even those who pierced Him.
- **Acts 2:36–37** – Spirit brings repentance after realization of crucifying the Messiah.
- **Isaiah 53:5** – He was pierced for our transgressions.
- **Matthew 24:30** – All peoples will mourn at the coming of the Son of Man.
- **Romans 11:26–27** – Promise of Israel's future repentance and salvation.

LESSON SCRIPTURE: **ISAIAH 53: 10-12**

PROPHECY TITLE

The Servant's Suffering and Triumph

Introduction

Isaiah 53 concludes in verses 10–12 by revealing the divine purpose behind the Servant's suffering. Though the Lord crushed Him, His suffering was not in vain; it served as an offering for sin, leading to the justification of many. The passage then transitions from death to triumph, stating that the Servant will see life, find satisfaction, and be exalted.

This prophecy is fulfilled in Jesus Christ. His death was God's will for our salvation, His resurrection affirmed His vindication, and He continues to intercede for us as our High Priest. These verses illustrate that the cross represented not defeat but victory, accomplishing redemption for many and glorifying the Servant.

Scripture Reference

Isaiah 53:10–12 (NIV) "Yet it was the LORD's will to crush him and cause him to suffer, and though the LORD makes his life an offering for sin, he will see his offspring and prolong his days, and the will of the LORD will prosper in his hand. [11] After he has suffered, he will see the light of life and be satisfied; by his knowledge my righteous servant will justify many, and he will bear their iniquities. [12] Therefore I will give him a portion among the great, " and he will divide the spoils with the strong, because he poured out his life unto death, and was numbered with the transgressors. For he bore the sin of many, and made intercession for the transgressors.**

Big Picture Insights

- **God's will** – Christ's suffering was divinely purposed.
- **Offering for sin** – sacrificial, substitutionary death.
- **Vindication** – Servant will see life, resurrection implied.
- **Justification** – many made righteous through Him.
- **Reward** – exalted and given honor among the great.
- **Suffering Servant → conquering Lord** – humiliation leads to glory.
- **Intercession** – Christ prays for His people, even as He dies.
- **Already/not yet** – fulfilled in cross and resurrection, consummated in final victory.
- **Covenantal fulfillment** – Servant becomes the source of the new covenant.
- **Pastoral assurance** – our salvation is secured in His finished work.

Verse -by-Verse Commentary

Isaiah 53:10 "Yet it was the LORD's will to crush him and cause him to suffer, and though the LORD makes his life an offering for sin, he will see his offspring and prolong his days, and the will of the LORD will prosper in his hand."

- This shocking affirmation shows that the cross was not an accident of history or merely human cruelty. It was God's sovereign will and eternal purpose to accomplish salvation through the crushing of His Servant.
- The Servant's life is described as a guilt offering, echoing Leviticus 5. Like the sacrificial lambs, His life was given to bear sin and restore fellowship between God and His people through substitutionary atonement.
- Resurrection hope is implied: "he will see his offspring and prolong his days." Though crushed, His life would continue. God's redemptive plan prospers eternally because of the Servant's obedience unto death and His triumph over the grave.

Isaiah 53:11 – "After he has suffered, he will see the light of life and be satisfied; by his knowledge my righteous servant will justify many, and he will bear their iniquities."

- This points directly to resurrection and vindication. The Servant does not remain in death but emerges to see "the light of life," confirming God's approval and the victory of His suffering.
- He will be satisfied, knowing His mission accomplished redemption. The agony of the cross becomes worth it because it secures forgiveness, reconciliation, and eternal life for countless souls who believe.
- The righteous Servant "justifies many," providing the foundation for the doctrine of justification. He bears iniquities, transferring guilt from sinners to Himself, so that they may stand righteous before God by faith.

Isaiah 53:12 – "Therefore I will give him a portion among the great, ⁿ and he will divide the spoils with the strong, because he poured out his life unto death, and was numbered with the transgressors. For he bore the sin of many, and made intercession for the transgressors."

- Exaltation follows humiliation. Like Philippians 2:8–11, this verse affirms that the Servant, after His obedience to death, is lifted high above all. His suffering leads to universal recognition of His glory and kingship.
- The Servant poured out His life unto death, willingly identifying Himself with sinners. Though innocent, He bore the lot of transgressors, dying the death of criminals in order to redeem them through His self-giving sacrifice.
- He bore the sin of many and interceded for them, fulfilled both on the cross — "Father, forgive them" (Luke 23:34) — and in His heavenly ministry where He continually intercedes for believers (Hebrews 7:25).

Discussion Questions

1. What does it mean that it was the Lord's will to crush the Servant?

2. How is the Servant's suffering described as a sacrificial offering?

3. How does verse 10 already point toward resurrection and vindication?

4. Why is justification ("make many righteous") central to this prophecy?

5. How does the Servant's exaltation connect to Philippians 2:8–11?

6. What does it mean that He both bore sin and interceded for sinners?

7. How does this prophecy assure us of the completeness of salvation?

Narrative Reflection

Isaiah 53:10–12 stands as the climax of the Servant Song and one of the most profound passages in all of Scripture. In these verses, the prophet moves from the sorrow of the Servant's suffering to the divine purpose behind it and the glorious outcome that follows. What was described earlier as rejection, oppression, and grief is now revealed to be part of God's sovereign plan, designed to bring about salvation for His people. Here we see the heart of the gospel laid bare: the suffering of the Servant is not an accident of history or merely the result of human cruelty, but the very will of God for the redemption of the world.

Verse 10 opens with words that are shocking in their directness: "Yet it was the Lord's will to crush him and cause him to suffer." At first, such a statement may strike us as harsh or even troubling. How could it be God's will to crush the Servant? The answer lies in the mystery of divine love and the unity of the Trinity. The Father did not act in cruelty toward the Son, nor did the Son resist the Father's will. Instead, in perfect harmony, the triune God purposed redemption through the Servant's suffering. The cross was not an afterthought or a tragic miscalculation; it was the plan of salvation from before the foundation of the world. Revelation 13:8 speaks of Christ as the Lamb slain from the creation of the world, underscoring that the Servant's crushing was foreordained as the means by which sin would be atoned for.

The verse goes on to describe the Servant's life as "an offering for sin." This language recalls the sacrificial system of Leviticus, particularly the guilt offering. In that system, an unblemished animal bore the guilt of the sinner, and its blood secured forgiveness. Yet those sacrifices were temporary and had to be repeated. Isaiah proclaims that the Servant Himself would become the final, perfect offering. In Him, the imagery of Leviticus finds its true fulfillment. Jesus Christ, unblemished and sinless, willingly offered His life to bear the guilt of humanity once for all. The book of Hebrews echoes this truth: unlike the priests who offered repeated sacrifices, Jesus offered Himself once and for all to take away sins (Hebrews 10:10–14).

Even in the midst of this solemn picture of suffering, hope shines through. Isaiah declares: "He will see his offspring and prolong his days, and the will of the Lord will prosper in his hand." Though the Servant is cut off from the land of the living, death will not have the final word. He will live again. His "offspring" are not physical descendants but the spiritual children born through His sacrifice — all who are justified by His work and brought into the family of God through faith. The Servant's days will be prolonged, pointing to resurrection life. The will of God, far from being thwarted by death, prospers precisely because of it. The mission of redemption cannot fail, for it is upheld by divine power and accomplished by the Servant's obedience.

Verse 11 continues the theme of vindication: "After he has suffered, he will see the light of life and be satisfied." Here resurrection is explicitly implied. The Servant, who endures suffering and death, will emerge into life again. This vision of resurrection not only affirms God's victory over death but also underscores the Servant's satisfaction in His completed work. The suffering He bore was agonizing beyond description, yet it was not in vain. He will look upon the redeemed multitudes — the fruit of His labor — and be satisfied. His death secures life for many, and this gives Him joy.

The verse further explains the outcome of His work: "By his knowledge my righteous servant will justify many, and he will bear their iniquities." This is the heart of the gospel. The Servant, righteous in Himself, justifies many. Justification is the central doctrine Paul expounds in Romans: sinners are declared righteous not because of their own merit but because the Servant bore their iniquities. The Servant's knowledge is not abstract information but experiential obedience, His faithful execution of God's saving plan. Through His suffering and obedience, He becomes the source of justification for all who believe. Our guilt is transferred to Him; His righteousness is credited to us.

Verse 12 concludes the Servant Song with a vision of exaltation and triumph: "Therefore I will give him a portion among the great, and he will divide the spoils with the strong." The imagery is that of a victorious warrior receiving the spoils of battle. The Servant, who humbled Himself unto death, is now exalted and honored. Philippians 2:8–11 echoes this theme: because He was obedient to death on a cross, God highly exalted Him and gave Him the name above every name. What appeared to be defeat at Calvary is revealed as the greatest victory in history — the triumph of God's love over sin, death, and Satan.

The verse continues: "Because he poured out his life unto death, and was numbered with the transgressors." Jesus fulfilled this prophecy literally by being crucified between two criminals (Luke 23:32–33). Though innocent, He was treated as guilty, identifying Himself fully with sinners. He did not merely die for sinners in the abstract; He died with sinners, counted among them in shame and execution. Yet in this very act, He bore the sin of many, taking their guilt upon Himself.

The final phrase deepens the picture: "and made intercession for the transgressors." Even as He hung on the cross, Jesus prayed, "Father, forgive them, for they do not know what they are doing" (Luke 23:34). His intercession did not end with His death. The risen and exalted Christ continues to intercede for His people at the right hand of God (Hebrews 7:25). This highlights the ongoing nature of His saving work. His sacrifice was once for all, but His intercession continues forever.

Isaiah 53:10–12 presents the full sweep of Christ's redemptive work: His sacrificial death, His resurrection life, His justification of sinners, His exaltation in glory, and His continuing intercession. It shows the paradox at the heart of the gospel: humiliation leads to exaltation, death leads to life, and suffering leads to glory. What seemed like the darkest moment in history becomes the centerpiece of God's plan of salvation.

For believers, these verses provide deep assurance. Our salvation is complete, finished, and secure. The Servant bore our sins fully; nothing remains for us to add. He justifies many — all who put their trust in Him — and He intercedes continually, ensuring that we are never abandoned. His exaltation guarantees that the cross was not failure but victory.

These verses also shape our discipleship. The Servant's path was one of suffering before glory, and the same may be true for us. As followers of Christ, we are called to take up our cross, endure trials, and trust that God will bring victory from suffering. Yet we do so with hope, knowing that our triumph is secured in His.

This final look at Isaiah 53:10–12 is the crescendo of the Servant Song and one of the most important passages in all of Scripture. It reveals that Christ's suffering was God's will, His death was a sacrificial offering, His resurrection brought satisfaction and life, His exaltation secured victory, and His intercession continues today. These verses present the gospel in prophetic form, fulfilled perfectly in Jesus Christ. For us, they are a source of assurance, comfort, and calling. Our salvation rests not in ourselves but in the Servant who was crushed, pierced, raised, exalted, and who now prays for us. Truly, in Isaiah 53:10–12, we behold the heart of God's redemptive plan.

Layers of Understanding

Historical Context

Isaiah's Servant Song was given to exiled Israel as a promise of hope. Redemption would not come through military might or political power, but through the Servant's willing suffering and ultimate vindication. His obedience and sacrifice assured God's people that restoration and victory would emerge from apparent defeat.

Jewish Understanding

Jewish interpreters often understood the Servant corporately as Israel itself, suffering on behalf of the nations or representing a faithful remnant. Christians, however, recognize its unique fulfillment in the Messiah, who embodies Israel's calling, bears its burdens, and accomplishes redemption through His obedience, suffering, death, and vindication.

New Testament Fulfillment

In the New Testament, Jesus is revealed as the true sin offering, the Lamb of God who takes away the sin of the world (John 1:29; Hebrews 9:26). Through His death and resurrection, justification flows to all who believe, restoring sinners into fellowship with God (Romans 5:18). Though humiliated and crucified, He was exalted to the highest place, receiving the name above every name (Philippians 2:9–11). His work did not end at the cross, for His intercession continues—first in His prayer for forgiveness while suffering (Luke 23:34), and now eternally in heaven as He pleads on behalf of His people (Hebrews 7:25).

Theological Significance Today

For believers, these verses assure us that Christ's work is finished and complete. He bore our sins, secured our justification, rose in triumph, and intercedes continually on our behalf. This truth encourages endurance and faithfulness, reminding us that suffering is never wasted but leads ultimately to glory in Him.

Cross-Reference Connections

- **Leviticus 5** – Guilt offering background.
- **Romans 5:18–19** – Justification for many through one man's obedience.
- **Philippians 2:8–11** – Exaltation after humiliation.
- **Luke 23:32, 34** – Numbered with transgressors; interceded for sinners.
- **Hebrews 7:25** – Christ intercedes continually for us.
- **Revelation 5:9–12** – The Lamb slain is worthy to receive honor and power.

Series 5 – Resurrection & Exaltation Prophecies

PROPHECY FULFILLED - STUDY LESSON - 33

LESSON SCRIPTURE: **PSALM 34: 20**

PROPHECY TITLE

None of His Bones Broken

Introduction

Psalm 34, attributed to David, celebrates God's deliverance of the righteous from trouble. In verse 20, David proclaims, "He protects all his bones; not one of them will be broken." While this initially serves as a general statement about God's protection, the New Testament identifies it as a prophecy fulfilled during Christ's crucifixion.

During the crucifixion, Roman soldiers broke the legs of the criminals to hasten their deaths. However, when they approached Jesus, they found Him already dead. Instead of breaking His legs, they pierced His side with a spear. John 19:36 refers directly to Psalm 34:20: "These things happened so that this scripture would be fulfilled: 'Not one of his bones will be broken.'"

This detail is significant as it connects Jesus to the Passover lamb. Exodus 12:46 and Numbers 9:12 specify that none of the lamb's bones should be broken. Jesus, the Lamb of God, perfectly fulfilled this requirement, demonstrating that His sacrifice was the true Passover offering.

Scripture Reference

Psalm 34:20 (NIV) "he protects all his bones, not one of them will be broken."

Big Picture Insights

- **Davidic psalm** – assurance of God's protection for the righteous.
- **Literal fulfillment** – Jesus' bones were not broken at crucifixion.
- **Roman custom** – breaking legs was common; omission fulfills prophecy.
- **Connection to Passover lamb** – none of its bones were to be broken.
- **Christ as Lamb of God** – perfect sacrifice without defect.
- **God's sovereignty** – even small details were divinely purposed.
- **Typology** – lamb imagery woven from Exodus to Christ.
- **Contrast** – thieves' legs broken, Jesus' not.
- **Theological meaning** – God preserves the body of His Son for resurrection.
- **Faith assurance** – every prophecy is fulfilled in Christ.

Verse -by-Verse Commentary

Psalm 34:20a – "He protects all his bones,…"

- The psalmist testifies to God's preserving care, portraying the righteous as shielded from ultimate harm. Though affliction may strike, God safeguards what is essential, proving His faithfulness to sustain His people.
- This prophecy finds literal fulfillment in Christ at the crucifixion. Despite brutal suffering, His bones were not broken, showing divine protection even in death and confirming the precision of God's word.

Psalm 34:20b – "…not one of them will be broken."

- The detail emphasizes God's meticulous care. In ancient times, broken bones often signified defeat or disgrace, yet here, wholeness is preserved by divine decree.
- John 19:33–36 cites this verse directly. Soldiers refrained from breaking Jesus' legs because He was already dead, fulfilling prophecy perfectly. The unbroken bones testify to Christ as the true Passover Lamb (Exodus 12:46).

Discussion Questions

1. Why is the detail of Jesus' unbroken bones significant?

2. How does this verse connect Christ to the Passover lamb?

3. What does John 19:36 teach us about prophecy fulfillment?

4. How does God's sovereignty over even small details encourage faith?

5. Why did God preserve Jesus' bones when others were broken?

6. How does this verse show continuity between Old Testament law and the cross?

7. What does this fulfillment teach us about Christ as the Lamb of God?

Narrative Reflection

Psalm 34:20 is a concise verse that, upon closer examination, reveals profound prophetic significance. Composed by David in a psalm praising God's deliverance, it asserts, "He protects all his bones; not one of them will be broken." In its immediate context, it offers reassurance to the righteous that God safeguards their lives even amid adversity. However, like many verses in the Psalms, its deeper meaning is fully realized in the life, death, and resurrection of Jesus Christ. What may seem like a minor promise becomes a striking prophetic detail linked to the crucifixion.

To grasp the weight of this prophecy, it is essential to understand the historical and physical realities of crucifixion. This method of execution was designed not only to kill but to inflict maximum pain and humiliation. Victims were nailed or tied to a wooden cross, positioned so that breathing became increasingly difficult. Death usually resulted from suffocation, as the victim could no longer push up against the nails in their feet to inhale.

Since some victims could linger for hours or even days, Roman soldiers sometimes expedited the process by breaking their legs. This action prevented the victim from pushing up, leading to a quicker death by suffocation. In John 19, the soldiers broke the legs of the two criminals crucified alongside Jesus. However, when they approached Him, they found He was already dead. Instead of breaking His legs, one soldier pierced His side with a spear, fulfilling another prophecy from Zechariah 12:10: "They will look on me, the one they have pierced."

John, who witnessed the crucifixion, immediately connected this event to Psalm 34:20: "These things happened so that the scripture would be fulfilled: 'Not one of his bones will be broken'" (John 19:36). While this detail may appear minor, John highlights it as evidence of God's complete faithfulness in fulfilling His word.

The first theological insight from Psalm 34:20 is the sovereignty of God in Christ's suffering. Even the smallest details fell within His control. The Roman soldiers acted on their own accord, yet their actions aligned perfectly with what had been foretold centuries earlier. Not one of Jesus' bones was broken—not in His hands, feet, or ribcage—despite the brutality of crucifixion.
This illustrates that prophecy is not a vague prediction but divine orchestration. The God who governs nations also ensures that the minutest details of His plan come to fruition. Believers can find comfort in

this truth. If God fulfilled such a precise prophecy amid violence and chaos, His promises to us are equally secure.

A second powerful layer of meaning connects Psalm 34:20 to the imagery of the Passover lamb. In Exodus 12:46, when God instituted the Passover, He commanded that none of the lamb's bones were to be broken. This rule is reiterated in Numbers 9:12 when the Passover is reaffirmed. The unbroken bones symbolized the lamb's wholeness and perfection.

Jesus died during Passover. John the Baptist identified Him as "the Lamb of God who takes away the sin of the world" (John 1:29), and Paul affirmed, "For Christ, our Passover lamb, has been sacrificed" (1 Corinthians 5:7). By ensuring that Jesus' bones remained unbroken, God proclaimed that Jesus is the true Passover lamb, whose sacrifice was unblemished, whole, and perfect—sufficient to cover the sins of His people once for all.

This connection enhances our understanding of the cross. Jesus did not die as a mere victim of injustice; He died as the Passover Lamb, fulfilling centuries of sacrificial symbolism. His preserved bones signify His flawless offering, accepted by God for the redemption of the world.

In its original context, Psalm 34 celebrated God's protection of the righteous. David wrote about deliverance from enemies and God's watchful care over His people. Yet, in the broader scope of biblical theology, only one person embodies true righteousness in its fullest sense—Jesus Christ.

When Psalm 34:20 states that God protects the bones of the righteous, it finds its ultimate fulfillment in Him. Though His body was pierced, His bones were preserved intact, fulfilling prophecy and preparing His body for resurrection. Death could not fully claim Him, for the Father preserved Him for vindication. His intact bones symbolize that His life, though surrendered, was not destroyed forever.

Another notable aspect of Psalm 34:20 is its interconnection with other passages of Scripture, weaving a seamless prophetic narrative across centuries. The psalmist proclaims God's protection, the law establishes the unbroken bones of the Passover lamb, and the Gospel writers document its precise fulfillment.

Together, these passages point to Jesus as the unifying thread of the Bible. Psalm, Torah, and Gospel converge on Him. Nothing is accidental; every verse and detail leads to the revelation of Christ as the true Lamb of God.

For believers, Psalm 34:20 transcends historical fulfillment; it serves as a personal assurance. If God was faithful to preserve even the smallest detail of Christ's crucifixion, how much more will He be faithful to preserve us? Jesus' intact bones remind us that suffering and death do not have the final word—resurrection awaits. This detail also calls us to deeper faith. In our own moments of suffering, it is easy to feel abandoned or overlooked. But if God honored a prophecy about bones written centuries prior, He will not forget us. His care encompasses every detail of our lives.

Finally, Psalm 34:20 directs our attention to Christ as the true Lamb. His sacrifice was sufficient, final, and perfect. The preservation of His bones is not merely a historical curiosity; it serves as a divine signature on the cross, declaring, "This is the Lamb I have provided. His offering is complete."

We no longer require the blood of Passover lambs, for Christ's blood has been shed once for all. His body, preserved intact, was raised on the third day. His sacrifice delivers us not only from physical death, as in the Exodus, but from eternal death.

Psalm 34:20 may be a brief verse, but it carries immense prophetic significance. It reveals God's sovereignty, fulfilling His word down to the smallest detail. It connects Christ to the Passover lamb, illustrating that His sacrifice was perfect and unblemished. It affirms His righteousness, preserved by God for resurrection. It demonstrates the continuity of prophecy across the Old and New Testaments. And it assures believers that God's promises never fail.

Jesus' bones were not broken, not due to the restraint of Roman soldiers, but because God's redemptive plan was unfolding precisely as decreed. Every detail, from the casting of lots for His garments to the piercing of His side, testifies that He is the Lamb of God who takes away the sin of the world. Psalm 34:20 serves as a reminder that in Christ, every promise of God is "Yes" and "Amen."

Layers of Understanding

Historical Context

Psalm 34 was written by David after God delivered him from danger, celebrating the Lord's faithfulness to protect the righteous. Verse 20 poetically assures that God guards every bone, symbolizing complete preservation and divine care even in times of suffering, danger, or apparent defeat.

Jewish Understanding

In Jewish tradition, this verse was generally read as God's protection over the faithful, not necessarily a messianic prophecy. Yet Christians recognize its deeper fulfillment in the Messiah, who alone embodies perfect righteousness and experiences God's ultimate preservation even through death itself.

New Testament Fulfillment

John 19:36 explicitly cites this verse after the soldiers chose not to break Jesus' legs on the cross. This detail links Him directly to the Passover lamb, whose bones were not to be broken (Exodus 12:46; Numbers 9:12), revealing Christ as God's unblemished sacrificial Lamb.

Theological Significance Today

Psalm 34:20 reminds believers of God's sovereign control, even over the smallest details of prophecy. Jesus' unbroken bones reveal Him as the perfect sacrifice, the true Passover Lamb. This fulfillment reassures Christians that God's promises are trustworthy and His redemptive plan is flawless and complete.

Cross-Reference Connections

- **John 19:33–36** – Jesus' bones not broken at crucifixion.
- **Exodus 12:46; Numbers 9:12** – Passover lamb's bones not broken.
- **1 Corinthians 5:7** – Christ our Passover lamb.
- **Zechariah 12:10** – Pierced side fulfilled alongside.
- **John 1:29** – Jesus as the Lamb of God.
- **Revelation 5:6** – The Lamb who was slain is exalted.

PROPHECY FULFILLED - STUDY LESSON - 34

LESSON SCRIPTURE: **PSALM 16: 10**

PROPHECY TITLE

You Will Not Abandon the Holy One to Decay

Introduction

Psalm 16 expresses confidence in God's protection and guidance. In verse 10, David declares, *"because you will not abandon me to the realm of the dead, nor will you let your faithful one see decay."* While David speaks from his own experience of trust, the New Testament reveals that these words extend beyond him.

Peter, in his Pentecost sermon (Acts 2:25–31), applies Psalm 16:10 directly to Jesus Christ. He points out that David died, was buried, and his body decayed, indicating that the verse cannot ultimately refer to him. Instead, it serves as a prophecy about the Messiah, whose body would not remain in the grave or experience corruption. Paul reinforces this interpretation in Acts 13:35–37.

This prophecy is fulfilled in the resurrection of Jesus. He was not abandoned to Sheol, nor did His body undergo decay. God raised Him from the dead on the third day, vindicating Him as the Holy One and securing salvation for all who trust in Him.

Scripture Reference

Psalm 16:10 (NIV) **"because you will not abandon me to the realm of the dead, nor will you let your faithful one see decay."**

Big Picture Insights

- **Davidic psalm** – originally a song of trust in God's deliverance.
- **Prophetic reach** – David's words transcend his own experience.
- **New Testament application** – Peter and Paul apply it to Jesus.
- **Not abandoned to Sheol** – Christ did not remain in the grave.
- **No decay** – body did not undergo corruption.
- **Resurrection** – God raised Him on the third day.
- **Vindication** – Jesus proven to be the Holy One.
- **Victory over death** – confirms hope of eternal life for believers.
- **Covenantal promise** – God's faithful one is preserved forever.
- **Pastoral assurance** – we too will be raised with Him.

Verse-by-Verse Commentary

Psalm 16:10a – "because you will not abandon me to the realm of the dead,…"

- The psalmist expresses confidence that God's covenant faithfulness extends beyond death. Unlike pagan fears of Sheol's permanence, trust in the Lord assures deliverance and continued fellowship with Him even after the grave.
- Peter applied this verse directly to Christ in Acts 2:25–27. While David died and was buried, Jesus rose, proving that God did not abandon Him to death but vindicated Him through resurrection.

Psalm 16:10b – "…nor will you let your holy one see decay."

- "Holy One" points beyond David to the Messiah, uniquely consecrated and preserved by God. Unlike ordinary flesh, Christ's body did not experience the corruption of decay, marking Him as distinct from all others.
- Paul emphasized this in Acts 13:35–37, showing that David's body decayed, but Jesus did not. The resurrection confirms Him as the Holy One, the eternal Son, and the guarantee of believers' resurrection hope.

Discussion Questions

1. How does Psalm 16:10 show both David's personal trust and Christ's prophetic victory?

2. Why do Peter and Paul insist this verse cannot apply to David himself?

3. What does it mean that Jesus did not see decay?

4. How does the resurrection vindicate Jesus as the "Holy One"?

5. How does this prophecy strengthen our faith in God's promises?

6. What comfort does it give believers regarding their own death?

7. How should we live in light of Christ's resurrection victory?

Narrative Reflection

Psalm 16 is one of David's most remarkable psalms, brimming with trust, confidence, and hope in God's preserving power. It serves as a song of refuge, where David recognizes that the Lord alone is his portion and security. While much of the psalm highlights David's assurance in God's present protection, verse 10 stands out as a prophetic declaration that transcends his own life: "because you will not abandon me to the realm of the dead, nor will you let your faithful one see decay." This promise extends beyond David's personal experience, directly pointing to the resurrection of the Messiah.

When David first spoke these words, he made a bold proclamation of trust in God's power over death. In the Old Testament, "the realm of the dead" (Hebrew *Sheol*) was understood as a shadowy existence where life ceased and human fellowship ended. Although David was confident that God could preserve him in danger, the words he penned reached beyond the common understanding of his time. They contained the promise that God's faithful one would not be left in the grave, nor would His body undergo decay.

The early church recognized that David's words could not be fully applied to him alone. On the day of Pentecost, the apostle Peter quoted this psalm extensively to explain the resurrection of Jesus. He reminded his listeners of a simple historical fact: "Fellow Israelites, I can tell you confidently that the patriarch David died and was buried, and his tomb is here to this day" (Acts 2:29). If David's body had decayed, then Psalm 16:10 could not pertain solely to him. Peter clarified that David, as a prophet, was speaking of someone greater—the Messiah whom God had promised. This Messiah would not remain in the grave but would rise before decay could set in. The prophecy was not about David's deliverance from earthly enemies, but about Christ's victory over death itself.

Paul echoed this point in his sermon recorded in Acts 13. Addressing the synagogue in Pisidian Antioch, Paul contrasted David and Jesus. He stated that David "served God's purpose in his own generation, fell asleep, was buried with his ancestors, and his body decayed. But the one whom God raised from the dead did not see decay" (Acts 13:36–37). Paul's argument reinforced Peter's: David's prophecy looked forward to Christ, whose resurrection fulfilled every word.

The fulfillment of this verse occurred with astonishing precision in the resurrection of Jesus. Crucified on Friday, His body was laid in the tomb of Joseph of Arimathea. According to Jewish reckoning, He rose on the third day, before His body could begin to corrupt. John's Gospel highlights the speed of the burial and the care with which His body was laid to rest, underscoring that He truly died. Yet, when the women arrived at the tomb on Sunday morning, they found it empty. The angels proclaimed the good news: "He is not here; he has risen, just as he said" (Matthew 28:6). In that moment, Psalm 16:10 was fulfilled.

Theologically, this prophecy underscores the uniqueness of Christ. Unlike David or any other person, His body did not see corruption. Death could not hold Him because He was sinless and holy. As Peter noted in Acts 2:24, "it was impossible for death to keep its hold on him." The wages of sin is death, but Christ, being without sin, could not be bound by its power. His resurrection was both a vindication of His identity as the Holy One of God and proof that His sacrifice on the cross was accepted by the Father.

This verse also highlights God's covenant faithfulness. Just as the Father did not abandon Christ to the grave, He will not abandon those who belong to Him. Paul elaborates on this truth in 1 Corinthians 15, where he refers to Christ as the "firstfruits of those who have fallen asleep." Just as the first portion of a harvest guarantees the rest, Christ's resurrection assures the resurrection of all who trust in Him. The victory He won over death is shared with His people. We, too, will not be abandoned to the grave but will be raised in imperishable, glorious bodies.

For believers today, Psalm 16:10 offers profound comfort. Death is humanity's greatest fear, casting a shadow over every life. Yet in Christ, that fear has been conquered. When we face the death of loved ones in Christ or confront our own mortality, this verse reassures us that death is not the end. Scripture teaches that at the moment of death, the believer's spirit goes immediately to be with the Lord, enjoying His presence in peace and joy. Meanwhile, the body rests in the grave, awaiting the day when God will raise it in glory at the resurrection. Thus, the grave is not our final destiny but a temporary resting place for physical body, while the soul is alive in Christ's presence. Our confidence rests not in vague hope but in the concrete reality of Christ's resurrection, which guarantees both our immediate communion with Him after death and our future bodily resurrection at His return. At the same time, this verse challenges us to live in resurrection hope. If Christ has truly risen and death has been defeated, our faith and labor are not in vain. Paul urges believers in 1 Corinthians 15:58: "Therefore, my dear brothers and sisters, stand firm. Let nothing move you. Always give yourselves fully to the work of the Lord, because you know that your labor in the Lord is not in vain." Resurrection hope should shape our daily lives, liberating us from fear and empowering us to live boldly for Christ.

Psalm 16:10 also enriches our worship. When we gather to celebrate the Lord's Supper or Easter, we do so knowing that the one who was crucified is also the one who rose, whose body did not see decay. Our songs of praise are grounded in this fulfilled prophecy, assuring us that every word of God is true and reliable.

Psalm 16:10 is much more than a comforting verse; it is a prophecy fulfilled with exactness in the resurrection of Christ. David's words of trust pointed beyond his experience to the Holy One who would conquer death. The apostles proclaimed this fulfillment as the essence of the gospel, echoing through the church ever since: Christ is risen! His body did not see decay, His grave could not hold Him, and His resurrection assures us of our own. For believers, this verse is both a source of comfort in the face of death and a call to live in the light of resurrection hope.

Layers of Understanding

Historical Context

Psalm 16 reflects David's confidence in God's protection and his assurance that God would not abandon him even in the face of death. While rooted in David's personal faith, the language clearly stretches beyond him to a future fulfillment.

Jewish Understanding

Traditionally, this verse was read as David's personal trust in God's care and deliverance from mortal danger. Some also saw it as the voice of the righteous sufferer. Christians, however, understand it as a prophecy uniquely fulfilled in the Messiah.

New Testament Fulfillment

The apostles applied Psalm 16:10 directly to Jesus. Peter on Pentecost (Acts 2:25–31) and Paul in Acts 13:35–37 both argued that David could not have been speaking of himself. The prophecy was fulfilled when Jesus rose from the dead on the third day.

Theological Significance Today

This verse assures believers that Christ's resurrection was foretold and accomplished. It gives comfort that we, too, will not be abandoned in death but raised with Him. It calls us to live in hope, worship in confidence, and endure in faith, knowing death has lost its sting.

Cross-Reference Connections

- **Acts 2:25–31** – Peter applies Psalm 16:10 to Jesus.
- **Acts 13:35–37** – Paul confirms the prophecy fulfilled in Christ's resurrection.
- **1 Corinthians 15:20–22** – Christ as firstfruits of resurrection.
- **Romans 6:9** – Death no longer has mastery over Him.
- **John 11:25–26** – Jesus, the resurrection and the life.
- **Revelation 1:18** – The Living One who holds the keys of death and Hades.

PROPHECY FULFILLED - STUDY LESSON - 35

LESSON SCRIPTURE: **HOSEA 6: 2**

PROPHECY TITLE

Raised on the Third Day

Introduction

Hosea, a prophet in the eighth century BC, ministered to the northern kingdom of Israel, urging the people to return to God after their repeated unfaithfulness. In Hosea 6:1–3, he speaks of repentance and renewal, proclaiming God's ability to heal, restore, and revive His people. Verse 2 is particularly striking: "After two days he will revive us; on the third day he will restore us, that we may live in his presence."

Initially, this verse addressed Israel's hope for renewal after judgment, but Christians interpret it as a prophetic foreshadowing of Christ's resurrection. Paul references it in 1 Corinthians 15:4, affirming that Jesus was raised on the third day "according to the Scriptures." Hosea's imagery of revival and restoration on the third day ultimately finds its fulfillment in the empty tomb, where Christ was resurrected, securing new life for all who believe.

Scripture Reference

Hosea 6:2 (NIV) **"After two days he will revive us; on the third day he will restore us, that we may live in his presence."**

Big Picture Insights

- **Historical context** – Israel called to repentance and promised restoration.
- **Poetic imagery** – "two days… third day" signals a short, decisive act of renewal.
- **Corporate revival** – initially about Israel as a nation.
- **Messianic fulfillment** – Christ raised on the third day.
- **New Testament connection** – Paul links the resurrection to "the Scriptures" (1 Cor. 15:4).
- **Restoration to life** – ultimate fulfillment in Christ's resurrection power.
- **Presence of God** – resurrection restores fellowship with Him.
- **Foreshadowing** – one of the earliest "third day" resurrection prophecies.
- **Continuity** – Israel's hope prefigures the church's hope in Christ.
- **Pastoral comfort** – God revives the broken, restores the fallen, and brings life out of death.

Verse-by-Verse Commentary

Hosea 6:2a – "After two days he will revive us…"

- The phrase signals God's nearness in rescue. Though judgment falls, restoration stands close at hand. "Two days" functions poetically, stressing swift mercy and certain revival for a repentant people under His covenant love and sovereign initiative.
- Read through the gospel lens, this anticipates resurrection life. The pattern—wounding then healing, tearing then binding—finds fullest expression in Christ, whose death and rising bring real revival to hearts, churches, and communities renewed by grace.

Hosea 6:2b – "…on the third day he will restore us…"

- "Third day" becomes a prophetic marker for decisive divine action. In Hosea's setting it promised national renewal; in salvation history, it foreshadows the resurrection, when God's restoration is complete, public, and victorious over sin, exile, and despair.
- The apostles recognized this pattern fulfilled in Jesus, raised on the third day "according to the Scriptures." Restoration here is not partial renovation but new-creation wholeness, inaugurating the age of life, hope, and reconciled fellowship with God.

Hosea 6:2c – "…that we may live in his presence."

- The goal of revival is communion: restored worship, covenant intimacy, and life before God's face. Presence, not merely pardon, is the promise—sustained relationship replacing estrangement, with joy, holiness, and service flowing from renewed fellowship.
- In Christ this is both now and future. By the Spirit we already share resurrection life, learning to walk with God daily; and we anticipate the consummation—unbroken presence forever—when faith becomes sight and death yields to everlasting joy.

Discussion Questions

1. What did Hosea's prophecy mean for Israel in its original context?

2. How does the imagery of "two days… third day" connect to resurrection hope?

3. Why is the "third day" so significant in the New Testament?

4. How does Paul's statement in 1 Corinthians 15:4 link to Hosea 6:2?

5. What does it mean to "live in His presence" through resurrection life?

6. How can this verse bring comfort in times of brokenness or repentance?

7. How does Hosea 6:2 encourage us to see God's power to restore even after judgment?

Narrative Reflection

Hosea 6:2 stands as one of the most striking verses in the prophetic writings, capturing the rhythm of judgment and restoration, death and life, despair and hope. Though penned in the 8th century B.C., it anticipates the gospel with imagery that becomes central to the New Testament proclamation of Christ's resurrection.

To grasp its depth, we begin in Hosea's world. Hosea prophesied during a time of spiritual adultery in Israel. The people had turned to idolatry, forsaking the covenant relationship with God. Hosea's own marriage to Gomer — a wife who was unfaithful — became a living parable of Israel's unfaithfulness. The message of the book alternates between warning of God's judgment and promises of His redeeming love.

Hosea 6:1–3 begins with a call to repentance: "Come, let us return to the LORD. He has torn us to pieces but he will heal us; he has injured us but he will bind up our wounds." The imagery is of God as both judge and healer, the one who wounds but also the one who heals. This paradox expresses God's covenant love: discipline is never meant to destroy, but to bring His people back to Himself.

Verse 2 builds upon this theme with an assurance of restoration: "After two days he will revive us; on the third day he will restore us, that we may live in his presence." For Hosea's original audience, this was poetic reassurance. "Two days" and "third day" were not intended as literal timetables but as symbolic markers. They communicated that God's restoration would come soon, decisively, and completely. The exile, punishment, or judgment would not last forever. God's love would have the final word.

But as with many prophetic passages, the words of Hosea reached beyond their immediate context. The Spirit of God embedded within them a deeper, messianic fulfillment. Centuries later, the apostles saw in Hosea's imagery a clear anticipation of the resurrection of Christ.

Paul summarizes the gospel in 1 Corinthians 15:3–4: "Christ died for our sins according to the Scriptures, that he was buried, that he was raised on the third day according to the Scriptures." One of the texts that shaped this understanding was Hosea 6:2. While no Old Testament verse states directly, "The Messiah will rise on the third day," Hosea's prophecy provided the poetic and prophetic foundation for this truth.

The resurrection of Jesus is the ultimate revival and restoration. On the cross, He bore the judgment of sin. In the grave, He entered the depths of death. Yet on the third day, He rose again, vindicated by the Father and triumphant over the grave. Hosea's pattern — after two days, revival; on the third day, restoration — is fulfilled perfectly in Christ's passion and resurrection.

The final phrase, "that we may live in his presence," underscores the goal of this restoration. For Israel, this meant being restored to God's covenant fellowship, symbolized in temple worship. For Christians, this reaches its ultimate fulfillment in the resurrection of Christ. Because He rose, we too are restored to God's presence — not temporarily, but eternally. This is both a present reality and a future hope. Even now, believers experience fellowship with God through the Spirit. Yet one day, in the resurrection, we will live in His presence forever, face to face.

The early church clung to this promise. The resurrection of Christ was not an isolated miracle but the firstfruits of what was promised in the Scriptures. Peter and Paul both drew from Hosea and other prophetic passages to demonstrate that Christ's rising on the third day was "according to the Scriptures." Hosea 6:2 was not merely an encouraging word to ancient Israel; it was God's plan for redemption revealed in advance.

For us today, this verse carries layers of assurance. First, it reminds us that God disciplines but also restores. Hosea's audience needed to hear that judgment would not last forever. In our lives, seasons of hardship and discipline may come, but God's purpose is always restoration. His reviving grace comes quickly, often sooner than we expect, and it is decisive.

Second, Hosea 6:2 points us directly to the resurrection of Jesus. The imagery of two days and the third day finds its fulfillment in Christ's victory over death. The resurrection is the center of the Christian faith, the guarantee that sin has been dealt with and eternal life secured. Without it, faith would be in vain; with it, hope is unshakable.

Third, the verse speaks to our own resurrection hope. Just as Christ was raised, so we will be. Paul ties our future resurrection directly to Christ's: "If we have been united with him in a death like his, we will certainly also be united with him in a resurrection like his" (Romans 6:5). The promise that we will "live in his presence" assures us that death does not end our story.

Finally, Hosea 6:2 challenges us to live as people of resurrection. To "return to the Lord" is to repent and embrace the life He offers. Revival begins with repentance, and restoration flows from God's grace. In seasons of personal or corporate brokenness, Hosea's words call us to trust that God can bring life out of death and hope out of despair.

205

Hosea 6:2 is a profound intersection of prophecy, poetry, and gospel truth. For ancient Israel, it meant that judgment would not last forever and that God's mercy would restore them. For the early church, it confirmed that Christ's resurrection was according to the Scriptures. For us today, it assures us that God revives, restores, and raises. After death, life; after separation, presence; after despair, hope. The "third day" is the day of victory, and because Christ rose, we too will live in His presence forever.

Layers of Understanding

Historical Context

Hosea spoke to a nation torn by idolatry and judgment, yet he proclaimed that God's mercy would restore them. "Two days... third day" conveyed that restoration would come quickly and decisively. For Israel, this was reassurance that exile and punishment would not end the covenant relationship but lead to renewal.

Jewish Understanding

Jewish readers understood Hosea 6:2 as a promise of national renewal after judgment. The imagery of revival and restoration affirmed God's mercy toward His people despite their unfaithfulness. While not universally read as messianic, it created patterns of expectation that Christians later recognized as fulfilled in the Messiah's resurrection on the third day.

New Testament Fulfillment

The New Testament applies Hosea 6:2 to Christ's resurrection. Paul in 1 Corinthians 15:4 declares that Jesus was raised "on the third day according to the Scriptures," echoing Hosea's language. Luke 24:46 confirms that the Messiah had to rise on the third day, making Hosea 6:2 a key prophetic foreshadowing.

Theological Significance Today

For believers, Hosea 6:2 assures us of God's power to restore what is broken. It comforts us in times of repentance and trial, reminding us that resurrection hope defines our faith. Through Christ's resurrection, we are revived to live in God's presence both now and forever, secure in His covenant love.

Cross-Reference Connections

- **Hosea 6:1–3** – Context of repentance and renewal.
- **1 Corinthians 15:3–4** – Christ raised on the third day according to the Scriptures.
- **Luke 24:46** – Jesus Himself ties resurrection to the third day.
- **John 14:19** – Because He lives, we will live also.
- **Romans 6:5** – United with Christ in resurrection.
- **Ephesians 2:4–6** – God made us alive with Christ, raising us up with Him.

LESSON SCRIPTURE: ISAIAH 25: 7-9

PROPHECY TITLE

Raised on the Third Day

Introduction

Isaiah 25 is a vision of God's final triumph over sin, sorrow, and death. In verses 7–9, Isaiah proclaims that God will destroy the shroud that covers all nations, wipe away every tear, and swallow up death forever. This prophecy anticipates the resurrection hope fulfilled in Jesus Christ.

The New Testament directly applies these words to the resurrection. Paul cites them in 1 Corinthians 15:54: "Death has been swallowed up in victory." John echoes them in Revelation 21:4, where God wipes away every tear in the new creation. Through Christ's resurrection, death has been defeated, and the promise of eternal life is secured for all who believe.

This vision also reflects the pastoral heart of God. Isaiah reveals that salvation is not only cosmic in scale — destroying death for all nations — but deeply personal in application, as God Himself wipes away tears from every face. It anticipates the end of grief, shame, and fear, pointing us toward a salvation that restores wholeness and joy.

Scripture Reference

Isaiah 25:7–9 (NIV) **"On this mountain he will destroy the shroud that enfolds all peoples, the sheet that covers all nations; [8] he will swallow up death forever. The Sovereign LORD will wipe away the tears from all faces; he will remove his people's disgrace from all the earth. The LORD has spoken. [9] In that day they will say, "Surely this is our God; we trusted in him, and he saved us. This is the LORD, we trusted in him; let us rejoice and be glad in his salvation."**

Big Picture Insights

- **Universal scope** – death and sorrow affect all nations.
- **Shroud destroyed** – God removes death's covering.
- **Swallow up death** – total victory over mortality.
- **Tears wiped away** – comfort and healing for all people.
- **Removal of disgrace** – sin and shame taken away.
- **Resurrection fulfillment** – Christ conquers death in His rising.
- **NT connections** – 1 Cor. 15:54; Rev. 21:4.
- **Covenantal promise** – God Himself guarantees this outcome.
- **Worshipful response** – rejoicing in salvation.
- **Pastoral comfort** – assurance of eternal life and hope.

Verse-by-Verse Commentary

Isaiah 25:7 – "On this mountain he will destroy the shroud that enfolds all peoples, the sheet that covers all nations;"

- **Universal shadow** – The "shroud" represents the universality of death and sorrow, covering every person and every nation without exception. It conveys humanity's helplessness under mortality, but God promises that this shadow will be lifted and destroyed forever by His saving act.
- **God's deliverance** – This verse assures us that death, which binds and limits humanity, is not beyond God's power to undo. His plan includes restoration, renewal, and the gift of eternal life, making His people free from death's suffocating hold.
- **Prophetic hope** – For Isaiah's audience, this was more than poetry. It was assurance that exile, oppression, and grief would not be the final story. The prophecy pointed forward to God's redemptive intervention, culminating in resurrection life through the Messiah.

Isaiah 25:8 – "he will swallow up death forever. The Sovereign LORD will wipe away the tears from all faces; he will remove his people's disgrace from all the earth. The LORD has spoken."

- **Total victory** – The language of "swallowing" signifies a complete reversal. Death, the great devourer of all humanity, will itself be devoured. Its defeat is permanent and absolute, leaving no remnant of its power to haunt or terrify the people of God.
- **Resurrection fulfilled** – Paul directly cites this prophecy in 1 Corinthians 15:54 to explain Christ's resurrection as the fulfillment of God's promise. Death has lost its sting because Jesus has risen, ensuring that those in Him share the same victory.
- **Wiping away tears** – This verse not only announces death's destruction but also declares the end of sorrow. God Himself will wipe away tears from all faces, echoing Revelation 21:4. Salvation is holistic, addressing both the cause and the pain of death.
- **Disgrace removed** – Humanity's shame, tied to sin's curse and mortality, will be undone. Through Christ's redemptive work, disgrace is replaced with honor. God restores His people's dignity, ensuring their eternal standing in His presence free from guilt and condemnation.

Isaiah 25:9 – "In that day they will say, "Surely this is our God; we trusted in him, and he saved us. This is the LORD, we trusted in him; let us rejoice and be glad in his salvation."

- **Confession of faith** – God's people recognize Him as Savior, publicly acknowledging that their trust was rightly placed. Faith becomes sight, and their declaration reveals the covenantal relationship in which God rescues His people, vindicating their hope in Him.
- **Joyful response** – Salvation evokes worship. The natural outcome of being delivered from death is rejoicing. This verse captures the celebratory atmosphere of the final day when mourning ends, and God's redeemed community gathers in eternal joy and thanksgiving.
- **Eschatological fulfillment** – This verse anticipates the ultimate day of resurrection when all God's promises culminate. Trust is vindicated, grief is silenced, and salvation is experienced in its fullness. The eternal feast of joy replaces uncertainty, suffering, and despair.

Discussion Questions

1. What does the "shroud" represent in verse 7?

2. How does Christ's resurrection fulfill the promise of swallowing death?

3. Why is the removal of disgrace linked with the defeat of death?

4. How does Revelation 21:4 connect to this prophecy?

5. What does verse 9 teach us about the proper response to salvation?

6. How can this passage comfort those grieving today?

7. How does this prophecy strengthen our hope for eternity?

Narrative Reflection

Isaiah 25:7–9 presents a triumphant vision that addresses humanity's deepest need and greatest fear: death. Throughout history, death has loomed over human life, bringing grief, separation, and despair. However, Isaiah boldly declares that God will destroy death, wipe away every tear, and turn sorrow into joy. These verses serve not only as poetic promises for ancient Judah but also as gospel truths fulfilled in Christ and anticipated in the new creation.

In verse 7, death is depicted as a suffocating "shroud" or "sheet" that envelops all people. In Hebrew culture, burial shrouds symbolize the finality of death, binding the body in preparation for the grave. Isaiah expands this imagery universally: every person, nation, and family lives under this covering. Death spares no one. Yet God promises to destroy this shroud. What humanity cannot lift, God will tear away.

Verse 8 intensifies the vision: "He will swallow up death forever." Death, which consumes all humanity, will itself be devoured. This metaphor is striking and powerful. In the ancient world, "swallowing" signified overwhelming victory, as when the sea swallows ships or the earth swallows rebels. Isaiah proclaims that death's dominion will be ended not partially or temporarily, but forever. This hope transcends national boundaries; it is cosmic in scope.

Paul echoes this imagery in 1 Corinthians 15:54 when he proclaims the resurrection: "Death has been swallowed up in victory." The resurrection of Jesus concretely fulfills Isaiah's promise. At the cross, sin was judged; in the resurrection, death was defeated. The empty tomb declares that death's reign is broken and will ultimately be abolished.

The prophecy extends beyond cosmic victory to deeply personal language: "The Sovereign Lord will wipe away the tears from all faces." The God who conquers death also comforts His people. He does not merely announce the end of grief; He personally wipes away tears. This imagery conveys intimacy and compassion, affirming that salvation is relational. God Himself will comfort His children.

The verse continues: "He will remove his people's disgrace from all the earth." Death is not only an enemy but also a reminder of sin's curse. Humanity's fall in Eden introduced both shame and mortality. To remove disgrace is to undo sin's consequences, restoring dignity, holiness, and fellowship with God. Revelation 21:4 echoes this promise: no more death, no more mourning, no more crying or pain. The end of tears comes not through denying grief but through destroying its cause.

Verse 9 shifts to the worshipful response of God's people: "Surely this is our God; we trusted in him, and he saved us." In that future day, salvation will be celebrated with joy. Trust, which often feels fragile in the present, will be vindicated. Faith will give way to sight, and God's people will rejoice in His deliverance. The final note is not grief but gladness, not fear but joy.

Isaiah 25:7–9 encapsulates the scope of salvation: cosmic, personal, and eternal. It assures us that God's plan extends beyond forgiving sin to include the undoing of death itself. The cross dealt with guilt; the resurrection defeated mortality; and the consummation will bring the removal of grief and shame forever. Salvation is holistic, touching every aspect of human existence.

For believers today, this passage offers profound comfort. In grief, we are assured that death does not have the final word. Every tear shed will one day be wiped away by God Himself. For those mourning loved ones in Christ, the promise of resurrection secures the hope that separation is temporary.

This promise also strengthens our confidence in God's faithfulness. Isaiah emphasizes his vision with certainty: "The Lord has spoken." God's word guarantees fulfillment. The soldiers at Jesus' tomb believed the grave had won, but the resurrection proved otherwise. If God has promised to swallow death forever, we can live with unshakable assurance that His word will come to pass.

Furthermore, this prophecy challenges us to live as resurrection people. If death is defeated, fear should not govern our lives. We are called to live with courage, generosity, and hope. We can take risks for the gospel, endure suffering, and face mortality with peace, knowing that death has already been conquered in Christ.

Isaiah 25:7–9 stands as one of Scripture's brightest promises. It proclaims that God will destroy the universal shroud of death, swallow it forever, wipe away every tear, and remove disgrace from the earth. Fulfilled in Christ's resurrection and awaiting final consummation, it assures us that life will triumph, joy will endure, and God's people will rejoice in His salvation.

Layers of Understanding

Historical Context

Isaiah prophesied to a people surrounded by threats of war, oppression, and mortality. His words of death's defeat gave hope beyond immediate struggles, pointing to God's final victory. For ancient Judah, this was assurance that their covenant Lord would not allow death and disgrace to reign forever but would intervene decisively.

Jewish Understanding

Jewish readers often interpreted Isaiah 25 as a vision of future messianic deliverance, where God would vindicate His people and extend salvation to the nations. The imagery of feasting and death's removal pointed to God's coming reign, offering hope for Israel's restoration, the healing of nations, and the triumph of divine justice.

New Testament Fulfillment

The New Testament applies this passage directly to Christ's resurrection. Paul cites Isaiah in 1 Corinthians 15:54 to proclaim death's defeat through Jesus. Revelation 21:4 echoes the wiping of tears, linking it with the new creation. Christ's resurrection fulfills the prophecy now, while its ultimate completion awaits His return and final judgment.

Theological Significance Today

For believers, Isaiah 25:7–9 assures victory over death and grief. It reminds us that death is not final, tears will be wiped away, and disgrace removed. This prophecy comforts the grieving, strengthens faith in God's promises, and calls us to live as people of hope, rejoicing in salvation already secured.

Cross-Reference Connections

- **1 Corinthians 15:54** – Death swallowed up in victory.
- **Revelation 21:4** – Tears wiped away, no more death.
- **Hosea 13:14** – God ransoms from death and the grave.
- **John 11:25–26** – Jesus, the resurrection and the life.
- **Romans 8:21** – Creation freed from decay and death.
- **Philippians 3:20–21** – Christ transforms our bodies for immortality.

LESSON SCRIPTURE: **PSALM 110:1**

PROPHECY TITLE
Sit at My Right Hand

Introduction

Psalm 110 is a royal psalm attributed to David, but it extends beyond David's kingship. In verse 1, David writes: "The Lord says to my lord: 'Sit at my right hand until I make your enemies a footstool for your feet.'" This verse depicts a divine dialogue in which Yahweh ("The Lord") speaks to David's "Lord."

Jesus referenced this psalm to provoke His listeners to reconsider their understanding of the Messiah (Matthew 22:41–46). How could David call the Messiah his "Lord" unless the Messiah was greater than him? The New Testament frequently applies this verse to Christ's exaltation after His resurrection (Acts 2:34–35; Hebrews 1:13), confirming that Jesus now reigns at the right hand of God while anticipating the ultimate defeat of His enemies.

This prophecy underscores both the authority of the risen Christ and the certainty of His victory. For believers, it serves as a reassurance that our Lord reigns now, and one day every enemy—sin, Satan, and death—will be placed under His feet.

Scripture Reference

Psalm 110:1 (NIV)   "The LORD says to my lord: "Sit at my right hand until I make our enemies a footstool for your feet."

Big Picture Insights

- **Divine dialogue** – Yahweh speaks to David's Lord.
- **Messianic identity** – points to one greater than David.
- **Right hand of God** – place of power and authority.
- **Enemies subdued** – final victory is certain.
- **Jesus' teaching** – He uses this verse to reveal His identity (Matt. 22).
- **Apostolic preaching** – Peter cites it at Pentecost (Acts 2:34–35).
- **Heavenly enthronement** – Christ exalted after resurrection.
- **Already and not yet** – He reigns now, final defeat of enemies still future.
- **Priestly-kingly role** – psalm also connects to Melchizedek (v. 4).
- **Believers' assurance** – our Lord reigns over all.

Verse-by-Verse Commentary

Psalm 110:1a – "The LORD says to my lord:…"

- David records a divine declaration, distinguishing between "the LORD" (Yahweh) and "my lord" (Messiah). This affirms the Messiah's authority even above David, pointing to Christ's exalted identity as Lord over all.
- Jesus highlighted this verse (Matthew 22:44), showing that the Messiah is not merely David's descendant but David's Lord. It reveals His divine nature and eternal authority, uniting kingship with deity.

Psalm 110:1b – "…Sit at my right hand…"

- The right hand signifies honor, power, and authority. God invites the Messiah to share His throne, granting ultimate rule and partnership in divine sovereignty, affirming the Messiah's co-reign with the Father.
- The New Testament cites this repeatedly (Acts 2:33–35; Hebrews 1:3), showing fulfillment in Christ's ascension. Seated at God's right hand, He rules as intercessor and king until all enemies are defeated.

Psalm 110:1c – "…until I make your enemies a footstool for your feet."

- God assures the Messiah of total victory. Enemies may oppose, but their resistance ends in subjugation. The footstool imagery emphasizes complete conquest under the authority of God's chosen King.
- Paul applies this to Christ's final triumph (1 Corinthians 15:25). All opposition—sin, death, and spiritual powers—will ultimately be brought under His reign, culminating in God's eternal kingdom of peace and justice.

Discussion Questions

1. Why is it significant that David calls the Messiah his "Lord"?

2. How does this verse point to the deity and authority of Christ?

3. What does it mean for Jesus to sit at God's right hand?

4. How do we see the "already/not yet" fulfillment in this verse?

5. What enemies has Christ already defeated, and which remain to be subdued?

6. How does this verse give believers confidence in Christ's present reign?

7. How should Christ's exaltation shape our worship and mission today?

Narrative Reflection

Psalm 110:1 occupies a unique position in Scripture as the most frequently quoted Old Testament verse in the New Testament. This is significant, as the psalm encapsulates themes of kingship, divine authority, victory over enemies, and the identity of the Messiah in a single sentence. When David, Israel's greatest king, wrote these words, he referred to something beyond the limits of his earthly reign. His throne in Jerusalem was temporary; the throne of the coming Messiah would be eternal.

The verse begins with, "The LORD says to my lord…" This introduces a profound mystery. The first "LORD" translates to Yahweh, the covenant God of Israel, while the second, "my lord," is striking because David — the reigning king — acknowledges someone else as his superior. In the cultural and patriarchal context of ancient Israel, fathers and ancestors were honored above their descendants. Yet, David refers to his own descendant as "Lord." This reversal indicates that the coming Messiah would not only be David's son but also his sovereign, possessing divine status.

Jesus highlighted this verse to challenge prevailing assumptions. In Matthew 22:41–46, He asked the Pharisees whose son the Messiah would be. Confidently, they responded, "The son of David." Jesus then cited Psalm 110:1, questioning their understanding. If David, inspired by the Spirit, called the Messiah "Lord," how could the Messiah merely be his son? The religious leaders were silenced, and the implication was clear: the Messiah was both human and divine.

The New Testament writers repeatedly referred to Psalm 110:1 to explain Christ's resurrection and exaltation. At Pentecost, Peter declared: "David did not ascend to heaven, and yet he said, 'The Lord said to my Lord: Sit at my right hand until I make your enemies a footstool for your feet'" (Acts 2:34–35). For Peter, this served as decisive proof that Jesus — risen and ascended — now reigns as both Lord and Christ. He had entered into glory, received authority from the Father, and was seated at His right hand.

The imagery of sitting at the right hand carries deep significance. In ancient royal courts, the seat at the king's right hand was the place of highest honor and power, indicating shared rule. In Christ's case, it signifies His victory over sin and His entrance into heavenly majesty. Hebrews 1:3 emphasizes this truth: after making purification for sins, Jesus "sat down at the right hand of the Majesty in heaven." Unlike earthly priests who stood daily to perform ongoing sacrifices, Jesus sat down because His sacrifice was once for all and fully sufficient. His position represents both rest and rule — His work complete, His reign active.

However, the psalm does not end with enthronement; it anticipates conquest: "until I make your enemies a footstool for your feet." This alludes to ancient warfare practices, where conquerors demonstrated their supremacy by placing their feet on the necks of their defeated foes. Applied to Christ, this signifies that His enemies will be utterly vanquished. Who are these enemies? The New Testament clearly identifies them as sin, death, and Satan. At the cross and the empty tomb, Christ secured a decisive victory. Yet Paul reminds us in 1 Corinthians 15:25–26 that Christ must reign "until He has put all His enemies under His feet. The last enemy to be destroyed is death."

Here, we encounter the tension often described by theologians as the "already and not yet." Christ already reigns, possesses authority, and has defeated the powers of darkness. Yet, the final realization of His victory lies in the future, when He returns in glory to consummate His kingdom. Revelation vividly portrays this, with the Lamb who was slain receiving worship from every creature while the enemies of God are cast into the lake of fire.

For believers, this psalm offers profound encouragement. The world may seem chaotic, enemies may still rage, and suffering may persist, but we know that Christ reigns even now. His position at the right hand of the Father is not merely symbolic; it is a reality. Nothing is outside His control. Every earthly ruler, every demonic power, and every force of sin is already subject to Him and awaits its final defeat.

This truth emboldens our prayers. We pray to a reigning Christ, not to one awaiting authority. It fuels our worship; each time we gather, we join heaven in praising the exalted King (Revelation 5:11–14). It strengthens our mission, for the gospel we proclaim is not just that Christ died, but that He rose, ascended, and reigns. Psalm 110:1 undergirds the Great Commission: we go into the nations with the authority of the enthroned Lord.

In our personal lives, this verse anchors us in assurance. The enemies we face — temptation, fear, guilt, death — are temporary. They may wound us, but they cannot conquer us. The risen Lord holds power over them. Just as the Father promised to make Christ's enemies His footstool, we too can trust that every foe will ultimately fall beneath His rule.

Thus, Psalm 110:1 is not a relic of David's court but a living prophecy fulfilled in Jesus Christ. It affirms His identity as David's greater Son and Lord, His exaltation at God's right hand, His present reign, and His assured victory over all enemies. It draws us into worship, steadies us in hope, and sends us into mission. Above all, it declares the supremacy of Christ — now and forever.

Layers of Understanding

Historical Context

Psalm 110 was a royal psalm celebrating God's support for Israel's king. In its immediate sense, it affirmed divine backing for David's rule. Yet its language surpassed any earthly king, pointing forward to the ultimate Messianic ruler whose reign would extend far beyond Israel's borders and endure eternally.

Jewish Understanding

Jewish interpreters recognized Psalm 110 as messianic, anticipating God's chosen ruler who would bring deliverance and establish justice. While some viewed it in terms of Israel's monarchy, others saw in it the promise of a greater King. Christians identify its fullest meaning in Jesus, the exalted Messiah who fulfills David's hope.

New Testament Fulfillment

The New Testament repeatedly cites Psalm 110:1 to affirm Christ's exaltation. Jesus applied it to Himself (Matthew 22), Peter proclaimed it at Pentecost (Acts 2), Hebrews declared it proof of Christ's superiority (Hebrews 1), and Paul tied it to final victory over death (1 Corinthians 15). Its fulfillment is comprehensive and climactic.

Theological Significance Today

For believers, Psalm 110:1 assures that Christ already reigns at God's right hand. His enthronement gives confidence in prayer, courage in mission, and comfort in trials. It reminds us that evil's defeat is guaranteed, inviting us to live faithfully under His Lordship, worship joyfully, and proclaim His kingdom to the nations.

Cross-Reference Connections

- **Matthew 22:41–46** – Jesus challenges the Pharisees with Psalm 110:1.
- **Acts 2:34–35** – Peter cites it at Pentecost.
- **Hebrews 1:13** – Christ's unique enthronement above angels.
- **1 Corinthians 15:25–26** – Christ reigns until all enemies defeated.
- **Philippians 2:9–11** – Every knee will bow, every tongue confess.
- **Revelation 5:11–14** – The enthroned Lamb worshiped by heaven.

PROPHECY FULFILLED - STUDY LESSON - 38

LESSON SCRIPTURE: JOEL 2:28-32

PROPHECY TITLE

The Spirit Poured Out on All People

Introduction

Joel's prophecy anticipates a time when God will act decisively in history, not only through judgment but also through renewal. In Joel 2:28–32, the Lord promises to pour out His Spirit on all people—men and women, young and old, slave and free. This democratization of the Spirit signifies a new era in God's redemptive plan.

The New Testament identifies the fulfillment of this prophecy on the Day of Pentecost. In Acts 2:16–21, Peter explains that the outpouring of the Spirit on the disciples marks the beginning of what Joel foretold. The manifestations of tongues of fire, prophecy, visions, and dreams all confirm that the Spirit has been poured out through the risen Christ.

However, Joel's words also point to the "great and dreadful day of the Lord." The prophecy encompasses both a "now" and "not yet" aspect: the Spirit has indeed been poured out, but the final day of the Lord is still to come. For believers, this passage assures us of the Spirit's presence and power in our lives while urging us to remain ready for Christ's return.

Scripture Reference

Joel 2:28–32 (NIV)   "And afterward, I will pour out my Spirit on all people. Your sons and daughters will prophesy, your old men will dream dreams, your young men will see visions. [29] Even on my servants, both men and women, I will pour out my Spirit in those days. [30] I will show wonders in the heavens and on the earth, blood and fire and billows of smoke. [31] The sun will be turned to darkness and the moon to blood before the coming of the great and dreadful day of the LORD. [32] And everyone who calls on the name of the LORD will be saved; for on Mount Zion and in Jerusalem there will be deliverance, as the LORD has said, even among the survivors whom the LORD calls."

Big Picture Insights

- **Spirit poured out** – not limited to prophets, kings, or priests.
- **All people included** – men and women, young and old, slave and free.
- **Signs and wonders** – cosmic events signal the day of the Lord.
- **Now and not yet** – fulfilled at Pentecost, consummated at the end of the age.

- **Salvation promise** – everyone who calls on the name of the Lord will be saved.
- **Universal invitation** – salvation is open to all nations and peoples.
- **Mount Zion focus** – salvation flows from God's covenant people.
- **Continuity** – ties OT prophecy to NT fulfillment.
- **Empowerment** – the Spirit equips believers for witness and service.
- **Hope** – God's Spirit presence assures us until Christ returns.

Verse-by-Verse Commentary

Joel 2:28–29 – "And afterward, I will pour out my Spirit on all people. Your sons and daughters will prophesy, your old men will dream dreams, your young men will see visions. [29] Even on my servants, both men and women, I will pour out my Spirit in those days."

- God's promise of pouring out the Spirit marks a radical break with the Old Testament pattern, where only select leaders or prophets experienced this empowerment. Here, all God's people are included without distinction of age, gender, or social class.
- The fulfillment begins at Pentecost (Acts 2:16–18), where Peter declares Joel's prophecy realized through the Spirit's descent. This universal scope demonstrates the inclusivity of God's plan and the Spirit's essential role in uniting the church.
- Prophecy, dreams, and visions signify the Spirit's activity across generations. Young and old alike share in God's revelation, showing that the Spirit communicates God's purposes through diverse means that equip believers for guidance, encouragement, and witness.

Joel 2:30–31 – "I will show wonders in the heavens and on the earth, blood and fire and billows of smoke. [31] The sun will be turned to darkness and the moon to blood before the coming of the great and dreadful day of the LORD."

- The imagery of blood, fire, smoke, darkened sun, and moon turned to blood reflects apocalyptic language associated with divine judgment. These cosmic signs declare God's sovereignty over creation and point to His decisive intervention in human history.
- At Christ's crucifixion, some of these signs appeared—such as the midday darkness (Matthew 27:45)—providing a foretaste of ultimate fulfillment. These events remind us that the death of Christ was both redemptive and cosmic in significance.
- Other aspects remain future, anticipating Christ's return when creation itself will bear witness to God's final judgment and renewal. The signs serve as warnings and reminders of the certainty of the "great and dreadful day of the Lord."

Joel 2:32 – "And everyone who calls on the name of the LORD will be saved; for on Mount Zion and in Jerusalem there will be deliverance, as the LORD has said, even among the survivors whom the LORD calls."

- This verse proclaims a universal invitation to salvation. Unlike earlier covenants often seen as limited to Israel, the promise now extends to "everyone," transcending barriers of ethnicity, culture, and social status. Salvation becomes available to all through faith.
- The verse is quoted in Acts 2:21 and Romans 10:13, underscoring its centrality in the gospel message. It assures us that no one is excluded from God's saving grace if they sincerely call upon Him in trust.

218

- Deliverance is rooted in God's covenant faithfulness. Salvation is not human achievement but God's gift, centered in Zion and fulfilled in Christ, through whom all nations are invited to experience deliverance and eternal life.

Discussion Questions

1. Why is the Spirit's outpouring on "all people" so significant?

2. How did Pentecost fulfill Joel's prophecy?

3. What does it mean that the prophecy has both "already" and "not yet" aspects?

4. How do prophecy, dreams, and visions show the Spirit's presence?

5. Why is the cosmic imagery of vv. 30–31 important for the day of the Lord?

6. How does the promise in verse 32 shape our understanding of salvation?

7. What does this passage teach us about the Spirit's role in empowering believers today?

Narrative Reflection

Few prophetic passages carry as much weight as Joel 2:28–32, bridging Old Testament expectation with New Testament fulfillment. In these verses, God promises a sweeping transformation of how His Spirit will interact with His people. What had once been limited to kings like David, prophets like Isaiah, or craftsmen like Bezalel in building the tabernacle, would now be extended to all God's people. This change represents nothing less than a new epoch in salvation history.

The promise begins with the striking phrase, "I will pour out my Spirit." The verb "pour out" suggests lavish abundance. God does not give sparingly but generously, flooding His people with His Spirit. This imagery recalls rain falling on dry land, restoring life to what was barren. In the same way, the Spirit brings vitality, renewal, and transformation to God's people.

Unlike earlier eras, this outpouring is for "all people." The Spirit's activity is no longer confined to a chosen few. Sons and daughters will prophesy, old men will dream dreams, and young men will see visions. Even slaves, both men and women, are included. This radical inclusivity breaks down traditional barriers of age, gender, and social class. The Spirit is for all, a reality the New Testament affirms when it declares that in Christ there is neither Jew nor Gentile, slave nor free, male nor female (Galatians 3:28).

The fulfillment of Joel's prophecy is seen most clearly at Pentecost. In Acts 2, as tongues of fire rested on the disciples and they proclaimed the mighty works of God in languages they had never learned, Peter stood up and explained, "This is what was spoken by the prophet Joel." Pentecost was the watershed moment when Joel's vision became reality. The Spirit who once empowered a select few now filled the entire community of believers, empowering them for mission.

Yet Joel's prophecy does not end with Pentecost. He also describes signs and wonders: blood, fire, smoke, the sun darkened, the moon turned to blood. These cosmic disturbances serve as markers of divine judgment and anticipate the day of the Lord. Some of these signs were foreshadowed in Christ's crucifixion, such as the midday darkness, underscoring that His death was not an isolated event but one of cosmic importance. Still, many of these signs remain to be fulfilled in the future, pointing to Christ's second coming.

This "already and not yet" tension is central to Joel's prophecy. The Spirit has already been poured out, and the church already lives in the age of the Spirit. Yet the final day of the Lord is still coming, bringing judgment on God's enemies and final salvation for His people. Christians live in the overlap of the ages: empowered by the Spirit now, while waiting for the consummation of God's kingdom.

The heart of the prophecy is found in verse 32: "Everyone who calls on the name of the Lord will be saved." This is one of the clearest statements of the universality of salvation in the Old Testament. It affirms that salvation is available to all who turn to God in faith. The New Testament repeatedly affirms this truth. Paul, in Romans 10, quotes Joel to show that salvation is not dependent on ethnicity or adherence to the law but on faith in Christ. The message is as simple as it is profound: whoever calls on the name of the Lord will be saved.

For the early church, this was revolutionary. No longer was salvation tied to national identity, temple rituals, or hereditary priesthood. Instead, salvation was rooted in calling upon the Lord Jesus Christ. The Spirit poured out at Pentecost was both the sign and the guarantee of this new reality.

Joel's prophecy highlights three major truths. First, it reveals the Spirit's role in empowering the people of God. The Spirit is not merely a personal comforter but the divine presence enabling prophecy, visions, and dreams — signs that God is at work. Second, it underscores the universality of salvation. God's grace is extended to all who call upon Him, regardless of background. Third, it points forward to the final day of the Lord, when God's purposes will be brought to completion and His kingdom fully revealed.

For believers today, this prophecy is deeply encouraging. It assures us that the Spirit is for all — not only for leaders, pastors, or missionaries but for every believer. Whatever our age, gender, or social position, the Spirit equips us for service. It also challenges us to live Spirit-filled lives, sensitive to God's leading through prophecy, dreams, and visions. Furthermore, it calls us to mission, as those who have received the Spirit are sent out to bear witness to Christ.

Finally, Joel 2:28–32 offers hope. In a world marked by uncertainty, conflict, and brokenness, the Spirit's presence reminds us that God has not abandoned His people. He has poured out His Spirit as a down payment of what is to come, guaranteeing that His promises will be fulfilled. The cosmic signs remind us that history is moving toward a climactic conclusion, and the promise of salvation for all who call upon the Lord assures us of His grace.

At its heart, Joel's prophecy encapsulates God's unfolding plan of salvation. It declares that the Spirit has been poured out, salvation is available to all, and history is moving toward the day when Christ will return. For us, it means living in the power of the Spirit now, trusting in God's promises, and awaiting the glorious day of the Lord with hope and expectation.

Layers of Understanding

Historical Context

Joel addressed a nation devastated by locust plagues, using their destruction as a picture of the coming "day of the Lord." His prophecy looked beyond immediate crisis, assuring Israel that judgment would give way to renewal. The Spirit's promised outpouring marked a new covenant reality, extending God's presence beyond Israel's leaders.

Jewish Understanding

For Jewish readers, Joel's words offered hope for national revival. They anticipated a restored Israel, empowered by God's Spirit, where prophecy and visions would guide the people. This was seen as a sign of God's faithfulness, with deliverance centered in Zion, affirming God's continuing covenant commitment to His chosen people.

New Testament Fulfillment

The New Testament identifies Joel's prophecy with Pentecost. Peter proclaimed it fulfilled in the Spirit's descent on the disciples (Acts 2). Paul quoted Joel in Romans 10:13 to affirm universal salvation. The cosmic imagery, however, awaits completion at Christ's return, showing that the prophecy encompasses both inauguration and consummation.

Theological Significance Today

Joel's prophecy assures believers that the Spirit empowers every Christian, not just a chosen few. It challenges the church to live Spirit-filled lives, exercising spiritual gifts in mission and service. It also reminds us that salvation is universally available, and that history is moving toward Christ's return and God's final victory.

Cross-Reference Connections

- **Acts 2:16–21** – Peter cites Joel at Pentecost.
- **Romans 10:13** – Everyone who calls on the Lord will be saved.
- **Matthew 27:45** – Darkness at Jesus' crucifixion recalls cosmic signs.
- **Revelation 6:12; 21:4** – Final day imagery and tears wiped away.
- **Numbers 11:29** – Moses longed for all God's people to have the Spirit.
- **John 7:37–39** – Jesus promises rivers of living water through the Spirit.

PROPHECY FULFILLED - STUDY LESSON - 39

LESSON SCRIPTURE: **DANIEL 7:13-14**

PROPHECY TITLE

The Son of Man Given Dominion

Introduction

In Daniel 7, the prophet has a vision of four beasts symbolizing worldly empires, followed by the enthronement of the Ancient of Days. In this dramatic moment, "one like a son of man" approaches God and is granted everlasting dominion.

This prophecy is crucial because it identifies the Messiah not only as Israel's king but also as the universal ruler over all nations. Jesus often referred to Himself as the "Son of Man," directly linking His mission to Daniel's vision (Matthew 26:64; Mark 14:62). After His resurrection, the apostles recognized His ascension and exaltation as the fulfillment of this prophecy.

Daniel 7:13–14 reassures us that Christ reigns with authority over every nation, and His kingdom will never end. For believers, this promise strengthens our hope in the unshakable reign of the Son of Man.

Scripture Reference

Daniel 7:13–14 (NIV)   "In my vision at night I looked, and there before me was one like a son of man, coming with the clouds of heaven. He approached the Ancient of Days and was led into his presence. 14 He was given authority, glory and sovereign power; all nations and peoples of every language worshiped him. His dominion is an everlasting dominion that will not pass away, and his kingdom is one that will never be destroyed."

Big Picture Insights

- **Heavenly vision** – Daniel sees beyond earthly kingdoms.
- **Son of Man** – human figure with divine authority.
- **Coming with the clouds** – imagery of divinity and heavenly vindication.
- **Ancient of Days** – God Himself enthroning the Messiah.
- **Universal reign** – all nations and languages serve Him.
- **Eternal dominion** – unlike earthly kingdoms, His kingdom never ends.
- **Messianic title** – Jesus' preferred self-designation points here.
- **NT fulfillment** – seen in Christ's resurrection, ascension, and exaltation.
- **Worshiped by all** – points to divine status.
- **Hope for believers** – kingdom secure despite worldly chaos.

Verse-by-Verse Commentary

Daniel 7:13 – "In my vision at night I looked, and there before me was one like a son of man, coming with the clouds of heaven. He approached the Ancient of Days and was led into his presence."

- The "Son of Man" figure is deliberately contrasted with the beastly kingdoms that precede him, emphasizing true humanity in contrast to corrupted power and brutality. He represents the dignity and righteousness of God's intended design for dominion.
- The imagery of "coming with the clouds of heaven" points to divine status, since cloud-riding is consistently associated with God in Scripture (Psalm 104:3; Isaiah 19:1). The phrase indicates glory, vindication, and heavenly origin.
- This figure is both human and divine, suggesting the mystery of incarnation fulfilled in Christ. His humanity identifies Him with us, while His divine authority demonstrates His role as the appointed ruler of heaven and earth.
- The prophecy finds its fulfillment in Christ's resurrection and ascension. Acts 1:9–11 and Revelation 1:7 confirm that He ascended on the clouds and will return in the same manner, uniting both exaltation and eschatological hope.

Daniel 7:14 – "He was given authority, glory and sovereign power; all nations and peoples of every language worshiped him. His dominion is an everlasting dominion that will not pass away, and his kingdom is one that will never be destroyed."

- The Ancient of Days entrusts this Son of Man with full rule, showing divine commissioning. Authority is not seized by violence but granted from heaven, underscoring His legitimacy and divine approval to reign eternally.
- The scope of His dominion is universal. All nations, tribes, and languages worship Him, revealing a kingdom that transcends boundaries and fulfills God's promise to Abraham that all nations would be blessed through his seed.
- His dominion is everlasting, explicitly contrasted with the temporal nature of earthly kingdoms. Unlike Babylon, Persia, Greece, or Rome, His reign cannot be destroyed, emphasizing permanence, stability, and divine sovereignty.
- The New Testament applies this directly to Jesus. After His resurrection, He declares, "All authority in heaven and on earth has been given to me" (Matthew 28:18). Philippians 2:9–11 confirms that every knee will bow before Him.

Discussion Questions

1. Why is it significant that the Messiah is called "Son of Man"?

2. What does the imagery of coming with the clouds reveal about His nature?

3. How does this vision contrast earthly kingdoms with Christ's kingdom?

4. How did Jesus use Daniel 7:13–14 to explain His mission?

5. What does it mean that all nations will worship Him?

6. How does this prophecy strengthen our faith in times of political or cultural upheaval?

7. How does the eternal nature of Christ's dominion give us hope today?

Narrative Reflection

Daniel 7:13–14 presents one of the Old Testament's most powerful and hope-inspiring visions, revealing God's purpose to establish an everlasting kingdom under the reign of the Son of Man. To grasp its full meaning, we must first consider the broader vision in Daniel 7. Daniel saw four beasts emerge from the sea, each representing successive empires that would dominate human history—Babylon, Medo-Persia, Greece, and Rome. These kingdoms, though powerful, were depicted as grotesque beasts, emphasizing their corruption, violence, and inhumanity.

Against this backdrop, the vision shifts to heaven. The Ancient of Days, clothed in radiant purity, takes His throne. His court sits in judgment, and the beasts' dominions are stripped away. Into this heavenly courtroom comes "one like a son of man." The contrast is striking. While the beasts symbolize dehumanized power, the Son of Man embodies true humanity, ruling as God intended—justly, righteously, and under divine commission.

Yet the Son of Man is more than a mere human ruler. He comes "with the clouds of heaven," an image consistently associated with divine appearances in Scripture. When Israel was led through the wilderness, God went before them in a pillar of cloud (Exodus 13:21). The psalmist declares that God "makes the clouds His chariot" (Psalm 104:3). To ride the clouds is to share in divine authority. Thus, Daniel presents a mysterious figure—human in appearance, yet divine in status.

This figure approaches the Ancient of Days, not as a subject in fear but as one worthy to stand in His presence. Remarkably, the Ancient of Days bestows upon Him authority, glory, and sovereign power. All nations and peoples worship Him. This act is profound, for in Israel's faith, worship belongs to God alone. That worship is directed to the Son of Man affirms His divine identity.

His dominion is described as everlasting. Unlike the beastly kingdoms, which rise and fall with violence and corruption, His kingdom will never pass away. It will not be overthrown by another empire, nor corrupted by sin. It is a kingdom of stability, righteousness, and eternal peace.

Jesus deliberately embraced this prophecy as His own identity and mission. Of all the titles available to Him—Messiah, Son of David, King of Israel—He most often referred to Himself as the "Son of Man." This was not a modest attempt to emphasize His humanity but a deliberate reference to Daniel 7. Over eighty times in the Gospels, Jesus used this title, anchoring His mission in this vision of universal dominion.

The clearest moment came during His trial before the Sanhedrin. Asked if He was the Messiah, Jesus replied: "From now on you will see the Son of Man sitting at the right hand of the Mighty One and coming on the clouds of heaven" (Matthew 26:64). His words directly echoed Daniel 7:13–14, claiming both divine authority and heavenly vindication. The religious leaders understood the claim as blasphemy, for Jesus identified Himself as the divine ruler of Daniel's vision.

The New Testament confirms that this prophecy was fulfilled in Jesus' resurrection and ascension. Peter proclaimed at Pentecost that God exalted Jesus to His right hand, giving Him authority as Lord and Messiah (Acts 2:33–36). Paul wrote that God exalted Him and gave Him the name above every name, so that every knee would bow (Philippians 2:9–11). John in Revelation saw the risen Christ coming with the clouds, fulfilling Daniel's vision (Revelation 1:7).

This vision also provides a powerful theological contrast between earthly kingdoms and Christ's kingdom. Human empires, no matter how strong, are temporary. They rise in violence, maintain power through oppression, and fall into corruption. In contrast, Christ's kingdom is eternal, righteous, and universal. It encompasses all nations, peoples, and languages. It is not bound by geography, culture, or politics, but transcends them all.

For believers, Daniel 7:13–14 offers deep encouragement in times of uncertainty. Like Daniel, we live in a world marked by beastly powers—governments that oppress, cultures that distort, and forces that corrupt. Yet above all of this stands the Son of Man, reigning with unshakable authority. His dominion cannot be threatened. His kingdom cannot be destroyed.

This vision also shapes our worship. Daniel saw all nations worshiping the Son of Man. Today, the church embodies this reality as people from every tribe and tongue gather to worship Christ. Our worship is both present reality and future anticipation of the universal adoration that will come at His return.

Finally, this prophecy gives us eternal hope. Sin, death, and evil do not have the final word. The Son of Man does. His kingdom is everlasting, His reign unshakable, and His promises certain. For those who belong to Him, this vision guarantees participation in His victory.

Daniel 7:13–14 brings us to the climax of hope, unveiling the Son of Man in His exaltation, entrusted with eternal dominion by the Ancient of Days. Fulfilled in Jesus Christ, this prophecy assures us of His present reign, calls us to faithful worship, and anchors our hope in His eternal kingdom.

Layers of Understanding

Historical Context

Daniel's vision was given during Israel's exile, a time when foreign empires seemed invincible. The beasts represented oppressive kingdoms, yet the vision reminded God's people that these powers were temporary. Above them, the Ancient of Days and the Son of Man revealed God's sovereignty and the promise of eternal dominion.

Jewish Understanding

Many Jewish interpreters viewed the "Son of Man" as a symbol of God's people, vindicated after suffering. Others saw Him as a messianic figure, God's chosen representative to bring justice and restoration. Christians see in Him the Messiah, combining true humanity with divine authority, fulfilling Israel's hope for universal deliverance.

New Testament Fulfillment

Jesus identified Himself as the Son of Man more than any other title, grounding His mission in Daniel 7. His resurrection, ascension, and exaltation fulfill the prophecy of dominion, as He declares authority over heaven and earth (Matthew 28:18). Revelation affirms His coming with clouds, uniting inauguration and final consummation.

Theological Significance Today

For believers, this prophecy assures us that Christ reigns with unchallenged authority over all nations. His kingdom cannot be destroyed, giving hope amid turmoil. It calls us to worship Him as divine King, trust His sovereignty in uncertain times, and live faithfully in anticipation of sharing in His eternal reign.

Cross-Reference Connections

- **Matthew 26:64; Mark 14:62** – Jesus identifies Himself with Daniel 7.
- **Acts 2:33–36** – Exalted at God's right hand, given authority.
- **Philippians 2:9–11** – Every knee will bow to Him.
- **Revelation 1:7** – Son of Man coming with clouds.
- **1 Corinthians 15:24–27** – Christ must reign until all enemies subdued.
- **Psalm 110:1** – Sit at my right hand until enemies made a footstool.

Series 6 – Messianic Kingdom Prophecies

PROPHECY FULFILLED - STUDY LESSON - 40

LESSON SCRIPTURE: **JEREMIAH 31:31-34**

PROPHECY TITLE

The Promise of a New Covenant

Introduction

Jeremiah began his ministry in 627 B.C., during the 13th year of King Josiah's reign (Jeremiah 1:2). His prophetic calling emerged in one of Israel's darkest periods, characterized by Judah's decline, the fall of Jerusalem, and the subsequent exile to Babylon. Amidst judgment and despair, God spoke through Jeremiah, offering a message of hope: He would establish a new covenant with His people. Unlike the previous covenant made at Sinai, which was inscribed on stone tablets and ultimately broken due to disobedience, this new covenant would be written on their hearts.

This prophecy is crucial for understanding the gospel. At the Last Supper, Jesus stated, "This cup is the new covenant in my blood" (Luke 22:20). The writer of Hebrews extensively references Jeremiah 31:31–34, illustrating that Christ fulfilled this prophecy by offering forgiveness and internal transformation through the Spirit (Hebrews 8:8–12; 10:16–17).

For believers today, Jeremiah's prophecy reassures us that our relationship with God is based not on external laws but on inward renewal, complete forgiveness, and unbreakable fellowship through Christ.

Scripture Reference

Jeremiah 31:31–34 (NIV)   "The days are coming," declares the LORD, "when I will make a new covenant with the people of Israel and with the people of Judah. ³² It will not be like the covenant I made with their ancestors when I took them by the hand to lead them out of Egypt, because they broke my covenant, though I was a husband to them," declares the LORD. ³³ "This is the covenant I will make with the people of Israel after that time," declares the LORD. "I will put my law in their minds and write it on their hearts. I will be their God, and they will be my people. ³⁴ No longer will they teach their neighbor, or say to one another, 'Know the LORD,' because they will all know me, from the least of them to the greatest," declares the LORD. "For I will forgive their wickedness and will remember their sins no more."

Big Picture Insights

- **New covenant** – different in nature from Sinai's covenant.
- **Internalized law** – written on hearts, not stone tablets.
- **Restored relationship** – God as their God, people as His.
- **Universal knowledge of God** – intimate, personal fellowship.
- **Full forgiveness** – sins remembered no more.
- **Fulfilled in Christ** – the cup of the new covenant in His blood (Luke 22:20).
- **Hebrews' emphasis** – superior covenant through Jesus (Hebrews 8, 10).
- **Spirit's role** – inward transformation (Ezekiel 36:26–27).
- **Continuity** – fulfills God's covenant promises to Abraham, Moses, and David.
- **Pastoral comfort** – assurance of forgiveness and intimacy with God.

Verse-by-Verse Commentary

Jeremiah 31:31 – "The days are coming," declares the LORD, "when I will make a new covenant with the people of Israel and with the people of Judah."

- The covenant at Sinai established Israel's identity but was broken repeatedly through rebellion. God's promise of a "new" covenant shows His faithfulness despite their failure and His intent to provide something greater than external laws.
- This covenant is rooted in God's initiative, not human strength. It points toward Christ, who inaugurates it in His blood (Luke 22:20), ensuring forgiveness, permanence, and transformation.
- The promise of a "new covenant" introduces hope beyond exile, demonstrating that failure does not end God's purposes. Instead, He brings renewal that surpasses what came before.

Jeremiah 31:32 – "³²It will not be like the covenant I made with their ancestors when I took them by the hand to lead them out of Egypt, because they broke my covenant, though I was a husband to them," declares the LORD."

- The Sinai covenant depended on obedience to laws given externally. Though God was faithful like a husband, Israel broke it through idolatry and injustice. This exposed the insufficiency of law without inward transformation.
- The new covenant is greater because it is not based on fragile human willpower but on God's grace and Spirit. It moves from external compulsion to internal transformation.
- Jeremiah highlights the contrast to show that God's redemptive plan always pointed beyond Sinai to something enduring and unbreakable.

Jeremiah 31:33 – "This is the covenant I will make with the people of Israel after that time," declares the LORD. "I will put my law in their minds and write it on their hearts. I will be their God, and they will be my people."

- This promise shows God's law no longer external but internalized. His people are transformed from within, shaped by Spirit-led obedience instead of mere outward compliance (Ezekiel 36:26–27).
- Relationship is central: "I will be their God, and they will be my people." Covenant is not simply about rules but restored fellowship.

- The Spirit's work ensures believers know God's will, desire His ways, and walk in faithfulness that flows from renewed hearts rather than imposed duty.

Jeremiah 31:34 – "No longer will they teach their neighbor, or say to one another, 'Know the LORD,' because they will all know me, from the least of them to the greatest," declares the LORD. "For I will forgive their wickedness and will remember their sins no more."

- Under the old covenant, priests and prophets mediated knowledge of God. Under the new, every believer enjoys direct access, from the least to the greatest, pointing to a universal fellowship.
- Forgiveness is the covenant's foundation. God promises not merely to cover sins but to erase them completely, remembering them no more.
- This is fulfilled in Christ's once-for-all sacrifice (Hebrews 10:16–18), where His blood secured eternal redemption and established intimacy between God and His people.

Discussion Questions

1. Why did the old covenant fail, and what makes the new covenant different?

2. What does it mean for God's law to be written on hearts rather than tablets?

3. How does this prophecy anticipate the work of the Holy Spirit?

4. What does universal knowledge of God imply for the people of God?

5. How does this prophecy point directly to Christ's sacrifice at the Last Supper?

6. Why is the promise of full forgiveness so central to this passage?

7. How should believers today live in light of being part of the new covenant?

Narrative Reflection

Jeremiah 31:31–34 stands out as one of the most hopeful and transformative passages in the Old Testament. It speaks directly to the despair of Judah's collapse and exile, while also extending far beyond their immediate circumstances. Central to Israel's story is the concept of covenant: God's binding relationship with His people, revealed through promises, laws, and signs. However, Israel consistently failed to uphold its end of the covenant, breaking God's commands and turning to idols. The exile was a tragic consequence of this failure. Yet, amidst this darkness, God promised not just to restore the old covenant but to establish something entirely new—an unbreakable covenant.

The term "new covenant" is remarkable. The covenant at Sinai was marked by thunder, lightning, and the voice of God. Inscribed on stone tablets, it symbolized God's holiness and the obligations of His people. However, from the incident of the golden calf onward, Israel repeatedly fell short. The old covenant highlighted humanity's need but could not address the problem of sinfulness. Jeremiah's prophecy recognizes this failure and declares that God Himself would take action to resolve it.

The new covenant is inward rather than outward. God promises: "I will put my law in their minds and write it on their hearts." Unlike stone tablets that could be disregarded, God's law would be inscribed within His people. This promise foreshadows the work of the Spirit. Centuries later, Ezekiel would describe God's promise of a new heart and Spirit (Ezekiel 36:26–27). The law, once external, would now be internal, leading to genuine obedience that flows from love rather than fear.

At the heart of the covenant is relationship: "I will be their God, and they will be my people." This phrase resonates throughout Scripture as the essence of God's purpose. The covenant is not merely legal but profoundly relational. Humanity, estranged by sin, would once again enjoy intimacy with the Creator. In this promise, we see God's ultimate desire—not just to govern His people but to dwell with them in unbroken fellowship.

Verse 34 expands this vision to universal access: "They will all know me, from the least of them to the greatest." Under the old covenant, knowledge of God was mediated by priests and prophets. The people relied on rituals and teachers to maintain their relationship with God. However, under the new covenant, knowledge of God would be direct and personal. Social status, education, and position would not dictate access; every believer, regardless of their standing, would know God intimately.

Forgiveness is foundational: "I will forgive their wickedness and remember their sins no more." The old covenant's sacrificial system served as a reminder of sin but could never fully remove it (Hebrews 10:1–

4). Year after year, sacrifices were made, yet guilt lingered. In contrast, the new covenant promises complete forgiveness. God pledges not only to forgive but to forget, choosing to remember sins no more. This profound assurance guarantees that reconciliation with God is both total and irreversible.

The New Testament identifies this prophecy as fulfilled in Christ. At the Last Supper, Jesus proclaimed, "This cup is the new covenant in my blood" (Luke 22:20). His death on the cross inaugurated the covenant that Jeremiah foresaw. His blood replaced the old sacrifices with a once-for-all offering, securing eternal redemption. The book of Hebrews directly quotes Jeremiah 31:31–34 to illustrate that Christ's sacrifice achieved what the old covenant could not: forgiveness, transformation, and intimacy with God (Hebrews 8:8–12; 10:16–18).

For the early church, this prophecy clarified the transition from temple rituals to a Spirit-filled community. God's presence was no longer confined to a temple; His Spirit resided within believers. Sacrifices were no longer repeated; Christ's sacrifice was final. Knowledge of God was no longer limited; every believer could know Him personally.

For us today, Jeremiah 31:31–34 remains both comforting and challenging. It comforts us by assuring us of God's forgiveness. Our sins are not just pardoned but erased from God's memory. This truth liberates us from guilt and fear, reminding us that our standing with God is secure, based not on our performance but on Christ's finished work.

It also assures us of God's presence. The promise that all will know Him means we are not left to second-hand faith. Through the Spirit, we enjoy direct fellowship with the living God. Prayer, worship, and obedience become expressions of an inward relationship rather than external duties.

Yet this prophecy also presents a challenge. If God's law is written on our hearts, our lives should reflect His character. We are called to embody love, justice, mercy, and holiness in our daily lives. If we are forgiven, we must extend forgiveness. If we know God, we must make Him known to others. The new covenant transforms not only our status before God but also our mission in the world.

Jeremiah 31:31–34 is the gospel in prophetic form. It announces a new covenant rooted in forgiveness, inward transformation, and intimate fellowship. Fulfilled in Christ's blood and sealed by the Spirit, it reassures us of God's unbreakable love. For the exiles of Jeremiah's day, it offered hope beyond failure. For us, it establishes the foundation of our faith and life in Christ. God has declared: "I will be their God, and they will be my people." This is the covenant reality we now inhabit—eternal, unshakable, and filled with hope.

Layers of Understanding

Historical Context

Jeremiah spoke during Judah's darkest collapse, when exile to Babylon revealed the nation's covenant failure. The old covenant, though glorious at Sinai, had been broken beyond repair. Into this despair, God promised a new covenant that would surpass the old — inward, lasting, and unbreakable — offering hope beyond judgment.

Jewish Understanding

For Jewish readers, this passage promised renewal after exile. It looked toward restoration of relationship with God and covenant faithfulness. Many saw it as national revival, when God would once again bless His people. Christians recognize its deeper fulfillment in Christ, the mediator of the new covenant for all nations.

New Testament Fulfillment

Jesus inaugurated the new covenant at the Last Supper, declaring His blood its foundation (Luke 22:20). Hebrews quotes Jeremiah to affirm its fulfillment in Christ's sacrifice, which provides full forgiveness and inward transformation. Through the Spirit, God's law is written on hearts, and believers enjoy direct access to intimate fellowship.

Theological Significance Today

This prophecy assures believers of complete forgiveness, inward renewal, and personal fellowship with God. It shifts religion from external duty to internal transformation. For Christians, it defines identity as covenant people empowered by the Spirit, called to reflect God's character and live in hope of His unbreakable promises through Christ.

Cross-Reference Connections

- **Luke 22:20** – Jesus' blood as the new covenant.
- **Hebrews 8:8–12; 10:16–18** – Jeremiah quoted as fulfilled in Christ.
- **Ezekiel 36:26–27** – Promise of new heart and Spirit.
- **2 Corinthians 3:3** – Law written not on tablets but on hearts.
- **Romans 8:1–4** – Law fulfilled in those who walk by the Spirit.
- **Revelation 21:3** – God dwelling with His people: "They will be His people."

LESSON SCRIPTURE: **EZEKIEL 36:25-28**

PROPHECY TITLE

A New Heart and a New Spirit

Introduction

Ezekiel, while prophesying to Israel in exile, addressed a people devastated by their sins and the loss of their land and temple. Yet, amid judgment, God delivered a message of hope: He promised not only to restore them to their land but also to transform them from within. In Ezekiel 36:25–28, God assures them of cleansing, a new heart, a new spirit, and His own Spirit residing within them.

This prophecy is fulfilled in the new covenant established by Christ and realized through the outpouring of the Holy Spirit. Jesus references this cleansing and renewal when He speaks of being "born of water and the Spirit" (John 3:5). Paul further describes believers as new creations (2 Cor. 5:17), empowered by the Spirit to live in obedience.

For Christians today, this passage reassures us that salvation involves not just external reform but profound inner renewal. God cleanses us, transforms us, and dwells within us, enabling us to truly live as His people.

Scripture Reference

Ezekiel 36:25–28 (NIV) **"I will sprinkle clean water on you, and you will be clean; I will cleanse you from all your impurities and from all your idols. [26] I will give you a new heart and put a new spirit in you; I will remove from you your heart of stone and give you a heart of flesh. [27] And I will put my Spirit in you and move you to follow my decrees and be careful to keep my laws. [28] Then you will live in the land I gave your ancestors; you will be my people, and I will be your God."**

Big Picture Insights

- **Cleansing from sin** – God removes impurity and idolatry.
- **New heart** – inner transformation replaces hardness with responsiveness.
- **New spirit** – renewal of inner life.
- **God's Spirit given** – indwelling presence enabling obedience.
- **Reversal of exile** – restored to land and covenant relationship.
- **Fulfilled in Christ** – His blood cleanses, His Spirit renews.
- **New birth** – "born of water and Spirit" (John 3:5).
- **Not external law** – obedience flows from inward change.

- **Believers as temple** – Spirit dwells within (1 Cor. 6:19).
- **Covenant promise** – "You will be my people, and I will be your God."

Verse-by-Verse Commentary

Ezekiel 36:25 – "I will sprinkle clean water on you, and you will be clean; I will cleanse you from all your impurities and from all your idols."

- The phrase draws from priestly rituals of purification (Numbers 19), where sprinkling water removed ceremonial uncleanness. Here, however, God Himself acts directly, cleansing His people not just outwardly but inwardly from sin and idolatry.
- This promise anticipates Christ's cleansing work, accomplished by His blood and applied by the Spirit's renewal (Hebrews 9:13–14). Salvation begins with divine initiative, not human reform.
- Idolatry is specifically addressed, showing that true cleansing is not partial but total — God removes every impurity that separated His people from Himself, preparing them for restored covenant fellowship.

Ezekiel 36:26 – "I will give you a new heart and put a new spirit in you; I will remove from you your heart of stone and give you a heart of flesh."

- In Hebrew thought, the heart represented the center of thought, will, and desire. Israel's "heart of stone" symbolized stubbornness, resistance, and spiritual death, unable to respond to God's commands or love.
- God promises to replace this lifeless heart with a "heart of flesh" — soft, responsive, and alive to Him. This signifies regeneration, the internal transformation that makes true obedience possible.
- This prophecy anticipates the new birth Jesus describes in John 3:5 and Paul's vision of new creation in Christ (2 Cor. 5:17). Conversion is not minor repair but complete inward renewal.

Ezekiel 36:27 – "And I will put my Spirit in you and move you to follow my decrees and be careful to keep my laws."

- Unlike the old covenant, where obedience was externally commanded but not internally empowered, the new covenant promises the indwelling Spirit to guide and transform. The Spirit's presence ensures real change rather than mere legal conformity.
- This prophecy was fulfilled at Pentecost (Acts 2), when the Spirit was poured out on all believers, marking the dawn of the church as God's Spirit-filled community.
- Paul expands this in Romans 8, teaching that the Spirit enables believers to fulfill God's righteous requirements. Obedience flows not from willpower but from God's Spirit dwelling within.

Ezekiel 36:28 – "Then you will live in the land I gave your ancestors; you will be my people, and I will be your God."

- This covenant formula appears repeatedly in Scripture and represents the goal of redemption: intimate, unbroken fellowship between God and His people.
- Restoration includes not only spiritual renewal but also the reversal of exile — God's people will live securely in the land, symbolizing covenant blessings and divine faithfulness.
- This promise finds its ultimate fulfillment in the church and will reach its climax in the new creation, where God will dwell with His people forever (Revelation 21:3).

Discussion Questions

1. What does it mean for God Himself to cleanse His people?

2. How does the image of a new heart describe salvation?

3. Why is the Spirit essential for true obedience?

4. How does this prophecy connect with Jesus' teaching on new birth in John 3?

5. What does it mean for believers to be God's people in this new covenant?

6. How does this passage encourage us when we feel spiritually hardened?

7. How does the Spirit's indwelling presence shape Christian living today?

Narrative Reflection

Ezekiel 36:25–28 presents a powerful prophetic vision of God's redemptive plan. It was addressed to exiles whose rebellion had led to judgment, the destruction of the temple, and the scattering of their people. Defiled by sin and feeling hopeless in exile, God declared His promise of inward transformation and lasting restoration.

The passage begins with a promise of cleansing: "I will sprinkle clean water on you, and you will be clean." In the Old Testament, the act of sprinkling water or blood symbolized purification from defilement (Numbers 19:13–19; Leviticus 14:7). While the people were familiar with these rituals, this cleansing would not be conducted by priests but by God Himself. It would go beyond mere ceremonial purification to cleanse the heart of impurity and idolatry. This foreshadows the cleansing achieved through the blood of Christ, which purifies the conscience (Hebrews 9:13–14), and the renewal brought about by the Spirit, referred to as "the washing of rebirth" (Titus 3:5).

Next, God promises transformation: "I will give you a new heart and put a new spirit in you." In Hebrew thought, the heart represents the core of one's inner life—intellect, will, and emotion. Israel's struggle stemmed not from a lack of law but from their inability to adhere to it. Their hearts were like stone—unresponsive, cold, and incapable of true obedience. God promises to replace this heart of stone with a heart of flesh—tender, responsive, and alive to Him. This signifies regeneration, a profound inner change enacted by the Spirit. Jesus affirmed this truth when He told Nicodemus, "No one can enter the kingdom of God unless they are born of water and the Spirit" (John 3:5). Paul later described believers as "new creations" in Christ (2 Cor. 5:17).

The prophecy intensifies further: "I will put my Spirit in you and move you to follow my decrees." The Spirit is not merely an external influence but God's indwelling presence. Under the old covenant, the law commanded obedience but did not empower it. In the new covenant, God provides what was previously lacking: His Spirit within His people. The Spirit guides, convicts, strengthens, and enables believers to fulfill God's will. This was dramatically fulfilled at Pentecost when the Spirit was poured out on the disciples (Acts 2), empowering them to boldly proclaim the gospel. Paul explains in Romans 8:4 that the righteous requirements of the law are fulfilled in those who walk according to the Spirit. Obedience becomes a natural outcome of God's indwelling presence rather than an external obligation.

The final verse culminates the covenant: "You will be my people, and I will be your God." This phrase, echoed throughout Scripture, expresses God's ultimate goal—restored fellowship with His people. The exile represented a broken relationship, while restoration symbolizes the renewal of covenant identity. The people would once again inhabit the land promised to their ancestors, a testament to God's faithfulness. Yet the ultimate fulfillment extends beyond physical land to the new creation, where Revelation 21:3 proclaims that God will dwell with His people forever.

From a theological perspective, Ezekiel 36:25–28 illustrates the failure of the old covenant and the success of the new covenant. The old covenant demanded obedience but could not transform hearts. The new covenant offers cleansing from sin, a new heart, and the Spirit's empowering presence. It transforms not just behavior but the very nature of individuals, reconciling God and His people by decisively addressing sin and enabling obedience from within.

For Christians today, this prophecy brings both encouragement and challenge. It reminds us that salvation is entirely God's work from beginning to end. We do not cleanse ourselves; God cleanses us. We do not transform our hearts; He replaces our hearts of stone with hearts of flesh. We do not obey in our own strength; the Spirit empowers us to follow His decrees. Salvation is wholly the work of God, ensuring that all glory belongs to Him.

At the same time, this passage calls us to live Spirit-filled lives. If God's Spirit dwells within us, our lives must reflect His presence. The Spirit not only comforts but also convicts, shaping our desires, guiding our decisions, and empowering our obedience. This requires rejecting idolatry and sin, as Israel was called to do, and embracing holiness, justice, and love as the fruits of God's presence within us.

Lastly, this prophecy affirms our identity: "You will be my people, and I will be your God." In a world characterized by alienation and brokenness, this covenant promise assures us that we belong to God. We are His people—cleansed, transformed, and indwelt by His Spirit. This truth gives us confidence in trials, comfort in failure, and hope for eternity.

Ezekiel 36:25–28 encapsulates the gospel prophetically, promising God's cleansing from sin, the gift of renewed hearts and spirits, and the transforming presence of His Spirit within His people. Fulfilled in Christ and sealed by the Spirit, it assures us of forgiveness, transformation, and eternal covenant fellowship. What Israel longed for in exile is our present reality in Christ and our future hope in the new creation.

Layers of Understanding

Historical Context

Ezekiel delivered this prophecy during the Babylonian exile, when Israel's sin had led to destruction of temple and land. The people were spiritually defiled and powerless to change. Against this backdrop, God promised cleansing, new hearts, and His Spirit, assuring His people that restoration would come not through them but through Him.

Jewish Understanding

For exiled Israel, Ezekiel's words promised more than a return to land — they foretold a transformation of the people themselves. Many Jews understood this as national renewal, where idolatry would be forsaken and faithfulness restored. The hope of a new heart sustained them as they longed for God's future redemption.

New Testament Fulfillment

The New Testament identifies Ezekiel's promise in Christ's work and the Spirit's outpouring. Jesus speaks of new birth "by water and Spirit" (John 3:5). At Pentecost, the Spirit indwells believers (Acts 2), empowering obedience. Paul affirms in 2 Corinthians 5:17 that anyone in Christ is a new creation, transformed by grace.

Theological Significance Today

This prophecy assures Christians that salvation is inward transformation, not external reform. God cleanses us, gives us new hearts, and dwells in us by His Spirit. It calls us to walk in Spirit-empowered obedience and reminds us that our covenant identity is secure: we are God's people, and He is our God.

Cross-Reference Connections

- **Numbers 19:13–19** – Ritual sprinkling for cleansing.
- **John 3:5** – Born of water and Spirit.
- **2 Corinthians 5:17** – New creation in Christ.
- **Romans 8:4, 9–11** – Spirit enables obedience and life.
- **Titus 3:5–6** – Washing of rebirth and renewal by the Spirit.
- **Revelation 21:3** – Fulfillment of covenant formula in new creation.

LESSON SCRIPTURE: ISAIAH 2:1-5

PROPHECY TITLE

Nations Streaming to the Mountain of the Lord

Introduction

Isaiah's vision in chapter 2 offers a stunning glimpse of the future: all nations united in peace to worship the Lord. In stark contrast to the violence, idolatry, and injustice prevalent in Isaiah's time, this prophecy anticipates a future when God's kingdom will be fully realized.

This prophecy is both a present reality and a future promise. It finds partial fulfillment in the spread of the gospel, as people from every nation come to Christ (Matthew 28:19; Acts 2:5–11). Ultimately, it points to the new creation when war will end and all nations will experience God's peace (Revelation 21:24–26).

For believers today, Isaiah 2:1–5 reassures us of the universality of God's kingdom, the authority of His Word as our guide for life, and the promise that His peace will one day reign completely. It also encourages us to "walk in the light of the Lord" in the present.

Scripture Reference

Isaiah 2:1-5 (NIV) **"This is what Isaiah son of Amoz saw concerning Judah and Jerusalem: ² In the last days the mountain of the LORD's temple will be established as the highest of the mountains; it will be exalted above the hills, and all nations will stream to it. ³ Many peoples will come and say, "Come, let us go up to the mountain of the LORD, to the temple of the God of Jacob. He will teach us his ways, so that we may walk in his paths." The law will go out from Zion, the word of the LORD from Jerusalem. ⁴ He will judge between the nations and will settle disputes for many peoples. They will beat their swords into plowshares and their spears into pruning hooks. Nation will not take up sword against nation, nor will they train for war anymore. ⁵ Come, descendants of Jacob, let us walk in the light of the LORD."**

Big Picture Insights

- **Last days vision** – points to the fullness of God's kingdom.
- **Exalted mountain** – symbol of God's reign and presence.
- **Nations streaming** – universal scope of God's salvation.
- **Word from Zion** – God's law and truth as standard for all.
- **Peace established** – war ceases, weapons turned to tools of life.
- **Messianic fulfillment** – Christ as the true temple (John 2:21).

- **Gospel expansion** – nations drawn through Christ and the Spirit (Acts 2).
- **Final consummation** – new creation where nations walk in God's light (Rev. 21).
- **Call to discipleship** – "walk in the light of the Lord" now.
- **Hope in troubled times** – assurance that peace is God's ultimate plan.

Verse -by-Verse Commentary

Isaiah 2:1 – "This is what Isaiah son of Amoz saw concerning Judah and Jerusalem:"

- This verse functions as an introduction, grounding the prophecy in a historical prophet (Isaiah son of Amoz) and a specific context (Judah and Jerusalem). It signals that what follows is both vision and divine revelation.
- The word "saw" implies more than physical sight — it indicates prophetic insight, a spiritual revelation of God's purposes. Isaiah is not describing wishful thinking but a vision of God's certain plan.
- The mention of Judah and Jerusalem ties the prophecy to God's covenant people, yet as the chapter unfolds, the scope expands to include all nations. It begins locally but widens universally, showing God's plan for Israel and the world.

Isaiah 2:2 – "In the last days the mountain of the LORD's temple will be established as the highest of the mountains; it will be exalted above the hills, and all nations will stream to it."

- "Last days" refers to the Messianic era inaugurated by Christ and completed in His return. Isaiah envisions a future beyond Judah's turmoil, when God's reign is exalted and recognized universally.
- Nations "streaming" reverses the scattering of Babel (Genesis 11). Instead of division, the peoples of the world unite under God's presence. The imagery of flowing upward highlights God's gravitational pull of glory.
- This vision partially unfolds in Pentecost (Acts 2), when diverse nations hear the gospel, and finds ultimate fulfillment in the new creation when all peoples walk in God's light (Revelation 21:24).

Isaiah 2:3 – "Many peoples will come and say, "Come, let us go up to the mountain of the LORD, to the temple of the God of Jacob. He will teach us his ways, so that we may walk in his paths." The law will go out from Zion, the word of the LORD from Jerusalem."

- The nations are not simply curious visitors but eager disciples, seeking God's teaching to live transformed lives. Learning His ways is paired with walking in His paths, showing obedience as the goal.
- "Law from Zion" recalls Sinai, but now God's instruction is not confined to Israel. It radiates outward, universalizing the covenant blessings through the gospel.
- This anticipates Jesus commissioning His disciples to teach all nations (Matthew 28:19–20) and the Word of the Lord spreading from Jerusalem in Acts. God's Word becomes the shared standard of all peoples.

Isaiah 2:4 – "He will judge between the nations and will settle disputes for many peoples. They will beat their swords into plowshares and their spears into pruning hooks. Nation will not take up sword against nation, nor will they train for war anymore."

- Weapons of destruction are repurposed into tools of cultivation and life. Isaiah's image shows not just an absence of war but the positive presence of flourishing. Peace is productive, creative, and life-giving.
- God Himself will arbitrate between nations, establishing justice that no human institution can secure. His rule removes hostility and replaces endless conflict with harmony.
- Christ's reconciling work (Ephesians 2:14–17) provides a foretaste, but complete fulfillment awaits the new creation, when violence is abolished and nations live under God's peace (Revelation 21:4).

Isaiah 2:5 – "Come, descendants of Jacob, let us walk in the light of the LORD.."

- Isaiah concludes with a summons to present discipleship. The vision of the future becomes motivation for living faithfully in the present. Hope leads to holiness.
- "Light of the Lord" signifies His Word, truth, and presence. Walking in it requires rejecting darkness and embracing God's ways, even when the world clings to violence and idolatry.
- The New Testament echoes this call: Jesus as the light of the world (John 8:12) and believers walking in His light (1 John 1:7).

Discussion Questions

1. What does the imagery of the "mountain of the Lord" symbolize?

2. How do we see this prophecy partially fulfilled in the gospel's spread?

3. What does it mean for God's Word to go out from Zion?

4. How does the vision of peace in verse 4 contrast with our world today?

5. What does "walking in the light of the Lord" look like for believers?

6. How does this prophecy encourage us to hope in God's ultimate plan?

7. How can Christians embody this vision of peace and unity now?

Narrative Reflection

This passage, Isaiah 2:1–5, stands as one of Scripture's clearest portrayals of hope and restoration. Delivered early in Isaiah's ministry, this prophecy addressed a people beset by idolatry, injustice, and political instability. In this uncertain context, Isaiah offers an inspiring vision of God's ultimate plan: His reign established, His Word proclaimed, and His peace embraced by all nations.

The vision begins with the declaration that "in the last days," the mountain of the Lord's temple will be exalted. In the ancient world, mountains symbolized strength and divine presence, often serving as sites for temples that brought worshippers closer to their gods. However, Isaiah envisions the Lord's mountain rising above all others—not in a physical sense, but in significance, authority, and permanence. This mountain represents God's reign and presence, revealed as supreme over all earthly powers.

What is particularly striking is the assertion that "all nations will stream to it." While rivers typically flow downward, here nations flow upward, illustrating the supernatural magnetism of God's glory. This image reverses the scattering at Babel (Genesis 11), where human pride led to division. Instead of confusion, Isaiah presents clarity; instead of division, there is unity. People from every tongue and tribe converge on God's presence. A partial fulfillment of this occurred at Pentecost (Acts 2), when Jews and converts from many nations heard the gospel in their own languages. Ultimately, Revelation 21:24–26 envisions the nations walking in the light of the Lamb, bringing their glory into the new Jerusalem.

In verse 3, the peoples are not passive spectators but eager disciples, saying, "Come, let us go up... He will teach us his ways, so that we may walk in his paths." This illustrates the essence of biblical faith: learning from God to live for God. The "law from Zion" expands Israel's covenant to include all nations, fulfilled when Christ commissions His disciples to teach all people (Matthew 28:19–20). Discipleship is central, with nations seeking instruction not merely out of curiosity, but for transformation.

Verse 4 envisions the outcome of God's reign: true peace. God will judge between nations and resolve disputes, delivering justice that human courts cannot achieve. Consequently, weapons are transformed into tools for cultivation: swords into plowshares, spears into pruning hooks. This represents more than disarmament; it signifies a profound transformation. Energy that was once dedicated to destruction now fosters life. This imagery resonates deeply in a world weary of conflict. Despite ongoing wars, Isaiah assures us that God's final word is peace. The repetition of this vision in Micah 4 underscores its importance to Israel's hope. In Christ, we experience this reality as He reconciles Jew and Gentile, breaking down hostility (Ephesians 2:14–17). The ultimate fulfillment will arrive in the new creation, where there will be no war or mourning (Revelation 21:4).

The prophecy concludes with a direct appeal: "Come, descendants of Jacob, let us walk in the light of the Lord." After revealing the end, Isaiah urges his people to live in light of it. Hope for the future inspires holiness in the present. If God's peace will one day fill the earth, then His people should embody peace now. If the nations will flock to His Word, His people must already live by it. This vision is not merely a distant dream but a present imperative.

Isaiah 2:1–5 teaches that God's kingdom is both universal and eternal. It is not confined to Israel's borders but extends to all nations. Unlike fragile human empires, it is everlasting. While human rulers often bring wars, God brings peace. His Word serves as the standard for all, and His judgment forms the foundation for justice.

For Christians, this passage unmistakably points to Christ. He is the true temple (John 2:21), exalted through resurrection and ascension. He draws all people to Himself (John 12:32). The gospel, starting in Jerusalem, now flows outward to every nation, fulfilling Isaiah's vision. Pentecost, with its multinational gathering, foreshadows the final gathering of the nations at the end of time. Christ is also the Prince of Peace, whose cross reconciles enemies and whose return will end conflict forever. For us today, Isaiah's vision offers profound comfort. The world is rife with war, division, and unrest. Yet God has declared that His ultimate plan is peace. History is not careening out of control; it is progressing toward God's goal. Nations will not always rage; one day they will worship. Violence will not always prevail; one day it will cease.

This vision also presents a challenge. Isaiah does not allow his hearers to remain passive. "Let us walk in the light of the Lord" calls us to embody the future now. As Christ's disciples, we are to be peacemakers in a world of conflict, truth-bearers in a culture of lies, and light-bearers in places of darkness. Walking in the light means aligning our lives with God's revealed Word and His promised future.

Isaiah 2:1–5 closes with both promise and command. It promises God's exalted reign, the gathering of nations, and the establishment of peace. It summons God's people to live now in anticipation of that reality, walking in His light and reflecting His peace. Partially fulfilled through Christ and His church, it will find its complete consummation upon Christ's return. Until then, we walk by faith, embodying the light of the coming kingdom.

Layers of Understanding

Historical Context

Isaiah spoke to Judah during the eighth century B.C., a time of idolatry, injustice, and looming threats from empires like Assyria. Amid instability, he cast a vision of God's final reign. The prophecy offered hope that beyond political turmoil, God's kingdom would bring peace, justice, and worldwide worship centered on Zion.

Jewish Understanding

For Israel, Isaiah's vision promised the exaltation of Zion and the recognition of Yahweh by all nations. It anticipated a time when Gentiles would stream to Jerusalem to learn God's ways and acknowledge His rule. This was seen as national vindication and global restoration, fulfilling God's covenant promises to Abraham and David.

New Testament Fulfillment

The prophecy begins to unfold in Christ. He is the exalted temple, and from Jerusalem the gospel spreads to the nations (Luke 24:47; Acts 2). Pentecost reverses Babel, uniting peoples in one Spirit. The Great Commission fulfills Isaiah's vision, with ultimate completion when nations walk in the Lamb's light (Revelation 21:24–26).

Theological Significance Today

Isaiah's vision assures believers that God's plan is peace, not war, and unity, not division. It calls us to live as people of the light, embodying God's Word and peace in our daily lives. Even amid conflict, we trust that God's universal reign and eternal justice will prevail through Christ.

Cross-Reference Connections

- **Micah 4:1–4** – Nearly identical prophecy of peace and nations streaming.
- **Matthew 28:19–20** – Gospel sent to all nations.
- **Acts 2:5–11** – Nations gathered at Pentecost.
- **John 12:32** – Jesus draws all people to Himself.
- **Ephesians 2:14–17** – Christ brings peace by breaking hostility.
- **Revelation 21:24–26** – Nations walk in the light of God's glory.

PROPHECY FULFILLED - STUDY LESSON - 43

LESSON SCRIPTURE: **ISAIAH 49: 6**

PROPHECY TITLE

A Light to the Nations

Introduction

Isaiah 49 is the second of the Servant Songs, where the Servant of the Lord is called, prepared, and commissioned for His mission. In verse 6, God states that it is "too small a thing" for the Servant merely to restore Israel; He will also be a light for the Gentiles, bringing salvation to the ends of the earth.

This prophecy broadens the scope of God's redemptive plan. The Messiah is not only the hope of Israel but of all nations. The New Testament consistently applies this to Christ. Simeon, holding the infant Jesus, declared Him to be "a light for revelation to the Gentiles" (Luke 2:32). Paul and Barnabas referenced Isaiah 49:6 in Acts 13:47, affirming their mission to the Gentiles as the fulfillment of this prophecy.

For believers today, Isaiah 49:6 serves as a reminder that the gospel is meant for everyone. Christ is the Savior of the world, and the church is called to share His light with all nations.

Scripture Reference

Isaiah 49:6 (NIV) **"he says: "It is too small a thing for you to be my servant to restore the tribes of Jacob and bring back those of Israel I have kept. I will also make you a light for the Gentiles, that my salvation may reach to the ends of the earth."**

Big Picture Insights

- **Servant's mission** – chosen and prepared by God.
- **Too small a thing** – Israel's restoration alone is insufficient.
- **Light to Gentiles** – mission expands to all nations.
- **Ends of the earth** – universal scope of salvation.
- **New Testament fulfillment** – Simeon (Luke 2:32), Paul (Acts 13:47).
- **Messiah's identity** – Savior not just for Israel, but the world.
- **Global gospel** – Christ's light shines everywhere.
- **Mission of the church** – called to continue the Servant's work.
- **Hope for all peoples** – no one excluded from God's plan.
- **Consummation** – final vision in Revelation of every tribe, tongue, and nation worshiping the Lamb.

Verse -by-Verse Commentary

Isaiah 49:6a "It is too small a thing for you to be my servant to restore the tribes of Jacob and bring back those of Israel I have kept…"

- Israel's restoration, though significant, was not the Servant's ultimate purpose. God's redemptive plan is expansive, never limited to one people or one land. His mission includes Israel but also surpasses it in scope.
- By calling this task "too small," God magnifies the greatness of the Servant's true mission: a salvation that embraces the world. This highlights the insufficiency of a narrow, nationalistic vision.
- Fulfilled in Christ, who reconciles Jew and Gentile into one family through the cross (Ephesians 2:14–16). The Servant gathers Israel but also builds a worldwide people for God.

Isaiah 49:6b "…I will also make you a light for the Gentiles…"

- Light symbolizes revelation, life, and divine guidance. For Gentiles in spiritual darkness, the Servant would be God's illumination, revealing His truth and salvation.
- Jesus claimed this directly: "I am the light of the world" (John 8:12). John affirms Him as "the true light that gives light to everyone" (John 1:9).
- This prophecy finds fulfillment in Christ's ministry and in the global mission of His church, empowered by the Spirit to extend His light to every culture and nation.

Isaiah 49:6c "…that my salvation may reach to the ends of the earth."

- God's ultimate aim is nothing less than worldwide salvation. The Servant's mission transcends ethnic, cultural, and geographic boundaries. Salvation is open to all who believe, regardless of heritage.
- This theme is realized in the Great Commission (Matthew 28:19) and confirmed in Acts 1:8, where disciples are called to witness "to the ends of the earth."
- Revelation 7:9–10 pictures its fulfillment: a multitude from every tribe and nation worshiping the Lamb. The Servant's mission culminates in a global family of redeemed people.

Discussion Questions

1. Why does God call restoring Israel alone "too small a thing"?

2. What does it mean that the Messiah is a "light for the Gentiles"?

3. How do Simeon and Paul apply this prophecy in the New Testament?

4. How does Isaiah 49:6 shape our understanding of the Great Commission?

5. What does this verse teach us about the inclusiveness of the gospel?

6. How does the Servant's mission inspire the church's global mission today?

7. In what ways are believers called to reflect Christ's light in their own communities?

Narrative Reflection

Isaiah 49:6 is one of the clearest revelations in the Old Testament regarding the universal reach of God's redemptive plan. Spoken during a time when Israel grappled with the fallout of exile and disobedience, this verse expands the hope of restoration beyond national borders to encompass global salvation. God declares that His Servant, chosen and prepared for this mission, will not only restore Israel but also bring light and salvation to all nations.

The Servant Songs of Isaiah (42, 49, 50, and 52–53) depict a divinely appointed figure who suffers and achieves salvation. In chapter 49, the Servant reflects on his calling: formed in the womb, equipped by God, and commissioned to bring Israel back. However, in verse 6, God challenges these expectations, stating, "It is too small a thing" for the Servant's mission to be limited to Israel's restoration. His purpose transcends one people or land; His salvation must reach the ends of the earth.

The imagery of light illustrates the nature of this mission. Light dispels darkness, reveals truth, and brings life. For Gentiles outside of Israel's covenant, the Servant serves as their illumination, guiding them to God. This prophecy anticipates Christ's ministry, who proclaimed, "I am the light of the world" (John

8:12). John further affirms that Jesus is "the true light that gives light to everyone" (John 1:9). Where Israel often failed to embody light for the nations, the Servant fulfills this role perfectly.

The New Testament consistently identifies Jesus as the fulfillment of Isaiah 49:6. When Simeon held the infant Jesus in the temple, he proclaimed, "My eyes have seen your salvation, which you have prepared in the sight of all nations: a light for revelation to the Gentiles, and the glory of your people Israel" (Luke 2:30–32). Simeon recognized that Christ's mission included both Israel and the nations, uniting them within God's plan.

Paul and Barnabas also explicitly applied Isaiah 49:6 to their missionary calling. In Acts 13, after facing rejection from the Jews, they declared: "We now turn to the Gentiles. For this is what the Lord has commanded us: 'I have made you a light for the Gentiles, that you may bring salvation to the ends of the earth'" (Acts 13:46–47). They saw themselves as participants in Christ's Servant mission, drawing theological grounding and confidence for their outreach to the Gentiles from this prophecy.

Theologically, Isaiah 49:6 highlights the expansive heart of God's mission. From the outset, God's covenant with Abraham contained a universal promise: "All peoples on earth will be blessed through you" (Genesis 12:3). Israel was chosen as the channel of blessing, but not as the sole recipient. The Servant fulfills that promise by extending salvation beyond Israel's borders.

For the church today, this passage offers both comfort and responsibility. It comforts us because most believers are Gentiles, grafted into God's family through Christ. Isaiah 49:6 reassures us that we were always included in God's plan, which was never meant to be narrow or exclusive but expansive and inclusive.

It also presents a challenge. If Christ is the light of the nations, then His followers are called to reflect that light. Jesus told His disciples, "You are the light of the world" (Matthew 5:14). The church's mission is to continue the Servant's work by proclaiming the gospel to every people group. The Great Commission (Matthew 28:19–20) serves as the practical outworking of Isaiah 49:6, as the disciples are commanded to make disciples of all nations.

This vision also encourages us in times of rejection or opposition to the gospel. Paul and Barnabas did not despair when some rejected their message; instead, they relied on Isaiah 49:6 and turned to the Gentiles. Similarly, when the church faces hostility or apathy, this prophecy reminds us that God's mission will prevail. His salvation will extend to the ends of the earth, regardless of human resistance.

The ultimate fulfillment of this prophecy is depicted in Revelation 7:9–10: "a great multitude that no one could count, from every nation, tribe, people, and language, standing before the throne and before the Lamb." The Servant's mission culminates in global worship, where the light of Christ has gathered the nations into one redeemed people.

Isaiah 49:6 emphasizes the global scope of God's redemptive plan. It tells us that restoring Israel alone would be "too small a thing." Instead, the Servant's mission is universal, bringing light to the Gentiles and salvation to the ends of the earth. Fulfilled in Christ, proclaimed by the apostles, and carried forward by the church, this prophecy assures us of God's inclusive salvation and invites us to participate in His mission.

Layers of Understanding

Historical Context

Isaiah 49 was spoken to Israel during a time of discouragement and exile. The nation longed for restoration, yet God revealed a plan far greater than national revival. The Servant would indeed restore Israel, but His mission would expand globally, reaching Gentiles and extending God's salvation to the ends of the earth.

Jewish Understanding

Some Jews interpreted this passage as Israel's collective role: to be a light to the nations by embodying God's law. Others awaited a personal Servant figure who would achieve it. Christians see the Servant as the Messiah, who perfectly fulfills this calling and brings both Israel and the nations into salvation.

New Testament Fulfillment

The New Testament applies Isaiah 49:6 directly to Jesus. Simeon praises Him as "a light for revelation to the Gentiles" (Luke 2:32). Paul and Barnabas quote the verse in Acts 13:47 as justification for their Gentile mission. Jesus Himself declares He is the light of the world, offering salvation universally.

Theological Significance Today

For modern believers, Isaiah 49:6 assures us that God's salvation is inclusive, reaching every nation, tribe, and people. It challenges the church to embrace global mission and calls each believer to reflect Christ's light in their own community. The prophecy reinforces our identity as participants in God's worldwide redemptive plan.

Cross-Reference Connections

- **Genesis 12:3** – Abraham's seed as blessing for all nations.
- **Isaiah 42:6** – Servant as light to the Gentiles.
- **Luke 2:32** – Simeon's song over the infant Jesus.
- **Acts 13:47** – Paul and Barnabas claim this prophecy.
- **John 1:9; 8:12** – Jesus as the light of the world.
- **Revelation 7:9–10** – Nations gathered in worship before the Lamb.

PROPHECY FULFILLED - STUDY LESSON - 44

LESSON SCRIPTURE: EZEKIEL 37: 24-28

PROPHECY TITLE

David My Servant Will Be King

Introduction

Ezekiel 37 is most famous for the vision of the valley of dry bones, which symbolizes God's power to restore Israel from exile. Following this vision, verses 24–28 describe what that restoration will entail. God promises that His servant David will reign as shepherd-king, His people will live in obedience, He will establish a covenant of peace with them, and His dwelling place will be among them forever.

Christians interpret this as a prophecy concerning the Messiah, the greater Son of David, who rules with justice, brings peace, and ensures God's presence with His people. Jesus identifies Himself as the Good Shepherd (John 10:11) and the promised King from David's lineage (Luke 1:32–33). The book of Revelation echoes this prophecy, proclaiming that God's dwelling will be with His people for all eternity.

For believers today, Ezekiel 37:24–28 reassures us that Christ reigns as our shepherd-king, that His covenant of peace is secure, and that God's presence dwells with us through the Spirit until it is fully realized in eternity.

Scripture Reference

Ezekiel 37:24–28 (NIV) **"My servant David will be king over them, and they will all have one shepherd. They will follow my laws and be careful to keep my decrees. 25 They will live in the land I gave to my servant Jacob, the land where your ancestors lived. They and their children and their children's children will live there forever, and David my servant will be their prince forever. 26 I will make a covenant of peace with them; it will be an everlasting covenant. I will establish them and increase their numbers, and I will put my sanctuary among them forever. 27 My dwelling place will be with them; I will be their God, and they will be my people. 28 Then the nations will know that I the LORD make Israel holy, when my sanctuary is among them forever."**

Big Picture Insights

- **Davidic king** – prophecy of a ruler from David's line.
- **One shepherd** – unity under God's chosen leader.
- **Obedience restored** – people walking in God's ways.
- **Covenant of peace** – everlasting covenant fulfilled in Christ.
- **Land promise** – security and permanence of God's people.
- **God's sanctuary** – His dwelling among them forever.

- **Messianic fulfillment** – Christ as Good Shepherd and eternal King.
- **Already and not yet** – fulfilled in Christ's first coming, consummated at His return.
- **Universal witness** – nations see God's holiness through His people.
- **Hope for the church** – Christ reigns, the Spirit dwells, eternity awaits.

Verse -by-Verse Commentary

Ezekiel 37:24 – "My servant David will be king over them, and they will all have one shepherd. They will follow my laws and be careful to keep my decrees."

- The title "my servant David" signals a future ruler from David's line rather than David himself, promising a king who embodies covenant faithfulness and shepherd-like care, uniting scattered tribes under righteous leadership and reversing the failures of Israel's former shepherds.
- "One shepherd" answers centuries of division and rivalry by establishing singular, benevolent rule. In contrast to the fractured monarchy after Solomon, God pledges undivided loyalty to one leader, healing political fragmentation and cultivating communal obedience rooted in shared devotion to God's law.
- In Christ, this shepherd-king arrives. Jesus names Himself the Good Shepherd who lays down His life for the sheep (John 10:11), gathering one flock from Jew and Gentile alike (John 10:16), creating a unified people under His sacrificial, wise, and gentle reign.

Ezekiel 37:25 – "They will live in the land I gave to my servant Jacob, the land where your ancestors lived. They and their children and their children's children will live there forever, and David my servant will be their prince forever."

- The promise of perpetual dwelling evokes covenant stability, not merely temporary reprieve. It stretches beyond post-exilic return to a lasting inheritance that anticipates the renewed creation, where God's people enjoy unthreatened belonging, security, and flourishing under divine protection.
- "Prince forever" highlights the permanence of messianic rule. Unlike dynasties toppled by foreign powers, this reign endures without succession crises, grounding hope in a ruler whose authority is anchored in God's oath and unassailable faithfulness to Davidic promises.
- The New Testament widens "land" toward the eschatological homeland (Hebrews 11:16), fulfilled when Christ reigns in the new heavens and new earth. Believers inherit with Him, experiencing eternal communion rather than fragile geopolitical sovereignty.

Ezekiel 37:26 – "I will make a covenant of peace with them; it will be an everlasting covenant. I will establish them and increase their numbers, and I will put my sanctuary among them forever."

- "Covenant of peace" (shalom) promises comprehensive wholeness—reconciliation with God, communal harmony, justice, and material well-being. It addresses enmity's root by healing hearts and relationships, not merely pausing hostilities or arranging pragmatic truces between rival factions.
- The covenant's "everlasting" nature surpasses Sinai's broken arrangements. Its durability rests on God's initiative and steadfast love, culminating in a relationship secured by divine oath rather than human performance, ensuring stability amid human frailty and historical upheaval.

- In Christ's blood the covenant is inaugurated (Luke 22:20; Hebrews 13:20). The cross ends hostility, making peace with God (Romans 5:1) and among His people (Ephesians 2:14–17), inaugurating a reconciled community animated by the Spirit's renewing power.

Ezekiel 37:27 – "My dwelling place will be with them; I will be their God, and they will be my people."

- God's intent is proximity, not mere patronage. "Dwelling place" recalls tabernacle and temple motifs, moving from localized presence to abiding nearness, saturating communal life with holiness and joy as God personally resides among His redeemed people.
- The covenant formula—"I will be their God, and they will be my people"—summarizes Scripture's heartbeat. It signals relational covenant, identity, belonging, and mutual delight, anchoring obedience in love rather than compulsion or fear.
- Presently fulfilled through the Spirit's indwelling (1 Corinthians 6:19) and the church as God's temple (Ephesians 2:21–22), this promise reaches consummation in Revelation 21:3, when God openly dwells with His people in unveiled, everlasting fellowship.

Ezekiel 37:28 – "Then the nations will know that I the LORD make Israel holy, when my sanctuary is among them forever."

- God's sanctuary among His people is not a private consolation but a public testimony. Divine presence forms a missional display, revealing God's holiness and character to watching nations through a transformed community shaped by worship, justice, and love.
- Holiness here is communicative: Israel's consecration broadcasts God's uniqueness. The people become a living signpost, demonstrating that true sacredness produces compassion, integrity, and peace, not isolation or prideful superiority over others.
- Revelation 21:24–26 anticipates global recognition of God's glory as the nations walk by His light. The church's holiness today foreshadows that reality, inviting the world to behold and enter the joy of God's kingdom.

Discussion Questions

1. What does it mean for Christ to be both King and Shepherd?

2. How does this prophecy connect to God's covenant promises to David?

3. Why is the "covenant of peace" called everlasting?

4. How is God's dwelling fulfilled both now and in the new creation?

5. What role does obedience play in this restored relationship?

6. How does this passage assure us of God's faithfulness to His promises?

7. How can the church today live as a witness to the nations of God's presence?

Narrative Reflection

Ezekiel 37:24–28 weaves together the thoughtful hopes of Israel's Scriptures into a cohesive vision of restoration: a righteous king to guide the people, a healed community committed to obedience, an everlasting covenant of peace, and God's enduring presence among them. Positioned right after the vision of the dry bones, these promises illustrate the true essence of resurrection from exile. God does not merely reassemble a nation; He transforms them into a holy people, crowned by a king whose reign is eternal.

The initial promise, "My servant David will be king over them, and they will all have one shepherd," intentionally evokes Israel's cherished memory of David—the shepherd-king who united the tribes, defeated their enemies, and brought stability. However, the prophecy extends beyond a mere historical reference. By Ezekiel's time, David had long since died; this phrase signals a forthcoming ruler from David's lineage whose leadership would mend the divisions that plagued the nation since the kingdom split after Solomon. Where selfish shepherds had exploited the flock, this king would sacrifice His life for the sheep. Jesus, the Good Shepherd, fulfills this vision: He gathers one flock from both Jew and Gentile, speaks, and His sheep recognize His voice, following Him into abundant life.

Unity under "one shepherd" encompasses more than politics; it embodies spiritual and ethical dimensions. Ezekiel underscores the importance of obedience—"They will follow my laws and be careful to keep my decrees." True restoration cannot be limited to repatriation or reconstruction; it requires a transformation of hearts. The new community learns to walk in God's ways not through coercion, but from a renewed desire. This anticipates the promises of the new covenant: God inscribes His law on hearts and places His

Spirit within, enabling joyful obedience. In the Messiah's kingdom, the demands of the law become a source of delight for the people.

The promise extends to land and lineage: "They… will live there forever, and David my servant will be their prince forever." The repetition of "forever" emphasizes a permanence that ancient Israel never experienced. Empires had invaded their territories, and exile had uprooted their families. Now, God promises unassailable security. The New Testament further deepens this promise beyond geographical boundaries. Hebrews teaches that the faithful seek a better country—a heavenly one. The land serves as a sign and foretaste of the renewed world, when Christ reigns in bodily form and His people inherit the earth. The "forever" of David's princehood also evolves into the enthronement of Jesus, whose resurrection assures a kingdom without end.

At the heart of this passage lies the "covenant of peace," an everlasting covenant. Shalom encompasses more than mere cessation of conflict; it signifies restored wholeness—right relationships with God, others, and creation. Exile had shattered Israel's sense of identity, safety, and fellowship with the Lord. God's covenant of peace addresses those fractures, binding His people into a community of flourishing under His protective care. This covenant is not fragile like Sinai's, broken by disobedience, but everlasting, secured by God's faithfulness. The New Testament identifies this covenant with the blood of Christ: "This cup is the new covenant in my blood" (Luke 22:20). Through His death and resurrection, Jesus secures peace with God (Romans 5:1) and peace between peoples once hostile (Ephesians 2:14–17).

The prophecy then ascends to its climax: "My dwelling place will be with them; I will be their God, and they will be my people." This covenant formula runs like a golden thread throughout Scripture. It was present in God's promise to Abraham, in the covenant at Sinai, and in the temple in Jerusalem. Yet all these earlier fulfillments were partial and vulnerable. In exile, the people lamented the loss of God's dwelling among them, symbolized by the destruction of the temple. Now God promises something greater—not just a building, but His very presence abiding with His people forever.

This promise finds fulfillment in several stages. In the incarnation, Jesus is Emmanuel, "God with us," dwelling among His people (John 1:14). In the present age, the Spirit makes the church God's temple (1 Corinthians 6:19; Ephesians 2:21–22). Yet Ezekiel's words look forward to the ultimate reality described in Revelation 21:3: "Now the dwelling of God is with men, and He will live with them. They will be His people, and God Himself will be with them and be their God." The temporary and symbolic gives way to permanent and visible reality: God's people in God's place under God's rule.

The passage concludes with a missional note: "Then the nations will know that I the Lord make Israel holy, when my sanctuary is among them forever." God's restoration of His people is not only for their benefit; it is for the sake of His name and witness among the nations. Israel's holiness is designed to reveal God's holiness, just as the church today is called to be a light to the world. The presence of God among His people becomes the strongest testimony to His reality and power. Holiness is never isolationist; it is compelling, drawing outsiders to the God who dwells with His people.

Ezekiel 37:24–28 integrates the great covenant promises of Scripture. It fulfills the Davidic covenant by promising an eternal ruler from David's line. It fulfills the new covenant by emphasizing inner transformation, obedience, and peace. It also brings to completion God's promise of His presence, moving from tabernacle to temple, from Christ to the Spirit, and ultimately to God's eternal dwelling with His people. For believers today, these promises hold immense significance. We live under the shepherding care of Christ, who rules as our King and lays down His life for us. We experience the covenant of peace, reconciled to God and one another by Christ's blood. We taste the presence of God now through the Spirit's indwelling, while longing for the day when God will dwell fully and visibly with His people.

This prophecy also speaks to our mission. Just as Israel's restored holiness was to serve as a testimony to the nations, so too the church's unity, holiness, and love bear witness to God's presence. Jesus said, "By this everyone will know that you are my disciples, if you love one another" (John 13:35). Our life together is not merely for our comfort but for God's glory among the nations.

In times of uncertainty, this vision anchors our hope. Political upheaval, cultural shifts, or personal trials cannot undo God's promises. Christ's reign is eternal, His covenant unbreakable, His presence secure. The nations may rage, but God's sanctuary is among His people forever. As Revelation reminds us, history ends not in chaos but in communion, with every tear wiped away in God's eternal dwelling.

Ezekiel 37:24–28, in the end, speaks of more than restoration—it lays bare the heartbeat of God's plan of redemption. His servant David, the Messiah, reigns as Shepherd-King. His covenant of peace brings reconciliation and wholeness. His dwelling transforms His people into a living testimony of His holiness. Fulfilled in Christ and consummated in eternity, these promises assure us that God's kingdom is both our present reality and our eternal hope.

Layers of Understanding

Historical Context

Addressed to exiles in Babylon after Jerusalem's fall, the prophecy promises more than repatriation. God pledges a Davidic ruler, unified people, covenant of peace, and restored presence. It reassures a shattered nation that true restoration is relational and royal—rooted in God's unbreakable commitments rather than fragile political arrangements or human merit.

Jewish Understanding

Many Jewish readers expected a future Davidic monarch to unite Israel, renew obedience, and restore temple presence. The "covenant of peace" signaled comprehensive peace (shalom). Hopes centered on national stability and sacred proximity, with the sanctuary among them testifying that God had truly returned to dwell with His consecrated people forever.

New Testament Fulfillment

Christ embodies "David my servant," the Good Shepherd uniting one flock. His blood installs the everlasting covenant of peace; His Spirit makes the church God's temple. Present fulfillment anticipates consummation when the risen King reigns visibly and God's dwelling is openly with His people in the renewed creation (Revelation 21:3).

Theological Significance Today

Believers live under Christ's shepherd-kingdom, participants in an everlasting covenant grounded in grace. The Spirit's indwelling makes the church a living sanctuary, calling us to unity, holiness, and peacemaking. Our communal life becomes mission: a visible testimony to the nations that God sanctifies a people with whom He delights to dwell.

Cross-Reference Connections

- **Ezekiel 34:23–24** – Promise of one shepherd from David's line.
- **John 10:11, 16** – Jesus the Good Shepherd, one flock under Him.
- **Luke 1:32–33** – Jesus will reign on David's throne forever.
- **Romans 5:1** – Peace with God through Christ.
- **Ephesians 2:14–17** – Christ is our peace, reconciling Jew and Gentile.
- **Revelation 21:3** – God's dwelling with His people forever.

PROPHECY FULFILLED - STUDY LESSON - 45

LESSON SCRIPTURE: ZECHARIAH 14: 8-9

PROPHECY TITLE

The Lord Will Be King Over All the Earth

Introduction

Zechariah's closing chapters depict an apocalyptic vision of God's ultimate victory. Following judgment and turmoil, the prophet envisions a time of renewal. In verses 8–9, living waters flow from Jerusalem in all directions, and the Lord is proclaimed as King over the entire earth.

This prophecy is fulfilled in Christ, who proclaimed Himself as the source of living water (John 7:37–39). It foreshadows the outpouring of the Spirit at Pentecost and the final renewal of creation described in Revelation 22:1–5, where the river of the water of life flows from the throne of God and the Lamb. The universal kingship of God, established through Christ's resurrection and ascension, will reach its culmination when every knee bows and every tongue confesses Him as Lord (Philippians 2:10–11).

For believers today, Zechariah 14:8–9 serves as a reminder that God's reign encompasses both the present and the future: Christ currently reigns at God's right hand, and one day His kingship will be recognized by all nations.

Scripture Reference

Zechariah 14:8-9 (NIV) **"On that day living water will flow out from Jerusalem, half of it east to the Dead Sea and half of it west to the Mediterranean Sea, in summer and in winter. ⁹ The LORD will be king over the whole earth. On that day there will be one LORD, and his name the only name."**

Big Picture Insights

- **Living water** – symbol of life, renewal, and the Spirit's unfailing supply.
- **Universal flow** – east and west, in every direction and every season.
- **God's kingship** – not confined to Israel but extended globally.
- **On that day** – signals eschatological fulfillment in history's climax.
- **Messianic hope** – Christ as the source of living water (John 7:37–39).
- **Already and not yet** – Spirit poured out now, fullness awaits Christ's return.
- **One Lord** – exclusive worship, the end of idolatry and false gods.
- **Cosmic renewal** – new creation envisioned in Revelation 22.
- **Mission focus** – church bears witness to God's reign now.
- **Pastoral comfort** – assurance that God's rule will be complete and uncontested.

Verse -by-Verse Commentary

Zechariah 14:8 – "On that day living water will flow out from Jerusalem, half of it east to the Dead Sea and half of it west to the Mediterranean Sea, in summer and in winter."

- The image of "living water" denotes a constant, life-giving supply, contrasting with stagnant or seasonal streams. It represents abundance, healing, and divine renewal flowing directly from God's presence to sustain His people.
- Its universal direction—east toward the Dead Sea and west toward the Mediterranean—signifies that no part of creation lies beyond God's renewing reach. This flow is inclusive, covering all lands and peoples, leaving nothing untouched.
- The mention of summer and winter underscores permanence. Unlike rivers that dry up in drought or freeze in winter, this water symbolizes the Spirit's unceasing presence, providing continual renewal across all times and seasons of history.
- In Christ, this finds fulfillment. He declares Himself the giver of living water (John 4:14; 7:37–39), offering eternal satisfaction and Spirit-filled life to all who believe. Pentecost becomes a foretaste of this prophetic vision.

Zechariah 14:9 – "The LORD will be king over the whole earth. On that day there will be one LORD, and his name the only name."

- This verse proclaims God's universal reign, contrasting ancient empires that claimed supremacy. Unlike earthly rulers, His kingship will be absolute, righteous, and eternal, bringing justice and order to a fractured and rebellious world.
- "On that day" points to the eschatological horizon when God's authority will be universally recognized, not just acknowledged by His covenant people. It signals the final stage of history when divine sovereignty is openly displayed.
- The phrase "one Lord" abolishes the confusion of idolatry. No rival gods will be worshiped; no competing allegiances will remain. All nations will confess the one true God as supreme, exclusive, and worthy of devotion.
- The New Testament connects this with Christ's exaltation (Matthew 28:18; Philippians 2:10–11). Revelation 11:15 echoes this prophecy: "The kingdom of the world has become the kingdom of our Lord and of his Messiah, and he will reign for ever and ever."

Discussion Questions

1. What does the imagery of "living water" symbolize in Scripture?

2. How does Jesus fulfill the promise of living water?

3. Why does the prophecy emphasize water flowing in all directions and seasons?

4. How does verse 9 connect to the Great Commission and Christ's present reign?

5. What does it mean that the Lord's name will be the only name?

6. How does this prophecy strengthen our hope for Christ's return?

7. How can believers today live as citizens under God's kingship?

Narrative Reflection

Zechariah 14:8–9 stands as a radiant climax in a book filled with visions of judgment, deliverance, and ultimate hope. These verses pull together the prophet's apocalyptic imagery into a single breathtaking vision: life-giving waters flowing outward from Jerusalem and the Lord reigning as King over the entire earth. For Zechariah's original audience—post-exilic Jews facing discouragement, vulnerability, and shattered expectations—this prophecy brought assurance that God's final plan was not defeat but renewal and triumph.

Verse 8 introduces the picture of "living water" flowing from Jerusalem. To ancient hearers, water symbolized life itself. In the dry and unpredictable climate of the Near East, a dependable water source could mean the difference between flourishing and famine. Here, however, the image transcends physical geography. Unlike seasonal wadis or man-made cisterns, this water flows perpetually—eastward toward the Dead Sea and westward toward the Mediterranean—indicating that God's blessing will reach every direction. The Dead Sea, a place of barrenness, will be touched by life, and the mighty Mediterranean, gateway to distant nations, will likewise receive the stream.

The detail that it flows "in summer and in winter" adds depth. Natural rivers in Israel often ran dry during hot summers or diminished in cold seasons. But the living waters of God are not bound by weather, time, or circumstance. They represent His Spirit, whose work never ceases. The contrast is clear: human provision is temporary and fragile, but divine provision is eternal and abundant.

This theme runs throughout Scripture. Jeremiah calls God "the spring of living water" (Jeremiah 2:13). Jesus expands the metaphor, offering the Samaritan woman water that becomes "a spring of water welling up to eternal life" (John 4:14). Later He cries out in Jerusalem, "Let anyone who is thirsty come to me and drink" (John 7:37), which John interprets as a promise of the Holy Spirit. At Pentecost, when the Spirit was poured out on believers, the vision of living water began to be fulfilled. Yet the picture remains eschatological as well, awaiting full consummation in the new creation. Revelation 22:1–2 portrays the river of the water of life flowing from the throne of God and of the Lamb, bringing healing to the nations. Zechariah's vision thus stretches across the ages—from exile, to Christ, to Pentecost, to eternity.

Verse 9 shifts the focus to kingship: "The Lord will be king over the whole earth." This proclamation answers Israel's long history of fragmented loyalty and idolatry. No longer will Yahweh be regarded as one deity among many; no longer will His reign seem limited to a small nation. On that day, His kingship will be universal. The competing claims of human rulers and false gods will collapse before His sovereignty.

The phrase "there will be one Lord, and his name the only name" emphasizes exclusivity. The divided allegiances of Israel's past—whether to Baal, Asherah, or the gods of neighboring peoples—will vanish. The Lord alone will be worshiped, His name confessed as supreme. For Christians, this points directly to Christ's exaltation. After His resurrection, Jesus declared that all authority in heaven and earth had been given to Him (Matthew 28:18). Paul echoes Zechariah's vision in Philippians 2:10–11, where he foresees every knee bowing and every tongue confessing that Jesus Christ is Lord. Revelation 11:15 resounds with the same promise: "The kingdom of the world has become the kingdom of our Lord and of his Messiah, and he will reign for ever and ever."

Theologically, Zechariah 14:8–9 integrates two grand themes: life and kingship. The living water symbolizes the gift of divine life through the Spirit, satisfying spiritual thirst and renewing creation. The kingship underscores God's sovereignty, ultimate justice, and uncontested authority. Together they paint a picture of salvation as abundant life lived under God's perfect reign.

For believers today, this vision offers profound encouragement. First, it assures us that Christ is already reigning. Though the world is full of chaos, wars, and rival powers, the reality of His resurrection and ascension testifies that His kingship has begun. He is enthroned at God's right hand, guiding history toward its consummation. Second, it strengthens our hope. We live in the "already and not yet"—already refreshed by the Spirit's living water, but not yet experiencing the fullness of God's reign. This dual reality calls us to patient endurance and joyful expectation.

Third, it challenges us to live now as subjects of the King. If Jesus is already Lord, our allegiance must be undivided. We are called to embody His reign by practicing justice, pursuing peace, and bearing witness to His name. As the church, we are streams of living water to a thirsty world, channels through which God's Spirit brings renewal. Our mission flows directly from this prophecy: proclaim Christ's kingship and invite all nations to drink deeply of His living water.

Finally, it gives us pastoral comfort. Many believers face hostility, discouragement, or uncertainty, just as Zechariah's audience did. But this passage reminds us that God's purposes cannot be thwarted. Living water still flows. The Lord still reigns. One day His kingship will be acknowledged universally, and His life-giving presence will restore all things.

In the end, Zechariah 14:8–9 gives us a prophetic glimpse of the final triumph of God's kingdom. It envisions a world where living waters flow without end and where God is acknowledged as King by all the earth. Fulfilled in Christ through the Spirit and awaiting final consummation at His return, this prophecy assures us that life and reign belong to God alone. For us, it is both a source of hope and a call to faithful living until that day arrives.

Layers of Understanding

Historical Context

Zechariah prophesied to post-exilic Judah, a small and vulnerable community. The vision of flowing waters and universal kingship reassured them that God's purposes extended beyond their immediate struggles. Restoration was not confined to land or temple—it anticipated global renewal, divine sovereignty, and God's presence bringing life to all creation.

Jewish Understanding

Jewish interpreters saw this prophecy as envisioning the day when Yahweh alone would be worshiped universally. Jerusalem, the source of living waters, symbolized the center of divine blessing. The imagery assured them that God's reign was not confined to Israel but would extend worldwide, vindicating their faith and exalting God's name among nations.

New Testament Fulfillment

The New Testament identifies Jesus as the source of living water (John 4:14; 7:37–39), fulfilled through the Spirit's outpouring at Pentecost. His resurrection confirmed His universal kingship (Matthew 28:18). Revelation 22 envisions the river of life flowing eternally, while Revelation 11:15 declares His kingdom established forever, echoing Zechariah's vision.

Theological Significance Today

For Christians, Zechariah 14:8–9 assures us that Christ reigns already, refreshing us with the Spirit's living water. It calls us to undivided allegiance, to mission, and to lives marked by justice and peace. Ultimately, it comforts us with the hope that His kingdom will be consummated, uncontested, and universally acknowledged forever.

Cross-Reference Connections

- **Jeremiah 2:13** – God as the spring of living water.
- **John 4:14; 7:37–39** – Jesus as the source of living water, Spirit given.
- **Matthew 28:18** – Christ given all authority in heaven and earth.
- **Philippians 2:10–11** – Every knee will bow to Jesus.
- **Revelation 11:15** – The kingdom of the world becomes Christ's kingdom.
- **Revelation 22:1–5** – River of life flows from God's throne.

LESSON SCRIPTURE: **HABAKKUK 2: 14**

PROPHECY TITLE

The Earth Filled with the Knowledge of the Glory of the Lord

Introduction

The prophet Habakkuk grappled with the problem of evil: why does God permit injustice, and why do wicked nations thrive? In response, God revealed that He would judge the proud and ultimately affirm His righteousness. Habakkuk 2:14 offers a powerful promise amid the turmoil: despite the prevalence of violence and idolatry, one day "the earth will be filled with the knowledge of the glory of the Lord as the waters cover the sea."

This prophecy resonates with and expands upon the hope found in Isaiah 11:9, envisioning a future where the knowledge of God permeates all of creation. For Christians, its ultimate fulfillment is seen in Christ, who embodies God's glory (John 1:14) and commissions His church to share that knowledge with the nations (Matthew 28:19–20). This promise will be fully realized in the new creation, where God's glory illuminates the city of God and fills the cosmos (Revelation 21:23–24).

For believers today, Habakkuk 2:14 serves as both a source of comfort and a call to mission. Although injustice may prevail for a time, God's glory will ultimately triumph, and we are invited to live as witnesses to that future reality.

Scripture Reference

Habakkuk 2:14 (NIV) **"For the earth will be filled with the knowledge of the glory of the LORD as the waters cover the sea."**

Big Picture Insights

- **Knowledge of glory** – not abstract ideas but experiential awareness of God's presence.
- **Global scope** – "the earth will be filled," leaving no corner untouched.
- **Certainty** – "will be filled" signals God's unshakable promise.
- **Imagery of waters** – total saturation, overwhelming and life-sustaining.
- **Echo of Isaiah 11:9** – a repeated prophetic hope.
- **Fulfilled in Christ** – the glory of God revealed in His face (John 1:14; 2 Cor. 4:6).
- **Already and not yet** – spreading now through the gospel, completed in the new creation.
- **Missionary vision** – church tasked with carrying knowledge of God to all nations.
- **Contrast** – present world filled with violence and idolatry, but future filled with glory.
- **Hope** – assurance that God's reign will define the world to come.

Verse -by-Verse Commentary

Habakkuk 2:14a "For the earth will be filled…"

- The prophecy envisions a global transformation, not confined to Israel or a single nation. It anticipates the whole earth saturated with divine reality, reversing humanity's rebellion that fractured creation's harmony with God.
- The verb is future and certain—God declares not possibility but inevitability. His plan cannot fail. For Habakkuk's audience living under Babylon's shadow, this was radical hope: empires rise and fall, but God's glory fills the earth.

Habakkuk 2:14b "…with the knowledge of the glory of the LORD…"

- Knowledge here is relational and empirical, not merely intellectual. It points to humanity's recognition and embrace of God's majesty and presence. This is the glory that once dwelt in tabernacle and temple but now shines through Christ.
- God's glory is His manifested presence—His holiness, justice, mercy, and power revealed. To know His glory is to encounter His reality personally and communally, transforming lives and societies.

Habakkuk 2:14c "…as the waters cover the sea."

- The comparison emphasizes completeness. Just as the sea cannot be separated from its waters, so the earth will be wholly saturated with God's glory—entire, unbroken, and all-encompassing.
- The imagery also evokes life, abundance, and unstoppable force. Just as water nourishes and reshapes landscapes, so God's glory renews creation, bringing healing, justice, and flourishing.

Discussion Questions

1. What does "knowledge of the glory of the Lord" mean in practical terms?

2. How does this prophecy contrast with the violence and idolatry of Habakkuk's time?

3. In what ways does Jesus reveal the glory of God to us?

266

4. How is this prophecy being fulfilled through the spread of the gospel today?

5. What does the image of waters covering the sea teach us about the scope of God's reign?

6. How does this verse give us hope when evil seems dominant in the world?

7. How can believers participate in filling the earth with knowledge of God's glory?

Narrative Reflection

Habakkuk 2:14 stands as one of the most sweeping promises in Old Testament prophetic literature. It envisions a world transformed from one of violence, oppression, and idolatry to one filled with the knowledge of God's glory. In this single verse, the prophet shifts the horizon of hope from despair over human injustice to confidence in God's ultimate victory.

Understanding the context of this verse is crucial. Habakkuk had expressed deep frustration to God regarding the injustice in Judah and had questioned God's plan to use Babylon—a more ruthless nation—as a tool for judgment. In response, God pronounces a series of woes against the arrogant and violent, but amid these woes, verse 14 shines brightly. While human kingdoms may wreak havoc across the earth, God promises that His glory will instead fill it.

The opening phrase, "the earth will be filled," conveys a sense of inevitability. This is not a vague hope but a divine certainty. Empires rise and fall; their legacies decay into dust. In contrast, God's glory will permeate the earth until it reaches every corner. This promise is universal, extending beyond Israel to encompass all peoples and lands. For those exiled under foreign domination, this assurance meant that Babylon would not have the final say—God would.

The content of this filling is "the knowledge of the glory of the LORD." In Hebrew thought, knowledge transcends mere information; it signifies a relational awareness. To "know" God's glory is to experience His presence, recognize His majesty, and be transformed by His reality. God's glory radiates His character—His holiness, justice, mercy, and power. In the Old Testament, God's glory filled the tabernacle (Exodus 40:34) and the temple (1 Kings 8:11). However, Habakkuk envisions a future where God's glory is not confined to a single sanctuary but spreads across the globe.

The imagery of waters covering the sea enhances this vision. Since the sea is water by definition, describing waters covering the sea signifies total saturation. Similarly, the knowledge of God's glory will be so pervasive that it defines existence itself. Just as water nourishes, sustains, and reshapes landscapes, God's glory will renew creation, bringing healing and life. This metaphor assures us that no part of creation will remain untouched by God's redeeming presence.

The New Testament links this promise to the person and work of Christ. John 1:14 states, "the Word became flesh and made his dwelling among us. We have seen his glory, the glory of the one and only Son." In Jesus, God's glory is revealed not through thunder or the temple but through flesh and blood. Paul echoes this in 2 Corinthians 4:6, writing, "God… made his light shine in our hearts to give us the light of the knowledge of God's glory displayed in the face of Christ." Christ fulfills Habakkuk's vision by revealing God's glory in personal and relational ways, demonstrating divine love, holiness, and mercy in action.

This prophecy also finds fulfillment in the mission of the church. Jesus' Great Commission (Matthew 28:19–20) instructs His disciples to make disciples of all nations and teach them to obey His commands. As the gospel spreads, so does the knowledge of the glory of the Lord. At Pentecost, the Spirit empowered the apostles to proclaim God's mighty works to people speaking various languages (Acts 2:5–11), foreshadowing global saturation. Missionary movements throughout history, despite facing challenges and setbacks, represent the ongoing fulfillment of Habakkuk's promise. Each conversion and every act of faithful witness contributes to the earth being filled with God's glory.

Yet, the prophecy exists in an "already and not yet" state. We witness glimpses now—the spread of the gospel, transformed lives, and the Spirit's presence in the church—but full saturation awaits the new creation. Revelation 21–22 depicts the culmination: the glory of God illuminating the city, with nations walking by its light. In this final vision, Habakkuk's prophecy reaches its ultimate fulfillment: the knowledge of God's glory will be complete, covering creation as waters cover the sea.

For believers today, Habakkuk 2:14 offers profound hope in a world still marked by violence, greed, and injustice. It reminds us that God's purposes extend beyond the rise and fall of nations. His glory will outlast tyranny and oppression. No matter how dark the present may seem, the future is filled with light. This truth anchors our faith and strengthens our endurance.

It also calls us to mission. If God's glory is destined to fill the earth, we are invited to participate in that filling by making His glory known now. Our words and actions testify to His majesty. Our worship proclaims His greatness. Our acts of justice and mercy reflect His character to the world. The church becomes both a sign and an instrument of Habakkuk's prophecy, witnessing to the glory of God in anticipation of its ultimate fulfillment.

Habakkuk 2:14 elevates our perspective beyond present injustices to the certainty of God's future. It promises a world filled with the knowledge of His glory—revealed in Christ, spreading through the gospel, and consummated in the new creation. For now, we live as witnesses, confident that what God has declared will surely come to pass: the earth will be filled with His glory, just as the waters cover the sea.

Layers of Understanding

Historical Context

Habakkuk spoke during Judah's decline, when Babylon loomed as God's instrument of judgment. Amid fears of violence and idolatry, this prophecy assured God's people of a greater future: empires would not define history; God's glory would. It promised cosmic renewal, offering hope to exiles that divine justice would saturate the world.

Jewish Understanding

For Jewish hearers, this verse echoed Isaiah 11:9, reinforcing the hope of a messianic age when the knowledge of God would flood the earth. It envisioned the restoration of justice, the end of idolatry, and the universal acknowledgment of Yahweh as the one true God, vindicating His people before the nations.

New Testament Fulfillment

The New Testament reveals the glory of God in Christ. John 1:14 identifies Jesus as God's glory in flesh, and 2 Corinthians 4:6 affirms that His face reveals divine majesty. Pentecost began the global spread of this knowledge. Revelation 21–22 depicts its consummation: the earth illuminated by God's glory forever.

Theological Significance Today

For Christians, this prophecy affirms that God's glory will ultimately triumph over injustice and idolatry. It comforts us in a broken world, inspires us with missionary urgency, and calls us to reflect His glory in daily life. It assures us that history's end is not chaos but the radiance of God's reign.

Cross-Reference Connections

- **Isaiah 11:9** – Parallel prophecy of earth filled with knowledge of the Lord.
- **Exodus 40:34** – God's glory fills the tabernacle.
- **John 1:14** – Christ reveals God's glory in flesh.
- **2 Corinthians 4:6** – God's glory displayed in Christ's face.
- **Matthew 28:19–20** – Church's mission to spread His glory.
- **Revelation 21:23–24** – Glory of God illuminates the new creation.

PROPHECY FULFILLED - STUDY LESSON - 47

LESSON SCRIPTURE: **MALACHI 4: 5-6**

PROPHECY TITLE

Elijah Before the Day of the Lord

Introduction

Malachi concludes the Old Testament with a hopeful message: before the day of the Lord fully arrives, God will send the prophet Elijah to prepare His people. This prophecy serves as a bridge between the Old and New Testaments.

The Gospels reveal that John the Baptist fulfills this prophecy (Luke 1:16–17; Matthew 11:14). He arrives "in the spirit and power of Elijah," calling Israel to repentance and preparing the way for Christ. Additionally, the prophecy holds eschatological significance, pointing to the final day of the Lord when judgment and renewal will occur.

For believers today, Malachi 4:5–6 reminds us that God provides preparation before His great acts of redemption. It emphasizes the importance of repentance, reconciliation, and being ready for Christ's return.

Scripture Reference

Malachi 4:5–6 (NIV) "See, I will send the prophet Elijah to you before that great and dreadful day of the LORD comes. ⁶ He will turn the hearts of the parents to their children, and the hearts of the children to their parents; or else I will come and strike the land with total destruction."

Big Picture Insights

- **Elijah promised** – God pledges to send a prophet like Elijah, known for boldness, fire, and covenant faithfulness.
- **Preparation for the day of the Lord** – repentance must precede God's great intervention in history.
- **John the Baptist** – fulfilled this prophecy in the "spirit and power of Elijah."
- **Hearts turned** – reconciliation of families symbolizes covenant renewal.
- **Urgency** – repentance averts destruction and opens the door to restoration.
- **Messianic link** – John prepared Israel for the Messiah's arrival.
- **Eschatological dimension** – ultimate fulfillment still awaits Christ's second coming.
- **Persistence** – Malachi closes the OT by anticipating NT fulfillment.
- **Pastoral comfort** – God sends warnings and messengers before judgment.
- **Present calling** – the church continues Elijah's task of preparing hearts.

Verse-by-Verse Commentary

Malachi 4:5 – "See, I will send the prophet Elijah to you before that great and dreadful day of the LORD comes."

- Elijah represents the quintessential prophet—zealous for God's honor, fearless in confronting idolatry, and fervent in calling Israel to repentance. Malachi promises a figure in this mold to appear before God's climactic intervention.
- Jesus affirms John the Baptist as this Elijah, who prepared the way for Him (Matt. 11:14; 17:12–13). Yet many Jewish interpreters also expect a final Elijah-like witness before the end.
- The sending of Elijah underscores God's mercy: He provides advance warning, a final chance for repentance before the day of judgment arrives.

Malachi 4:6 – "He will turn the hearts of the parents to their children, and the hearts of the children to their parents; or else I will come and strike the land with total destruction."

- Repentance is not only vertical (toward God) but horizontal (toward others). This verse envisions reconciliation within families, which are the foundation of covenantal life in Israel. Healing begins in the home.
- John the Baptist fulfilled this through his call to repentance, baptizing and urging restoration of relationships as part of readiness for Messiah's coming.
- The warning that follows is stark: without repentance, judgment will fall, leaving devastation. The Hebrew phrase for "total destruction" suggests a curse, the opposite of blessing, reminding God's people that holiness and reconciliation are not optional.

Discussion Questions

1. Why is Elijah, specifically, promised to return before the day of the Lord?

2. How does John the Baptist fulfill this prophecy?

3. What does it mean to "turn the hearts" of parents and children?

4. How does repentance prepare people for God's redemptive work?

5. What is the significance of this prophecy as the final words of the Old Testament?

6. How does this passage shape our understanding of Christ's first coming?

7. How should we live in readiness for Christ's second coming?

Narrative Reflection

Malachi 4:5–6 acts as a pivotal transition between the Testaments, concluding the Old with a promise and igniting anticipation for the New. These two brief yet profound verses offer both warning and hope, predicting the arrival of Elijah before the "great and dreadful day of the Lord" and emphasizing reconciliation as the fruit of repentance.

The image of Elijah would have deeply resonated with Malachi's audience. Elijah was the prophet who boldly confronted Ahab and Jezebel, called down fire from heaven, and challenged Israel to choose between Yahweh and Baal (1 Kings 18). He did not die but was taken to heaven in a whirlwind (2 Kings 2:11), fueling hopes for his return. His name, meaning "My God is Yahweh," symbolized a steadfast devotion to the Lord. For Malachi's listeners, the promise of Elijah's return indicated that God's covenant voice would once again be clearly heard.

The "day of the Lord" in prophetic literature has a dual nature: it is great because it brings deliverance and judgment. Malachi's prophecy underscores God's mercy; before that day arrives, He will send Elijah. God does not take pleasure in judgment but allows space for repentance, demonstrating that preparation precedes redemption.

The mission of this Elijah figure is described as "turning hearts." This phrase transcends mere sentiment; in biblical thought, the heart represents the center of will and decision. Turning hearts signifies repentance and a reorientation of life toward God, as well as reconciliation within families. Sin fractures relationships, starting at home. Estrangement between parents and children reflects a community broken in its covenant obligations. Conversely, when hearts turn, families are reconciled, restoring covenant life.

The New Testament identifies John the Baptist as the fulfillment of this promise. Luke 1:16–17 records the angel Gabriel's words to Zechariah, stating that John would "go on before the Lord, in the spirit and power of Elijah... to turn the hearts of the parents to their children." John's attire of camel's hair and his wilderness ministry echoed Elijah's style. Jesus Himself affirmed that John was the Elijah to come (Matt. 11:14). John's fiery preaching of repentance, his preparatory baptism, and his declaration of Jesus as "the Lamb of God" demonstrate how he prepared Israel for the Messiah.

However, Malachi's prophecy also extends beyond John. While John fulfilled it during Christ's first coming, the prophecy also carries an eschatological perspective that points to the end. From a pretribulational view — which I hold — Christians will not be present during the tribulation, having been raptured by Christ beforehand. Yet many, myself included, believe that some will be persuaded to the faith during the first half of the tribulation. Anticipating this time, God will send two Elijah-like witnesses who will appear. Revelation 11 describes these witnesses with powers reminiscent of Moses and Elijah, testifying before the end. The spirit of Elijah persists wherever God raises up voices of repentance and reconciliation in preparation for Christ's return. Theologically, these verses reveal God's mercy and patience. Before judgment, God sends a prophet; before destruction, He offers reconciliation. He desires that none should perish but that all should repent (2 Pet. 3:9). The significance of the Old Testament ending with this promise is profound. Rather than concluding in despair, it ends with hope—God will not leave His people unprepared.

For Christians today, Malachi 4:5–6 conveys several important lessons. First, it reminds us that repentance is the doorway to redemption. Without repentance, hearts remain hardened, families remain fractured, and destruction looms. With repentance, God brings restoration and blessing. Second, it calls us to value reconciliation. The turning of hearts between parents and children symbolizes covenant renewal. When families embody love and faithfulness, communities flourish, and God's glory is revealed. Third, it challenges us to be Elijah-like in our witness. The church's role is to prepare people for Christ's return, calling them to repentance, reconciliation, and readiness.

The closing words of the Old Testament also emphasize continuity. The story of God's people does not conclude with Malachi; rather, it anticipates something greater. The centuries of silence following Malachi were not the end but a pause before fulfillment. When the Gospels open, they do so with John the Baptist—the promised Elijah—crying out in the wilderness, "Prepare the way of the Lord." The bridge is complete: the last promise of the Old directly connects with the first proclamation of the New.

As a final thought Malachi 4:5–6 serves as a fitting close to the Old Testament and a powerful anticipation of the New. It promises Elijah before the great and dreadful day of the Lord, fulfilled in John the Baptist, who prepared the way for Christ's first coming, while also pointing forward to the ultimate preparation before His return. It reminds us that repentance and reconciliation are vital in God's plan, and that His mercy always provides a messenger before judgment falls. These final verses of the Old Testament leave us with hope and urgency: God's redemption is coming, and we must be ready.

Layers of Understanding

Historical Context

Malachi ministered in the post-exilic period when Israel struggled with apathy, corruption, and broken covenant relationships. His prophecy warned of judgment but promised Elijah's return before the day of the Lord. For Israel, this meant God would not act without first sending a prophet to call them back to repentance.

Jewish Understanding

Jewish expectation often took this literally: Elijah, who never died, would physically return before Messiah. To this day, Jewish Passover traditions include an empty seat for Elijah, symbolizing hope for his coming. Elijah represented covenant renewal, repentance, and preparation for God's ultimate intervention in history to establish His kingdom.

New Testament Fulfillment

The Gospels identify John the Baptist as the Elijah figure who prepared the way for Jesus. Luke 1:17 and Matthew 11:14 link John directly to Malachi's prophecy. His ministry of repentance and reconciliation inaugurated Christ's work. Revelation 11 extends the prophecy forward, envisioning Elijah-like witnesses preparing the world for during the final tribulational period.

Theological Significance Today

Malachi's prophecy assures believers that God provides warning and preparation before judgment. It calls the church to carry Elijah's mantle in preaching repentance and reconciliation. Families, communities, and nations are transformed when hearts turn back to God and one another. Ultimately, it summons us to readiness for Christ's return in glory.

Cross-Reference Connections

- **1 Kings 18** – Elijah confronts idolatry and calls Israel back.
- **2 Kings 2:11** – Elijah taken up in a whirlwind.
- **Luke 1:16–17** – John the Baptist comes in the spirit and power of Elijah.
- **Matthew 11:14; 17:12–13** – Jesus identifies John as Elijah.
- **Mark 1:2–4** – John prepares the way of the Lord.
- **Revelation 11:3–6** – Two witnesses with Elijah-like power testify before the end.

LESSON SCRIPTURE: **PSALM 118: 17-23**

PROPHECY TITLE

The Rejected Stone Becomes the Cornerstone

Introduction

Psalm 118 is a psalm of thanksgiving, often sung during Israel's festivals to celebrate God's deliverance and steadfast love. Among its verses is a profound prophecy: the psalmist proclaims that he will live to declare God's works, and that the stone rejected by the builders will become the cornerstone.

This imagery of the cornerstone became pivotal in the New Testament. Jesus applied it to Himself (Matthew 21:42; Mark 12:10–11), while Peter and Paul viewed it as a prophecy fulfilled through Christ's death and resurrection (Acts 4:11; Ephesians 2:20). Though rejected, Jesus became the foundation of God's new temple, the church.

For believers today, Psalm 118:17–23 holds both personal and cosmic significance. It reassures us that God delivers His people from death, points us to Christ as the cornerstone of our salvation, and encourages us to trust His plan, even when the world turns away from Him.

Scripture Reference

Psalm 118:17–23 (NIV)   "I will not die but live, and will proclaim what the LORD has done. [18] The LORD has chastened me severely, but he has not given me over to death. [19] Open for me the gates of the righteous; I will enter and give thanks to the LORD. [20] This is the gate of the LORD through which the righteous may enter. [21] I will give you thanks, for you answered me; you have become my salvation. [22] The stone the builders rejected has become the cornerstone; [23] the LORD has done this, and it is marvelous in our eyes.

Big Picture Insights

- **Deliverance** – the psalmist spared from death to declare God's mighty works.
- **Discipline** – God's chastening brings humility, but not destruction.
- **Gates of righteousness** – entry into God's presence marked by thanksgiving.
- **Salvation** – God Himself is the source of deliverance.
- **Rejected stone** – symbol of Christ despised by men but exalted by God.
- **Cornerstone** – foundation of God's new covenant community, the church.
- **Divine reversal** – what men reject, God establishes.
- **New Testament fulfillment** – cited by Jesus, Peter, and Paul.
- **Marvelous in our eyes** – God's work is astonishing, contrary to human expectation.
- **Assurance** – Christ the cornerstone secures our faith and hope.

Verse -by-Verse Commentary

Psalm 118:17 – "I will not die but live, and will proclaim what the LORD has done."

- The psalmist affirms deliverance from death, promising testimony of God's saving work. Life preserved is not for self-indulgence but for public praise, turning survival into proclamation of God's power and covenant faithfulness.
- In Christ, this finds ultimate fulfillment through resurrection. Jesus overcame death, living eternally to declare the Father's glory. Believers share in this victory, delivered from spiritual death to proclaim salvation's power to the world.

Psalm 118:18 – "The LORD has chastened me severely, but he has not given me over to death."

- Affliction is acknowledged as God's discipline, yet not abandonment. The psalmist recognizes that even severe trial is limited by God's mercy, who preserves life for continued service and worship.
- Jesus endured God's judgment on sin at the cross, yet was not abandoned to death (Acts 2:31). Resurrection reveals that divine discipline brings redemption, not destruction, securing hope for all believers.

Psalm 118:19 – "Open for me the gates of the righteous; I will enter and give thanks to the LORD."

- Deliverance leads to access. The psalmist longs to enter God's presence through the gates, symbolizing restored fellowship and worship. Gratitude replaces despair as he approaches the Lord with thanksgiving.
- Jesus is the true gate (John 10:9), granting believers access into God's presence. His resurrection opened the way for all who trust Him to enter with thanksgiving and worship into God's eternal kingdom.

Psalm 118:20–21 – "This is the gate of the LORD through which the righteous may enter. I will give you thanks, for you answered me; you have become my salvation."

- The righteous enter only through God's provision. The psalmist responds with gratitude, acknowledging God Himself as salvation. Deliverance is not chance but personal encounter with the saving God.
- Christ embodies this truth. He is the gate of salvation, and through Him the righteous enter eternal life. His resurrection secures thanksgiving, for God has answered humanity's deepest need through the gift of His Son.

Psalm 118:22–23 – "The stone the builders rejected has become the cornerstone; the LORD has done this, and it is marvelous in our eyes."

- The rejected stone elevated to cornerstone signifies God's reversal of human judgment. What was despised becomes the foundation of His saving plan, marvelous and undeniable in its wonder.
- Jesus directly fulfills this. Rejected by leaders yet exalted in resurrection, He is the cornerstone of God's new temple, the Church. Believers marvel at God's wisdom in turning rejection into redemption.

Discussion Questions

1. How does the psalmist view his deliverance—as personal relief or as a testimony?

2. What role does God's discipline play in deepening faith and trust?

3. How are the "gates of righteousness" fulfilled in Christ?

4. Why is thanksgiving central to salvation in verses 19–21?

5. How does the rejected stone becoming the cornerstone point directly to Christ?

6. Why does the psalmist emphasize that this reversal is "the Lord's doing"?

7. How should believers today build their lives on Christ the cornerstone?

Narrative Reflection

Psalm 118:17–23 stands at the heart of Israel's worship and at the crossroads of biblical prophecy. It is both thanksgiving for deliverance and a prophetic vision fulfilled in Jesus Christ. The psalm, sung at festivals like Passover, celebrated God's steadfast love and His power to save. These verses, however, move beyond Israel's immediate history to reveal God's ultimate plan: the rejected stone becoming the cornerstone.

The passage begins with the psalmist's declaration: "I will not die but live, and will proclaim what the Lord has done." Deliverance is not for self-preservation but proclamation. God preserves life so His works may be declared among His people. This theme recurs throughout Scripture: salvation is never merely private but always public, meant to glorify God and invite others to trust Him. For Christians, this points to resurrection life. In Christ, death no longer has the final word. We are preserved eternally to declare God's works forever.

Verse 18 acknowledges divine chastening. The psalmist has endured suffering that he interprets as God's discipline, but he affirms that God did not hand him over to death. This balance between chastening and mercy mirrors the believer's experience. God disciplines to correct and sanctify, not to destroy. For Israel, exile was severe chastening, yet not final death. For Christ, the cross was the ultimate chastening for sin, yet resurrection vindicated Him, proving that death could not hold Him. For believers, trials may be severe, but God's mercy preserves us for eternal life.

Verses 19–20 shift to worship imagery. The psalmist calls for the gates of righteousness to be opened, so that he may enter and give thanks. This is temple language: entering God's presence through His appointed gate. Righteousness is the condition of entry, but it is God who grants it. In the New Testament, Jesus identifies Himself as the gate: "I am the gate; whoever enters through me will be saved" (John 10:9). Through Christ's righteousness, believers gain access to God's presence with thanksgiving. The gates are opened not by our merit but by His grace.

Verse 21 continues the theme of gratitude: "I will give you thanks, for you answered me; you have become my salvation." Salvation is not a generic deliverance but God Himself acting as Savior. This personal recognition—"You have become my salvation"—echoes the experience of countless saints who find in God not only help but life itself. For Christians, this verse foreshadows the incarnation: salvation is not an idea but a person, Jesus Christ, who embodies and secures God's saving work.

Verses 22–23 bring the prophetic climax: "The stone the builders rejected has become the cornerstone; the Lord has done this, and it is marvelous in our eyes." The imagery of builders rejecting a stone suggests human leaders discarding what God values. Yet the rejected stone becomes the very foundation of God's construction project. In Israel's immediate context, this may have symbolized the nation itself—despised by empires yet chosen by God. But in the fullness of revelation, it points directly to Christ. Jesus cited this verse in Matthew 21:42 to confront the religious leaders who rejected Him. Peter echoed it in Acts 4:11, declaring Jesus the cornerstone rejected by Israel's leaders but chosen by God. Paul applied it to the church, built on the foundation of apostles and prophets, with Christ as the chief cornerstone (Eph. 2:20).

This divine reversal is "marvelous in our eyes." What humans despise, God exalts. What seems weak, God uses as strength. The cross epitomizes this paradox: rejected by men, Jesus became the Savior of the world. The marvel of Easter morning is that rejection turned into resurrection, and death became the doorway to life.

For believers today, Psalm 118:17–23 is profoundly encouraging. It reminds us that God preserves us for proclamation, disciplines us for restoration, and grants us access into His presence through Christ. It anchors us in thanksgiving, calling us to recognize God as our salvation. Most importantly, it directs us to Christ the cornerstone. Though rejected by many, He remains the foundation of our faith and the hope of the world.

This passage also challenges us. If Christ is the cornerstone, then our lives must be built on Him. Our identity, security, and mission flow from Him. We cannot build on shifting sands of cultural approval or personal ambition. The cornerstone determines the shape of the whole structure; so too Christ must define our lives and the church.

The passage ends with awe: "The Lord has done this, and it is marvelous in our eyes." Salvation is God's doing, not ours. The exaltation of the rejected stone is His work alone. Our response is wonder, gratitude, and worship. We marvel at the mystery of grace—that the crucified Messiah is Lord of all.

The message of Psalm 118:17–23 is one of salvation, thanksgiving, and fulfillment in Christ. It assures us that life is preserved to witness, discipline reshapes rather than ruins, and salvation rests in the Lord. The once-rejected stone has become the cornerstone, and this work is wondrous.

Layers of Understanding

Historical Context

Psalm 118 likely arose as a thanksgiving psalm for deliverance, sung at temple festivals such as Passover. Its imagery of gates and thanksgiving reflects temple worship, while its confidence in God's deliverance reflects Israel's survival amid enemies. For Israel, it celebrated national preservation and God's steadfast covenant love.

Jewish Understanding

In Jewish tradition, this psalm affirmed God's covenant faithfulness and celebrated deliverance from enemies. The "rejected stone" was often seen as Israel itself, despised by nations yet chosen by God. Sung in pilgrim festivals, it gave hope that God's preservation of His people would culminate in renewed blessing and vindication.

New Testament Fulfillment

Jesus identified Himself as the rejected stone made cornerstone (Matt. 21:42). Peter proclaimed this in Acts 4:11, applying it to Christ's rejection and resurrection. Paul declared the church built on this cornerstone (Eph. 2:20). The psalm's vision of deliverance and salvation finds ultimate fulfillment in Christ's death, resurrection, and exaltation.

Theological Significance Today

For believers, this passage underscores God's power to preserve life, redeem suffering, and overturn human rejection. It calls us to thanksgiving, to proclaim His works, and to build our lives on Christ the cornerstone. It assures us that rejection and suffering are never final when God is the one building.

Cross-Reference Connections

- **Exodus 40:34–35** – God's glory filling the tabernacle.
- **John 10:9** – Jesus as the gate for the sheep.
- **Matthew 21:42** – Jesus identifies Himself as the cornerstone.
- **Acts 4:11** – Peter declares Christ as the rejected stone.
- **Ephesians 2:20** – The church built on Christ the cornerstone.
- **1 Peter 2:4–6** – Believers as living stones built on Christ.

LESSON SCRIPTURE: **EXODUS 12: 1-14**

PROPHECY TITLE

The Passover Lamb and the Blood of Deliverance

Introduction

Exodus 12:1–14 records one of the central turning points in God's redemptive plan: the institution of the first Passover. On the eve of Israel's deliverance from slavery, God commanded His people to mark themselves by the blood of a lamb. While Egypt's firstborn would fall under judgment, those covered by the blood would live.

This passage lays the foundation for Israel's identity as a redeemed nation, forever remembered in the annual Passover feast. Yet more profoundly, it foreshadows Christ, the true Passover Lamb (1 Corinthians 5:7), whose blood secures salvation from sin and death. For believers today, Exodus 12:1–14 reveals God's power to save through substitutionary sacrifice and calls us to live as people covered by the Lamb's blood.

Scripture Reference

Exodus 12:1-14 (NIV)   The LORD said to Moses and Aaron in Egypt, [2] "This month is to be for you the first month, the first month of your year. [3] Tell the whole community of Israel that on the tenth day of this month each man is to take a lamb [t] for his family, one for each household. [4] If any household is too small for a whole lamb, they must share one with their nearest neighbor, having taken into account the number of people there are. You are to determine the amount of lamb needed in accordance with what each person will eat. [5] The animals you choose must be year-old males without defect, and you may take them from the sheep or the goats. [6] Take care of them until the fourteenth day of the month, when all the members of the community of Israel must slaughter them at twilight. [7] Then they are to take some of the blood and put it on the sides and tops of the doorframes of the houses where they eat the lambs. [8] That same night they are to eat the meat roasted over the fire, along with bitter herbs, and bread made without yeast. [9] Do not eat the meat raw or boiled in water, but roast it over a fire—with the head, legs and internal organs. [10] Do not leave any of it till morning; if some is left till morning, you must burn it. [11] This is how you are to eat it: with your cloak tucked into your belt, your sandals on your feet and your staff in your hand. Eat it in haste; it is the LORD's Passover. [12] "On that same night I will pass through Egypt and strike down every firstborn of both people and animals, and I will bring judgment on all the gods of Egypt. I am the LORD. [13] The blood will be a sign for you on the houses where you are, and when I see the blood, I will pass over you. No destructive plague will touch you when I strike Egypt. [14] "This is a day you are to

commemorate; for the generations to come you shall celebrate it as a festival to the LORD—a lasting ordinance."

Big Picture Insights

- **New beginning** – God resets Israel's calendar, anchoring identity in redemption.
- **Spotless lamb** – chosen without defect, prefiguring Christ's sinlessness.
- **Blood on the doorposts** – God's judgment passes over those covered.
- **Meal of remembrance** – lamb, unleavened bread, and bitter herbs tell the story of salvation.
- **Judgment and mercy** – Egypt judged, Israel spared by the blood.
- **Permanent memorial** – Israel commanded to remember redemption yearly.
- **Christ the fulfillment** – Jesus, the Lamb of God, fulfills the Passover.
- **Faith response** – protection requires obedience to God's instructions.
- **Holiness** – unleavened bread symbolizes purity, separation from sin.
- **Hope in Christ** – believers live as people redeemed by His blood.

Verse-by-Verse Commentary

Exodus 12:1–2 – "The LORD said to Moses and Aaron in Egypt, ² "This month is to be for you the first month, the first month of your year."

- God restructured Israel's calendar so that redemption, not creation or conquest, became the anchor of time. Salvation was to define their identity. Likewise, in Christ, believers mark new life from conversion, where the old has passed and the new has come.
- By tying time to deliverance, God ensured that every year began with a reminder of His saving power. The rhythm of their lives would always circle back to His grace, just as Christian worship continually recalls Christ's resurrection.

Exodus 12:3–6 – Tell the whole community of Israel that on the tenth day of this month each man is to take a lamb ᵗ for his family, one for each household. ⁴ If any household is too small for a whole lamb, they must share one with their nearest neighbor, having taken into account the number of people there are. You are to determine the amount of lamb needed in accordance with what each person will eat. ⁵ The animals you choose must be year-old males without defect, and you may take them from the sheep or the goats. ⁶ Take care of them until the fourteenth day of the month, when all the members of the community of Israel must slaughter them at twilight

- Each household was instructed to choose a lamb without defect, demonstrating that only perfection could suffice before a holy God. This foreshadowed Christ, who lived a sinless life, fulfilling God's standard of holiness, and offering Himself as the perfect Lamb of God.
- The lamb was to be kept four days, fostering familiarity and underscoring the personal cost of its death. This reflects how Christ dwelt among humanity, drawing near in relationship, before being offered as the substitutionary sacrifice to reconcile God's people through His own life-blood.

282

Exodus 12:7 – Then they are to take some of the blood and put it on the sides and tops of the doorframes of the houses where they eat the lambs.

- The blood applied visibly to the doorposts became the sign of faith and obedience. It was not the lamb's life alone but its blood, publicly displayed, that brought safety. In the same way, Christ's shed blood applied through faith secures salvation.
- The doorframe imagery symbolizes covering and passage. Israel entered homes marked by blood, protected within. Believers likewise abide under Christ's blood, safe from judgment, knowing God Himself declares, "When I see the blood, I will pass over you," promising refuge in His provision.

Exodus 12:8–11 – That same night they are to eat the meat roasted over the fire, along with bitter herbs, and bread made without yeast. ⁹ Do not eat the meat raw or boiled in water, but roast it over a fire—with the head, legs and internal organs. ¹⁰ Do not leave any of it till morning; if some is left till morning, you must burn it. ¹¹ This is how you are to eat it: with your cloak tucked into your belt, your sandals on your feet and your staff in your hand. Eat it in haste; it is the LORD's Passover.

- Eating the lamb ensured participation in salvation: the sacrifice was not only killed but consumed. This prefigures communion, where believers share in Christ's body and blood, spiritually nourished by His once-for-all sacrifice, finding strength for the journey of faith.
- Unleavened bread represented both purity and haste. Israel had no time for fermentation, symbolizing urgency in leaving bondage behind. For Christians, leaven pictures sin; we are called to live unleavened lives, pursuing holiness, ready to depart the old life at God's command.
- Bitter herbs recalled the harshness of slavery, ensuring redemption was never forgotten or romanticized. Believers were to remember sin's bondage, not to dwell in shame but to magnify the greatness of God's deliverance. Gratitude grows when freedom is measured against former enslavement.
- The command to eat in haste, belt fastened and staff in hand, emphasized readiness. Redemption was not to be delayed but embraced in faith. Likewise, believers are called to watchfulness, living as travelers prepared for Christ's return, eager for the greater Exodus to come.

Exodus 12:12–13 – On that same night I will pass through Egypt and strike down every firstborn of both people and animals, and I will bring judgment on all the gods of Egypt. I am the LORD. ¹³ The blood will be a sign for you on the houses where you are, and when I see the blood, I will pass over you. No destructive plague will touch you when I strike Egypt.

- God declared judgment against Egypt's gods and firstborn, showing His supremacy over all powers. Deliverance came not by Israel's merit but by God's gracious distinction. Christ's cross likewise defeats sin, death, and Satan, proving God's sovereignty and freeing His people from all enslaving powers.
- The blood was the decisive factor: where it was applied, judgment passed over. This illustrates substitutionary atonement—death had already fallen on another. In Christ, believers are safe, for He bore the penalty in our place. Faith in His blood alone secures eternal life.

Exodus 12:14 – This is a day you are to commemorate; for the generations to come you shall celebrate it as a festival to the LORD—a lasting ordinance.

- God instituted Passover as a perpetual ordinance, ensuring each generation would remember redemption's cost. Memory sustains faith, keeping alive the story of God's saving power. The church mirrors this in the Lord's Supper, proclaiming Christ's death until He comes in glory.
- The feast was both remembrance and identity formation. Israel was to see themselves as redeemed people defined by the blood of the lamb. At the cross, Christians discover their identity, shaped by Christ's sacrifice, which forms the foundation of our worship, guides our obedience, and propels our mission as God's redeemed community.

Discussion Questions

1. Why does God reset Israel's calendar around the Passover?

2. How does the spotless lamb point to Christ's sacrifice?

3. What is the significance of the blood on the doorposts?

4. How does the meal's symbolism (bread, lamb, herbs) speak to our salvation?

5. Why is remembrance so central in God's plan for His people?

6. How does the Passover reveal both judgment and mercy?

7. In what ways does Christ fulfill the meaning of Passover for believers today?

Narrative Reflection

Exodus 12:1–14 is a foundational biblical text that recounts Israel's redemption from Egypt while anticipating the gospel of Jesus Christ. It serves not only as history but also as prophecy in symbolic form, directing us to the Lamb who takes away the sins of the world.

The chapter begins with a profound proclamation: "This month is to be for you the first month, the first month of your year" (12:2). God reorients Israel's calendar around redemption, marking a new beginning based on His mighty act of deliverance from Egypt. Similarly, in Christ, our lives are transformed; we speak of life before and after Him, with redemption marking the true start of our story.

God instructs each household to choose a lamb without blemish (12:3–6), emphasizing the necessity of a perfect sacrifice. The lamb was to be kept for four days, fostering both anticipation and attachment to the sacrifice, making it a deeply felt experience rather than a mechanical one. Christ embodies this imagery perfectly as the Lamb without blemish, tested and found innocent, yet sacrificed for us. As Peter notes, we were redeemed "with the precious blood of Christ, a lamb without blemish or defect" (1 Peter 1:19).

The blood of the lamb was applied to the doorframes (12:7), marking the crucial distinction between life and death. While judgment loomed over Egypt, those marked by the blood would be spared. God declared, "When I see the blood, I will pass over you" (12:13). Salvation depended not on Israel's strength, merit, or morality, but solely on God's provision of the lamb and their faith in applying its blood. In Christ, we see the same truth: we are saved not by our works but by His blood, received through faith (Romans 5:9).

The meal of the lamb, unleavened bread, and bitter herbs (12:8–11) encapsulated the full experience of salvation. The lamb represented the substitute who died in their stead. The unleavened bread signified purity and urgency, urging Israel to leave sin and Egypt behind without delay. The bitter herbs served as a reminder of the suffering of slavery, ensuring that redemption was never taken lightly. In the New Testament, Jesus reinterprets this meal at the Last Supper, identifying Himself as the true Lamb whose body and blood bring salvation (Luke 22:19–20). For the church, the Lord's Supper continues the fulfillment of Passover.

God's declaration in verses 12–13 intertwines judgment and mercy. Egypt's firstborn faced judgment, while Israel's firstborn lived under the protection of the blood. This duality points directly to the cross, where God's judgment fell upon Christ, the Lamb, allowing His people to live. The same act that judged sin also provided salvation for the world.

Finally, verse 14 instructs Israel to keep this day as a lasting memorial. God foresaw that future generations would need reminders of His mighty act. Memory sustains identity; thus, Israel would annually reenact the Passover story, teaching their children that redemption was achieved by the blood of the lamb. For Christians, this memorial persists in the Lord's Supper. Each time we break bread and drink the cup, we proclaim the Lord's death until He comes (1 Corinthians 11:26). This act of remembrance keeps the gospel alive in our hearts and serves as a testimony to the world.

Exodus 12:1–14 reveals God's dual nature as Judge and Redeemer. He does not overlook sin; judgment is inevitable. Yet He provides a substitute, sparing His people through the blood of another. This principle culminates in Christ, who bore our judgment so that we might experience God's mercy. Additionally, it illustrates that salvation requires a personal faith response. It was not enough for the lamb to be slain; its blood had to be applied to the door. Likewise, while Christ's death is sufficient for all, it is only effective for those who trust in Him. Faith personalizes salvation.

Today, Exodus 12 calls us to live as a redeemed people. We are covered by the blood of the Lamb, liberated from bondage, and called to holiness. The unleavened bread encourages us to cast aside sin; the bitter herbs remind us of sin's slavery; and the lamb symbolizes Christ's sacrifice. Together, these elements cultivate a life of gratitude, obedience, and witness.

As a final thought, Exodus 12:1–14 is not only Israel's story but ours as well. The lamb foreshadows Christ, the blood foresees the cross, the meal anticipates the Supper, and the memorial points to the church's ongoing proclamation. God judges sin but saves through the Lamb. Our call is clear: trust in the blood of Christ, remember His salvation, and live as His redeemed people.

Layers of Understanding

Historical Context

Spoken on the eve of the Exodus, these instructions prepared Israel for deliverance. The first Passover became Israel's defining act of redemption, marking their transition from slavery to freedom. Every detail emphasized God's initiative, Israel's obedience, and the power of the lamb's blood to shield from judgment and secure salvation.

Jewish Understanding

For Israel, Passover became the central festival of remembrance. Each year they recalled God's mighty deliverance from Egypt and retold the story to future generations. The symbols of lamb, bread, and bitter herbs shaped their national identity, reminding them that they were redeemed people called to live in covenant faithfulness to God.

New Testament Fulfillment

The New Testament identifies Christ as the true Passover Lamb (1 Cor. 5:7). His blood secures deliverance from sin and death, fulfilling the imagery of Exodus 12. At the Last Supper, Jesus declared the bread and cup to be His body and blood — the new covenant of salvation for His people.

Theological Significance Today

For believers, Exodus 12 assures us that salvation is by grace through the blood of Christ. It calls us to obedience, purity, and remembrance. It teaches that judgment is real, but God provides a substitute. Covered by the blood, we live in gratitude, holiness, and hope, proclaiming Christ until He comes.

Cross-Reference Connections

- **Isaiah 53:7** – The lamb led to slaughter.
- **John 1:29** – Jesus, the Lamb of God.
- **Luke 22:19–20** – The new covenant in Christ's blood.
- **1 Corinthians 5:7–8** – Christ, our Passover Lamb.
- **Revelation 5:9–10** – The Lamb slain, worthy of worship.

LESSON SCRIPTURE: **NUMBER 21: 4-9**

PROPHECY TITLE

The Bronze Serpent and the Lifted Savior

Introduction

Numbers 21:4–9 recounts a significant episode during Israel's wilderness wanderings. Frustrated and rebellious, the people complained against God and Moses, resulting in judgment in the form of venomous serpents. Yet, in His mercy, God provided a means of salvation: those who looked upon a bronze serpent raised on a pole were healed and lived.

This passage serves not only as a historical account but also as a prophetic foreshadowing of Christ. Jesus Himself made this connection in John 3:14–15, stating that just as Moses lifted up the serpent, so must the Son of Man be lifted up, so that whoever believes in Him may have eternal life. The bronze serpent symbolizes the cross: judgment faced, salvation offered, and healing granted through faith.

For believers today, Numbers 21:4–9 underscores both the seriousness of sin and the sufficiency of Christ. Sin's poison leads to death, but God has provided the remedy — His Son, lifted up for our salvation. Our call is to look to Him in faith.

Scripture Reference

Numbers 21:4–9 (NIV) **"They traveled from Mount Hor along the route to the Red Sea, ᶜ to go around Edom. But the people grew impatient on the way; ⁵ they spoke against God and against Moses, and said, "Why have you brought us up out of Egypt to die in the wilderness? There is no bread! There is no water! And we detest this miserable food!" ⁶ Then the LORD sent venomous snakes among them; they bit the people and many Israelites died. ⁷ The people came to Moses and said, "We sinned when we spoke against the LORD and against you. Pray that the LORD will take the snakes away from us." So Moses prayed for the people. ⁸ The LORD said to Moses, "Make a snake and put it up on a pole; anyone who is bitten can look at it and live." ⁹ So Moses made a bronze snake and put it up on a pole. Then when anyone was bitten by a snake and looked at the bronze snake, they lived."**

Big Picture Insights

- **Complaint in the wilderness** – sin often rises from discontent.
- **Judgment by serpents** – sin brings death and destruction.
- **Intercession of Moses** – mediator appeals to God for mercy.
- **Bronze serpent lifted** – God provides a visible sign of salvation.
- **Healing by faith** – those who looked lived.
- **Picture of Christ** – serpent on the pole foreshadows the cross.
- **Lifted up** – fulfilled in Jesus' crucifixion and exaltation (John 3:14–15).
- **Salvation by grace** – not earned, but received through faith.
- **Warning against sin** – judgment is real, but so is mercy.
- **Assurance for believers** – Christ has borne sin's curse, granting eternal life.

Verse -by-Verse Commentary

Numbers 21:4–5 – They traveled from Mount Hor along the route to the Red Sea, ᶜ to go around Edom. But the people grew impatient on the way; ⁵ they spoke against God and against Moses, and said, "Why have you brought us up out of Egypt to die in the wilderness? There is no bread! There is no water! And we detest this miserable food!"

- Israel's discontent over food and hardship revealed hearts unwilling to trust God's provision. Complaints distorted reality, despising manna as "worthless." Sin often begins with ingratitude, blinding us to God's blessings and leading us into rebellion against His care and promises.
- Grumbling was more than dissatisfaction; it was rejection of God's authority. By scorning His gifts, Israel effectively accused God of failure. In the wilderness, discontent exposed unbelief. The lesson is clear: sin poisons gratitude and reveals a deeper problem, distrust of God's goodness.

Numbers 21:6 – Then the LORD sent venomous snakes among them; they bit the people and many Israelites died.

- God's judgment came swiftly: venomous serpents among the people. The "fiery" description likely referred to the burning pain of the bite, symbolizing the deadly poison of sin. Just as the serpent in Eden brought death, so sin's wages remain death.
- The serpents demonstrated that rebellion has consequences. Israel's murmuring was not trivial but deadly. The poison in their veins mirrored the poison of sin in the soul. Only God's intervention could save them. Judgment was deserved, yet God's purpose was to bring repentance and dependence upon His mercy.

Numbers 21:7 – The people came to Moses and said, "We sinned when we spoke against the LORD and against you. Pray that the LORD will take the snakes away from us." So Moses prayed for the people.

- The people confessed their sin, acknowledging rebellion against God and Moses. Repentance began with recognition of guilt. They pleaded with Moses, their mediator, to pray for deliverance. The law condemned, but intercession opened the door to grace.
- Moses' role highlights the necessity of a mediator. The people could not save themselves, nor could they plead directly apart from God's appointed intercessor. This foreshadows Christ, the greater Mediator, who intercedes for sinners and secures redemption through His own sacrifice.

Numbers 21:8–9 – The LORD said to Moses, "Make a snake and put it up on a pole; anyone who is bitten can look at it and live." ⁹ So Moses made a bronze snake and put it up on a pole. Then when anyone was bitten by a snake and looked at the bronze snake, they lived."

- God's remedy was unusual: a bronze serpent lifted on a pole. Those bitten had only to look and live. Healing came not from medicine or ritual but from faith in God's provision. The lifted serpent became a visible sign of grace.
- The paradox is profound: the image of the very thing that caused death became the means of healing. Likewise, Christ became sin for us (2 Corinthians 5:21). By bearing sin's curse on the cross, Christ gives us life. Faith directs us to look to Him, and in that act of trust we are lifted up, receiving the gift of salvation.

Discussion Questions

1. Why did Israel's complaints in the wilderness provoke God's judgment?

2. How do the fiery serpents symbolize the reality of sin?

3. What role did confession and Moses' intercession play in Israel's deliverance?

4. Why was the bronze serpent God's chosen means of salvation?

5. How does Jesus' teaching in John 3:14–15 connect this passage to the cross?

6. What does it mean to "look and live" in the context of salvation?

7. How should this story shape the way believers respond to sin and God's mercy today?

Narrative Reflection

Numbers 21:4–9 illustrates both the tragedy of human sin and the triumph of divine grace. The wilderness setting is significant: Israel was on its way to the Promised Land but had not yet entered. This place of testing continually revealed the hearts of the people. Instead of expressing gratitude for their deliverance from slavery, they often grumbled against God's provision.

Verses 4–5 depict their complaint. As the journey became long and arduous, frustration mounted. The people grew impatient, speaking against both God and Moses. Their disdain for manna is particularly striking: "We detest this miserable food." What God had provided as daily sustenance, they regarded as worthless. Ingratitude morphed into contempt. Their complaint was not merely about food or discomfort but reflected a lack of trust. Their dissatisfaction revealed unbelief in God's wisdom and goodness.

In verse 6, judgment comes swiftly. God sends fiery serpents among them, resulting in many deaths. The serpents vividly symbolize the consequences of sin. Since Eden, the serpent has represented rebellion and death. Here, the fiery serpents' venom burned like judgment in their veins, making the invisible reality of sin's deadly nature starkly visible. The rebellion that seemed trivial now proved fatal.

In verse 7, the people recognize their sin and turn to Moses. Confession is crucial: "We sinned when we spoke against the Lord and against you." Their words express both repentance and helplessness. They cannot undo the bite, remove the serpents, or cure the poison; they can only appeal for mercy. They ask Moses to intercede—to pray that God might deliver them. This highlights the necessity of a mediator. The law condemned, but the mediator petitioned. This foreshadows Christ, our Mediator, who pleads not with animal sacrifices but with His own blood.

God's response is surprising. In verses 8–9, He commands Moses to create a bronze serpent and lift it high on a pole. The means of salvation mirrors the instrument of judgment. The people are not told to fight, heal, or remove the serpents; they are simply instructed to look. Whoever looked upon the bronze serpent lived. Healing came not through effort or ritual but through faith in God's provision.

This paradox is rich with meaning. The image of the serpent, typically a curse, becomes a means of blessing. This foreshadows Christ. As Paul writes in 2 Corinthians 5:21, "God made him who had no sin to be sin for us, so that in him we might become the righteousness of God." On the cross, Christ bore the likeness of sinful flesh, condemned in our place (Romans 8:3). What brought death became the very means of life.

Jesus makes this connection explicit in John 3:14–15: "Just as Moses lifted up the snake in the wilderness, so the Son of Man must be lifted up, that everyone who believes may have eternal life in him." The bronze serpent prefigured the cross. Just as Israel looked and lived, so believers now look to the crucified Christ to receive eternal life. The requirement is faith—to look with trust upon God's provision.

This story teaches several lessons about salvation. First, it highlights the seriousness of sin. Complaining may seem trivial, but at its root, it is rebellion against God's goodness. Sin is deadly, like venom in the bloodstream, with no human cure. Second, it underscores the necessity of repentance. The people confessed their sin and sought God's mercy. Third, it reveals the sufficiency of faith. Healing came simply by looking—not by merit, work, or ritual. Salvation is God's gift, received through trust in His provision.

For believers today, the message is clear. We too have been bitten by sin and poisoned by death. Judgment is deserved. But God has provided a remedy in His Son. Christ, lifted on the cross, bore our sin. All who look to Him in faith will live. The bronze serpent was temporary, but the cross is eternal.

This passage also emphasizes the centrality of Christ's cross in the gospel. Salvation does not come from human wisdom or effort but from the crucified Savior. The church's task is to lift Him up before the world, proclaiming that life is found in Him alone.

Finally, this story points us toward eternal hope. While serpents may still surround us in a fallen world, the cure has been given. One day, when Christ returns, death itself will be destroyed, and sin's venom will be erased forever. Until then, we live by looking daily to Christ, the lifted Savior, who gives us life now and eternal life to come.

This passage is more than a wilderness story; it is a gospel picture. It reveals sin's poison, God's judgment, the need for a mediator, and the power of faith in God's provision. Fulfilled in Christ, it teaches us that salvation is found not in ourselves but in the One lifted up for us. Look to Him and live.

Layers of Understanding

Historical Context

Israel, weary in the wilderness, grumbled against God and Moses. Their contempt for manna revealed unbelief. God judged with fiery serpents, leading to confession and intercession. The bronze serpent, lifted high, became the God-ordained means of healing — not by effort but by faith in His provision.

Jewish Understanding

For Israel, this story highlighted both judgment and mercy. It reinforced that rebellion leads to death, but repentance brings God's provision. The bronze serpent became a national reminder of God's power to save, though later it was misused (2 Kings 18:4). Its original purpose was to testify to God's gracious salvation.

New Testament Fulfillment

Jesus declared the bronze serpent a type of His crucifixion (John 3:14–15). Just as looking brought healing, faith in Christ lifted on the cross brings eternal life. Paul echoes this by saying Christ became sin for us (2 Cor. 5:21), turning judgment into salvation through His sacrificial death.

Theological Significance Today

This passage shows that sin's poison leads to death, but God has provided a remedy in Christ. Salvation is not earned but received through faith. Believers are called to look to Christ daily, trusting His cross for forgiveness, healing, and life, and to proclaim Him as the lifted Savior.

Cross-Reference Connections

- **Genesis 3:14–15** – The serpent's role in the curse and promise of redemption.
- **John 3:14–15** – Christ lifted up as fulfillment of the bronze serpent.
- **Romans 8:3** – God condemns sin in the flesh through Christ.
- **2 Corinthians 5:21** – Christ became sin for us.
- **Hebrews 7:25** – Christ as intercessor and mediator.

PROPHECY FULFILLED - STUDY LESSON - 51

LESSON SCRIPTURE: **DANIEL 9: 24-26**

PROPHECY TITLE

Seventy Weeks and the Anointed One

Introduction

Daniel 9:24–26 contains one of the most debated and profound prophecies in Scripture. In response to Daniel's prayer of confession and intercession, the angel Gabriel reveals a timeline of "seventy weeks" (seventy sevens), set apart for God's purposes of redemption, judgment, and restoration. These verses anticipate the coming of the Anointed One, His being "cut off," and the unfolding of God's plan for His people.

Christians recognize this prophecy as pointing directly to the Messiah, Jesus Christ, whose ministry fulfills the promise. His atoning death, described as being "cut off," brings reconciliation and inaugurates the new covenant. The prophecy also looks ahead to desolations and final fulfillment, making it both a foundation of messianic hope and a cornerstone of biblical eschatology.

For believers today, Daniel 9:24–26 reminds us of God's sovereign control of history, His faithfulness to His covenant promises, and His provision of salvation through Christ. It calls us to trust His timing and to rest in the assurance that His redemptive plan is certain.

Scripture Reference

Daniel 9:24-26 (NIV)   "Seventy 'sevens' are decreed for your people and your holy city to finish transgression, to put an end to sin, to atone for wickedness, to bring in everlasting righteousness, to seal up vision and prophecy and to anoint the Most Holy Place. ²⁵ "Know and understand this: From the time the word goes out to restore and rebuild Jerusalem until the Anointed One, ^g the ruler, comes, there will be seven 'sevens,' and sixty-two 'sevens.' It will be rebuilt with streets and a trench, but in times of trouble. ²⁶ After the sixty-two 'sevens,' the Anointed One will be put to death and will have nothing. The people of the ruler who will come will destroy the city and the sanctuary. The end will come like a flood: War will continue until the end, and desolations have been decreed.

Big Picture Insights

- **Seventy weeks** – symbolic timeline of God's redemptive plan.
- **Six divine purposes** – ending sin, atonement, and establishing everlasting righteousness.
- **The Anointed One** – prophecy of the Messiah's coming.
- **Cut off** – Messiah's sacrificial death for His people.

294

- **Rebuilding Jerusalem** – physical and spiritual restoration amid opposition.
- **Vision and prophecy sealed** – fulfillment through Christ.
- **Destruction foretold** – city and temple destroyed in A.D. 70.
- **Already/not yet** – partial fulfillment in Christ, final consummation ahead.
- **God's sovereignty** – history unfolds on His timetable.
- **Assurance for believers** – salvation and everlasting righteousness secured in Christ.

Verse -by-Verse Commentary

Daniel 9:24 – "Seventy 'sevens' are decreed for your people and your holy city to finish transgression, to put an end to sin, to atone for wickedness, to bring in everlasting righteousness, to seal up vision and prophecy and to anoint the Most Holy Place."

- The seventy sevens symbolize a divinely appointed period in which God's plan for Israel and Jerusalem will be completed. The number carries symbolic weight, suggesting fullness, completion, and God's sovereign determination over history.
- Six purposes are outlined: to finish transgression, end sin, atone for wickedness, bring everlasting righteousness, seal up vision and prophecy, and anoint the Most Holy Place. These point beyond Israel's immediate restoration to Christ's atoning work and the consummation of His kingdom.

Daniel 9:25 – "Know and understand this: From the time the word goes out to restore and rebuild Jerusalem until the Anointed One, ᵍ the ruler, comes, there will be seven 'sevens,' and sixty-two 'sevens.' It will be rebuilt with streets and a trench, but in times of trouble."

- Gabriel specifies a timeline beginning with a decree to restore Jerusalem and culminating in the arrival of the Anointed One. This points to Christ's coming in history, God's definitive intervention on behalf of His people.
- The timeline is divided into seven weeks, sixty-two weeks, and a final week. The first 69 weeks extend to the Messiah's coming, fulfilled in Christ's ministry. Many interpreters note a prophetic pause before the final week, corresponding to the church age before the tribulation.
- Jerusalem will be rebuilt "in times of trouble," underscoring that restoration does not erase opposition. God's people are always refined through hardship, yet His promises stand. The rebuilding anticipates Christ Himself, who declared His body the true temple to be raised in three days.

Daniel 9:26 – "After the sixty-two 'sevens,' the Anointed One will be put to death and will have nothing. The people of the ruler who will come will destroy the city and the sanctuary. The end will come like a flood: War will continue until the end, and desolations have been decreed."

- The Messiah is "cut off," signifying rejection and death. This anticipates the crucifixion of Jesus, where He bore sin's penalty and appeared to be left with nothing, though His death secured the eternal purposes of God.
- The destruction of the city and sanctuary points historically to the fall of Jerusalem in A.D. 70. This fulfilled the prophecy of judgment, showing that rejection of the Messiah has consequences. It also anticipates future desolations, reminding us that history moves toward final judgment and redemption.

Discussion Questions

1. What is the significance of God setting a fixed period of "seventy sevens" for His plan?

2. How do the six purposes in verse 24 connect to Christ's ministry?

3. Why is it important that the Anointed One is "cut off" in verse 26?

4. How does this prophecy strengthen our faith in God's control of history?

5. In what ways does the destruction of Jerusalem illustrate both judgment and fulfillment?

6. How does this prophecy shape Christian hope for the final consummation of God's plan?

7. How should believers respond to God's precise, sovereign timing in unfolding His promises?

Narrative Reflection

Daniel 9:24–26 is one of the most significant prophetic passages in Scripture, generating centuries of study, debate, and devotion. It was given in response to Daniel's heartfelt prayer for his people's restoration following seventy years of Babylonian exile. Having read Jeremiah's prophecy about the duration of the exile, Daniel sought God's mercy for Jerusalem as the time approached its end. However, the angel Gabriel's response far exceeded Daniel's immediate concerns. Rather than simply addressing the conclusion of the seventy years, God unveiled a broader timeline of "seventy sevens" (or seventy weeks), extending to the coming of the Messiah and the fulfillment of His redemptive plan.

Verse 24 introduces the decree of seventy sevens for Daniel's people and the holy city. This period, whether viewed symbolically or chronologically, signifies a divinely appointed timeframe in which God's plan regarding sin, righteousness, prophecy, and His dwelling among His people will be fulfilled. Six specific purposes are outlined: to finish transgression, put an end to sin, atone for wickedness, bring in everlasting righteousness, seal up the vision and prophecy, and anoint the Most Holy Place. Collectively, these purposes point to the work of Christ in His atoning death and resurrection, as well as to the eventual establishment of His kingdom.

Verse 25 details the structure of the seventy weeks: seven sevens, sixty-two sevens, and a final seven. From the decree to restore and rebuild Jerusalem to the arrival of the Anointed One, there would be a total of sixty-nine sevens (seven plus sixty-two). Many interpreters equate this to 483 years, depending on whether they use prophetic years (360 days) or solar years (365 days). Ongoing debates focus on the starting point—Cyrus's decree in 538 B.C., Artaxerxes' decree in 458 B.C., or Nehemiah's commission in 445 B.C.—but the key truth remains: God established a timeline leading directly to the Messiah's appearance.

This prophecy highlights not only the certainty of the Messiah's coming but also the conditions of Jerusalem at that time: "rebuilt with streets and a trench, but in times of trouble." Ezra and Nehemiah recount the significant opposition and challenges faced by the returning exiles as they sought to rebuild. This pattern spiritually prepares us for Christ, who arrived in the fullness of time amid rejection, opposition, and suffering.

Verse 26 delivers a startling declaration: "After the sixty-two sevens, the Anointed One will be cut off and will have nothing." The Messiah would come, but instead of immediate victory, He would be rejected and killed. This perfectly describes the crucifixion of Jesus Christ, who was cut off not for His sins, but for ours. To human perception, He appeared to have nothing—rejected by His people, abandoned by His disciples, and crucified outside the city walls. Yet, in God's sovereign plan, Christ being cut off secured atonement and everlasting righteousness. The cross, far from being a defeat, marked the climactic fulfillment of Daniel's prophecy.

The prophecy further predicts destruction: "The people of the ruler who will come will destroy the city and the sanctuary." This was fulfilled in A.D. 70 when the Romans under Titus destroyed both Jerusalem and the temple. This catastrophic event confirmed Jesus' own words in Matthew 24:2, where He stated that not one stone of the temple would be left on another. It served as both a historical judgment and a prophetic sign that God's purposes were advancing toward ultimate fulfillment.

Many interpreters recognize a prophetic "pause" between the 69th and 70th weeks. The timeline leads up to the Messiah's coming and death, after which history seems to shift. Instead of progressing immediately into the final seven, there exists a gap often understood as the church age—the interval between Christ's first and second comings. During this time, the gospel is preached to the nations, and the Spirit gathers a people from every tribe and tongue. In this interpretation, the 70th week is anticipated as a future event, commonly linked to the tribulation described in Daniel 9:27 and elaborated upon in Matthew 24 and Revelation.

For those with a pretribulational perspective, this pause underscores the mystery of God's plan: Israel's prophetic clock halted with the rejection of the Messiah and will resume in the last days. The church, raptured before the tribulation, will be with Christ, while Daniel's people, Israel, will again become the focus during the final week. Others perceive the 70th week as symbolically fulfilled in the destruction of Jerusalem or spiritually through Christ's atoning work and ongoing kingdom. Regardless, the structure of the 69 and 70 weeks emphasizes God's precision in redemptive history.

This prophetic pause imparts two lessons. First, God's plan transcends our immediate expectations. Daniel prayed for an end to seventy years of exile, but God unveiled seventy sevens that extend far beyond. Second, God's plan unfolds with purpose and certainty. The Anointed One has come, been cut off, and provided atonement. The final fulfillment, whether viewed futuristically or spiritually, is assured.

From a theological perspective, Daniel 9:24–26 affirms God's sovereignty over time and history, showcasing His precision in foretelling the coming of Christ centuries in advance. It underscores the centrality of the cross, where the Messiah was cut off for our sins, and points toward the ultimate consummation when transgression will be finished, sin will be ended, and everlasting righteousness will prevail.

This subject is complex and requires a deep exploration of many related books of the Bible, along with a careful analysis of the book of Revelation. I have written a commentary on Revelation and, for those desiring a more detailed study, I would humbly recommend my book *Miracles, Signs, Symbols, and Judgment: God's Plan for the End Times.* For believers today, this prophecy offers both assurance and exhortation. We can trust that God keeps His promises with exactness. The same God who foretold the Messiah's death and the temple's destruction will also fulfill the promise of Christ's return and the final establishment of His kingdom. We are called to live in readiness, knowing that history is progressing toward its appointed end. The prophetic pause reminds us that we exist in the in-between—already redeemed through Christ, yet still awaiting the final consummation of all things.

Daniel 9:24–26 is a prophecy of breathtaking scope. It predicts the Messiah's atoning death, establishes a timeline of redemptive history, and foresees both destruction and ultimate restoration. The seventy sevens frame God's plan, the 69 weeks highlight the precision of His timing, and the pause directs us to the mystery of the church age and the hope of Christ's return. Throughout, we see that God governs history, Christ fulfills His promises, and His people are called to live in faith, hope, and readiness for the day when everlasting righteousness is revealed.

Layers of Understanding

Historical Context

Daniel, exiled in Babylon, prayed for mercy and restoration after reading Jeremiah's prophecy. Gabriel revealed a greater plan: seventy "sevens" decreed for Israel and Jerusalem. This timeline pointed not only to the rebuilding of the city but to the coming of the Messiah, His sacrifice, and ultimate restoration.

Jewish Understanding

Jewish readers saw this as God's promise of restoration and the coming of an anointed leader. Some connected it to Zerubbabel or later Maccabean figures, though the prophecy's scope clearly stretched beyond. The focus remained on God's covenant faithfulness and the hope that transgression would be ended and righteousness established.

New Testament Fulfillment

The New Testament applies this prophecy to Christ. Jesus is the Anointed One, cut off at the cross (John 3:14–15). His death secured atonement and inaugurated everlasting righteousness. The temple's destruction in A.D. 70 fulfilled the prophecy of judgment. His resurrection and return consummate the full realization of Daniel's vision.

Theological Significance Today

For believers, this prophecy assures us that God controls history and fulfills His promises with precision. Christ's atoning work has ended sin's power and brought righteousness. Though we live amid trouble and waiting, we trust His sovereignty, rest in His cross, and anticipate the consummation of His kingdom at His return.

Cross-Reference Connections

- **Jeremiah 25:11–12** – Seventy years of exile.
- **Isaiah 53:5–8** – The Servant "cut off" for our transgressions.
- **Matthew 24:2** – Jesus foretells temple destruction.
- **John 19:30** – "It is finished" as Christ fulfills atonement.
- **2 Corinthians 5:21** – Christ made sin for us.
- **Revelation 11:15** – The kingdom of Christ consummated.

PROPHECY FULFILLED - STUDY LESSON - 52

LESSON SCRIPTURE: ISAIAH 65: 17-25

PROPHECY TITLE

The New Heavens and the New Earth

Introduction

Isaiah 65:17–25 presents a grand vision of ultimate restoration. In stark contrast to Israel's sin and exile, God promises a renewal so profound that it is characterized as a new creation: *"See, I will create new heavens and a new earth."* This prophecy not only anticipates Israel's return from exile but also foretells God's final redemptive work.

The New Testament explicitly links this prophecy to the Christian hope for eternity. Revelation 21–22 closely mirrors Isaiah's language, describing the new heaven, new earth, and new Jerusalem where God dwells with His people and wipes away every tear. This promise has already begun with Christ's resurrection and will be fully realized upon His return.

For believers today, Isaiah 65:17–25 serves as a foundation for our hope in the certainty of God's eternal plan. It reminds us that the story of redemption does not conclude at the cross or even with the resurrection, but culminates in the renewal of all things.

Scripture Reference

Isaiah 65:17–25 (NIV)   "See, I will create new heavens and a new earth. The former things will not be remembered, nor will they come to mind. [18] But be glad and rejoice forever in what I will create, for I will create Jerusalem to be a delight and its people a joy. [19] I will rejoice over Jerusalem and take delight in my people; the sound of weeping and of crying will be heard in it no more. [20] "Never again will there be in it an infant who lives but a few days, or an old man who does not live out his years; the one who dies at a hundred will be thought a mere child; the one who fails to reach a hundred will be considered accursed. [21] They will build houses and dwell in them; they will plant vineyards and eat their fruit. [22] No longer will they build houses and others live in them, or plant and others eat. For as the days of a tree, so will be the days of my people; my chosen ones will long enjoy the work of their hands. [23] They will not labor in vain, nor will they bear children doomed to misfortune; for they will be a people blessed by the LORD, they and their descendants with them. [24] Before they call I will answer; while they are still speaking I will hear. [25] The wolf and the lamb will feed together, and the lion will eat straw like the ox, and dust will be the serpent's food. They will neither harm nor destroy on all my holy mountain," says the LORD."

Big Picture Insights

- **Promise of cosmic renewal** - new heavens and a new earth.
- **Former things forgotten** - sorrow and sin no longer remembered.
- **Joy-filled creation** - Jerusalem and her people a delight to God.
- **End of weeping** - sorrow and loss banished.
- **Life extended** - longevity, blessing, and fulfillment of God's promises.
- **Fruit of labor** - people enjoy their work without oppression.
- **Covenant blessing** - descendants secure in God's favor.
- **God's nearness** - He answers before they call.
- **Peace in creation** - predator and prey reconciled, violence ended.
- **Final vision** - points to Revelation's promise of eternal renewal.

Verse -by-Verse Commentary

Isaiah 65:17 – "See, I will create new heavens and a new earth. The former things will not be remembered, nor will they come to mind."

- God promises more than restoration; He declares re-creation, transforming the cosmos itself. The old order, marred by sin and death, will be forgotten. Revelation 21 echoes this, where God unveils an entirely renewed creation for His redeemed people.
- The phrase emphasizes both continuity and transformation. God does not discard creation but renews it, redeeming His original design. The "former things" — sorrow, sin, rebellion — will no longer dominate memory, as God's new reality overshadows every former grief.

Isaiah 65:18–19 – But be glad and rejoice forever in what I will create, for I will create Jerusalem to be a delight and its people a joy. ¹⁹ I will rejoice over Jerusalem and take delight in my people; the sound of weeping and of crying will be heard in it no more.

- God delights in His people as they delight in Him. Joy is the defining mark of the renewed creation. No weeping will remain, for God Himself wipes away tears, ensuring a community marked by divine fellowship and everlasting gladness.
- Jerusalem, often a city of rebellion and judgment, is transformed into God's joy. The reversal is radical: once a byword of sorrow, now it is the epicenter of gladness. God Himself rejoices over His people, fulfilling Zephaniah 3:17's promise of divine delight.

Isaiah 65:20 – Never again will there be in it an infant who lives but a few days, or an old man who does not live out his years; the one who dies at a hundred will be thought a mere child; the one who fails to reach a hundred will be considered accursed.

- The curse of premature death is removed; children live, the elderly thrive, and even at 100 years, life is considered only beginning. This imagery reveals God's reversal of death's power, a foretaste of the resurrection hope fulfilled in Christ.
- The language suggests not only longevity but quality of life. Life is no longer cut short by curse or calamity. God's blessing ensures His people live fully under His covenant promises, secure in His goodness.

Isaiah 65:21–23 – They will build houses and dwell in them; they will plant vineyards and eat their fruit. ²² No longer will they build houses and others live in them, or plant and others eat. For as the days of a tree, so will be the days of my people; my chosen ones will long enjoy the work of their hands. ²³ They will not labor in vain, nor will they bear children doomed to misfortune; for they will be a people blessed by the LORD, they and their descendants with them.

- Unlike Israel's exile, where enemies consumed their labor, here the people enjoy the fruit of their hands. Work is no longer vain or exploited but becomes a joyful participation in God's purposes.
- Families, too, are blessed, with children not doomed to misfortune but inheriting God's covenant favor. Generational blessing replaces generational curse. God's people flourish in security, echoing Psalm 128's vision of households rooted in the fear of the Lord.

Isaiah 65:24 – Before they call I will answer; while they are still speaking I will hear.

- The intimacy of God with His people is astounding: before they call, He answers. This shows not only divine responsiveness but covenant intimacy. God's presence ensures constant fellowship, removing barriers between Creator and redeemed creation.
- This anticipates Christ's promise in John 16:24, where prayer in His name brings fullness of joy. In the renewed world, the communion between God and His people is unbroken, immediate, and deeply personal.

Isaiah 65:25 – The wolf and the lamb will feed together, and the lion will eat straw like the ox, and dust will be the serpent's food. They will neither harm nor destroy on all my holy mountain," says the LORD."

- Wolves and lambs feed together, lions eat straw, and the serpent is reduced to dust. Violence, predation, and enmity are erased. This is Eden restored, but greater — creation living in harmony under God's reign.
- The serpent eating dust recalls Genesis 3:14, showing evil's final defeat. God's holy mountain becomes a realm where nothing harms or destroys, anticipating the peace of Revelation 21:4 and 22:3, where the curse is fully removed.

Discussion Questions

1. What does the promise of a "new heavens and new earth" reveal about God's ultimate plan for creation?

2. How does this prophecy connect to Revelation 21–22?

3. Why is joy central to the vision of Jerusalem's renewal?

4. How does this passage reverse the curses of Genesis 3?

5. What does the imagery of fruitful labor and generational blessing mean for believers today?

6. How does verse 24 shape our understanding of prayer and God's presence?

7. What does verse 25 reveal about the harmony of the new creation?

Narrative Reflection

Isaiah 65:17–25 provides a vivid depiction of God's ultimate plan: not just to repair creation, but to renew it entirely. This passage transcends Israel's return from exile, offering a sweeping vision of new heavens and a new earth. For exiles who witnessed their land devastated and their city destroyed, this promise signifies more than mere restoration. It reveals the essence of God's redemptive plan: everlasting joy, flourishing life, covenant intimacy, and cosmic peace.

The vision commences with God's declaration, "I will create new heavens and a new earth" (v. 17). Creation is not discarded but transformed; the old order of sorrow, sin, and death is set aside. This idea resonates centuries later in Revelation 21:1–4, where John sees this reality fulfilled in Christ: a new creation where God dwells with His people and wipes away every tear. In Isaiah, the promise is so comprehensive that "the former things will not be remembered." The traumas and tragedies of the past will vanish in the brilliance of God's renewal.

Jerusalem, often a city of grief and rebellion, transforms into a city of joy (vv. 18–19). God delights in His people, and they find their joy in Him. This transformation is profound; instead of weeping and sorrow, there is only laughter and rejoicing. God is depicted as rejoicing over His people, fulfilling the vision in Zephaniah 3:17 of God singing over His redeemed. Joy is central to the renewed creation — a joy that flows from communion with God Himself.

Verse 20 shifts focus to life and blessing. No longer will infants die in their infancy or elders perish prematurely. Longevity is so abundant that one who dies at 100 is regarded as still a child. While death is not completely absent, the anguish of untimely death is removed, anticipating the resurrection life fulfilled in Christ's victory over death. This imagery conveys abundance of days, security, and covenant blessing.

Verses 21–23 highlight fruitful labor and family blessings. In exile, Israel had toiled in vain, with foreigners reaping the fruits of their labor. Here, they will enjoy the outcomes of their work. Labor becomes fruitful and fulfilling rather than oppressive. Families thrive, with children born to blessings rather than misfortune. God's covenant favor extends through generations, ensuring a legacy of peace and prosperity under His reign. This reverses the curses of Deuteronomy and embodies the blessings promised to Abraham and his descendants.

Verse 24 reveals the closeness of God's relationship with His people: "Before they call, I will answer; while they are still speaking, I will hear." Prayer becomes immediate and unhindered, illustrating a covenant bond so intimate that God anticipates their requests. The communication gap between heaven and earth is erased, with God's presence constant, His care immediate, and His fellowship unbroken.

Finally, verse 25 depicts peace within creation itself. Wolves and lambs coexist, lions eat straw, and the serpent — symbol of evil since Eden — is consigned to dust. This is not merely poetic imagery but a portrayal of Eden restored, with creation reconciled under God's reign. Violence, predation, and fear are abolished. God's holy mountain becomes a sanctuary where nothing harms or destroys. Revelation 22 echoes this vision: the curse removed, the tree of life restored, and the nations healed.

Religiously, Isaiah 65:17–25 weaves together the central threads of biblical hope in a vision both rich and comprehensive. Creation is not abandoned but renewed, affirming God's enduring commitment to the world He made. Joy becomes the defining mark of the redeemed community, as God Himself delights in His people. Life flourishes free from the curse, with death's sting removed and longevity secured. Work and family are restored to their rightful fruitfulness under God's blessing, no longer touched by futility or misfortune. Prayer reflects unbroken communion with God, for He answers even before His people call. Finally, creation itself is reconciled, with peace extending to every corner of existence — even to the animals — signaling that the harmony lost in Eden has been fully restored. For believers today, this passage offers both hope and challenge. It reassures us that history is moving toward God's renewal rather than despair. Every sorrow, injustice, and loss will be swallowed up in the joy of God's new creation. It challenges us to live now as citizens of that future reality. If the future is defined by peace, we are called to be peacemakers. If it is characterized by joy, we should cultivate rejoicing even amid trials. If creation itself will be renewed, we are called to steward it well, anticipating its liberation from decay.

In conclusion, Isaiah 65:17–25 is a prophetic masterpiece that unveils the destiny of God's people and the world. It points beyond exile to new creation, beyond sorrow to joy, beyond curse to blessing, and beyond death to life. Fulfilled in Christ and consummated at His return, this vision anchors our hope. It assures us that the story concludes not in ruin but in renewal, not in despair but in delight. With this vision before us, we are called to live as people of hope, rejoicing in the Lord's promises and walking in the light of His coming kingdom.

Layers of Understanding

Historical Context

Isaiah spoke to a weary people burdened by judgment and exile. His vision of new creation transcended immediate concerns, assuring them that God's final word would be renewal, not ruin, lifting their eyes to ultimate restoration.

Jewish Understanding

Many saw this as the hope of Israel's restoration — Jerusalem renewed, peace secured, and long life restored. Yet the imagery pointed beyond the return from exile to a greater eschatological future.

New Testament Fulfillment

The New Testament affirms Isaiah's vision fulfilled in Christ. Revelation 21:1–4 promises a new heaven and earth without sorrow or death. 2 Peter 3:13 assures believers of a creation where righteousness dwells. Romans 8:18–21 portrays creation groaning for liberation, awaiting freedom from decay and sharing in the glory of God's redeemed children.

Theological Significance Today

This passage assures believers of the hope of cosmic renewal in Christ. It calls us to live as people of joy, peace, and holiness, embodying the values of the coming kingdom even while awaiting its consummation.

Cross-Reference Connections

- **Revelation 21:1–4** – New heavens and new earth fulfilled in Christ.
- **Revelation 22:1–5** – River and tree of life restore creation's harmony.
- **2 Peter 3:13** – Believers await the new creation of righteousness.
- **Romans 8:18–21** – Creation groans, awaiting liberation.
- **Zephaniah 3:17** – God rejoices over His people with singing.
- **Psalm 128** – Families and labor blessed under God's favor.

About the Author

David G. Brown has faithfully served as an ordained elder for over forty years and has devoted more than four decades to teaching Scripture at the adult level. His ministry is marked by a deep commitment to biblical inquiry, especially in the areas of Revelation, prophecy, and the foundational doctrines of the Christian faith.

He is the author of *Miracles, Signs, Symbols, and Judgment: God's Plan for the End Times*—a comprehensive, verse-by-verse commentary on Revelation. Written to address growing spiritual confusion and cultural drift, it aims to make complex theology clear and spiritually enriching. He has also authored *It Is All About You: From Eden to Eternity—How God Never Forgot His Creation*, which demonstrates how, through His Word, God has interacted with His creation to draw us near to Him. In a world where many question God's presence and plan, David affirms a vital truth: the Creator remains actively involved with His creation. (Included at the back of *It Is All About You* is a guided worksheet for each chapter, making it an ideal resource for personal reflection, small-group study, or discipleship training.)

His theological depth is matched by his hands-on commitment to missions. A former board member of Haiti Outreach Ministries, David has participated in more than twenty-five short-term mission trips and disaster relief efforts. His life reflects tangible obedience to the Great Commission, combining local service with global impact.

Concerned by the rise of biblical illiteracy within both the church and society, David presents *Prophecy Fulfilled* as a timely resource to ground believers in Scripture and strengthen their confidence in God's promises.

David and his wife, Linda, reside in Richmond, Virginia, where they celebrate over fifty years of marriage. He has also served as a football official for more than thirty years and enjoys restoring antique cars, building and refinishing furniture, and engaging in various construction projects. Yet above all, his greatest passion remains unchanged: teaching the Word of God and helping others grow in their understanding of divine truth.